Cassandra Admin DBA Guide

Cassandra Admin DBA Guide

Prasad Bagewadi

Cassandra Admin DBA Guide
by Prasad Bagewadi

ISBN 13: 9781072205135

Printing History:
    July 2019 : First Edition.

Typeset by Amnet Systems.

This book is dedicated to the memory of my parents Pandurang Bagewadi and Prabha Bagewadi.

Table of Contents

Foreword

"**N**OSQL database? Are you crazy?" is the reaction you would have received if you had mentioned it 30 years ago. This was around the time I was starting as an Ingres DBA. Back then, "NOSQL" database was not practically possible when RDBMS was making its way in. My first job was to write COBOL codes on Ingres system, the most structured you could have gotten in DBMS. Since then, a lot has changed. Since the evolution of Facebook, Yahoo, and Google in the last few years, relational databases are struggling to meet the business requirements. Typical challenges are managing large volumes of data, high availability, agility to business changes, different data formats, and easy maintenance. Though hardware innovations such as faster CPU, bigger memory, and faster(SSD) disks the speed of innovation is much slower compared to the speed of digital transformation, social media, and internet of things. So the urgency to find alternatives led to the innovation of massively distributed processing and distributed databases. The attractive factor of distributed databases is that most of them are open source and there are no big bucks to spend for trying. If you have worked on structured databases, moving to unstructured databases is a major shift. Sometimes it is scary even to imagine the concept. Though NOSQL cannot fully replace SQL, I see the adoption to NOSQL is increasing drastically in all industry verticals. The exciting news is NOSQL is going to stay and is going to impact many database fundamentals that we know.

I know Prasad as an excellent, hardworking Sybase (RDBMS) DBA. When I heard him supporting Cassandra, I asked him how he made the shift. After reading this book, he is not only an expert, but he has mastered it. The proof is in the book. Prasad made Cassandra learning much easier, starting from the basics all the way to the advanced capabilities of Cassandra. Since Prasad came from a strong relational databases background, throughout this book, he compared and highlighted the differences and strengths/weaknesses of relational databases and Cassandra to help us easily understand them better. I am confident this book will help anyone for making the adoption of NOSQL technology, or to advance their career on managing and architecting in Cassandra. I hope you find this book enjoyable, informative, and useful.

- Raju Chidambaram
Co-founder/CTO, Dobler Consulting Inc.

Preface

Why has this book been written?

I started my career as a developer. I developed many applications using Clipper, Assembly language routines, and Microsoft C. Later, I started working on Oracle and Sybase. From 1996 I am working as DBA with major wall-street firms, mainly working with SAP Sybase and replication technology. A few years ago I decided to change the technology I was working. I did not want to work on traditional RDBMS such as Oracle, Microsoft SQL, or SAP Sybase anymore. As my most experience was as DBA, my incline was towards NoSQL databases. I took some courses and online classes on Hadoop and MongoDB. But what attracted me the most was Apache/DataStax Cassandra. I started self-learning and spent hundreds of hours on building and rebuilding Cassandra clusters. During my learning process, I have to go to different websites and blog posts to understand the basics of Cassandra. This whole learning process encouraged me to write this book.

In recent years a growing number of companies have adopted NoSQL/Cassandra. These organizations need scalable, highly available, and secured databases such as Cassandra. When it comes to supporting such environments, it takes a lot of effort to train the staff, and I hope this book can fill that void space.

How will this book help you?

- This book focusses on administration part of Cassandra only and does not cover any application level coding. This makes sure that readers who bought the book by reading its title, find more value.

- Unlike most books on Cassandra, this book has been filled with actual examples with commands and output. When you read only theory, it's become difficult to understand, and you don't know what to expect while working on a real Cassandra cluster at work.
- All the examples listed in this book can be tested on your laptop, which will give you actual hands-on experience.

Is this book for you?

Cassandra Admin DBA Guide book is intended for a variety of readers. This book should be useful to you if you are:

- Database administrator currently working with any RDBMS such as SAP Sybase, Oracle, SQL Server, MySQL, or any other NoSQL such as MongoDB, HBASE, CouchDB and would like to understand Cassandra.
- Sybase DBA/Oracle DBA, who would like to change technology and move to Cassandra and they are looking for a book which will give you enough knowledge and hands-on to become an expert at beginner's level in Cassandra Administration.
- A developer who is working on Cassandra and like to know more about the architecture, beginner level internals and want to do hands-on.
- A developer currently working on a live Cassandra project, you may not have the permissions/access/opportunity to work on Administration tasks. For such developers, this is an ideal book, where you can learn the Administration part of Cassandra by creating your test environment.
- A Manager leading an Analytics team or in the operational role, and would like to work on Cassandra to increase your knowledge, which may help your decision making in technology strategy.
- A student, analyst, data scientist, or a technical savvy person who want to know more about Cassandra.
- Someone who just wants to learn more about Cassandra in general!

This book is NOT for you

- If you are a developer, who is looking for Java or any other code examples for using Cassandra.
- If you are looking in-depth knowledge on CQL or Cassandra internals. This is purely a basic Cassandra Administration book, which covers decent information about administrating a Cassandra cluster.

Examples in this book

The examples, data model, presented in this book, are only for demonstration and understanding. By no means, these are perfect examples or design, because it is not.

While every effort has been made and every precaution has been taken in the preparation of this book, the author or the publisher will not be held liable for damages resulting from use of the information from this book. Information from this book is sold without any warranty. Any code examples, data model examples, steps on doing certain activity may have errors and use it without any warranty.

Conventions used in this book

The following fonts are used in this book

Italics used for file names, figures & table and column names in most places.

Gray area text is used mostly for CQL output, command and outputs. The gray area text contains different fonts and sizes in many places. This was mainly done to fit the text in the window.

About the Author

Prasad Bagewadi has over 20 years of IT experience, most of it working as a Database Administrator on Wall Street. He has worked in companies like American Express, JP Morgan, Chase, Lehman Brothers, Merril Lynch/Bank of America, Credit Suisse, UBS, Wells Fargo as DBA. He has received a Bachelor's degree in Science from Mysore University in India and has settled down in New Jersey since the mid-90's. He currently works in Greater Philadelphia and New York City area. In his free time, he loves playing tennis and spending time with his family, whether it be hiking or traveling. Prasad, being an avid reader, also likes reading business and motivational books.

www.linkedin.com/in/prasadbagewadi

About the Reviewer

G ayathri Govindhan is a Database Engineer and Architect and working in database systems for over 25 years. She has a Masters in Computer Science, from New Jersey Institute of Technology, Newark, NJ.

She has wide experience with a variety of OLTP and Big Data databases, like Sybase, SQL Server, MySQL, MariaDB, PostgreSQL, Netezza, Cassandra and Paraccel. These days she works as a AWS Solutions Architect helping migrate databases from on premise to Cloud.

Acknowledgement

Writing this book has been a fun and exciting journey. This book took hundreds of hours from family time on weekdays and weekends. When things were not going in the right direction, I naturally was little stressed out and my wife and two lovely daughters were very accommodative.

Writing this book has proved to be a fun, exciting, and challenging journey in all. Although hundreds of hours were taken away from family time on weekdays and weekends, my family has been my rock through it all. My wife Sheetal Bagewadi, is someone I owe the most credit to for helping me through the course of the making of this book. Her continuous belief in me has helped me make the best version of this book possible. I also have to thank my two lovely daughters, Sohini Bagewadi and Saniya Bagewadi. Unlike them, I have done my education in a language that is not English. Naturally, that has had a slight interference with some of my sentence structures. My daughters have given their time out of their busy school lives to help me with endless hours of proof-reading and editing. I truly could not have done it without their support.

Next I would like to say thanks to Manjunath Subramanya for his constant encouragement for writing this book. Gayathri for her help in technical proofreading. Having a second pair of eyes who understand the meaning of this book was super helpful.

I would also like to thank Ankit Patel from Datastax and Gopinath Murugan. Working with you has been an invaluable experience for me.

CHAPTER 1

Big Data and Cassandra

C assandra is a distributed, fault-tolerant, master-less peer-to-peer, linearly scalable, and decentralized database. Cassandra was created at Facebook, based on a distributed design from Amazon's Dynamo and Google's BigTable.

Databases

In 1970 Edgar Codd coined the term "RDBMS" (relational database management system). The RDBMS has become very popular over the last four decades. Many RDBMSs are available in the market, like Oracle, Sybase, MS SQL Server, MySQL, and Informix. The common definition of RDBMS is the storage of data in a collection of columns and rows in the form of a table. SQL (structured query language) is used to do various operations on the data, like data definition language (DDL), data manipulation language (DML—INSERT, UPDATE, and DELETE), and SELECT. SQL was officially adopted as an ANSI standard in 1986. It has been extended by several vendors with proprietary syntaxes, such as Microsoft's and SAP's (formerly Sybase) T-SQL and Oracle's PL-SQL.

In the 1980s and 1990s, big and small companies transformed their front office and back office by storing data in RDBMSs, moving from human-intensive manual work to computerized data processing and printing. As companies heavily invested in information technology, they started finding different sources of data that can be stored and processed for business advantage. Product and service data, customer data, employee data, accounting, and various types of transactions, including point of sales, provided companies with unique insights about their businesses and helped speed up their processes. Data processing gave them the ability to

1

identify market trends and customers' buying patterns, as well as to do better forecasting, all of which ultimately helped manage their businesses with fewer overheads.

In the mid-90s, I was working on a data warehouse project for a large tobacco company in Kuala Lumpur, Malaysia. Product costs, product inventory, and customer transaction history were all loaded into a Sybase server, and data were analyzed to forecast region-wide sales, inventory readiness, product costing, and revenue. Computerizing this task saved them thousands of human-intensive hours. This type of forecasting which used to take weeks before, they were able to complete this in a few minutes.

Internet Age

As the Internet was commercialized in the mid-1990s, all companies started going online. A new data source in the form of web clicks became a new asset to the companies to analyze the data and obtain new insight into product sales and customer behavior. Online companies started collecting data, as they realized the analysis of data could lead them to achieve the following:

- Better customer understanding
- Better customer service
- Significant competitive advantage over brick-and-mortar companies

The perfect example is the success of Netflix, which transformed the online-entertainment industry. Brick-and-mortar companies, which refused to go online vanished.

The 20th century was an industrial age. Big companies needed a massive amount of land, money, and workers to generate wealth and reach the market cap of over 100 billion dollars. The 21st century is very innovative, and great technological innovations always kept the companies on the top. Today's capital for these companies is people and data. People are in the form of customers (for Amazon it's Prime members, and for Netflix it's members.) and users (for Facebook, Twitter, and other social-media companies). Data is in the form of clicks generated by people (for Google) and other companies. Most of the data is generated by the people, which is stored and processed to increase the revenue of these companies. In the 21st century, you need to know how you can collect your data and buy data from other companies where it is required. This way the data can provide ideas for new revenue-generating products or services to stay ahead of the competition.

Let's look at a hypothetical example of cable-television advertising. Cable advertising targets the area that matters to the advertising company the most. Different types of advertisements are shown in different neighbourhoods. This ensures customers see the advertisement most relevant to their needs. When a large audience is exposed to properly targeted advertisements, it has a big impact, providing a higher return of investment for the advertisement company. Let's say a pharmaceutical company with blood pressure medication, and diabetes medication can target their advertisement in two adjacent towns, based on the data collected from pharmacies in the area. If Town A has more BP medication sold and Town B has more diabetes medications sold, it makes sense for the pharmaceutical company to show relevant advertisements in each town. The pharmaceutical company can show more BP medication advertisements in Town A and diabetes medication advertisements in Town B. This is more effective in terms of getting sales, rather than showing 50%–50% in both the towns. It's all about the data.

Cassandra Origination

As companies moved from storing the data, to analyzing the data, they started to grow the amount of data they were collecting. This was the time when processors were slow, and computer memory and hard disk to store the data were expensive. Companies need to significantly invest in hardware if they want to analyze and take advantage of the data.

Social media was a game changer for the amount of data generated. The companies found it profitable to store and process this data. Social-media posts, sensor data, machine-generated logs, web clicks, and so on generate huge volumes of data that runs into terabytes and petabytes, which companies not only wanted to store but also process this data. RDBMS and database management tools were never designed for the terabyte and petabyte of data volume and their processing. Due to the velocity at which this unstructured data was generated, it was impossible to store and process this data using available RDBMS technology. Companies like Amazon, Yahoo, Google, and Facebook have to find a new way to store and process the data they were collecting.

Google developed the GFS (Google File System) and BigTable. GFS provides fast access to data using commodity hardware. BigTable was Google's core technology, designed to scale across thousands of machines and made it easy to add more machines and horizontally scalable. BigTable was compressed, log-structured storage that was optimized for GFS.

Hadoop was developed by Doug Cutting, based on GFS papers, and deployed at Yahoo in 2006.

Amazon runs a massive worldwide e-commerce platform that serves millions of customers, using thousands of servers located across multiple datacenters around the world. In 2004, Amazon's rapid growth started to hit the upper limit of its Oracle database. To meet the reliability and scaling, the company's engineers created a new proprietary database called DynamoDB, which is a key-value store. The engineers behind Amazon Dynamo published the Dynamo Papers in 2007. The papers were highly influential and inspired to create Cassandra.

Apache Cassandra was initially developed by Avinash Lakshman and Prashant Malik at Facebook. It was based on the Amazon Dynamo database and Google's BigTable. Avinash Lakshman was one of the authors of Amazon's Dynamo. Facebook originally developed Apache Cassandra for its messenger platform to power their inbox search. In 2010 it became the main project for Apache.

Jonathan Ellis and Matt Pfeil were using Cassandra at Rackspace. In 2010, they left Rackspace and formed a company called Riptano in Austin, Texas. Later they renamed their company as DataStax and moved the headquarters to Santa Clara, California. DataStax created its proprietary version of Cassandra and called it DataStax Enterprise (DSE). DSE is the first commercial distribution of the Cassandra database. Over the period, they enhanced Cassandra to include advanced security, search capability through Solr, graph database, spark for analytics and OpsCenter to monitor the entire cluster.

Scalability

Until the middle of 2000, most of the data was stored and processed in RDBMSs. Vertical scalability or scaling up is easily achievable by adding more memory, disk space and upgrading to the faster CPU. The costs of the CPU, memory, and disk keep falling over the years, which allowed companies to invest more money in the hardware to scale up the environment. The performance was achieved by tuning the software code, normalizing the data model, and caching more data in memory to reduce disk I/O. But there is a limit for vertical scalability. Traditional databases cannot be tuned to access and process terabyte and petabyte of data. I have experienced in supporting so many applications in Sybase ASE, which grew from a few gigabytes into terabytes in a few years. Every year or two, we used to migrate these database servers to bigger and better hardware. This used to temporarily fix the performance issues, which was not productive.

Cassandra and many other NoSQL databases are horizontally scalable. Cassandra is a massively scalable, distributed, decentralized, highly available, partition-tolerant, eventual consistent database. To understand Cassandra and its architecture, you need to know about CAP theorem.

CAP Theorem

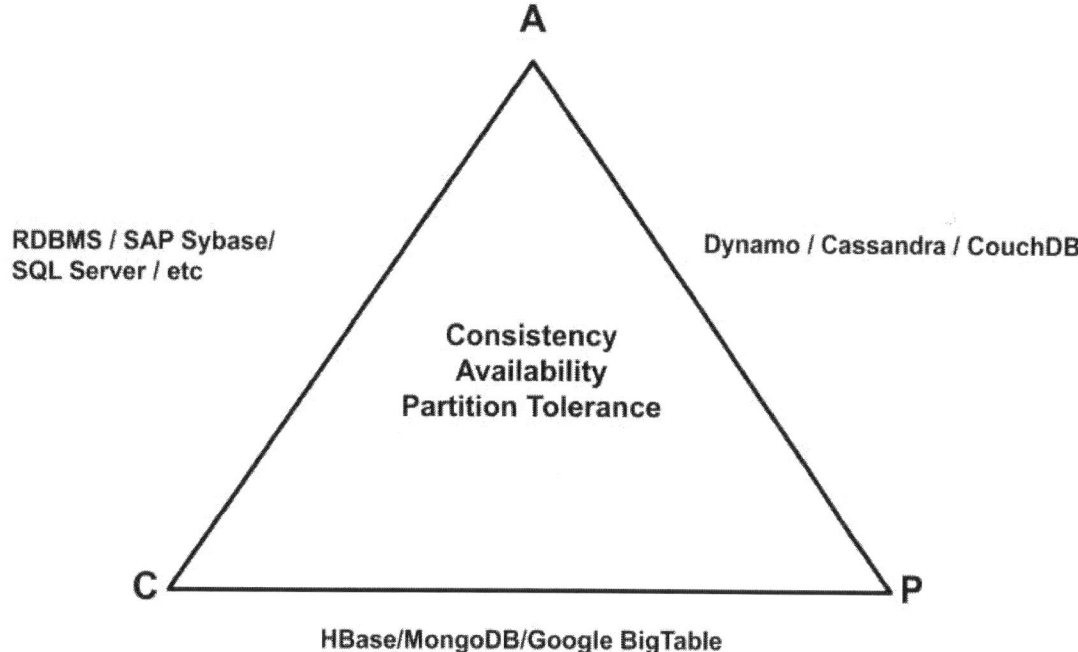

Figure 1.1: CAP theorem

CAP theorem, also known as Brewer's theorem, states that it is impossible for a distributed database or data store to guarantee consistency, availability, and partition tolerance all at once. You cannot build a distributed database that is continually available, consistent, and tolerant of any partition failure. Any two requirements can be met as shown in Figure 1.1 below.

Consistency: All nodes contain same data at the same time.

Availability: Data can be read or write all the time.

Partition Tolerance: System continues to operate despite failure of any part of the system or node.

Cassandra is classified as an AP system, meaning that availability and partition tolerance are guaranteed. But Cassandra can be tuned with replication factor and consistency level to meet good consistency. If you design the cluster and replication factors appropriately and tune the consistency to the higher level, Cassandra can be a CP (consistency and partition tolerance).

CHAPTER 2

Basic Cassandra Architecture

n this chapter, we will examine basic Cassandra architecture. If you are from an RDBMS background, you will notice a lot of new terms when you are learning Cassandra.

Cassandra is a distributed, fault-tolerant, master-less peer-to-peer, linearly scalable, and decentralized database. It is designed to handle large volumes of data while providing fault tolerance and high availability with no single point of failure.

Cassandra Cluster

A Cassandra cluster is a set of peer-to-peer nodes that are logically and physically configured as a distributed database. All the nodes in the cluster have the same cluster name. All the nodes will have the same list of seed nodes. Preferably two seed nodes from each datacenter is the best practice. Seed nodes are used during startup and bootstrapping to discover other nodes in the cluster. These two configurations can be found in *$CASSANDRA_HOME/conf/casandra.yaml*.

cluster_name: <name of the cluster>
seeds: <IP addresses of nodes>

A node is one Cassandra instance. In Figure 2.1, nodes N1 to N8 are part of the same cluster. A cluster is sub grouped into datacenters and racks for replication and failover purposes.

Rack is a logical set of nodes. Nodes N1 & N2 are configured as RAC1, N3 & N4 as RAC2 in datacenter US-EAST. Similarly, nodes N5 & N6 as RAC1 and N7 & N8 are configured as RAC2 in datacenter US-WEST.

Datacenter is a logical set of RACK and nodes. In the below picture, nodes N1,N2,N3 & N4 are configured as US-EAST datacenter, whereas nodes N5,N6,N7 & N8 are configured as US-WEST datacenter.

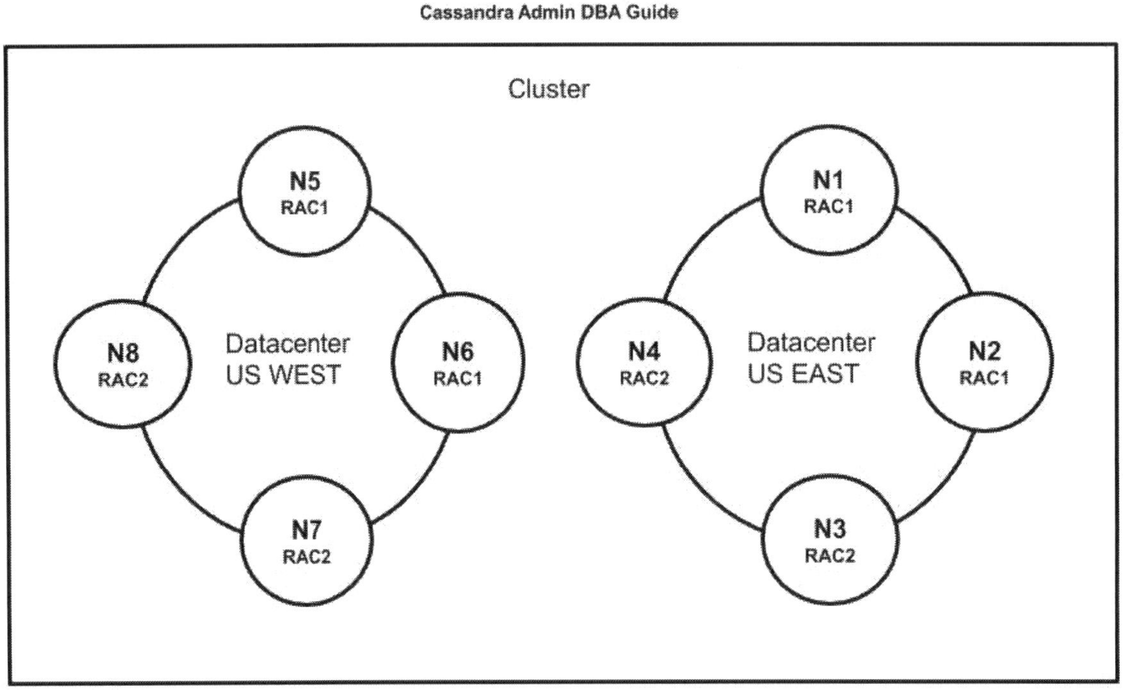

Figure 2.1: Cassandra Cluster

Master-Less Peer-to-Peer Architecture

Cassandra is designed with the master-less peer-to-peer architecture. There is no concept of a master node and slave node in Cassandra. In the traditional mater-slave model, slaves synchronize their data with the master. In master-slave architecture, unavailability or node failure of the master is a potential cause for a single point of failure. Cassandra can handle big workloads across multiple nodes with no single point of failure due to the network or nodes going down. It can achieve the workload by distributing the data across the cluster. Cassandra has been built to be highly available and easily scalable. Each node in Cassandra is structurally identical, and it's designed to be fault tolerant.

Figure 2.2 shows a simple four-node Cassandra cluster. Clients can connect to any node to read and write data. The node to which the client is connected is called the coordinator node.

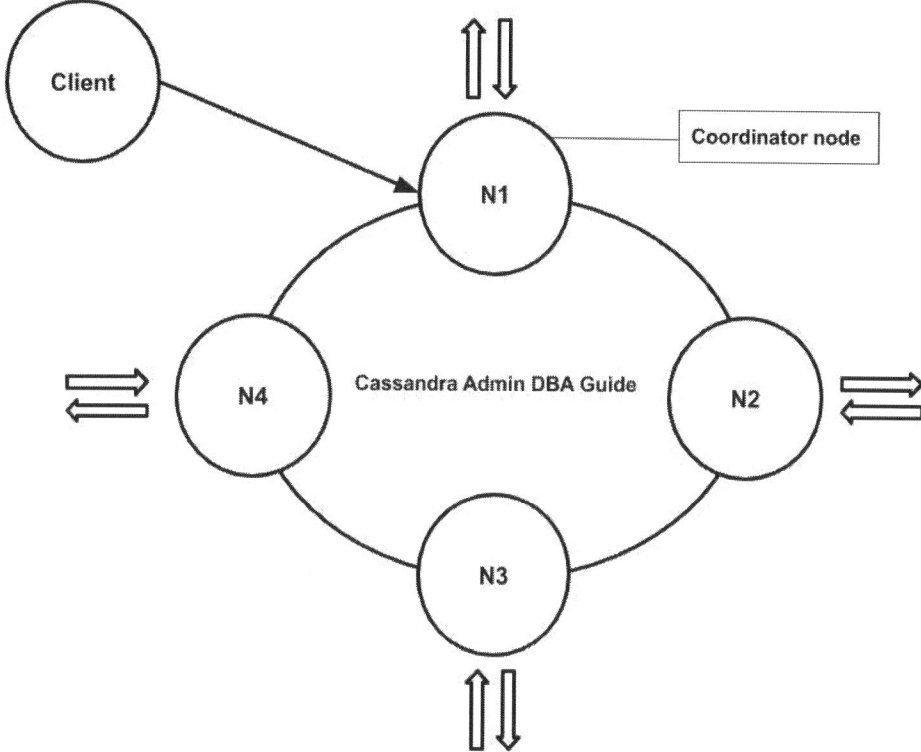

Figure 2.2: Coordinator node

Gossip Protocol

Cassandra uses gossip protocol for communication within the cluster, to support decentralization and partition tolerance. Each node in the cluster discovers information about other nodes by exchanging status about itself and other nodes. The gossiper runs every second on each node, and it exchanges status information with up to three random nodes in the cluster. It's like a heartbeat, checking node state, location, and timestamp. This communication between the nodes makes them learn about one another in the cluster.

For example, in *Figure 2.2*, if node N3 is dead, rest of the nodes soon will know that node N3 is unreachable, and the coordinator node will save any write pending to the node N3 as hints.

The main purpose of the gossip protocol is failure detection. The "gossip" name came from the concept of human gossiping.

It is best practice to use the same list of seed nodes for all nodes to prevent any gossiping issues. In multiple datacenter clusters, include at least two nodes from each datacenter in the seed list. If you include only one node, gossip has to communicate with another datacenter if you have to bootstrap that seed node. When you include at least one node from each datacenter in the seed list, it makes gossip performance optimal. Do not include every node in the seed list as it will reduce gossip performance.

In a Cassandra cluster, some nodes are configured as seed nodes; these nodes need to startup first. As other nodes join the cluster, they gossip with the seed node and quickly learn about all other nodes in the cluster.

During cluster expansion, while adding nodes, which is called bootstrapping, the new joining nodes talk to the seed node to obtain information about other nodes in the cluster.

Data Partition

Cassandra is a distributed database. When data is written, it is written transparently and saved across all the nodes in the cluster. Each node is responsible for that part of the data.

The most common partitioning used is Murmur3Partitioner. This can be configured in the *cassandra.yaml* file. Below you see that node is configured to use Murmur3Partitioner.

```
# partitioners and token selection.
partitioner: org.apache.cassandra.dht.Murmur3Partitioner
```

Note that once a cluster is initialized with a specific partitioner, it cannot be changed. Cassandra dynamically partitions the data over a set of nodes in the cluster, which can be visualized as a ring (the terminology is taken from Amazon Dynamo). It partitions the data across all nodes using consistent hashing using the hash of the row key. Murmur3Partitioner uses a maximum possible range of hash values from -2^{63} to $+2^{63}-1$. These are called token values. When a row is inserted into a table, Cassandra applies the hash function to the partition key and creates a consistent token value. Based on the token value for that partition key, the row is inserted in the appropriate node, which owns that token range Cassandra key.

Figure 2.3 shows a four-node Cassandra cluster with single token ranges.

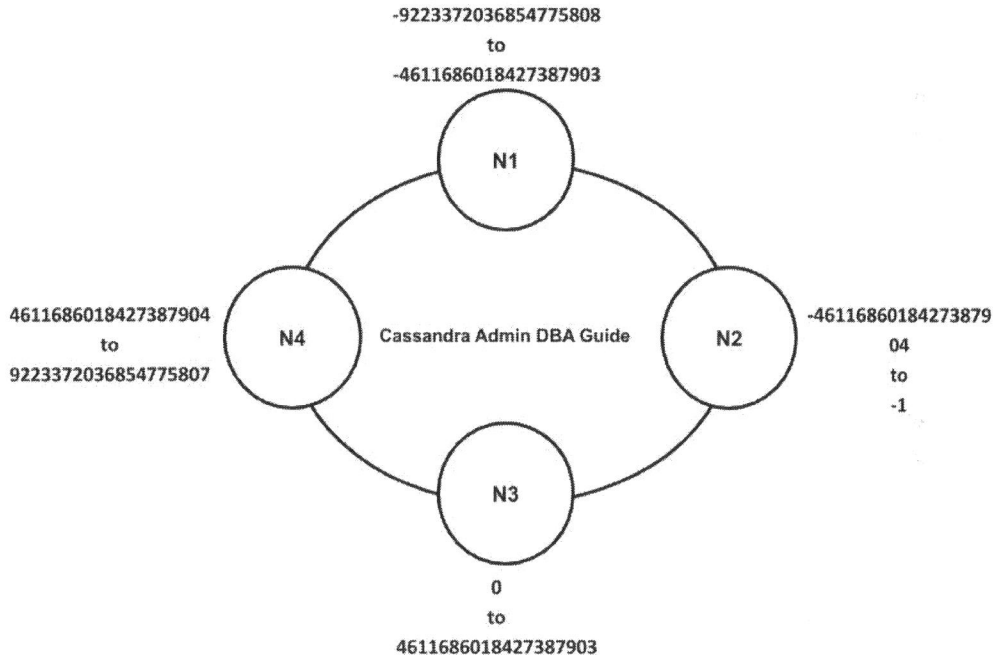

Figure 2.3: Partition and tokens

For the Cassandra token calculator, you can refer to the website https://www.geroba.com/cassandra/cassandra-token-calculator/.

In *Figure 2.4* the result set displays the token range for a four-node cluster using Murmur3Partitioner.

Cassandra Token Calculator

Partitioner	⦿ Murmur3Partitioner ○ RandomPartitioner
Number of nodes	4
Result	-9223372036854775808 -4611686018427387904 0 4611686018427387904

Calculate Tokens

Figure 2.4: Token calculator

For simplicity and our understanding, let's assume that the entire cluster's token-range distribution is from −100 to 100. In *figure 2.5*, you will see that four nodes—N1, N2, N3, and N4—are evenly owning a range of tokens. When a row is inserted, Cassandra applies a hash function to the partition key (*Cust_ID*), and it will generate a consistent token value for that particular keyspace.table.*Cust_ID* value in the range of −100 to 100. Based on this token value, it will send a write to the node that owns that token range. From the figure, you can see that for Cust_ID = 'A001', the token value generated is −25, which is owned by node N2.

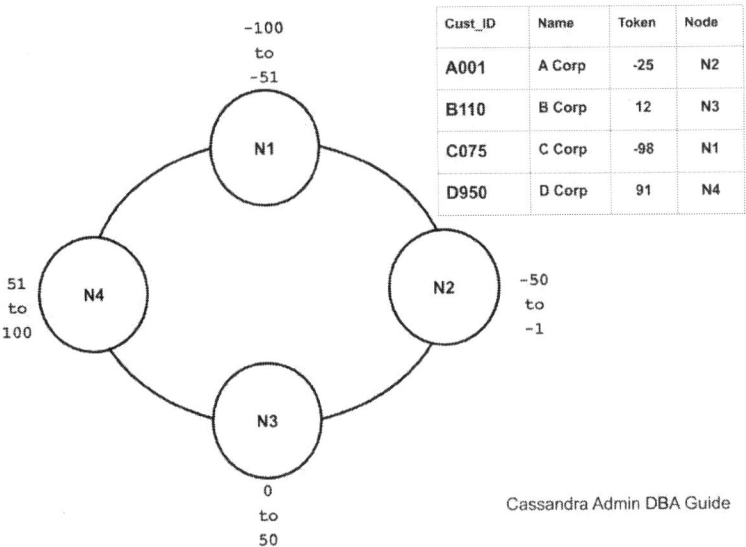

Cust_ID	Name	Token	Node
A001	A Corp	-25	N2
B110	B Corp	12	N3
C075	C Corp	-98	N1
D950	D Corp	91	N4

Cassandra Admin DBA Guide

Figure 2.5: Cassandra token ring

Replication

Cassandra replication is easy to set up and maintain. Unlike traditional RDBMS products, there is no need to get another product to replicate the data. Traditional RDBMS was never built with horizontal scalability in mind. Replication features were added later to the core product to give a feel of horizontal scalability. RDBMS replication setup and maintenance involve complexity with no guarantee of live recovery in many cases.

In a Cassandra cluster, all nodes involved in the replication are grouped as logical, physical or Geo-distributed datacenters. There is no additional piece of software you need to run to set up replication.

While working as a DBA for a large financial company in the early 2000s, they had a very complex replication setup. They had a massive replication of tables across hundreds of database servers that were geo-distributed across the United States, Europe, and Asia. The company was using Sybase ASE and Replication Server from SAP. Some of the key points and observations are as follows:

- One organization-wide database was replicated to hundreds of different Sybase servers across all the regions. That means if there are any changes to the existing DDL, you need to modify the definition and subscriptions for those hundreds of servers.
- There was no easy way to understand the flow of replication by querying system metadata. We had to manually maintain a list of the source and target servers for a quick understanding of the flow.
- Thousands of tables from many keyspaces (ASE database/Oracle Schema) were replicated by complex definitions. Many table replications were bi-directional between the United States and Europe, with complex logic to update the tables.
- The purpose of this setup was workload separation to run reports without affecting transactional loads and making data available for disaster recovery in different Geo-locations by keeping the master copy in one place.
- The major amount of DBA resources and work was involved in the following:
  1. Maintaining the complex setup, which required high-level of expertise.
  2. Monitoring the threads and latency of the replication.
  3. Performance tuning of the server and replication server to reduce latency.

The above-listed tasks and complexity used to take 60%–70% of DBA time in supporting day-to-day activities, which was very hectic. The good news is Cassandra was built with all these in mind, which is incredible. In Cassandra, replication is built as out of the box, which does not need additional products. It's very easy and simple to set up, and very little to almost no maintenance of replication is required.

In Cassandra, replication is set at keyspace level. A keyspace is equivalent to the database in SAP ASE/SQL Server or schema in Oracle. You cannot set replication at table level. Set up the replication at the time of creating keyspace by providing replication strategy and replication factor information. For example:

```
create keyspace first_ks with replication={'class':'SimpleStrategy','replication_factor':3};
```

SimpleStrategy is used only in a single datacenter and one rack. This is mostly used in the development environment. Replication factor represents the number of replica to maintain. In the preceding example, you are creating keyspace "first_ks" with SimpleStrategy, and you are defining the number of copies to maintain as 3. The replication factor affects your read and write consistency-levels.

SimpleStrategy places the first replica based on the node determined by the partitioner. Additional replicas are placed on the next nodes clockwise in the ring according to the token range.

Figure 2.6 shows the placement of the first replica, second replica, and third replica based on the token value and token range owned by each node in the cluster. This is assuming each node is configured with a single token range. You will learn more about virtual nodes (vnodes) in later chapters.

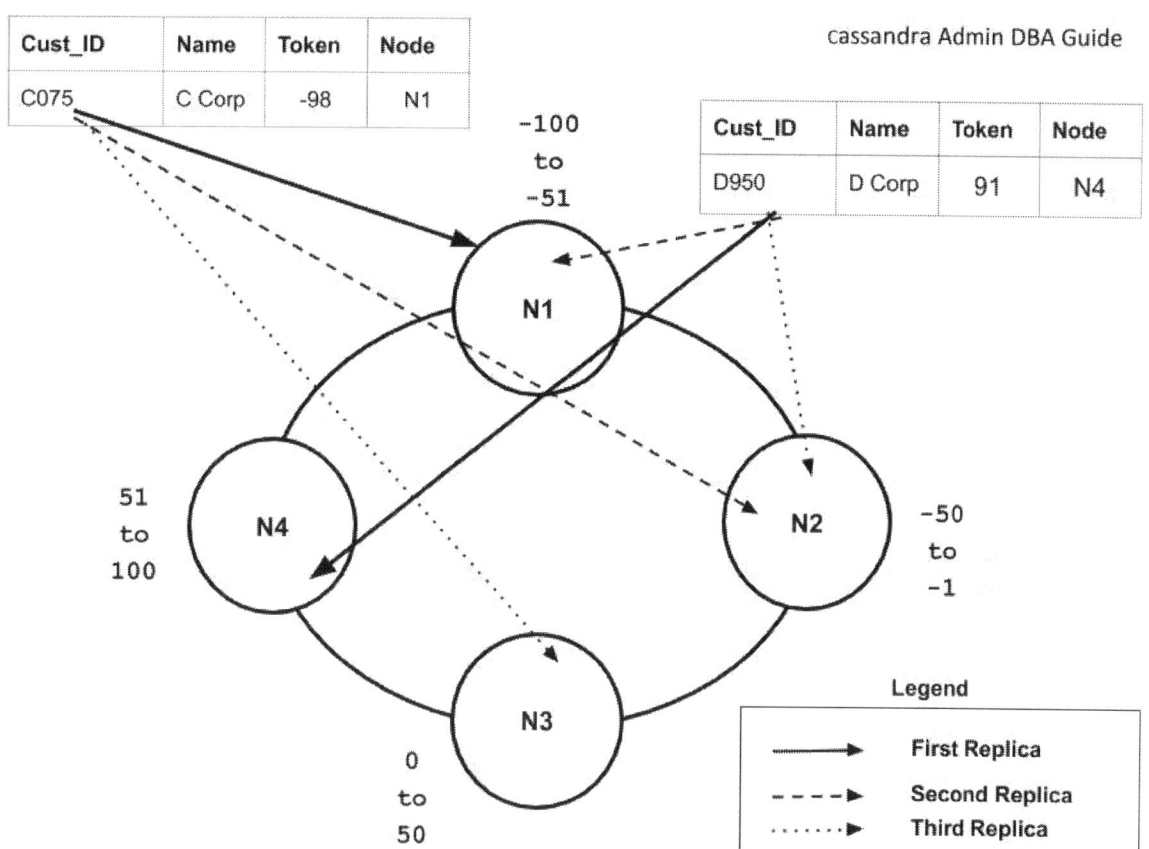

Cust_ID	Name	Token	Node
C075	C Corp	-98	N1

Cust_ID	Name	Token	Node
D950	D Corp	91	N4

-100
to
-51

51
to
100

-50
to
-1

0
to
50

Legend

First Replica
Second Replica
Third Replica

Figure 2.6: Replication Simple Strategy

NetworkTopologyStrategy is used when you configure clusters across multiple datacenters. In this strategy, we can specify the replication factor (number of replicas) for each datacenter. This strategy is datacenter aware, and make sure that replicas are not placed on the same rack. Cassandra uses snitches to discover overall network topology, which is configured in *cassandra-rackdc.properties* file. When we write data, this strategy places replicas in each datacenter. It places the first replica based on the node determined by the partitioner and subsequent replicas in the ring clockwise until it reaches the first node with a different rack configuration. When configuring NetworkTopologyStrategy, very close attention needs to be paid to configure it properly. For example, each rack should have the same number of nodes in the datacenter. Otherwise, the disk usage of some nodes will be more, and it can create hot spots in the cluster.

```
create keyspace second_ks with replication =
{ 'class' : 'NetworkTopologyStrategy, 'US-EAST':3, 'US-WEST':1 };
```

The preceding example sets three replicas in the "US-EAST" datacenter and one replica in the "US-WEST" datacenter.

Figure 2.7 is a comparison of how the second replica is selected based on the replication strategy. In SimpleStrategy, since there is no concept of datacenter or rack, the second replica will be the next node in the Cassandra ring after the primary node was selected based on the token value generated from the partitioner. In the case of NetworkTopologyStrategy, since it is datacenter and rack aware, it will skip node N2 for the second replica, as both nodes N1 and N2 belong to the same rack, which is RAC1. The second replica is placed on node N3, which is RAC2.

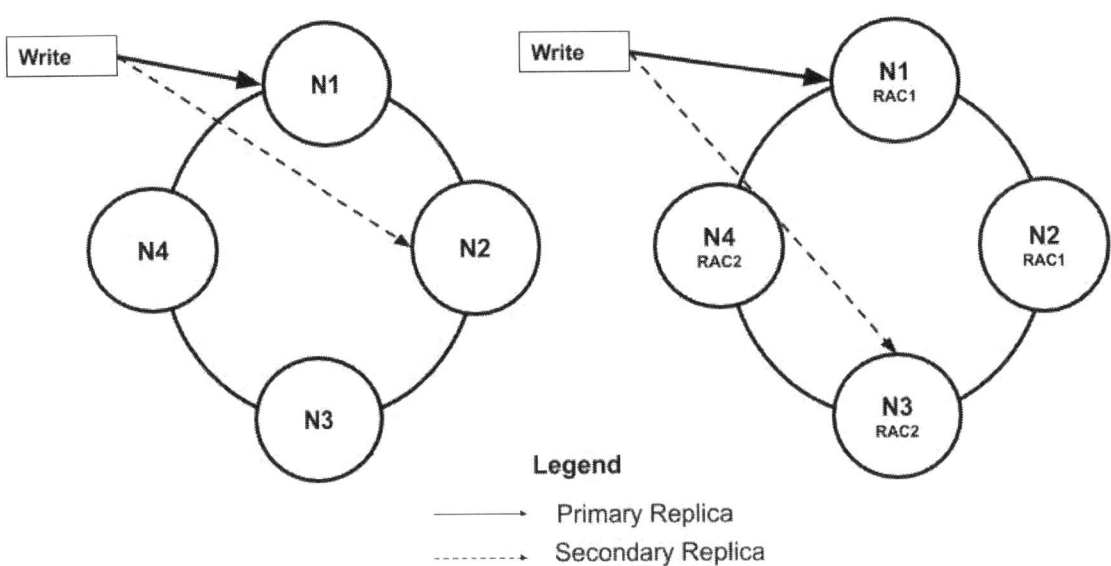

Cassandra Admin DBA Guide

SimpleStrategy replication_factor = 2   NetworkTopologyStrategy dc1 replication_factor = 2

Figure 2.7: SimpleStrategy vs NetworkTopologyStrategy

Some of the use cases of replication are as follows:

Workload separation: By replicating to different datacenters, it is possible to separate transactional workload from reporting workload. In this case replication strategy would look similar to { 'dc_transaction':3, 'dc_report',3 }.

Geographic location: If cluster data is accessed by clients from two different geographic locations, such as the United States and Europe, to lower the latency, Europe clients can connect to datacenters in Europe. Both datacenters will be part of the same cluster. In this case replication strategy would look similar to { 'dc_US':3, 'dc_EUROPE',3 }.

Live backup: Backing up database in a distributed system is not easy. For example, we can set up a cluster with a datacenter, which can be dedicated as a live backup. In this case replication strategy would look similar to { 'dc_main':3, 'dc_backup',3 }. If you would like to save disk spaces, you can set up as { 'dc_main':3, 'dc_backup',2 }.

Below is an example of settings with the all above use cases. Note that this is only a theoretical discussion to illustrate how the configuration would look.

```
{ 'dc_newyork':3, 'dc_nj_report':3, 'dc_london':3, 'dc_nj_backup':2 }
```

Consistency

Cassandra is a linearly scalable and highly available distributed database. It's an AP (available/partition-tolerant) system as per the CAP theorem. This means Cassandra can provide availability and partition tolerance. Consistency means all the users see the same data even when the system is going through concurrent updates. In a distributed system, such as Cassandra, to make it "available" and "partition-tolerant," data is usually replicated to multiple nodes and datacenters. When you update the data, it may take some time to reach every node where it is supposed to be replicated. This creates a possibility where a user reads the data from a node where the write has not yet reached, and the data is inconsistent. This data will eventually become consistent.

In below *Figure 2.8*, you can read about Cassandra's consistency level and its implications.

Consistency Level	Implication
ANY	This is applicable for write operation only. Ensures that write is successful on one node or by co-ordinator write to hints. If hint is stored, co-ordinator will later attempt to deliver the writes to all replicas. Not suggested for production use.
ONE	One node need to respond for read/write.
LOCAL_ONE	One node need to respond for read/write. In a multi datacenter, read/write will not be sent to replicas for remote data center.
TWO	Two nodes need to respond for read/write.
THREE	Three nodes need to respond for read/write.
QUORUM	Majority of replicas need to respond. [(replication factor/2) + 1] for a given keyspace, if replication_factor = 3, means for QUORUM, 2 nodes need to respond. For replication_factor = 7, 4 nodes need to respond. For example, from example above { 'dc_US':3, 'dc_EUROPE',3 }, if you are performing read/write connected to any node in any datacenter, any 4 nodes need to respond. This means QUORUM response can be from both datacenters.
LOCAL_QUORUM	Same as QUORUM but only for local data center. For example, from example above { 'dc_US':3, 'dc_EUROPE',3 }, if you are performing read/write connected to any node in dc_US datacenter, any 2 nodes need to respond from dc_US datacenter. Unless you have a strong use case to use QUORUM, you can use LOCAL_QUORUM. For example, if you have written all your application with QUORUM and you are connected to dc_US, you need at least four nodes to respond and if dc_EUROPE is down for whatever reason, all read/write will start failing. But with LOCAL_QUORUM, even dc_EUROPE is down, you can continue to operate with dc_US datacenter.
EACH_QUORUM	Majority of nodes need to respond from all datacenters. For example, from example above { 'dc_US':3, 'dc_EUROPE',3 }, if you are performing read/write, two nodes need respond from dc_US datacenter and two nodes need to respond from dc_EUROPE.
ALL	Every replica must respond; this include all datacenters. Consistency ALL reduce the availability. Note that storing hint by co-ordinator for write operation is not considered as success for consistency ALL.

Figure 2.8: Cassandra consistency

Cassandra's consistency is tunable. You can change consistency for a set of queries. Lower the consistency, higher the availability. A higher consistency level means that more nodes need to respond, thus lower availability. How consistency level responds, is based on the replication factor of the keyspace and not the total number of nodes in the datacenter or cluster.

Consistency ONE or ANY is not suggested in production or even in development or QA unless there is a clear use case. Take an example of a four-node (N1, N2, N3, and N4) cluster with replication_factor (RF) = 3. Say the writes are at consistency QUORUM and the data is updated for the given keyspace.table.partition on nodes N1 and N2 and failed to write on node N3. In this case, the write is successful on two nodes out of three, which satisfied the consistency QUORUM. Since the write failed on node N3, it has inconsistent data. Now if you run a SELECT query at consistency level ONE and if the coordinator selects node N3 to run your query, you will get incorrect, old data. If you write back the updated data, based on the old data, it will overwrite the data on nodes N1 and N2, which are incorrect.

When a strong consistency is required, write at QUORUM, and read at the QUORUM level.

When W + R > RF, it's strong consistency.

R = Read replicas

W = Write replicas

RF = Replication factor

For example, in replication={'class':'SimpleStrategy','replication_factor':3}, QUORUM means two nodes need to respond to read or write.

R+W (2+2) > RF (3) satisfies the strong consistency need. When you write at the QUORUM level and read at the QUORUM level, it means it is immediately consistent.

Commit Logs, Memtables, and SSTable

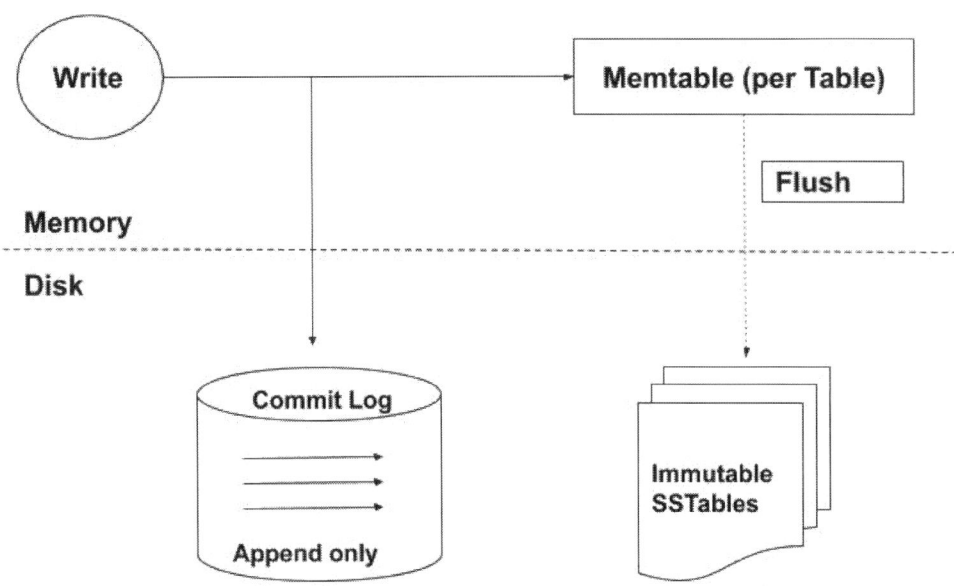

Cassandra Admin DBA Guide

Figure 2.9: Cassandra write

Commit logs, memtables, and SSTable is key to Cassandra's write performance. Writes are first written to the commit log and then in-memory table structure (memtable). A write is successful once it is written to both the commit log and memtable. Memtable is flushed to SSTable once it reaches the threshold.

Memtable is an in-memory structure for every CQL table and its indexes. Data in memtable is sorted by the row key of the table.

Memtable is flushed to SSTable when the number of objects stored in it reaches the threshold. Memtables are sorted key structure, and when it is flushed to the disk as SSTable, it is written sequentially. Each flush creates a new SSTable. These SSTables eventually get merged by compaction process into new SSTables. SSTable stands for "sorted strings table". This concept is borrowed from Google's Bigtable. SSTables are actual data files in Cassandra.

As you can see in *Figure 2.9*, each flush creates a new SSTable with sorted data from memtable. If a data row is updated multiple times and flushed multiple times, that data row will be in multiple SSTables and memtable.

cassandra.yaml file has settings which allow you to configure commit log and data directory.

commitlog_diectory: Allow you to configure location of the commitlog.
data_file_directories: Allow you to configure location of the datafiles.

Tombstones

Cassandra tombstones are nothing but delete. Tombstones are generated when an entire row is deleted, or a just a cell (value of a column in a row) is deleted. If anyone from RDBMS background might be surprised to hear how it's possible to delete just a column value. Yes, it is possible. Cassandra does not store "null" values. This means when you delete a cell or even just update a column value for a given row with "null", Cassandra deletes the cell and generates a tombstone.

In RDBMS, when a row is deleted, the row gets removed, or marker is updated, and the actual data page that contains the row gets updated. Deleting a row in a distributed database system and replicated database system like Cassandra is trickier and complicated. In Cassandra, the deletion of a row or cell is a write operation. Cassandra is designed to write optimized performance, and every write operation is sequential and append-only.

When a row is deleted, Cassandra does not immediately remove data. It is written or marked in the memtable as deleted. When memtable get flushed, the "delete" is written to the SSTable. Tombstones exist in SSTables and are removed by the compaction process after *gc_grace_seconds* has passed. This is designed to avoid any zombie data. For this reason, do not expect that the deletion of a large number of rows will free up the disk space immediately. Default gc_grace_seconds is set to ten days.

How deleted data can reappear?

To explain this, say there is a three-node cluster with nodes N1, N2, and N3 and the replication factor is set to 3. Delete operation on TableA was run at 11:00 a.m. with a QUORUM. Delete succeeded on nodes N1 and N2 and failed on N3, as it was down. As two nodes acknowledged the delete, QUORUM was successful.

11:00 a.m.: DELETE a row from TableA excecuted. Nodes N1 and N2 acknowledged, but N3 failed, as it was down.

If node N3 is up before *gc_grace_seconds* (default ten days) and if you happen to read the same row with QUORUM, the partial read repair is triggered, and node N3 will get the tombstone mark from node N1 or N2. And data will be consistent across the cluster.

If node N3 is up after gc_grace_seconds, compaction process might have removed the tombstone for that particular row in TableA on nodes N1 and N2. So there is no existence of that row on any other node. So when you read the data, Cassandra treats this as new data and propagates it to the entire cluster.

So it is very important to run repairs. Run repairs on all the nodes within *gc_grace_seconds* periods. If a node is down for an extended period, then bootstrap it again.

Hinted Handoff

Imagine a scenario in your office. You (write request) wanted to give a message to your colleague (node N3), and you walk up to his cubicle and find that he is not there! You see his neighbor (coordinator) and ask him to deliver your message when he comes back. This is what is exactly happening in Cassandra's hinted handoff. I know nowadays you don't walk to your colleagues to deliver messages when you can slack it.

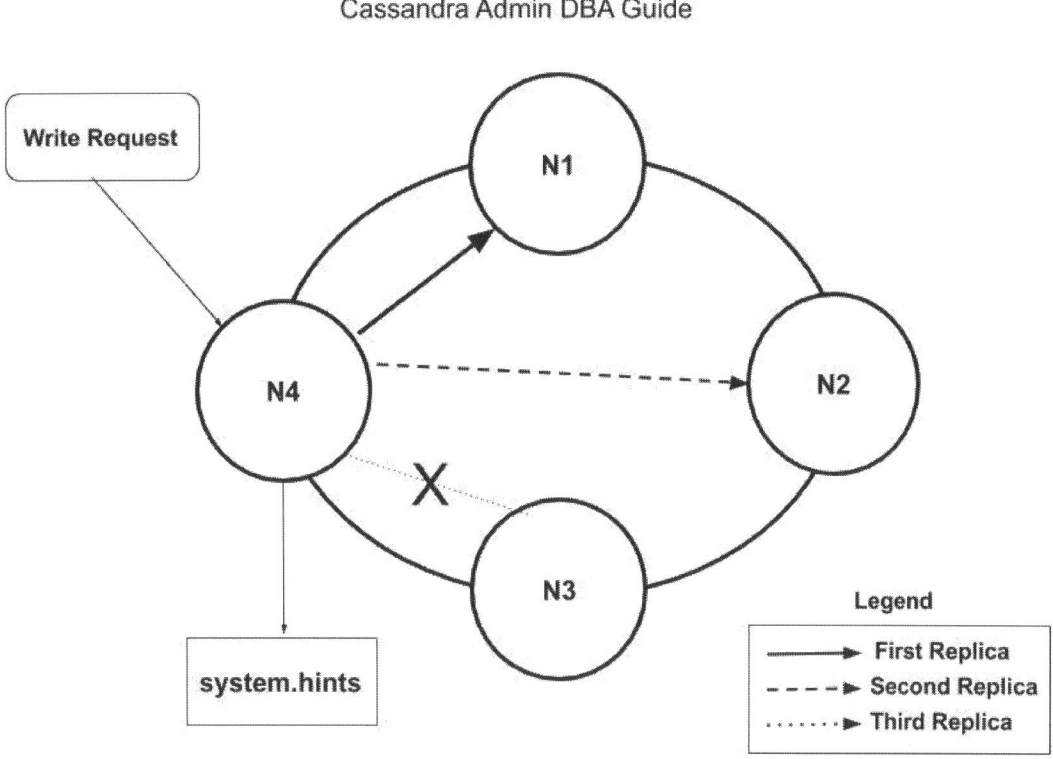

Figure 2.10: Hinted Handoff

Hinted handoff is a feature that optimizes the consistency process's anti-entropy when a node is not available. Take a look at *Figure 2.10*.

1. A write request comes to the coordinator node N4 and assumes that the write needs to be written to three replicas—nodes N1, N2, and N3.
2. Node N4 writes to nodes N1 and N2 and finds that node N3 is not reachable. N3 could be temporarily unavailable due to network issues/down.
3. Node N4 stores the writes for N3 into its *system.hints*.
4. Node N4 acknowledges back as write is successful.

cenario:

s written at the QUORUM level, it is still considered as successful as two out
e nodes were available.

2.   Jes N2 and N3 both were down and write is written at QUORUM, then write is
co..sidered as fail. In this case, hints will not be stored.

Hinted handoff can be enabled or disabled in the *cassandra.yaml* file.

May either be "true" or "false" to enable globally
hinted_handoff_enabled: true

Hinted handoff is stored only for the duration of max_hint_window_in_ms. Default value is
three hours. So if the node is down for more than three hours and recovers, run repair to
re-replicate the missed data.

this defines the maximum amount of time a dead host will have hints
generated. After it has been dead this long, new hints for it will not be
created until it has been seen alive and gone down again.
max_hint_window_in_ms: 10800000 # 3 hours

Removing a node or decommissioning a node automatically removes all the hints. So if you are
planning to decommission a node, check to make sure all hints are applied from that node.

System Keyspace

Like RDBMS, Cassandra stores metadata about the cluster in its internal keyspaces. These
keyspaces contain details about Cassandra database objects and cluster-related configurations.
In SAP Sybase and SQL Server, a *master* database is used to keep information about server
settings, disk information, tables, index, and view information, and tempdb is used as a work
space for sorting and storing intermediate results. Oracle database has a tablespace called
SYSTEM, which is used for a similar purpose.

Note that as Cassandra's version changes and improvements are made, the system keyspace and table information might change. If you are building any custom scripts around these, make sure to check when you migrate to a newer version of Cassandra. In earlier versions of Cassandra, there was only *system* keyspace, which was containing *schema_columnfamilies*, which stores information of all tables (used to refer as column family) and *schema_keyspaces*, which stores information of all keyspaces. In the latest version, these two are named different and moved under new keyspace *system_schema*. Columnfamily is now referred to as table whereas *schema_keyspaces* is named as *keyspaces*.

Below output displays all keyspaces and tables in those keyspaces. Once you go through the installation chapter and install Cassandra on one node, you can run the following cql commands.

```
cassandra@host1:~$ $CASSANDRA_HOME/bin/cqlsh -u cassandra -pcassandra 192.168.1.32
Connected to CADG_cluster at 192.168.1.32:9042.
[cqlsh 5.0.1 | Cassandra 3.10 | CQL spec 3.4.4 | Native protocol v4]
Use HELP for help.
cassandra@cqlsh> desc keyspaces;

demo system_schema system_auth system system_distributed system_traces

cassandra@cqlsh> use system;
cassandra@cqlsh:system> desc tables;

available_ranges       peers          batchlog      transferred_ranges
batches              compaction_history size_estimates hints
prepared_statements     sstable_activity   built_views
"IndexInfo"          peer_events      range_xfers
views_builds_in_progress paxos          local

cassandra@cqlsh:system> use system_schema ;
cassandra@cqlsh:system_schema> desc tables;
```

```
tables   triggers   views   keyspaces  dropped_columns
functions aggregates indexes types      columns

cassandra@cqlsh:system_schema>
cassandra@cqlsh:system_schema> select keyspace_name,replication from keyspaces;

 keyspace_name  | replication
----------------------+-------------------------------------------------------------------------------
      system_auth | {'class': 'org.apache.cassandra.locator.SimpleStrategy', 'replication_factor': '1'}
    system_schema |                         {'class': 'org.apache.cassandra.locator.LocalStrategy'}
 system_distributed | {'class': 'org.apache.cassandra.locator.SimpleStrategy', 'replication_factor': '3'}
           system |                         {'class': 'org.apache.cassandra.locator.LocalStrategy'}
    system_traces | {'class': 'org.apache.cassandra.locator.SimpleStrategy', 'replication_factor': '2'}
             demo | {'class': 'org.apache.cassandra.locator.SimpleStrategy', 'replication_factor': '1'}

(6 rows)
cassandra@cqlsh:system_schema>
```

All metadata about system tables and user tables data is stored in data_file_directories, and commitlog is stored in *commitlog_directory*, which can be found in the *cassandra.yaml* file.

```
cassandra@host1:/usr/local/cassandra/conf$ grep -B 10 commitlog_directory cassandra.yaml
# Directories where Cassandra should store data on disk. Cassandra
# will spread data evenly across them, subject to the granularity of
# the configured compaction strategy.
# If not set, the default directory is $CASSANDRA_HOME/data/data.
# data_file_directories:
#     - /var/lib/cassandra/data

# commit log. when running on magnetic HDD, this should be a
# separate spindle than the data directories.
# If not set, the default directory is $CASSANDRA_HOME/data/commitlog.
# commitlog_directory: /var/lib/cassandra/commitlog
```

As shown in the below output, the default directory for storing data is *$CASSANDRA_HOME/data/data*. In this directory, the individual directory will be created for each keyspace. Within each keyspace, one folder is created for each table. Cassandra appends a unique id as a postfix for each table. In below output, you can see the data directory has keyspaces.

```
cassandra@host1:~$ cd $CASSANDRA_HOME/data/data
cassandra@host1:/usr/local/cassandra/data/data$ ls -lrt
total 24
drwxrwxr-x  26 cassandra cassandra  4096 Nov 10 20:41 system
drwxrwxr-x  12 cassandra cassandra  4096 Nov 10 20:41 system_schema
drwxrwxr-x   4 cassandra cassandra  4096 Nov 10 20:41 system_traces
drwxrwxr-x   5 cassandra cassandra  4096 Nov 10 20:41 system_distributed
drwxrwxr-x   6 cassandra cassandra  4096 Nov 10 20:41 system_auth
drwxrwxr-x   8 cassandra cassandra  4096 Nov 19 21:34 demo
cassandra@host1:/usr/local/cassandra/data/data$ cd demo
cassandra@host1:/usr/local/cassandra/data/data/demo$ ls -lrt
total 24
drwxrwxr-x 4 cassandra cassandra 4096 Nov 19 21:32 tablesplit-f6cc7af0ec6811e8953c855e44da35b5
drwxrwxr-x 4 cassandra cassandra 4096 Nov 20 16:15 test-631288a0e55511e8be1e4fa05a863635
drwxrwxr-x 4 cassandra cassandra 4096 Nov 20 16:15 tombstone_test-55e78da0eaec11e8a943d330b5c3dec0
drwxrwxr-x 4 cassandra cassandra 4096 Nov 20 16:15 tbl_tombstone-4ed5ee50eaea11e8a943d330b5c3dec0
drwxrwxr-x 4 cassandra cassandra 4096 Nov 20 16:15 tombstone_tbl-90418c80eae711e8a943d330b5c3dec0
drwxrwxr-x 4 cassandra cassandra 4096 Nov 20 23:52 tablesplit-c2392c30ec6c11e8953c855e44da35b5
cassandra@host1:/usr/local/cassandra/data/data/demo$
```

Keyspace "demo" has five tables. You can observe that there are two directories for table *'tablesplit'*. When you drop a table, Cassandra does not drop the directory. In this case, the table has been dropped and created again. For the right directory, you can query *system_schema.tables*. As you can find in the next output, directory with id 'c2392c30-ec6c-11e8-953c-855e44da35b5' as postfix, is the current one.

```
cassandra@cqlsh:system_schema> select keyspace_name,table_name,id
                          from tables where keyspace_name='demo';
```

27

```
keyspace_name | table_name     | id
---------------+----------------+-------------------------------------
          demo |      tablesplit | c2392c30-ec6c-11e8-953c-855e44da35b5
          demo |    tbl_tombstone | 4ed5ee50-eaea-11e8-a943-d330b5c3dec0
          demo |             test | 631288a0-e555-11e8-be1e-4fa05a863635
          demo |     tombstone_tbl | 90418c80-eae7-11e8-a943-d330b5c3dec0
          demo |   tombstone_test | 55e78da0-eaec-11e8-a943-d330b5c3dec0

(5 rows)
cassandra@cqlsh:system_schema>
```

Single Token vs VNODE

Here are some differences between them.

Single Token: Each node is assigned a specific token range. In the *cassandra.yaml* file, set *initial_token* for that node.

```
Initial_token: -4611686018427387904
```

When you set *initial_token* to a number, it means it's a single token setup. From this initial token to the next initial token set up by another node or to the end of the ring, all ranges will be owned by this physical node.

VNODE : Instead of assigning a single token range to a node, multiple smaller token ranges are assigned.

In *cassandra.yaml* file, set *num_token* to a number of vnodes.

```
num_token:16
```

num_token represents the number of token range owned by this physical node.

To understand better, let's assume the entire token range is represented from 0 to 99. Now we will see how this can be distributed in a five-node single-token cluster and five-node vnode cluster with *num_token = 4*. Note that actual range given below is just an example.

Single token range

Node	Range
Node1	0-19
Node2	20-39
Node3	40-59
Node4	60-79
Node5	80-99

vnode with num_token=4

Node	Range (four ranges)
Node1	0-4, 25-29, 50-54, 75-79
Node2	5-9, 30-34, 55-59, 80-84
Node3	10-14, 35-39, 60-64, 85-89
Node4	15-19, 40-44, 65-69, 90-94
Node5	20-24, 45-49, 70-74, 95-99

Single Token: When you add or remove node, you need to manually recalculate token to rebalance.

VNODE: When you add or remove node, tokens are automatically rebalanced. Also, number of vnodes, num_token can be set at node level.

CHAPTER 3
Installation of Cassandra

This chapter will cover the steps to install and run Cassandra on a virtual Linux host. You can choose any of the Linux OS for installation. Some examples are CentOS, RHEL, Ubuntu, Mac & Windows. In this chapter, we will install Cassandra on virtual machines using Ubuntu.

Once Cassandra is running on a single host, we can connect using *cqlsh* and run few CQL (Cassandra query language) commands. Installing Cassandra on one node will give you a hand-on experience and confidence, which is most important in learning new technology.

VM Ubuntu Installation

Installing Cassandra, configuring multiple node cluster, learning needs more than one Linux box. In this chapter, we are using Oracle VM VirtualBox and installing Cassandra ion Ubuntu 12.04.

Oracle VM can be downloaded from https://www.virtualbox.org/. At the time of writing this book, Oracle VM and all other software downloaded were free of charge. Do make sure to check the current charges or if there are any licensing fees.

For the installation, Ubuntu ISO disk image, ubuntu-12.04.4-desktop-amd64, was downloaded from one of the publicly available sites.

Note that the exact steps to install and configure Ubuntu may vary based on the version you use, and it may change in future. These are guidelines only.

From Oracle VM, select "New" to create a new virtual machine (VM).

Name the first machine as cc1 (Cassandra Cluster 1).

Step 1 : Select OS Type as Linux.

Select Version as Other Linux (64-bit). Based on your Windows machine, select either 32-bit or 64-bit. When Version was selected as "Ubuntu (64 bit) on AMD laptop, there was an issue with configuring static IP address for the machine. Play around few configuration to make sure it works.

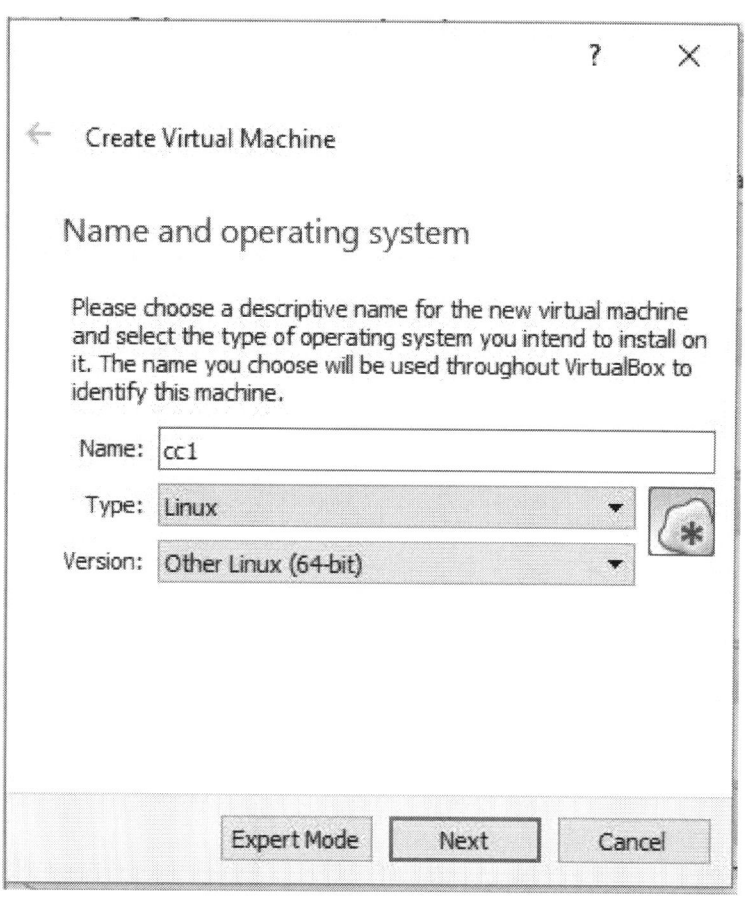

Figure 3.1: Select OS screen

Step 2 : Allocate memory for the machine. Allocate at least 1 GB of memory. recommendation is to use a laptop or desktop with a minimum of 16 GB of memory. This allows you to run 6-8 VM machines at the same time.

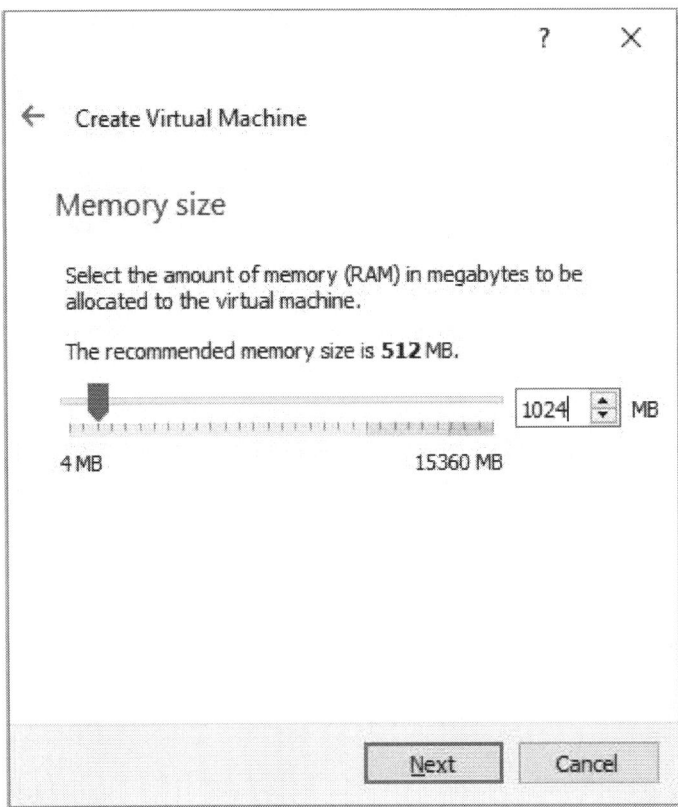

Figure 3.2: Allocate memory.

Step 3 : Allocate the virtual hard disk. Follow the screenshots.

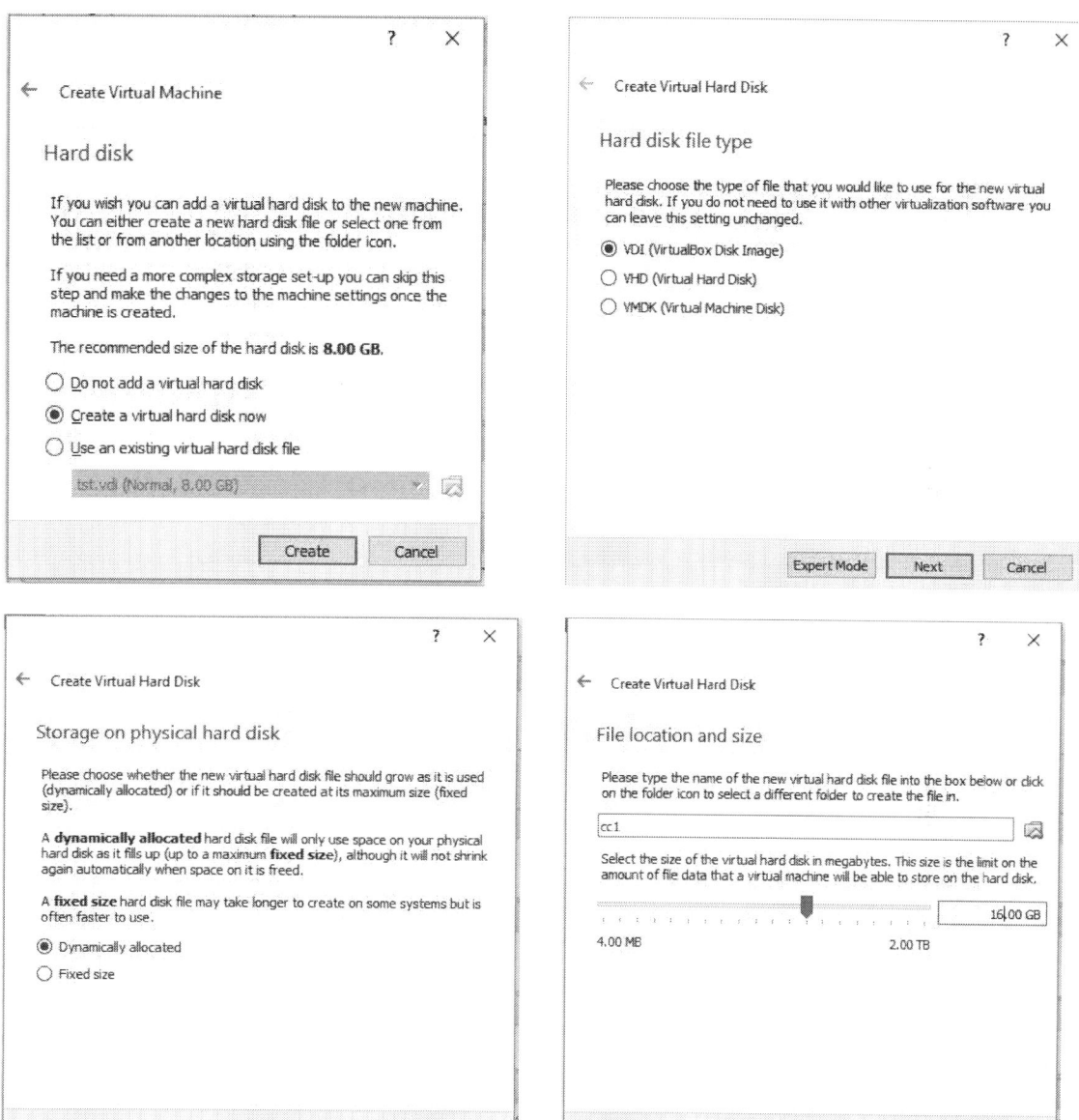

Figure 3.3: Allocate virtual harddisk.

Step 4 : New VM Settings

Go to the settings for new cc1 machine and uncheck Floppy for System setting to change the boot order.

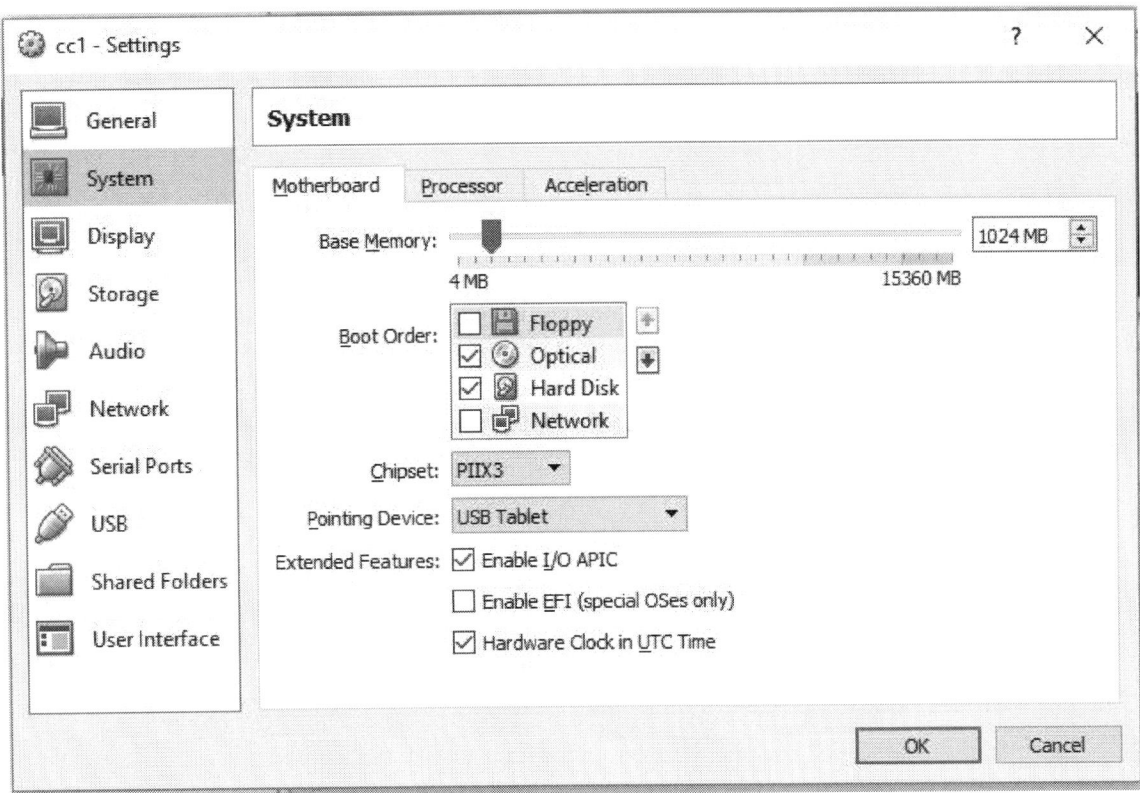

Figure 3.4: Boot order

Step 5 : Configure boot image

Click on *Storage*, and from StorageTree click on *Empty* as shown in Figure 3.5. In Attributes, keep the Optical Drive as IDE Secondary Master, and click on the Disk icon to select Ubuntu ISO image as shown in Figure 3.6.

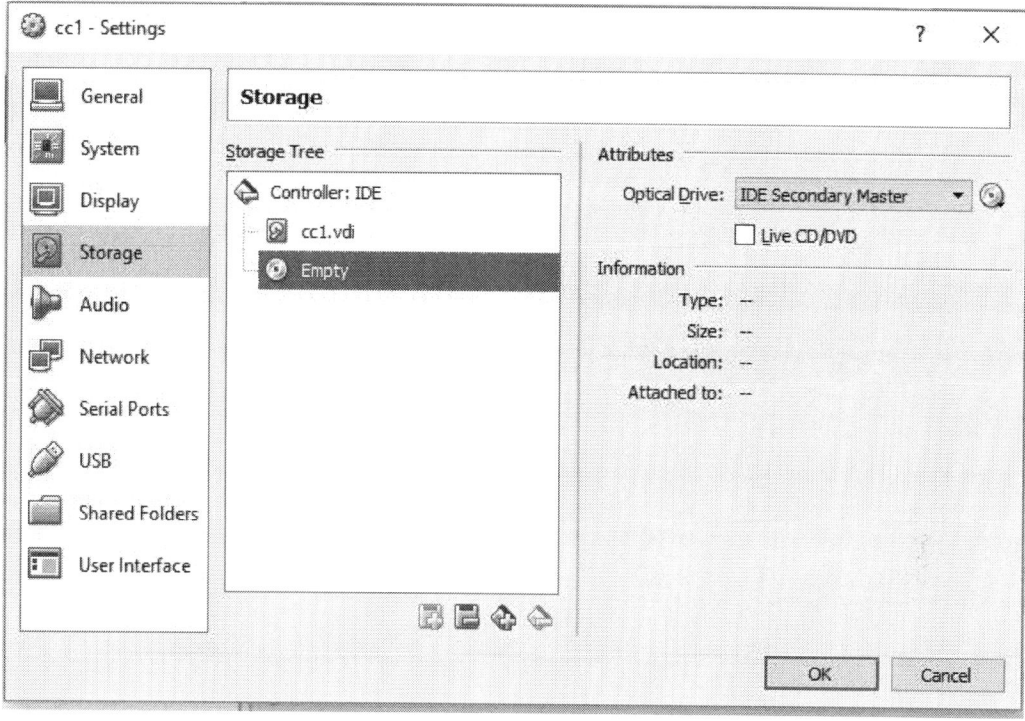

Figure 3.5: Storage settings

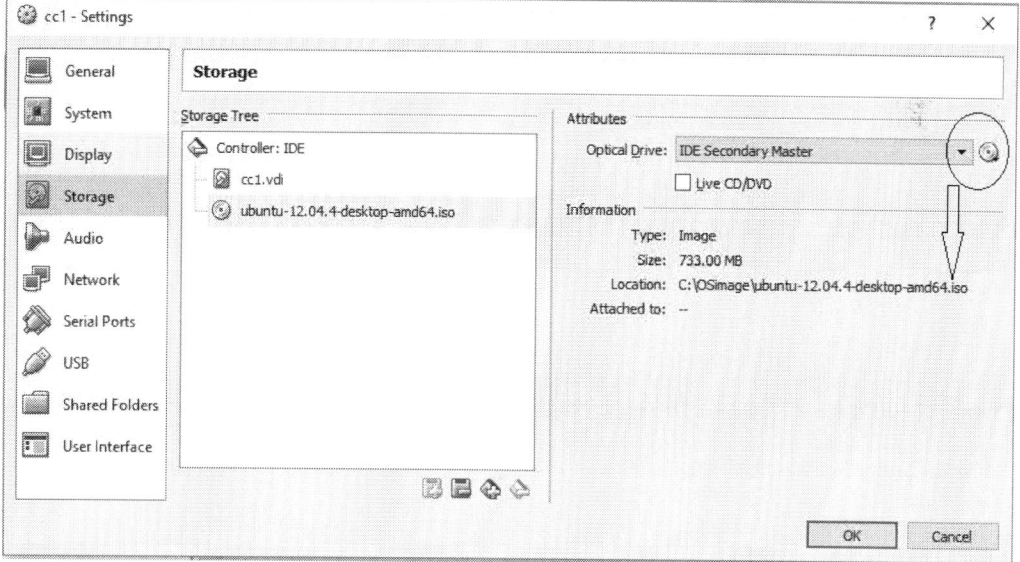

Figure 3.6: ISO image selection

Step 6 : Cassandra ID creation.

Start the cc1 machine, and continue with the configuration. When it comes to creating user, complete the information as listed below.

Username "Cassandra" is created with password as "cass123" as shown in *Figure 3.7*.

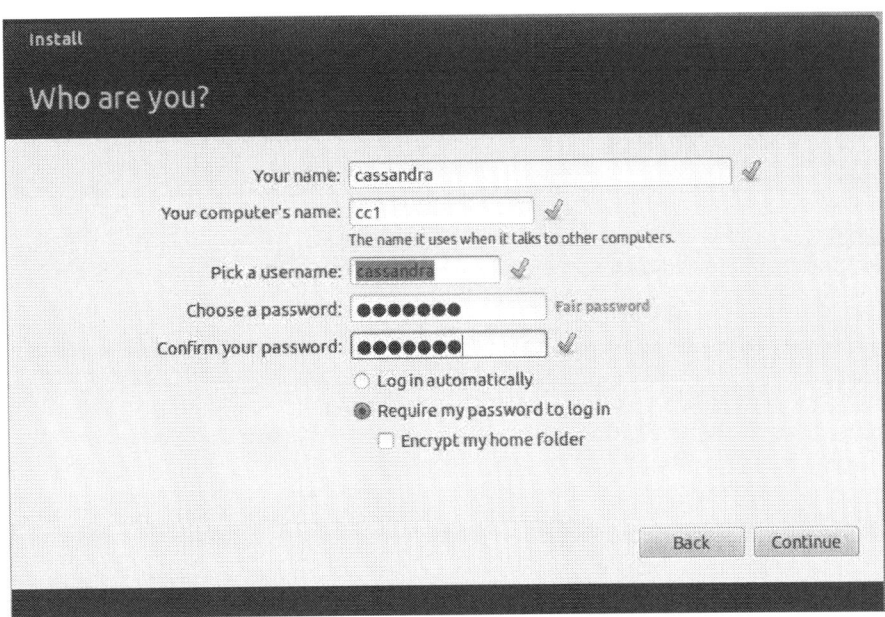

Figrue 3.7: Cassandra username

Once the installation of Ubuntu is complete, restart the cc1 machine. Now we can proceed with the installation of Cassandra.

Java Installation

Java is the main prerequisite for Cassandra. It is recommended to use the latest version of Oracle Java 8. Install Oracle Java by downloading from the Oracle website. Follow the method below, which was found on many public websites.

```
cassandra@cc1:~$ sudo add-apt-repository ppa:webupd8team/java
cassandra@cc1:~$ sudo apt-get update
```

This will update all the packages.

```
cassandra@cc1:~$ sudo apt-get install oracle-java8-installer
```

To install java run the above command. A text-only UI will appear with Terms and Conditions. Once you select "Yes" to agree to the Oracle Java Binary Agreement, Java 8 will continue with the installation. Once Java is installed, run the command below to make the Oracle Java default

```
cassandra@cc1:~$ sudo apt-get install oracle-java8-set-default
```

Verify that java is installed and it's version.

```
cassandra@cc1:~$ java -version
java version "1.8.0_121"
Java(TM) SE Runtime Environment (build 1.8.0_121-b13)
Java HotSpot(TM) 64-Bit Server VM (build 25.121-b13, mixed mode)
cassandra@cc1:~$
```

JAVA_HOME will be set up to /usr/lib/jvm/java-8-oracle. You can check this by:

echo $JAVA_HOME

If the variable is not set, you can set up JAVA_HOME in ~/.bashrc.

You can run the following command to get the path for $JAVA_HOME.

echo $(dirname $(dirname $(readlink -f $(which javac))))

Cassandra Download and ID Setup

Cassandra installation can be done by a tarball or through a package manager. In this section Cassandra installation is done by using tarbal. Install Cassandra tarball by downloading Apache Cassandra 3.10.

On your Ubuntu machine browser, go to http://cassandra.apache.org/download/, and click on the 3.10 link. Copy the complete URL of the mirror site, and run *wget* to download the tarball.

```
cassandra@cc1:~$ pwd
/home/cassandra
cassandra@cc1:~$wget http://apache.claz.org/cassandra/3.10/apache-cassandra-3.10-bin.tar.gz
cassandra@cc1:~$ ls -l *gz
-rw-rw-r-- 1 cassandra cassandra 37608621 Feb  3 17:56 apache-cassandra-3.10-bin.tar.gz
cassandra@cc1:~$
```

We will install Cassandra in /usr/local. Now untar the file using below command using *sudo*.

```
cassandra@cc1:~$sudo tar -xvf apache-cassandra-3.10-bin.tar.gz -C /usr/local/
```

Now cd to /usr/local and you will see that entire tarball is copied under apache-cassandra-3.10.

```
cassandra@cc1:~$ cd /usr/local
cassandra@cc1:/usr/local$ ls -lrt
total 36
drwxr-xr-x    2 root root  4096 Feb  4 2014 src
drwxr-xr-x    2 root root  4096 Feb  4 2014 sbin
drwxr-xr-x    2 root root  4096 Feb  4 2014 include
drwxr-xr-x    2 root root  4096 Feb  4 2014 games
drwxr-xr-x    2 root root  4096 Feb  4 2014 etc
drwxr-xr-x    2 root root  4096 Feb  4 2014 bin
drwxr-xr-x    3 root root  4096 Feb  4 2014 lib
drwxr-xr-x    7 root root  4096 Feb  4 2014 share
lrwxrwxrwx   1 root root     9 Apr  1 22:33 man -> share/man
drwxr-xr-x 10 root root  4096 Apr  8 01:51 apache-cassandra-3.10
```

Create a symbolic link of Cassandra to the downloaded binary. For readability, some lines *of ls -lrt* have been removed from the below output.

```
cassandra@cc1:/usr/local$ sudo ln -s /usr/local/apache-cassandra-3.10 /usr/local/cassandra
cassandra@cc1:/usr/local$ ls -lrt
[...]
drwxr-xr-x   10  root root   4096 Apr  8 01:51 apache-cassandra-3.10
lrwxrwxrwx   1  root root      32 Apr  8 01:53 cassandra -> /usr/local/apache-cassandra-3.10
```

As you can see, directory apache-cassandra-3.10 and the symbolic link are both owned by root. We need to change the ownership to cassandra id under cassandra group.

```
cassandra@cc1:/usr/local$ sudo chown -R cassandra:cassandra /usr/local/apache-cassandra-3.10/
cassandra@cc1:/usr/local$ sudo chown -R cassandra:cassandra /usr/local/cassandra
cassandra@cc1:/usr/local$ ls -l
[...]
drwxr-xr-x   10 cassandra cassandra  4096 Apr  8 01:51 apache-cassandra-3.10
lrwxrwxrwx   1 cassandra cassandra      32 Apr  8 01:53 cassandra -> /usr/local/
apache-cassandra-3.10
cassandra@cc1:/usr/local$
```

The reason to create the symbolic link is, when we install a new version of Cassandra, all we have to do is point the symbolic link to the new binaries. Thus we don't need to change any environment variables or scripts you may develop, which will refer to the current binary as /usr/local/cassandra. We will see that in the upgrade chapter.

Now set up $CASSANDRA_HOME to /usr/local/cassandra in the .bashrc file.

Start Cassandra

The basic setup of Cassandra is done. Now you can start Cassandra on this node. To start, run:

```
cassandra@cc1:/usr/local$ $CASSANDRA_HOME/bin/Cassandra -f
```

This will start the Cassandra process in the foreground. Since we ran this in foreground, keep this window open. And open a new terminal, and run cqlsh to connect to the database.

```
cassandra@cc1:~$ $CASSANDRA_HOME/bin/cqlsh
Connected to Test Cluster at 127.0.0.1:9042.
[cqlsh 5.0.1 | Cassandra 3.10 | CQL spec 3.4.4 | Native protocol v4]
Use HELP for help.
cassandra@cqlsh> desc keyspaces;

demo system_schema system_auth system system_distributed system_traces

cassandra@cqlsh>
```

Once cqlsh connects, it displays the Cassandra cluster name, cqlsh version, and Cassandra version. "desc keyspaces" displays the system keyspaces.

One of the very important command line programs you will be extensively using is nodetool. This is located in the *$CASSANDRA_HOME/bin* directory. Running nodetool status will give you the status of the entire cluster. Since we are running Cassandra on a single node, nodetool status displays the status of one node. UN stands for "up and normal."

```
ccassandra@cc1:~$ $CASSANDRA_HOME/bin/nodetool status
Datacenter: datacenter1
========================
Status=Up/Down
|/ State=Normal/Leaving/Joining/Moving
--  Address    Load        Tokens   Owns      Host ID                                Rack
                                    (effective)
UN  127.0.0.1  103.68 Kib  256      100.0%    4d66d841-3932-4d3b-a281-090c51ec868f  rack1
```

Congratulations! You have installed Cassandra, and it is running on a node cluster now.

✳ ✳ ✳

CHAPTER 4

CQL

C QL stands for Cassandra Query Language. CQL is the primary language to communicate with Cassandra database cluster. You can run CQL using *cqlsh* (CQL shell), DataStax DevCenter or third-party client. CQL is created similar to SQL used in relational databases like Oracle/SAP Sybase/SQL Server/MySQL. This similarity makes it easy to transition from RDBMS to Cassandra. There are many CQL, and SQL commands are almost the same.

This chapter provides enough information to understand the data types, data definition, and data manipulation commands. For in-depth details about the syntax and complete usage of all the commands refer to online documentation at cassandra.apache.org or datastax.com.

CQL Data Types

Following are the built in CQL data-types for columns in Cassandra table.

CQL data-type	Constant	Description
Asci	string	ASCII character string
Bigint	integer	64-bit signed long
Blob	blob	Arbitrary bytes (hexadecimals)
Boolean	boolean	true or false
Counter	integer	Distributed Counter column (64-bit signed value). Used for increments.
Date	integer, string	Date value as yyyy-mm-dd or 32-bit unsigned int which is days since epoch (Jan 1, 1970).

Decimal	integer, float	Variable-precision decimal
Double	integer float	64-bit IEEE-754 floating point
Float	integer, float	32-bit IEEE-754 floating point
Inet	string	IP address as string in IPv4 or IPv6 format.
Int	integer	32-bit signed int
Smallint	integer	16-bit signed int
Text	string	UTF8 encoded string
Time	integer, string	64-bit unsigned as nanoseconds from midnight.
timestamp	integer, string	Number of milliseconds since epoch time (Jan 1, 1970). Represent as string or integer. Example 1996-07-24 9:50:30.123.
Timeuuid	uuid	Version 1 UUID
Tinyint	integer	8-bit signed int
Uuid	uuid	Standard UUID
Varchar	string	UTF8 encoded string
Varint	integer	Arbitrary-precision integer
Set		Sorted collection of one or more elements. { 'cassandra','nosql','ring'}
Map		JSON style array of key-value pairs. {'Books':10,'People':25}
List		List of non-unique literals. {'roger','rafa','novak','andy'}

Figure 4.1: CQL Datatypes

Counter

The column with counter datatype is a special column to store an integer value which is changed in increments. Counter columns are useful in data models where you need to keep track of certain activity by incrementing the number — for example, the number of webpage clicks, number of click on a product.

Some limitations of counter columns are

- All non-counter columns in the table must be part of the PRIMARY KEY.

- Counter columns cannot be part of PRIMARY KEY.
- Counter column updates are not idemptotent.

Data Definition

In Cassandra, a cluster is a container for keyspaces. A keyspace is equivalent to a database in SAP-ASE or SQL Server or schema in Oracle. Each keyspace contains sets of tables. Each keyspace can be configured with its replication placement on datacenter and replication factor, which are globally applied to all the tables in that keyspace.

If you are from an RDBMS background, where your entire server was running on one single machine, it's slightly confusing in the beginning about how and where each table data is stored. You can find a detailed explanation about this in the next *Chapter 5, Cassandra Data Modeling* under the topic *"Location of the Data"*.

Keyspace

To create a keyspace, you need to specify its name and replication strategy. Since we have only one node cluster, we will define the replication strategy as 'SimpleStrategy' and replication factor as 1.

Run *'describe keyspaces'* or *'desc keyspaces'* to list existing keyspace's.

```
cassandra@cc1:~$ $CASSANDRA_HOME/bin/cqlsh
Connected to Test Cluster at 127.0.0.1:9042.
[cqlsh 5.0.1 | Cassandra 3.10 | CQL spec 3.4.4 | Native protocol v4]
Use HELP for help.
cqlsh> DESC KEYSPACES;


system_traces  system_schema  system_auth  system  system_distributed


cqlsh> CREATE KEYSPACE first_ks with replication={'class':'SimpleStrategy','replication_factor':1};
cqlsh> DESC KEYSPACES;
```

```
system_schema system_auth system first_ks system_distributed system_traces

cqlsh>
```

MetaData

system_schema.keyspaces table stores the information about keyspaces in the cluster.

```
cqlsh> use system_schema;
cqlsh:system_schema> DESC tables;

tables    triggers  views   keyspaces dropped_columns
functions aggregates indexes types    columns

cqlsh:system_schema> SELECT keyspace_name,replication
                     FROM system_schema.keyspaces WHERE keyspace_name='first_ks';

 keyspace_name | replication
---------------+---------------------------------------------------------------------------
    first_ks   | {'class': 'org.apache.cassandra.locator.SimpleStrategy', 'replication_factor': '1'}

(1 rows)
cqlsh:system_schema>
```

Use "ALTER KEYSPACE" to alter the replication factor, strategy, and durable writes. Keyspace name cannot be altered once it is created. Below example alters the keyspace and sets the replication strategy to 'NetworkTopologyStrategy' and configures replication_factor = 1 in each datacenter, NewYork_DC & NJ_DC.

```
ALTER KEYSPACE node_mgmt WITH replication=
    {'class':'NetworkTopologyStrategy','NewYork_DC' : 1, 'NJ_DC':1};
```

Use "DROP KEYSPACE" to drop a keyspace. Cassandra takes a snapshot (backup) of all tables before it drops the keyspace. Note that, the actual physical directory on the disk will not be dropped. You need to manually remove the folder to cleanup and clear the disk space.

Table (Column Family)

CREATE and ALTER TABLE command have many options, and we will not be discussing all of them in detail here. The table in Cassandra is also referred to as column family, and it can be created using 'CREATE TABLE' command. Create table consists of the column definition, primary key, optional clustering column, and optional table properties.

General Syntax of CREATE TABLE is

```
CREATE TABLE [IF NOT EXISTS] [keyspace.]table_name (
  column_definition [ ]
  PRIMARY KEY (column1 [, column2 ...])
[WITH table_options
  | CLUSTERING ORDER BY (column1(ASC | DESC) ( , column2 (ASC | DESC) )) ]
```

Primary Key uniquely identifies a row in the table, and every table must define a primary key. The primary key is composed of partition key + clustering columns. A table always has at least a partition key; in this case, the primary key will be its partition key. The simplest and smallest definition of table creation will be as listed below.

```
CREATE TABLE simpletbl ( col1 text PRIMARY KEY);
```

Here is an example of create table and insert few rows.

```
cqlsh> USE first_ks;
cqlsh:first_ks> CREATE TABLE  mytbl
          ... (
          ... a int,
          ... b text,
```

```
        ... c text,
        ... d text,
        ... e text,
        ... PRIMARY KEY (a,b)
        ... );
cqlsh:first_ks> INSERT INTO mytbl ( a,b,c,d,e ) VALUES
(1,'b1','c1','d1','e1');
cqlsh:first_ks> INSERT INTO mytbl ( a,b,c,d,e ) VALUES
(2,'b2','c2','d2','e2');
cqlsh:first_ks> SELECT * FROM mytbl;

 a | b  | c  | d  | e
---+----+----+----+----
 1 | b1 | c1 | d1 | e1
 2 | b2 | c2 | d2 | e2

(2 rows)
cqlsh:first_ks>
```

When you insert data into Cassandra table, all the rows belong to the same partition key will be stored on the same node.

In the above example, the partition key is column 'a' and clustering key is column 'b'. Clustering keys are typically used for enforcing row uniqueness and ordering of rows within the partition.

The above CREATE TABLE definition does not include all the table properties which include compression, compaction type, read repair settings, *gc_grace_seconds* and more. To view the complete table definition, you can run DESCRIBE TABLE command as displayed in the below output.

```
cqlsh:first_ks> DESC TABLE mytbl;
```

```
CREATE TABLE first_ks.mytbl (
    a int,
    b text,
```

```
    c text,
    d text,
    e text,
    PRIMARY KEY (a, b)
) WITH CLUSTERING ORDER BY (b ASC)
    AND bloom_filter_fp_chance = 0.01
    AND caching = {'keys': 'ALL', 'rows_per_partition': 'NONE'}
    AND comment = ''
    AND compaction = {'class': 'org.apache.cassandra.db.compaction.
SizeTieredCompactionStrategy', 'max_threshold': '32', 'min_threshold': '4'}
    AND compression = {'chunk_length_in_kb': '64', 'class': 'org.apache.cassandra.io.compress.
LZ4Compressor'}
    AND crc_check_chance = 1.0
    AND dclocal_read_repair_chance = 0.1
    AND default_time_to_live = 0
    AND gc_grace_seconds = 864000
    AND max_index_interval = 2048
    AND memtable_flush_period_in_ms = 0
    AND min_index_interval = 128
    AND read_repair_chance = 0.0
    AND speculative_retry = '99PERCENTILE';

cqlsh:first_ks>
```

SizeTieredCompactionStrategy is the default compaction strategy unless you mention it during the creation of the table. Also, *gc_grace_seconds*, *read_repair_chance*, and all other properties are taken the default values.

MetaData

Table *system_schema.tables* stores all the information about the existing tables in the cluster. Column 'id', which is table identification string in hexadecimal, is used in creating a directory in the *$CASSANDRA_HOME/data/data* directory.

```
cqlsh:first_ks> SELECT * FROM system_schema.tables
               WHERE keyspace_name='first_ks' AND table_name='mytbl';


keyspace_name | table_name | bloom_filter_fp_chance | caching                          | cdc
| comment | compaction                                                                |
compression | crc_check_chance | dclocal_read_repair_chance | default_time_to_live |
extensions | flags     | gc_grace_seconds | id                    | max_index_interval |
memtable_flush_period_in_ms | min_index_interval | read_repair_chance | speculative_retry

---------------+-----------+----------------------+---------------------------------------+-----+--------+-----
---------------------------------------------------------------------------------------+--------
----------------------------------------------------------------+----------------+-----------------------------
--+-------------------+-----------+-------------+-----------------+-----------------------------------+-------------
----------+--------------------------+-------------------+-------------------+------------------

   first_ks |    mytbl |          0.01 | {'keys': 'ALL', 'rows_per_partition': 'NONE'} | null |
| {'class': 'org.apache.cassandra.db.compaction.SizeTieredCompactionStrategy',
'max_threshold': '32', 'min_threshold': '4'} | {'chunk_length_in_kb': '64', 'class':
'org.apache.cassandra.io.compress.LZ4Compressor'} |            1 |           0.1 |
0 |       {} | {'compound'} |      864000 | 7673d720-f124-11e8-a99d-db9b270363a1 |
2048 |                0 |         128 |       0 |   99PERCENTILE

(1 rows)
```

As you can see in the below output, table name and table id 7673d720-f124-11e8-a99d-db9b270363a1 (hexadecimal string) is used to create the directory under keyspace *first_ks*. Cassandra creates this unique directory to avoid problems arising from the repeated drop and recreate of the same table. If you drop and recreate the table, it will generate a new hexadecimal id, which will be used to create the new directory. In this case, you need to remove the old directory manually on all the nodes.

```
cassandra@cc1:/usr/local/cassandra/data/data/first_ks$ pwd
/usr/local/cassandra/data/data/first_ks
cassandra@cc1:/usr/local/cassandra/data/data/first_ks$ ls -lrt
total 4
drwxrwxr-x 3 cassandra cassandra 4096 Nov 25 21:39 mytbl-7673d720f12411e8a99ddb9b270363a1
cassandra@cc1:/usr/local/cassandra/data/data/first_ks$
```

Alter table command can be used add/drop column, modify datatype of the column and change table properties like compaction strategy. For complete syntax refer online documentation for your Cassandra version documentation.

In the below output, alter command has run to change the compaction strategy of the table, set *read_repair_chance* to 0.1 and also we have added a new column.

```
cqlsh> ALTER TABLE first_ks.mytbl WITH compaction =
       { 'class' : 'LeveledCompactionStrategy'} AND read_repair_chance=0.1;


cqlsh> ALTER TABLE first_ks.mytbl ADD  a_newcol int;


cqlsh> DESC TABLE first_ks.mytbl;

CREATE TABLE first_ks.mytbl (
    a int,
    b text,
    a_newcol int,
    c text,
    d text,
    e text,
    PRIMARY KEY (a, b)
) WITH CLUSTERING ORDER BY (b ASC)
    AND bloom_filter_fp_chance = 0.01
    AND caching = {'keys': 'ALL', 'rows_per_partition': 'NONE'}
    AND comment = ''
    AND compaction = {'class': 'org.apache.cassandra.db.compaction.LeveledCompactionStrategy'}
    AND compression = {'chunk_length_in_kb': '64', 'class': 'org.apache.cassandra.io.compress.
LZ4Compressor'}
    AND crc_check_chance = 1.0
    AND dclocal_read_repair_chance = 0.1
    AND default_time_to_live = 0
    AND gc_grace_seconds = 864000
    AND max_index_interval = 2048
    AND memtable_flush_period_in_ms = 0
```

```
   AND min_index_interval = 128
   AND read_repair_chance = 0.1
   AND speculative_retry = '99PERCENTILE';

cqlsh>
```

In this version of Cassandra, ALTER TABLE <table_name> ALTER <colname> TYPE <new_type> was not allowed.

```
cqlsh> ALTER TABLE first_ks.mytbl ALTER a_newcol TYPE bigint;
InvalidRequest: Error from server: code=2200 [Invalid query] message="Altering of types is not allowed"
```

DROP TABLE

Drop table command drops the table.

```
cqlsh:first_ks> DROP TABLE first_ks.mytbl ;
cqlsh:first_ks> SELECT * FROM first_ks.mytbl ;
InvalidRequest: Error from server: code=2200 [Invalid query] message="unconfigured table mytbl"
cqlsh> exit
cassandra@cc1:/usr/local/cassandra/data/data/first_ks$ pwd
/usr/local/cassandra/data/data/first_ks
cassandra@cc1:/usr/local/cassandra/data/data/first_ks$ ls -l
total 4
drwxrwxr-x 4 cassandra cassandra 4096 Nov 26 20:21
mytbl-7673d720f12411e8a99ddb9b270363a1
cassandra@cc1:/usr/local/cassandra/data/data/first_ks$
```

Note that, drop table only removes the entry from metadata, i.e., *system_schema.tables*, but it will not drop the data from all the nodes. If you drop the table and recreate it, the directory with the old *'id'* will not be dropped from the data directory. As you can see in the above output, the old directory 'mytbl-7673d720f12411e8a99ddb9b270363a1' was not removed.

TRUNCATE TABLE

Truncate Table command truncates all the existing data without removing the table itself.

For both the drop table and truncate table, depending on the *auto_snapshot* setting in *cassandra.yaml* file, it creates a snapshot in each node. By default, this value is 'true' as listed below.

```
cassandra@cc1: $ cd $CASSANDRA_HOME/conf
cassandra@cc1:/usr/local/cassandra/conf$ grep auto_snapshot cassandra.yaml
auto_snapshot: true
```

In the output below, when the table mytbl was dropped, Cassandra created a snapshot by creating a new directory with the timestamp of drop table time. It is recommended to set *auto_snapshot* to *'true'* on a production cluster.

```
cassandra@cc1:/usr/local/cassandra/data/data/first_ks$ pwd
/usr/local/cassandra/data/data/first_ks

cassandra@cc1:/usr/local/cassandra/data/data/first_ks$ ls -l
mytbl-7673d720f12411e8a99ddb9b270363a1/
total 8
drwxrwxr-x 2 cassandra cassandra 4096 Nov 25 21:39 backups
drwxrwxr-x 3 cassandra cassandra 4096 Nov 26 20:21 snapshots

cassandra@cc1:/usr/cassandra/data/data/first_ks$ ls -l
mytbl-7673d720f12411e8a99ddb9b270363a1/snapshots/
total 4
drwxrwxr-x 2 cassandra cassandra 4096 Nov 26 20:21 dropped-1543281716563-mytbl

cassandra@cc1:/usr/local/cassandra/data/data/first_ks$ ls -l
mytbl-7673d720f12411e8a99ddb9b270363a1/snapshots/dropped-1543281716563-mytbl/
total 44
-rw-rw-r-- 1 cassandra cassandra   31 Nov 26 20:21 manifest.json
-rw-rw-r-- 1 cassandra cassandra   43 Nov 25 22:26 mc-1-big-CompressionInfo.db
```

```
-rw-rw-r-- 1 cassandra cassandra    74 Nov 25 22:26 mc-1-big-Data.db
-rw-rw-r-- 1 cassandra cassandra    10 Nov 25 22:26 mc-1-big-Digest.crc32
-rw-rw-r-- 1 cassandra cassandra    16 Nov 25 22:26 mc-1-big-Filter.db
-rw-rw-r-- 1 cassandra cassandra    16 Nov 25 22:26 mc-1-big-Index.db
-rw-rw-r-- 1 cassandra cassandra 4742 Nov 25 22:26 mc-1-big-Statistics.db
-rw-rw-r-- 1 cassandra cassandra    56 Nov 25 22:26 mc-1-big-Summary.db
-rw-rw-r-- 1 cassandra cassandra    92 Nov 25 22:26 mc-1-big-TOC.txt
-rw-rw-r-- 1 cassandra cassandra   860 Nov 26 20:21 schema.cql
cassandra@cc1:/usr/local/cassandra/data/data/first_ks$
```

Data Manipulation

SELECT

SELECT command retrieves the data from the table. It is not recommended to retrieve data without a WHERE condition. As table's data is evenly distributed on the entire cluster, select without a where clause has to retrieve all the data from all the node which is a very expensive operation.

The basic SELECT syntax is listed below. For complete syntax for your version of Cassandra, check online resources.

```
SELECT [* | select_expression | DISTINCT partition | JSON ]
FROM [keyspace name.] table_name
WHERE partition_value [AND clustering_filters]
GROUP BY [partition|static column]
[ORDER BY PK_COLUMN ASC|DESC]
[LIMIT n]
[ALLOW FILTERING]
```

Let's review a few SELECT queries by example. For this, we will create the below table and insert some data, as listed below. The partition key of this table is *user_id,* and clustering columns are *category* and *purchase_dt*.

```
cqlsh> CREATE TABLE first_ks.saletran (
   ...        user_id text,
   ...        category text,
   ...        product text,
   ...        purchase_dt timestamp,
   ...        amt float,
   ...        PRIMARY KEY (user_id, category, purchase_dt));
cqlsh>

cqlsh> SELECT * FROM first_ks.saletran  ;
```

user_id	category	purchase_dt	amt	product
novak_m	clothing	2017-02-02	75	ties
novak_m	sports	2016-12-01	100	racketw
andy_f	clothing	2016-12-21	50	t-shirt
andy_f	sports	2016-12-21	79	racketw
andy_f	sports	2016-12-25	200	sunglass
andy_f	sports	2017-01-01	99	racketw
roger_n	sports	2016-12-01	100	racketw
roger_n	sports	2016-12-21	200	shoes
roger_n	sports	2017-01-01	99	racketb
rafa_d	clothing	2016-12-21	55	t-shirt
rafa_d	clothing	2016-12-25	95	ties
rafa_d	sports	2017-01-21	300	rcketb

```
(12 rows)
```

SELECT with "LIMIT <n>" to limit the output to specified 'n' number of rows.

```
cqlsh> SELECT * FROM first_ks.saletran LIMIT 4;
```

user_id	category	purchase_dt	amt	product
novak_m	clothing	2017-02-02	75	ties
novak_m	sports	2016-12-01	100	racketw

```
    andy_f |  clothing |  2016-12-21 |   50 |  t-shirt
    andy_f |    sports |  2016-12-21 |   79 |  racketw

(4 rows)
```

SELECT with partition key in the WHERE clause.

```
cqlsh> SELECT * FROM first_ks.saletran WHERE user_id='novak_m';

 user_id | category | purchase_dt | amt | product
---------+----------+-------------+-----+---------
 novak_m | clothing |  2017-02-02 |  75 |    ties
 novak_m |   sports |  2016-12-01 | 100 | racketw

(2 rows)
```

SELECT with partition key in the WHERE clause with JSON output.

```
cqlsh> SELECT JSON * FROM first_ks.saletran WHERE user_id='novak_m';

 [json]
--------------------------------------------------------------------------------

 {"user_id": "novak_m", "category": "clothing", "purchase_dt": "2017-02-02 00:00:00.000Z",
"amt": 75.0, "product": "ties"}

 {"user_id": "novak_m", "category": "sports", "purchase_dt": "2016-12-01 00:00:00.000Z", "amt":
100.0, "product": "racketw"}

(2 rows)
```

If you run select from the table without the leading clustering column, the query will give an error. In the below example, the complete primary key is "PRIMARY KEY (user_id, category, purchase_dt)". Select will fail if you omit leading clustering key 'category'.

```
cqlsh> SELECT * FROM first_ks.saletran
     WHERE user_id='novak_m' AND purchase_dt='2017-02-02';
InvalidRequest: Error from server: code=2200 [Invalid query] message="PRIMARY KEY column
"purchase_dt" cannot be restricted as preceding column "category" is not restricted"
```

The same query will work if you omit *purchase_dt* and include *category*.

```
cqlsh> SELECT * FROM first_ks.saletran
     WHERE user_id='novak_m' AND category='clothing';

 user_id  | category  | purchase_dt  | amt | product
----------+-----------+--------------+-----+---------
 novak_m  | clothing  | 2017-02-02   |  75 |    ties

(1 rows)
cqlsh>
```

The reason for this how Cassandra stores data internally. Clustering columns specify the order of the data within a single partition. Cassandra read contiguous data from disk and clustering column determine on-disk sort order as listed below in the *sstabledump* output. This is the reason when it comes to passing the clustering keys, you must provide all the columns leading up to the last one.

```
sstable dump. Only partial data is displayed

[novak_m]@0 Row[info=[ts=1543289990106890] ]: clothing, 2017-02-01 19:00-0500 | [amt=75.0
ts=1543289990106890], [product=ties ts=1543289990106890]

[novak_m]@54 Row[info=[ts=1543289990106890] ]: sports, 2016-11-30 19:00-0500 | [amt=100.0
ts=1543289990106890], [product=racketw ts=1543289990106890]

[andy_f]@89 Row[info=[ts=1543289990106890] ]: clothing, 2016-12-20 19:00-0500 | [amt=50.0
ts=1543289990106890], [product=t-shirt ts=1543289990106890]
```

Following is an example of using IN with partition keys and clustering column.

```
cqlsh> SELECT * FROM first_ks.saletran
       WHERE user_id IN ('roger_n','andy_f');


 user_id | category | purchase_dt | amt | product
---------+----------+-------------+-----+----------
  andy_f | clothing |  2016-12-21 |  50 |  t-shirt
  andy_f |   sports |  2016-12-21 |  79 |  racketw
  andy_f |   sports |  2016-12-25 | 200 | sunglass
  andy_f |   sports |  2017-01-01 |  99 |  racketw
 roger_n |   sports |  2016-12-01 | 100 |  racketw
 roger_n |   sports |  2016-12-21 | 200 |    shoes
 roger_n |   sports |  2017-01-01 |  99 |  racketb


(7 rows)
cqlsh> SELECT * FROM first_ks.saletran
       WHERE user_id IN ('novak_m','rafa_d')
       AND category IN ('sports','clothing');


 user_id | category | purchase_dt | amt | product
---------+----------+-------------+-----+---------
 novak_m | clothing |  2017-02-02 |  75 |    ties
 novak_m |   sports |  2016-12-01 | 100 | racketw
  rafa_d | clothing |  2016-12-21 |  55 | t-shirt
  rafa_d | clothing |  2016-12-25 |  95 |    ties
  rafa_d |   sports |  2017-01-21 | 300 |  rcketb


(5 rows)
```

A select expression using sum(), min(), max() & avg() with group by on partition key returns the aggregate result. Note in this case Cassandra warning at the bottom of the result set. If your query is spanning more than 1 partition, it will not be efficient, and Cassandra gives warning about this. The second query retrieves single partition for which Cassandra does not show any warnings.

```
cqlsh> SELECT user_id,min(amt),max(amt),avg(amt),sum(amt)
      FROM first_ks.saletran GROUP BY user_id;


user_id  | system.min(amt) | system.max(amt) | system.avg(amt) | system.sum(amt)
---------+-----------------+-----------------+-----------------+----------------
novak_m |              75 |             100 |            87.5 |           175
 andy_f |              50 |             200 |             107 |           428
 roger_n |             99 |             200 |             133 |           399
  rafa_d |              55 |             300 |             150 |           450

(4 rows)

Warnings :
Aggregation query used without partition key
cqlsh> SELECT user_id,avg(amt),sum(amt)
      FROM first_ks.saletran
      WHERE user_id='andy_f' GROUP BY user_id,category;


user_id | system.avg(amt) | system.sum(amt)
--------+-----------------+----------------
 andy_f |              50 |             50
 andy_f |             126 |            378

(2 rows)
cqlsh>
```

GROUP BY without a declared order of primary key returns error. In the below query you are missing 'category' column which precedes 'purchase_dt'.

```
cqlsh> SELECT user_id,purchase_dt,sum(amt)
      FROM first_ks.saletran
      GROUP BY user_id, purchase_dt;
InvalidRequest: Error from server: code=2200 [Invalid query] message="Group by currently only
support groups of columns following their declared order in the PRIMARY KEY"
```

The SELECT query must have a partition key in the WHERE clause. If a select is run without a non-partition key in where clause, it will fail with below message suggesting to run with 'ALLOW FILTERING'. When 'ALLOW FILTERING' is used, Cassandra is internally skipping over the data. This is unpredictable as Cassandra does not know how much data it will skip over. Cassandra may read all data from all the nodes and skip over all and return 0 rows. This is ok if you always return most of the data. But it is highly recommended that you keep this type of query only for development. It is not recommended to run ALLOW FILTERING in production cluster.

```
cqlsh> SELECT * FROM first_ks.saletran
       WHERE product='racketw';
InvalidRequest: Error from server: code=2200 [Invalid query]
message="Cannot execute this query as it might involve data filtering
and thus may have unpredictable performance. If you want to execute this
query despite the performance unpredictability, use ALLOW FILTERING"
cqlsh>
cqlsh> SELECT * FROM first_ks.saletran
       WHERE product='racketw' ALLOW FILTERING;

 user_id | category | purchase_dt | amt | product
---------+----------+-------------+-----+---------
 novak_m |   sports |  2016-12-01 | 100 | racketw
  andy_f |   sports |  2016-12-21 |  79 | racketw
  andy_f |   sports |  2017-01-01 |  99 | racketw
  roger_n |  sports |  2016-12-01 | 100 | racketw

(4 rows)
cqlsh>
```

If you do not want to use ALLOW FILTERING, you can create an index on the non-partition column. Creating Index on such column, Cassandra will allow you to query the data. Unlike in RDBMS, creating an index can impact performance greatly

```
cqlsh> SELECT * FROM first_ks.saletran
        WHERE product='racketw';
InvalidRequest: Error from server: code=2200 [Invalid query]
message="Cannot execute this query as it might involve data filtering
and thus may have unpredictable performance. If you want to execute this
query despite the performance unpredictability, use ALLOW FILTERING"
cqlsh> CREATE INDEX saletran_product ON first_ks.saletran (product);
cqlsh> SELECT * FROM first_ks.saletran WHERE product='racketw';

 user_id | category | purchase_dt | amt | product
---------+----------+-------------+-----+---------
 novak_m |   sports |  2016-12-01 | 100 | racketw
  andy_f |   sports |  2016-12-21 |  79 | racketw
  andy_f |   sports |  2017-01-01 |  99 | racketw
 roger_n |   sports |  2016-12-01 | 100 | racketw

(4 rows)
cqlsh>
```

Metadata for index is stored at *system_schema.indexes*.

```
cqlsh> SELECT * FROM system_schema.indexes;

keyspace_name | table_name | index_name      | kind       | options
--------------+------------+-----------------+------------+--------------------
      first_ks |   saletran | saletran_product | COMPOSITES | {'target': 'product'}

(1 rows)
cqlsh>
```

INSERT

If you are from a pure RDBMS background, you should learn a new term called 'UPSERT'. In Cassandra, every INSERT or UPDATE is actually work as UPSERT. If you are inserting a row which already exists, it updates the row. Similarly, if you are updating a row, which does not exist, it inserts the row. Surprised! Cassandra is a distributed database which is designed to avoid reads before it writes. The exception is when you use 'IF NOT EXISTS' with INSERT command. When you use IF NOT EXISTS, Cassandra has to read the data to check the existence of the row, which might incur a performance penalty. In a write-heavy application, this will impact the performance.

General short syntax for INSERT is

```
INSERT INTO [keyspace name.] table_name ( column names...)
VALUES ( value1, value2 ) [ IF NOT EXISTS ]
[ USING TTL | TIMESTAMP ]
```

Every update or insert to every column has a timestamp entry. During read repair or reconciliation, Cassandra pulls data from all replicas in the form of a checksum, and it uses the timestamp value to determine the most recent data. You can input TIMESTAMP in microseconds. If not specified, the current time in microseconds will be written.

TTL – Time-to-live is designed for deleting columns when their time to live is known when they are written. When you insert a row with TTL of 600 seconds, which is 10 minutes, all TTL column value is automatically marked as deleted (tombstone) after requested amount of time.

In the below output, we created a 'ttl_test' table and inserted 2 rows. The second row is inserted with a TTL of 60 seconds. After insertion timestamp + 60 seconds, this entire row will be marked as deleted and becomes tombstone.

```
cqlsh> USE first_ks ;
cqlsh:first_ks> CREATE TABLE ttl_test ( id int primary key, comment text);
cqlsh:first_ks> INSERT INTO ttl_test( id,comment ) VALUES ( 1, 'row 1');
cqlsh:first_ks> INSERT INTO ttl_test( id,comment ) VALUES ( 2, 'row 2')
                USING TTL 60;
cqlsh:first_ks> SELECT * FROM ttl_test ;

 id | comment
----+---------
```

```
 1 |   row 1
 2 |   row 2

(2 rows)
```

WAIT FOR 60 SECONDS AND RUN SELECT AGAIN

```
cqlsh:first_ks> SELECT * FROM ttl_test ;

 id | comment
----+---------
  1 |   row 1

(1 rows)
```

Multiple INSERT with same primary key update the value (UPSERT). In traditional RDBMS, when you insert a row with a primary key which already exists, it will throw a primary key violation error. In Cassandra, it overwrites the data which you need to be aware of.

```
cqlsh:first_ks>
cqlsh:first_ks> INSERT INTO ttl_test( id,comment ) VALUES ( 1, 'row 1');
cqlsh:first_ks> INSERT INTO ttl_test( id,comment ) VALUES ( 2, 'row 2');
cqlsh:first_ks> SELECT * FROM ttl_test ;

 id | comment
----+--------------
  1 |     row 1
  2 |     row 2

(2 rows)
cqlsh:first_ks> INSERT INTO ttl_test( id,comment ) VALUES ( 2, 'row 2 inserted again');
cqlsh:first_ks> SELECT * FROM ttl_test ;

 id | comment
----+-------------------------
```

```
1 |                 row 1
2 | row 2 inserted again

(2 rows)
cqlsh:first_ks>
```

UPDATE

General short syntax for UPDATE is

```
UPDATE  [keyspace name.] table_name
[ USING TTL | TIMESTAMP ]
SET assignment, assignment
WHERE cluase
[ IF EXISTS | IF condition [AND condition] . . . ];
```

Let's review few self-explanatory UPDATE examples

```
cqlsh:first_ks> CREATE TABLE utable (
                id        int primary key,
                comment   text,
                status    text);
cqlsh:first_ks> INSERT INTO utable ( id,comment,status )
                VALUES ( 1, 'Row 1', 'x');
cqlsh:first_ks> INSERT INTO utable ( id,comment,status )
                VALUES ( 2, 'Row 2', 'y');
cqlsh:first_ks> SELECT * FROM utable ;

 id | comment | status
----+---------+--------
  1 |   Row 1 |      x
  2 |   Row 2 |      y
```

```
(2 rows)
cqlsh:first_ks> UPDATE utable SET status='y' WHERE id=1;
cqlsh:first_ks> UPDATE utable
                SET comment='Row 3 not exists', status='x'
                WHERE id=3 IF EXISTS;


 [applied]
 -----------
      False


cqlsh:first_ks> SELECT * FROM utable ;

 id | comment | status
----+---------+--------
  1 |   Row 1 |      y
  2 |   Row 2 |      y

(2 rows)
```

In the above output, UPDATE of ID=3 fails due to the use of IF EXISTS clause. If you omit "IF EXISTS", Cassandra execute the UPDATE as UPSERT. As shown in the below output, a row with id=3 does not exist in the table. When UPDATE is run with partition key in the WHERE clause, it uses the SET assignment value(s) and the where clause partition key value and INSERT a row.

```
cqlsh:first_ks> SELECT * FROM utable ;

 id | comment | status
----+---------+--------
  1 |   Row 1 |      y
  2 |   Row 2 |      y

(2 rows)
cqlsh:first_ks> UPDATE utable
                SET comment='Row 3 not exists', status='x'
```

```
                    WHERE id=3;
cqlsh:first_ks> SELECT * FROM utable ;

 id | comment          | status
----+------------------+--------
  1 |           Row 1  |      y
  2 |           Row 2  |      y
  3 | Row 3 not exists |      x

(3 rows)
```

Update can be run with conditional IF clause to make sure you don't overwrite the value if some column value does not match.

```
cqlsh:first_ks> SELECT * FROM utable ;

 id | comment          | status
----+------------------+--------
  1 |           Row 1  |      y
  2 |           Row 2  |      y
  3 | Row 3 not exists |      x

(3 rows)
cqlsh:first_ks> UPDATE utable
                SET comment='Row 1 update'
                WHERE id=1 IF status='N';

 [applied] | status
-----------+--------
    False  |      y

cqlsh:first_ks> UPDATE utable
                SET comment='Row 1 update'
                WHERE id=1 IF status='N' AND comment='Row 1';
```

```
 [applied] | status | comment
-----------+--------+---------
    False  |    y   |   Row 1

cqlsh:first_ks>
```

DML on set, list & map

Let's see few examples of INSERT, DELETE & UPDATE on set, list & map data types.

List

Use LIST type when the order of elements matters or to be maintained. Also, use a LIST when you want to store duplicate values. The LIST is not unique and maintains the order. Below a few examples of INSERT, UPDATE, UPSERT, and DELETE are self-explanatory. Note that for list values, you need to input all the values separated by "," (comma) and within square braces [].

```
cqlsh:first_ks> CREATE TABLE cust (  id int PRIMARY KEY,
                                name text,
                                stock_watchlist list<text> );
cqlsh:first_ks> INSERT INTO cust( id,name,stock_watchlist)
            VALUES (1, 'Roger',['FB','AMZN','BABA']);
cqlsh:first_ks> SELECT * FROM cust;

 id | name  | stock_watchlist
----+-------+-------------------------
  1 | Roger | ['FB', 'AMZN', 'BABA']

(1 rows)
cqlsh:first_ks>-- Below UPDATE, adding of duplicate 'AMZN' does add it to the end of the list.
```

```
cqlsh:first_ks> UPDATE cust
              SET stock_watchlist = stock_watchlist + ['GOOG','AMZN']
              WHERE id=1;
cqlsh:first_ks> SELECT * FROM cust;


 id | name  | stock_watchlist
----+-------+------------------------------------------
  1 | Roger | ['FB', 'AMZN', 'BABA', 'GOOG', 'AMZN']


(1 rows)
```
cqlsh:first_ks>-- **Below UPDATE, adding 'TSLA' to the beginning maintains the order**
```
cqlsh:first_ks> UPDATE cust
              SET stock_watchlist = ['TSLA']+stock_watchlist
              WHERE id=1;
cqlsh:first_ks> SELECT * FROM cust;


 id | name  | stock_watchlist
----+-------+--------------------------------------------------
  1 | Roger | ['TSLA', 'FB', 'AMZN', 'BABA', 'GOOG', 'AMZN']


(1 rows)
```

cqlsh:first_ks>**Below UPDATE, removal of 'AMZN' does remove all entries from the list.**
```
cqlsh:first_ks> UPDATE cust
              SET stock_watchlist = stock_watchlist - ['AMZN']
              WHERE id=1;
cqlsh:first_ks> SELECT * FROM cust;


 id | name  | stock_watchlist
----+-------+----------------------------
  1 | Roger | ['TSLA', 'FB', 'BABA', 'GOOG']


(1 rows)
cqlsh:first_ks> DELETE stock_watchlist[0] FROM cust WHERE id=1;
cqlsh:first_ks> SELECT * FROM cust;
```

```
 id | name  | stock_watchlist
----+-------+------------------------
  1 | Roger | ['FB', 'BABA', 'GOOG']

(1 rows)
```

cqlsh:first_ks>-- Below UPDATE does an UPSERT by setting id & name column.
cqlsh:first_ks> UPDATE cust
              SET name='John'
              WHERE id=2; ← **UPSERT**
cqlsh:first_ks> SELECT * FROM cust;

```
 id | name  | stock_watchlist
----+-------+------------------------
  1 | Roger | ['FB', 'BABA', 'GOOG']
  2 | John  |                   null

(2 rows)
```

SET

In SET type values are unique and no order is maintained. The values are sorted. Below are few examples of INSERT, UPDATE, UPSERT and DELETE which are self-explanatory. Note that for SET values, you input all the values separated by "," (comma) with curly brackets {}.

cqlsh:first_ks> CREATE TABLE customer (id int PRIMARY KEY,
                                            name text,
                                            sports set<text>);
cqlsh:first_ks> INSERT INTO customer (id,name, sports)
              VALUES (1,'Novak',{ 'Tennis', 'Golf' });
cqlsh:first_ks> SELECT * FROM customer;

```
 id | name  | sports
----+-------+--------------------
```

```
  1 | Novak | {'Golf', 'Tennis'}
```

(1 rows)

cqlsh:first_ks>-- Below UPDATE added duplicate 'Golf' which is ignored.

cqlsh:first_ks> UPDATE customer
               SET sports = sports + {'Golf'}
               WHERE id = 1;

cqlsh:first_ks> SELECT * FROM customer;

```
 id | name  | sports
----+-------+-------------------
  1 | Novak | {'Golf', 'Tennis'}
```

(1 rows)

cqlsh:first_ks>-- Below UPDATE added 'Basket Ball', which is added in the beginning by sorted order.

cqlsh:first_ks> UPDATE customer
               SET sports = sports + {'Basket Ball'}
               WHERE id = 1;

cqlsh:first_ks> SELECT * FROM customer;

```
 id | name  | sports
----+-------+---------------------------------
  1 | Novak | {'Basket Ball', 'Golf', 'Tennis'}
```

(1 rows)

cqlsh:first_ks>-- Below UPDATE, removal of 'Golf' .

cqlsh:first_ks> UPDATE customer
               SET sports = sports - {'Golf'}
               WHERE id = 1;

cqlsh:first_ks> SELECT * FROM customer;

```
 id | name  | sports
----+-------+---------------------------
  1 | Novak | {'Basket Ball', 'Tennis'}
```

(1 rows)

cqlsh:first_ks>-- Below UPDATE, removal of nonexistent 'Cricket' has no effect

cqlsh:first_ks> UPDATE customer

            SET sports = sports - {'Cricket'}

            WHERE id = 1;

cqlsh:first_ks> SELECT * FROM customer;

```
 id | name   | sports
----+--------+---------------------------
  1 | Novak  | {'Basket Ball', 'Tennis'}
```

(1 rows)

cqlsh:first_ks>-- Below UPDATE, removal of nonexistent of 'Cricket' does not UPSERT.

cqlsh:first_ks> UPDATE customer

            SET sports = sports - {'Cricket'}

            WHERE id = 2;

cqlsh:first_ks> SELECT * FROM customer;

```
 id | name   | sports
----+--------+---------------------------
  1 | Novak  | {'Basket Ball', 'Tennis'}
```

(1 rows)

cqlsh:first_ks>-- Below UPDATE, addition of 'Basket Ball' does UPSERT by setting null to the name.

cqlsh:first_ks> UPDATE customer

            SET sports = sports + {'Basket Ball'}

            WHERE id = 2;

cqlsh:first_ks> SELECT * FROM customer;

```
 id | name   | sports
----+--------+---------------------------
  1 | Novak  | {'Basket Ball', 'Tennis'}
  2 |  null  |            {'Basket Ball'}
```

```
(2 rows)
cqlsh:first_ks>
```

MAP

MAP datatype is used to store {key, value} pair of elements.

```
cqlsh:first_ks> CREATE TABLE cust (    id int PRIMARY KEY,
                                       name text,
                                       phone map<text,text>  );
cqlsh:first_ks> INSERT INTO cust (id,name,phone)
                VALUES ( 1,'Rafa',{ 'home':'123-456','offie':'987-6543' } );
cqlsh:first_ks> INSERT INTO cust (id,name,phone)
                VALUES ( 2,'Andy',{ 'mobile':'654-7890' } );
cqlsh:first_ks> SELECT * FROM cust;

 id | name | phone
----+------+----------------------------------------
  1 | Rafa | {'home': '123-456', 'offie': '987-6543'}
  2 | Andy |                    {'mobile': '654-7890'}

(2 rows)
cqlsh:first_ks> SELECT JSON * FROM cust;

 [json]
-----------------------------------------------------------------------
{"id": 1, "name": "Rafa", "phone": {"home": "123-456", "offie": "987-6543"}}
            {"id": 2, "name": "Andy", "phone": {"mobile": "654-7890"}}

(2 rows)
cqlsh:first_ks> UPDATE cust
                SET phone = phone + {'mobile':'234-7654'}
                WHERE id=1;
```

70

```
cqlsh:first_ks> SELECT * FROM cust;

id | name | phone
----+---------+---------------------------------------------------------------
 1 |  Rafa | {'home': '123-456', 'mobile': '234-7654', 'offie': '987-6543'}
 2 | Andy |                                        {'mobile': '654-7890'}

(2 rows)
cqlsh:first_ks> DELETE  phone['home'] FROM cust WHERE id=1;
cqlsh:first_ks> SELECT * FROM cust;

id | name | phone
----+---------+-------------------------------------------------------
 1 |  Rafa | {'mobile': '234-7654', 'offie': '987-6543'}
 2 | Andy |                       {'mobile': '654-7890'}

(2 rows)
```

Batch statements

BATCH command is used to apply all the DML statements (such as INSERT, DELETE & UPDATE) as a group to achieve atomicity and isolation for a single partition or only atomicity when updating multiple partitions.

```
General syntax
BEGIN [ UNLOGGED | LOGGED ] BATCH
[USING TIMESTAMP epoch_microseconds]

...
CQL

...
APPLY BATCH;
```

In the above general syntax, 'LOGGED' works with only Datastax version of Cassandra.

71

If you are running five inserts, five updates, and two deletes as individual statements, the chances are that one of them could fail. The failed statement can cause the data to go out of sync. When you group them these twelve individual statements in a BATCH, either all will succeed or none, ensuring atomicity.

If multiple partitions are modified in the batch, Cassandra uses the batch log to ensure all modifications are written. It ensures guaranteed write of all grouped statements. If the timestamp is not specified for each statement, then all statements will be applied with the same timestamp, either generated by the coordinator node or the timestamp provided at the batch level.

Batch involving multiple partitions is a definite anti-pattern. Avoid multiple partitions BATCHING as much as possible unless eventual atomicity must be needed. If multiple partitions are involved, batches are logged by default and Cassandra writes these batch to the *batchlog* system table as a blob data. Once it successfully writes the batch, it removes the *batchlog* data. This is a big performance penalty as it has to write to 2 other nodes if your RF is set to 3.

Although logged batch ensures atomicity and eventual consistency, it does not give batch isolation unless the batch operation is writing to a single partition. In multiple partition batch operations like below example, the clients can read first updated rows from the batch, say *custno*=500, while other rows are still being updated on the node.

```
BEGIN BATCH USING TIMESTAMP 1545369701
UPDATE customer SET name='R Steel' WHERE custno=500;
UPDATE customer SET name='Tejesh S' WHERE custno=700;
UPDATE customer SET name='Jeremy K' WHERE custno=800;
UPDATE customer SET name='M Evans' WHERE custno=900;
APPLY BATCH;
```

If you run large batch operations with multiple partition update, it places a big burden on the coordinator node, and performance would degrade considerably. You might see heap issues on the coordinator node and it can increase latency.

Note that statements in the batch are not applied sequentially. If you are updating the same column multiple times for the same partition, it is not guaranteed that it will apply the DML sequentially.

For example

If you apply the below batch, it is not guaranteed that status will be equal to 'T' at the end of the batch. CQL statements within the batch can be applied in any order. To force a particular ordering, you must specify per-statement timestamps.

```
cassandra@cqlsh:demo> BEGIN BATCH
                      UPDATE test SET status='Z' WHERE id=3;
                      UPDATE test SET status='X' WHERE id=3;
                      UPDATE test SET status='T' WHERE id=3;
                      APPLY batch;
cassandra@cqlsh:demo> SELECT * FROM test;

id | city       | status
---+------------+--------
 1 | New York   |   Y
 2 | Paris      |   N
 3 | Tokyo      |   Z

(3 rows)
```

When to use logged Batches?

Basic rules of data modeling in Cassandra involves duplicating data into multiple tables based on the queries run against that table. Cassandra data modeling is all about duplicating data by de-normalization. When you de-normalize the tables, you need to maintain the relations and data integrity manually when you modify the data.

Consider *Figure 4.2* below. Table *'ticker'* and *'customer'* are de-normalized in *'cust_ticker'*. We can show all the customers who follow a ticker. If you delete a customer, you need to delete all the ticker he follows from the *cust_ticker* table. If you run delete on customer and *cust_ticker* as two separate statements and one of them fails, it will leave orphaned data in one of the tables. In this case, you can use batching.

Cassandra Admin DBA Guide

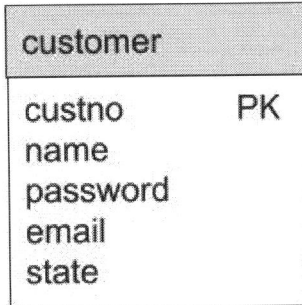

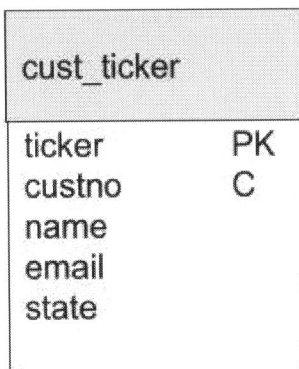

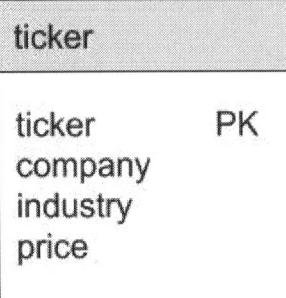

Figure 4.2: cust_ticker table

Materialized View

In some RDBMS, views are just a definition or query stored in the system table which does not contain any data. These views can be used just like normal tables or joining with other tables.

A materialized view is introduced in Cassandra 3.0. In Cassandra, materialized views are a standard table, which is automatically maintained by the Cassandra server. When a base table is updated, appropriate updates are applied to the underlying view tables. At a glance, this looks very helpful and great feature as you don't have to manually maintain the de-normalized tables, but care must be taken to review the performance impact of views in your use case.

Let's look at simple table and view creation.

```
cqlsh:first_ks>
cqlsh:first_ks> CREATE TABLE first_ks.customer (   custno int PRIMARY KEY,
                                                    loginname text,
                                                    name text,
                                                    state text,
                                                    phone map<text,text> );
```

```
cqlsh:first_ks> INSERT INTO customer(custno,loginname,name,state,phone)
              VALUES (100,'bill_001','Bill','NJ',{'mobile': '123-4567'} );
cqlsh:first_ks> INSERT INTO customer(custno,loginname,name,state,phone)
              VALUES (200,'warren_2','Warren','NY',{'mobile': '321-6789'} );
cqlsh:first_ks> INSERT INTO customer(custno,loginname,name,state,phone)
              VALUES (300,'jeff00','Jeff','NJ',{'mobile': '123-9876'} );
cqlsh:first_ks> INSERT INTO customer(custno,loginname,name,state,phone)
              VALUES (400,'mark9','Mark','PA',{'mobile': '876-9876'} );
cqlsh:first_ks> INSERT INTO customer(custno,loginname,name,phone)
              VALUES (500,'mike1','Michael',{'mobile': '123-4567'} );
cqlsh:first_ks>
cqlsh:first_ks> SELECT * FROM customer;

 custno | loginname | name    | phone                     | state
--------+-----------+---------+---------------------------+-------
    500 |     mike1 | Michael | {'mobile': '123-4567'} |  null
    200 |  warren_2 |  Warren | {'mobile': '321-6789'} |    NY
    100 |  bill_001 |    Bill | {'mobile': '123-4567'} |    NJ
    400 |     mark9 |    Mark | {'mobile': '876-9876'} |    PA
    300 |    jeff00 |    Jeff | {'mobile': '123-9876'} |    NJ

(5 rows)
cqlsh:first_ks>
```

Syntax of Materialized view

```
CREATE MATERIALIZED VIEW [ IF NOT EXISTS ] materialized_view_name AS
SELECT_STATEMENT <columna_names>
WHERE_clause
PRIMARY KEY ( primary_key ) --must contain all primary column from base table.
WITH table_options
```

Limitation of Creating view.

1) The primary key of the view must contain all columns from the primary key of the base table. In the above case, 'custno' is the primary key in the base table. This means the primary key of the view must contain the column 'custno'.

2) Along with the full base primary key, you can add only one additional column for the primary key of the view.

Now let's create a view based on the base table. For the view, we will provide *state* & *custno* as primary key.

When creating a view, you can filter columns that are not part of the base table's primary key. As you can see in the below CREATE VIEW statement, the column *state* was not a part of the primary key in the base table and may contain a null value. When you create a view, you can filter out such *null* rows.

```
cqlsh:first_ks> CREATE MATERIALIZED VIEW cust_by_state
            AS
            SELECT * FROM first_ks.customer
            WHERE state IS NOT NULL
            AND custno IS NOT NULL
            PRIMARY KEY(state,custno)
            WITH comment = 'customer by state of customer table';
cqlsh:first_ks>
SELECT * FROM cust_by_state;


 state | custno | loginname | name   | phone
-------+--------+-----------+--------+-----------------------
    NJ |    100 |  bill_001 |   Bill | {'mobile': '123-4567'}
    NJ |    300 |    jeff00 |   Jeff | {'mobile': '123-9876'}
    PA |    400 |     mark9 |   Mark | {'mobile': '876-9876'}
    NY |    200 |  warren_2 | Warren | {'mobile': '321-6789'}

(4 rows)
cqlsh:first_ks>
```

As you can see from the above output, *cust_by_state* view did not include the row where *custno*=500 for which state was inserted as null. If you update the base table and run a SELECT on the view, you would see that Cassandra internally inserted this updated row.

```
cqlsh:first_ks> UPDATE customer SET state='NJ' WHERE custno=500;
cqlsh:first_ks> SELECT * FROM cust_by_state;


 state | custno | loginname | name    | phone
-------+--------+-----------+---------+---------------------------
    NJ |    100 |  bill_001 |    Bill | {'mobile': '123-4567'}
    NJ |    300 |    jeff00 |    Jeff | {'mobile': '123-9876'}
    NJ |    500 |     mike1 | Michael | {'mobile': '123-4567'}
    PA |    400 |     mark9 |    Mark | {'mobile': '876-9876'}
    NY |    200 |  warren_2 |  Warren | {'mobile': '321-6789'}

(5 rows)
cqlsh:first_ks>
```

How do you confirm that UPDATE of the base table has updated the view table? When you run the UPDATE, turn tracing on, which displays and record the details in the *system_traces* *keyspace*. The above UPDATE was run with "TRACING ON".

```
cqlsh:first_ks> tracing on;
Now Tracing is enabled
cqlsh:first_ks> UPDATE customer SET state='NJ' WHERE custno=500;

Tracing session: d21b0c30-fa91-11e8-ac0d-3550c4f85976
```

The tracing output contains activity, timestamp, source, client and elapsed time. Let's just retrieve the activity to see what does Cassandra do internally with the UPDATE. As you can see from the below output, UPDATE on customer table created mutations for the materialized view. At the end of the tracing, you see that the data is updated and added to memtable for both the tables, *customer & cust_by_state*. The first commitlog update is for *customer* and the second commitlog update is for the *cust_by_state* table.

```
cqlsh:system_traces> SELECT activity FROM events
                     WHERE session_id=d21b0c30-fa91-11e8-ac0d-3550c4f85976;


 activity
----------------------------------------------------------------------------------
                         Parsing UPDATE customer SET state='NJ' WHERE custno=500;
                                                              Preparing statement
                                                   Determining replicas for mutation
                                                            Appending to commitlog
                          Creating materialized view mutations from base table replica
                                        Executing single-partition query on customer
                                                        Acquiring sstable references
                                                         Key cache hit for sstable 1
                 Skipped 0/1 non-slice-intersecting sstables, included 0 due to tombstones
                                          Merged data from memtables and 1 sstables
                                                   Read 1 live and 0 tombstone cells
                                                   Determining replicas for mutation
                                                            Appending to commitlog
                                                     Adding to cust_by_state memtable
                                                       Adding to customer memtable

(15 rows)
```

The metadata for the views are stored in the *system_schema.views* table.

```
cqlsh:system_traces> SELECT keyspace_name, view_name,
                     base_table_id, base_table_name, where_clause
                     FROM system_schema.views ;


 keyspace_name | view_name      | base_table_id
 | base_table_name | where_clause
---------------+----------------+------------------------------------
+----------------+------------------------------------------
      first_ks | cust_by_state | 20465e30-fa8f-11e8-ac0d-3550c4f85976 |
customer | state IS NOT NULL AND custno IS NOT NULL
```

```
(1 rows)

cqlsh:system_traces> SELECT keyspace_name,table_name,id
                     FROM system_schema.tables
                     WHERE keyspace_name='first_ks'
                     AND table_name='customer';

 keyspace_name | table_name | id
---------------+------------+-----------------------------------
      first_ks |   customer | 20465e30-fa8f-11e8-ac0d-3550c4f85976

(1 rows)
cqlsh:system_traces>
```

Now let's create a view to verify the limitation of one additional column in the view.

```
cqlsh:system_traces> CREATE MATERIALIZED VIEW cust_by_loginname_state AS
                     SELECT * FROM first_ks.customer
                     WHERE loginname is NOT NULL
                     AND state is NOT NULL
                     AND custno IS NOT NULL
                     PRIMARY KEY( loginname, state, custno );
InvalidRequest: Error from server: code=2200 [Invalid query] message="unconfigured table
customer"
cqlsh:system_traces>
```

In the above case, we are trying to create a view and we are trying to add two columns – *loginname* & *state* in addition to the base tables primary key *'custno'*. Cassandra throws error on this.

You can create view's with custom filtering. Let's create a view by filtering *state*='NJ'.

```
cqlsh:first_ks>
cqlsh:first_ks> CREATE MATERIALIZED VIEW cust_by_state_NJ
        AS
```

```
        SELECT * FROM first_ks.customer
        WHERE state = 'NJ'
        AND custno IS NOT NULL
        PRIMARY KEY(state,custno)
        WITH comment = 'view of cust table where state = to NJ';

cqlsh:first_ks> SELECT * FROM cust_by_state_NJ;

 state | custno | loginname | name     | phone
-------+--------+-----------+----------+------------------------
    NJ |    100 |   bill_001 |     Bill | {'mobile': '123-4567'}
    NJ |    300 |    jeff00 |     Jeff | {'mobile': '123-9876'}
    NJ |    500 |     mike1 |  Michael | {'mobile': '123-4567'}

(3 rows)
cqlsh:first_ks>
```

You can use DROP MATERIALIZE VIEW and drop a view. Use ALTER MATERIALIZE VIEW to modify any table options.

Data Export & Import

COPY command can be used to import and export data to and from Cassandra. It's part of CQL shell.

```
Syntax :
COPY tablename [( column list )]
FROM 'filename' [WITH option = 'value' [AND ...]]
COPY tablename [( column list )]
TO 'filename' [WITH option = 'value' [AND ...]]
```

COPY TO export the data from a table to a text file. Each row is written to the target file with columns separated with a delimiter. *COPY FROM* imports the data from a text file into an existing table. If no columns are specified, all columns from the table will be imported or exported. A

80

subset of columns may be specified by adding the comma-separated column list. When you are importing using COPY FROM, unspecified columns will be inserted as null values.

Use COPY command to import or export for small amount of data. Documentation does not say about maximum row size or limit on the number of rows, but If you want to bulk-load large data, use *sstableloader*.

Following COPY command creates a text file with columns delimited with '~' .

```
cqlsh:first_ks> COPY first_ks.customer (custno,loginname,name,phone,state)
      ... TO '/home/cassandra/customer.txt' WITH DELIMITER = '~';
Reading options from the command line: {'delimiter': '~'}
Using 1 child processes


Starting copy of first_ks.customer with columns [custno, loginname, name, phone, state].
Processed: 5 rows; Rate:     9 rows/s; Avg. rate:     18 rows/s
5 rows exported to 1 files in 0.290 seconds.
cqlsh:first_ks> exit
cassandra@cc1:~$ cat /home/cassandra/customer.txt
500~mike1~Michael~{'mobile': '123-4567'}~NJ
200~warren_2~Warren~{'mobile': '321-6789'}~NY
100~bill_001~Bill~{'mobile': '123-4567'}~NJ
400~mark9~Mark~{'mobile': '876-9876'}~PA
300~jeff00~Jeff~{'mobile': '123-9876'}~NJ
```

You can specify HEADER = true to export column names.

```
cqlsh> COPY first_ks.customer TO '/home/cassandra/customer.txt'
      WITH DELIMITER = '~' AND HEADER=true;
Reading options from the command line: {'header': 'true', 'delimiter': '~'}
Using 1 child processes


Starting copy of first_ks.customer with columns [custno, loginname, name, phone, state].
Processed: 5 rows; Rate:     24 rows/s; Avg. rate:     24 rows/s
5 rows exported to 1 files in 0.211 seconds.
```

```
cqlsh> exit
cassandra@cc1:~$ cat /home/cassandra/customer.txt
custno~loginname~name~phone~state
500~mike1~Michael~{'mobile': '123-4567'}~NJ
200~warren_2~Warren~{'mobile': '321-6789'}~NY
100~bill_001~Bill~{'mobile': '123-4567'}~NJ
400~mark9~Mark~{'mobile': '876-9876'}~PA
300~jeff00~Jeff~{'mobile': '123-9876'}~NJ
```

COPY...FROM will load the data into the target table.

```
cqlsh> TRUNCATE TABLE first_ks.customer;

cqlsh> COPY first_ks.customer
       FROM '/home/cassandra/customer.txt'
       WITH DELIMITER = '~' AND HEADER=true;
Reading options from the command line: {'header': 'true', 'delimiter': '~'}
Using 1 child processes

Starting copy of first_ks.customer with columns [custno, loginname, name, phone, state].
Processed: 5 rows; Rate:    8 rows/s; Avg. rate:    12 rows/s
5 rows imported from 1 files in 0.430 seconds (0 skipped).

cqlsh> SELECT * FROM first_ks.customer ;

 custno | loginname | name    | phone                   | state
--------+-----------+---------+-------------------------+-------
    500 |     mike1 | Michael | {'mobile': '123-4567'} |   NJ
    200 |  warren_2 |  Warren | {'mobile': '321-6789'} |   NY
    100 |  bill_001 |    Bill | {'mobile': '123-4567'} |   NJ
    400 |     mark9 |    Mark | {'mobile': '876-9876'} |   PA
    300 |    jeff00 |    Jeff | {'mobile': '123-9876'} |   NJ

(5 rows)
cqlsh>
```

If you are looking to COPY selected rows using where clause, it is not possible with the below version of Cassandra. You can write your script to extract data using SELECT [..] WHERE clause to save in a file and import that data.

Materialized views were introduced in Version 3.0 which allows you to create filter out the data, but as of Cassandra 3.10 | CQL spec 3.4.4, it does not allow to export the data.

```
cqlsh> SELECT * FROM first_ks.cust_by_state ;

 state | custno | loginname | name    | phone
-------+--------+-----------+---------+----------------------------
    NJ |    100 |   bill_001|    Bill | {'mobile': '123-4567'}
    NJ |    300 |     jeff00|    Jeff | {'mobile': '123-9876'}
    NJ |    500 |      mike1| Michael | {'mobile': '123-4567'}
    PA |    400 |      mark9|    Mark | {'mobile': '876-9876'}
    NY |    200 |   warren_2|  Warren | {'mobile': '321-6789'}

(5 rows)
cqlsh> COPY first_ks.cust_by_state TO '/home/cassandra/customer.txt'
      WITH DELIMITER = '~' AND HEADER=true;
Column family 'cust_by_state' not found
cqlsh:first_ks> show version;
[cqlsh 5.0.1 | Cassandra 3.10 | CQL spec 3.4.4 | Native protocol v4]
```

Some of options you can use with COPY commands are listed below. Refer documentation for complete set of options.

MAXPARSEERRORS - The maximum number of parsing errors to ignore. Default value is -1, which means unlimited.

MAXINSERTERRORS - The maximum number of insert errors to ignore. Default is 1000.

ERRFILE - File will be created to store all the rows that could not be imported. By default, this create import_<ks>_<table>.err. In the given example here, it will create a file import_first_ks_customer.err.

HEADER - For COPY TO, controls whether the first line in the output file will contain the column names. For COPY FROM, specifies whether the first line in the input file contains column names. Default is false.

NUMPROCESSES - The number of child worker processes to create for COPY tasks. Default is max of 4 for COPY FROM and 16 for COPY TO. For both commands max will be (num_cores - 1).

```
cqlsh> COPY first_ks.customer FROM '/home/cassandra/customer.txt'
      WITH DELIMITER = '~'
      AND HEADER=true
      AND MAXPARSEERRORS=5
      AND ERRFILE='/home/cassandra/error_file.txt';
Reading options from the command line: {'maxparseerrors': '5', 'header': 'true', 'delimiter': '~', 'errfile': '/home/cassandra/error_file.txt'}
Using 1 child processes

Starting copy of first_ks.customer with columns [custno, loginname, name, phone, state].
Failed to import 1 rows: ParseError - Invalid row length 4 should be 5,  given up without retries
Failed to process 1 rows; failed rows written to /home/cassandra/error_file.txt
Processed: 6 rows; Rate:     9 rows/s; Avg. rate:     14 rows/s
6 rows imported from 1 files in 0.422 seconds (0 skipped).
cqlsh> exit
cassandra@cc1:~$ cat /home/cassandra/error_file.txt
600~Larry00~Larry~CA
cassandra@cc1:~$
```

RDBMS vs Cassandra

If you are from RDBMS background and looking for a command like below, it will not work in Cassandra.

- INSERT INTO keyspace.table SELECT * FROM keyspace.another_table;
- If you INSERT INTO with the same primary key twice – you get an error as **primary key constraint** for the second INSERT.
- In Cassandra – there are no constraints. It will overwrite the row as an UPSERT.
- COPY FROM and COPY TO are equivalent to 'bcp out' and 'bcp in' in SAP Sybase or SQL Server and SQL*Loader in Oracle.

CHAPTER 5

Cassandra Data Modeling

I f you are from an RDBMS background, you might carry over the same RDBMS data modeling techniques and apply them to Cassandra. Cassandra data modeling is all about duplicating data by de-normalizing your tables as Cassandra does not have Joins. You need to prepare your queries first before you design your tables.

Your organization has chosen Cassandra for one or more reasons:

1. The volume of data: The current volume or future expected volume of the data you are going to process or store, is in terabyte and petabyte.
2. The speed of data: Your organization is looking for a write-heavy, high-velocity database.
3. You are looking for high availability or readily available data storage for your application.
4. Your organization is looking for a linearly scalable database rather than the old way of scaling vertically by moving to new hardware very often.

All of these points are very important for data modeling. To achieve the best possible data modeling, you need to know Cassandra architecture first. If you are not familiar with the Cassandra architecture, do spend some time and learn about it.

CQL (Cassandra Query Language) manages all Cassandra DDL/DML commands. CQL is the primary language for communicating with the Cassandra database, and it's similar to SQL. This similarity between CQL & SQL makes new people think it's just like RDBMS. Cassandra tables are not the same as RDBMS table. The DDL & DML in CQL is almost similar to SQL, with some differences in the syntax.

No JOINS

In Cassandra, you cannot join tables. There is a performance cost for Cassandra to give join capability. In a distributed database, like Cassandra, your table's data are stored on tens or even hundreds of nodes based on the cluster configuration. Providing capability of table join requires a lot of disk I/O, CPU, and network traffic for the amount of data to transfer and merge. What is the solution if you cannot join the tables? The Solution is, you duplicate the data by de-normalization based on your query requirement.

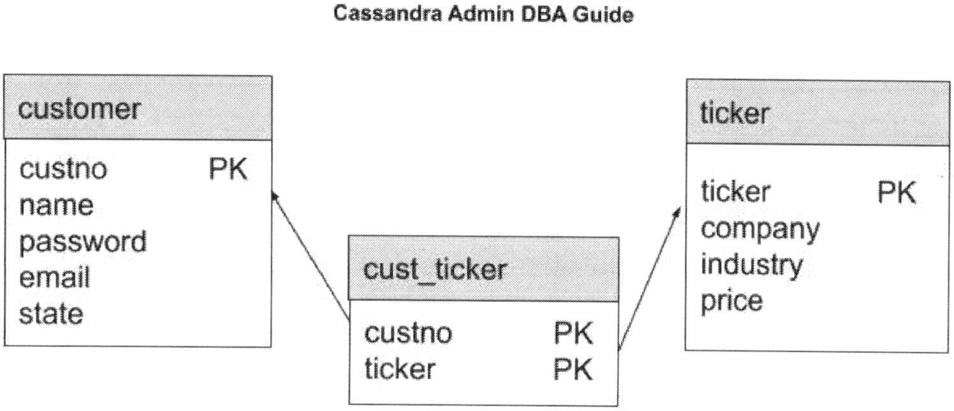

Cassandra Admin DBA Guide

Figure 5.1: customer & ticker – RDBMS data model.

In the *Figure 5.1* data model, designed for RDBMS, the *customer* table and *ticker* table have their respective information. If we want to store information on customers who follow the tickers, we will create a table like *cust_ticker*. This data modeling is normalized by removing repeated data.

To list all customers who follow a particular ticker, you would typically write a JOIN query as below.

```
SELECT c.custno, c.name, c.email, c.state
FROM customer c, ticker t, cust_ticker x
WHERE   t.ticker = "BAC"
```

```
AND      t.ticker = x.ticker
AND      x.custno = c.custno
```

In Cassandra, you cannot join tables. The solution is to de-normalize and duplicate the data as shown in *Figure 5.2*. A new table *cust_ticker* needs to be created with a PRIMARY KEY as (*ticker, custno*). The partition key ticker will store all customers in one big partition, and the clustering key will be *custno*. Note that, *name*, *email* and *state* data is duplicated in this table and will not have any foreign key or referential integrity to the customer table. Data consistency in both *customer* and *cust_ticker* table needs to be maintained by the application.

Cassandra Admin DBA Guide

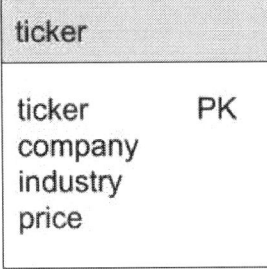

customer			cust_ticker			ticker	
custno	PK		ticker	PK		ticker	PK
name			custno	C		company	
password			name			industry	
email			email			price	
state			state				

Figure 5.2: customer & ticker – Cassandra data model.

Once you duplicate data in *cust_ticker* table, you will write a simple query to retrieve the data for a give ticker.

```
SELECT custno, name, email, state
FROM cust_ticker
WHERE ticker = 'BAC';
```

Note that the data modeling in Figure 5.2 is used for demonstration purposes only. The data modeling represented here is incorrect. For example, if 1 million customers watch the ticker 'BAC', there will be a big wide row with partition key value as 'BAC' will be sitting on one node. You will learn about a wide row later in this chapter.

Primary Key, Partition Key & Clustering Key

Cassandra does not have joins, foreign keys, and constraints. So in a way, data modeling in Cassandra is simple. Cassandra data modeling is all about de-normalizing tables and duplicating data, which is why the important thing is defining your partition key and primary key. Let's go in detail about the primary key, partition key, and clustering key.

Cassandra Admin DBA Guide

Primary Key = ((PartitionKey1, PartitionKey2, ..n), ClusteringKey1, ClusteringKey2,..n)

The primary key uniquely identifies a row and is comprised of a partition key and clustering key. While designing the primary key, make sure that at least one column (clustering key) ensures the uniqueness of the row. Otherwise, your UPDATE and INSERT (UPSERT) will overwrite the existing data.

A partition key can be simple or composite. A partition key is described as a composite when there is more than one partition key is defined. A partition key (simple or composite) determines the data locality. All the rows sharing the same partition key are stored on the same node. That's why you need to pay attention while designing tables and the primary key.

All listed columns after the partition key are clustering columns. Clustering columns specify the order of the data rows within that partition.

Primary key examples

Following *Figure 5.3* has examples of the primary key.

Cassandra Admin DBA Guide

	PRIMARY KEY Definition	Partition Key	Clustering Key
1	(uid)	uid	
2	(uid, name)	uid	name
3	(uid, state, name)	uid	state, name
4	((state, uid))	state, uid	
5	((state, uid), name)	state, uid	name
6	((state, uid), year, tran_type)	state, uid	year, tran_type

Figure 5.3: Partition keys

Example 1. In *Figure 5.3*, *uid* is the partition key, and there is no clustering key. When a table has a simple partition key (no composite partition key) and no clustering key, you can define the primary key in two different ways.

```
CREATE TABLE data_modeling.example1
(
    uid    int PRIMARY KEY,
    name   text
);


Or


CREATE TABLE data_modeling.example1
(
    uid    int,
    name   text,
    PRIMARY KEY (uid)
);
```

Example 2. When you mention PRIMARY KEY (*uid, name*), the first column is always the partition key and the second column is the clustering key.

Example 3. When you mention PRIMARY KEY (*uid, state, name*), the first column is always the partition key and second & third columns are the clustering keys. All rows belong to the same partition key (*uid* - in this case), is stored on the same node. Data rows will be sorted by *state* & *name* within that partition key.

Example 4. When you mention PRIMARY KEY ((*state, uid*)), since you are enclosing both *state* & *uid* in '()', both columns are considered as partition keys. In this case, it is referred to as the composite key. As you can see, there is no clustering column defined here.

Example 5. When you mention PRIMARY KEY ((*state, uid*), *name*), since you are enclosing both *state* & *uid* in '()', both columns considered as partition keys which is a composite key and *name* is a clustering column.

Example 6. When you mention PRIMARY KEY ((*state, uid*), *year, tran_type*), since you are enclosing both *state* and *uid* in '()', both columns considered as partition keys. When you have more than one columns in a partition key, it is referred to as a composite key. '*Year'* and '*tran_type'* are clustering columns in this case. Within the partition (*state, uid*), the rows are sorted by clustering columns. In this case, those are '*year'* and '*tran_type'*.

Valid & Invalid WHERE clause

When you define clustering columns, it is critical that the order of the clustering columns matter in WHERE clause. Take an example of PRIMARY KEY ((*state, uid*), *year, tran_type*) and assume that there are no secondary indexes.

In WHERE clause

- You must pass all the partition keys, but the clustering keys are optional.
- When it comes to passing the clustering keys, you must provide all the columns leading up to the last one. Take an example of PRIMARY KEY ((a, b)) e, f, g, h. If you want to pass 'g' in your WHERE clause, you must provide values for 'e' and 'f, but 'h' is optional.

Valid queries in WHERE clause are

- state = 'NJ' and uid = 100
- state = 'NJ' and uid = 100 and year = 2017
- state = 'NJ' and uid = 100 and year = 2017 and tran_type = 'Options'

Invalid queries in WHERE clause are

- state = 'NJ'
- state = 'NJ' and uid = 100 and tran_type = 'Options'

In the above invalid query example, *'tran_type'* is used in the where clause, but its leading clustering column *'year'* is left out.

Partition hotspotting

When you use multiple columns as the partition key, it breaks the partition data into smaller chunks. Use the proper composite partition key to avoid the hotspotting. When the partition is big, it can put pressure on the heap memory, and the overall performance can be an issue. Let's study a hypothetical example below.

```
CREATE TABLE data_modeling.temparature
(
    station     int,
    year        int,
    month       int,
    day         int,
    temp        int,
    humidity    int,
    collect_time timestamp,
    w_data      blob,
    PRIMARY KEY ((station, year), month, day)
);
```

In our hypothetical example, we are collecting and storing the temperatures from multiple weather stations. For this, we have created a table as listed above.

Let's look at the partition size (*station, year*), of the table if each weather station collects temperatures every hour and inserts a row with the above primary keys.

No. of rows inserted per day / station = 24 rows / day

No. of rows inserted per year / station = 24 (hours) * 365 (days) = 8,760 rows / year

Assume that, each data row size is 10 KB. The amount of data/year, per station, will be 85 MB, which, each read will fetch for the partition.

8,760 (rows/year) * 10 KB (row size) = 87,600 KB = 85.54 MB

Data modeling needs to address future business needs and changes where it is possible. Sometimes it's a tough call, but in some cases, it is easy to spot. In this case, when you started the discussion with your project team and gathering the specifications, it was decided to store hourly temperature data for each weather station.

If the business decides to collect temperatures every minute for every station, what do you think will happen to the partition size? Let's calculate.

No. of rows inserted per day / station = 60 (min) * 24 (24 hours) = 1440 rows / day

No. of rows inserted per year / station = 1440 * 365 days = 525,600 rows / year

The amount of data / year, per station will be

525,600 (rows/year) * 10 KB (row size) = 5,256,000 KB = 5,132 MB = 5.01 GB

Your Queries and frequency and amount of data insertion drive data modeling decisions here. Once you start collecting data every minute, as calculated above, with the current partition of (station, year), the table will have 5 GB partition size instead of 85 MB partition size! This change may lead to performance issue as read/write traffic increases and the read latency increases. For every table design, you need to brain storm with the team to make sure that you are addressing any future needs.

While designing the table and partition keys, instead of PRIMARY KEY ((station, year), month, day), if you define it as PRIMARY KEY ((station, year, month), day), you will be able to withstand the changes to data collection frequency and amount of data you read per partition. Business decision to change temperature collection frequency from every hour to every minute will make the partition (station, year, month) size to 426 MB, which is still acceptable.

This hypothetical example shows how designing the partition keys affects the partition size and performance of the cluster. Keep in mind that, for retrieving entire partition data from the table, all partition key values must be supplied in the WHERE clause as explained above in the valid queries topic.

Location of the data

Cassandra dynamically partitions the data over all the nodes (in a datacenter) in the cluster. It does this by consistently hashing the partition key of the table. A partitioner is a hash function which calculates the "token" of a partition key and writes the data to a node which owns that token range. As you can see in below example, *token()* function hash the value and generate a token number. Every time you hash the same value, it will generate the same token number. In below output, you can see that token number generated for *custcode* (values 'custB' & 'custA') are different. The token number generated for the static value 'Sample_HashingKey' is the same.

```
cassandra@cqlsh> SELECT custcode, name,token(custcode), token('Sample_HashingKey')
                 FROM data_modeling.customer;

 custcode | name        | system.token(custcode) | system.token('Sample_HashingKey')
----------+-------------+------------------------+----------------------------------
    custB | Customer B  |   -7658416167795438757 |              -4593142858293621375
    custA | Customer A  |    3407154596510871911 |              -4593142858293621375

(2 rows)
```

Let's look at a few simple examples of primary keys and partition keys and how the data does spread across a four node cluster.

```
CREATE TABLE data_modeling.customer (
    custno          int PRIMARY KEY,
    add1            text,
    email           text,
    name            text,
    password        text,
    state           text,
    zipcode         text
);
CREATE TABLE data_modeling.cust_by_email (
    email           text PRIMARY KEY,
    custno          int,
    password        text
);
CREATE TABLE data_modeling.cust_by_state (
    state   text,
    name            text,
    custno          int,
    email           text,
    password        text,
    PRIMARY KEY (state, name)
);
```

In the above output, the customer table has a simple primary key which is *custno*, which is also a partition key. When a row is inserted, it is written to a node in the cluster based on the token value generated by hashing of *custno*. The entire possible token range is divided and owned by each node in the datacenter of the cluster. For details, refer "Data Partition" in *Chapter 2, Cassandra Basic Architecture.*

Table *cust_by_state* has the primary key as (*state, name*). So if there are more than one customers in a state, all the rows with the same '*state*' are stored on the same node.

We have inserted below data in these three tables.

```
cqlsh:data_modeling> SELECT * FROM customer;

 custno| add1 | email         | name  | password| state | zipcode
 ------+------+---------------+-------+---------+-------+---------
    500|   xx | custE@__com   | custE |     xx  |   NJ  |  12345
    200|   xx | custB@__com   | custB |     xx  |   NY  |  12345
    100|   xx | custA@__com   | custA |     xx  |   NJ  |  12345
    400|   xx | custD@__com   | custD |     xx  |   NJ  |  12345
    300|   xx | custC@__com   | custC |     xx  |   PA  |  12345
    600|   xx | custF@__com   | custF |     xx  |   NY  |  12345
    700|   xx | custG@__com   | custG |     xx  |   NJ  |  12345

(7 rows)
cqlsh:data_modeling> SELECT * FROM cust_by_email ;

 email          | custno | password
 ---------------+--------+----------
  custE@__com   |    500 |     xx
  custF@__com   |    600 |     xx
  custD@__com   |    400 |     xx
  custB@__com   |    200 |     xx
  custA@__com   |    100 |     xx
  custC@__com   |    300 |     xx
  custG@__com   |    700 |     xx

(7 rows)
cqlsh:data_modeling> SELECT * FROM cust_by_state  ;

 state | name  | custno | email         | password
 ------+-------+--------+---------------+----------
    NJ | custA |    100 | custA@__com   |     xx
    NJ | custD |    400 | custD@__com   |     xx
    NJ | custE |    500 | custE@__com   |     xx
```

```
NJ  |  custG  |     700  |  custG@__com  |        xx
PA  |  custC  |     300  |  custC@__com  |        xx
NY  |  custB  |     200  |  custB@__com  |        xx
NY  |  custF  |     600  |  custF@__com  |        xx


(7 rows)
cqlsh:data_modeling>
```

Below, Figure 5.4 shows how the data is stored on these nodes. Tables, customer & cust_by_ email have a simple partition key, and based on their token value, are written to the nodes which owns those token range. Table cust_by_state partition key is 'state'. This means that all the rows with the same partition key value are stored as a wide row. We have four rows with a value of state=NJ, and as you can see, those are all stored as one wide row on node N2.

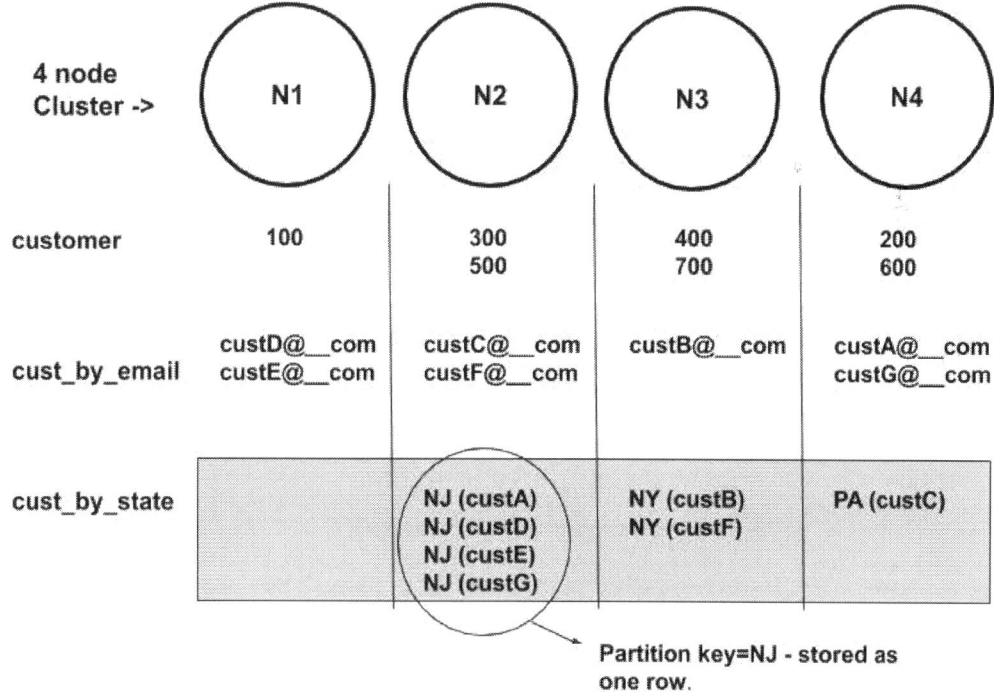

Figure 5.4: Data distribution

As a data modeler, you should have already sensed the problem here. For example, if the table *cust_by_state* has 30 million rows, out of which 20 million belong to state 'NJ,' it will create one huge wide row with partition key = 'NJ.' This wide row, could be a significant data modeling issue because it creates hotspotting, which may lead to a performance issue.

UPSERT

For Cassandra, UPDATE is synonymous with INSERT. Every INSERT & UPDATE is an UPSERT. INSERT can update an existing row, and UPDATE can insert a row if it does not exist. Let's look at an example. Note that in Cassandra there is no unique constraint enforcement. While designing the table, make sure your primary key is unique. In Cassandra data modeling, when we say design your queries first before the tables, this means including your UPDATE and INSERTs too. If your INSERT accidentally overwrites any data without any error, there will not be any versioned data to recover, and the data will be gone.

Now lets' look at an example of UPSERT. For this, we will use the data from *cust_by_state* table from the above output. There are 7 rows in the *cust_by_state* table, and as you see there are no customers belong where *state*='CA'. Now we will run below UPDATE command with *state*='CA'. If you run such an UPDATE in traditional RDBMS, you would get a message saying '0 rows affected', as there are no rows satisfying *state*='CA'. But in Cassandra, this UPDATE will run as UPSERT, and it will INSERT a row using the value provided in the WHERE clause.

UPDATE cust_by_state SET custno=1000 WHERE state='CA' and name='custX';

```
cqlsh:data_modeling> SELECT * FROM cust_by_state
                     WHERE state='CA';


 state | name | custno | email | password
-------+------+--------+-------+----------

(0 rows)
cqlsh:data_modeling> UPDATE cust_by_state
                     SET custno=1000
                     WHERE state='CA'
```

```
                    AND name='custX';
cqlsh:data_modeling> SELECT * FROM cust_by_state
                    WHERE state='CA';

 state | name  | custno | email | password
-------+-------+--------+-------+----------
    CA | custX |   1000 |  null |     null

(1 rows)
cqlsh:data_modeling> SELECT * FROM cust_by_state;

 state | name  | custno | email        | password
-------+-------+--------+--------------+----------
    NJ | custA |    100 | custA@__com  |       xx
    NJ | custD |    400 | custD@__com  |       xx
    NJ | custE |    500 | custE@__com  |       xx
    NJ | custG |    700 | custG@__com  |       xx
    PA | custC |    300 | custC@__com  |       xx
    NY | custB |    200 | custB@__com  |       xx
    NY | custF |    600 | custF@__com  |       xx
    CA | custX |   1000 |         null |     null

(8 rows)
cqlsh:data_modeling>
```

As you can see in the above output, UPDATE has inserted a row using the values provided in the WHERE clause.

Now let's look at an example of INSERT command. In traditional RDBMS, when you insert a row with an existing primary key, your INSERT will fail with a "duplicate primary key" error. In Cassandra, there is no unique constraint enforcement, and your INSERT statement will actually UPDATE the row if it already exists. In below example, you will see that the INSERT has updated the row.

99

```
cqlsh:data_modeling> SELECT * FROM cust_by_state WHERE state='CA';

 state | name  | custno | email | password
-------+-------+--------+-------+----------
    CA | custX |   1000 |  null |     null

(1 rows)
cqlsh:data_modeling> INSERT INTO cust_by_state ( state, name, custno, email, password )
                     VALUES ( 'CA', 'custX', 1100, 'custX@__com', 'yy' );
cqlsh:data_modeling> SELECT * FROM cust_by_state WHERE state='CA';

 state | name  | custno | email        | password
-------+-------+--------+--------------+----------
    CA | custX |   1100 | custX@__com  |       yy

(1 rows)
cqlsh:data_modeling>
```

In Cassandra, primary & foreign key constraints or referential integrity is not enforced. Cassandra is write optimized, and it does not do a read before it writes, unless you use the clause IF EXISTS. As you saw in the INSERT example above, we actually overwrote *custno* from 1000 to 1100, which is supposed to be, by design is a referential integrity issue with customer and *cust_by_email* tables. In Cassandra when you duplicate data, application layer needs to maintain the data consistency across the related tables.

If you do not want INSERT to update the data and UPDATE to insert the data, you can use IF & IF EXISTS command. Below example is self-explanatory.

```
UPDATE cust_by_state SET custno=1000 WHERE state='CA' and name='custX' IF EXISTS;

UPDATE account SET status='yes' WHERE acc_no=100 IF status=NULL;
I
NSERT INTO cust_by_state ( state,name,custno,email,password)
VALUES ('CA','custX',1100,'custX@__com','yy') IF EXISTS;
```

Partition Size and Limitations

As a data modeler, you need to know how to calculate the partition size while designing the tables. In Cassandra, the partition is the basic unit for replication. All data for the single partition must fit on a single node.

Limitation of partition size is the available disk space on the node. As you read earlier, Cassandra does not break partition. It treats it as one atomic unit, which needs to be fit on one node.

The number of cells in a partition has a limit of 2 Billion. The cells are equal to (rows*columns) in any given partition.

Single column value size is limited to 2 GB. The best practice is to have the size of the column value under 10 MB unless your use case requires you to go for a higher limit.

For other limitations, please refer the online documentation for the version you are using. Note that you should verify these values for your current version as well.

Calculating Partition Cells

In general, the number of cells = (number of rows * columns) in any given partition. This method is a quick way of estimating the number of cells in that partition.

If you study Cassandra's internal data storage, you will see that the partition key and static column values are not repeated in every row. Static column values are stored only once at the beginning of the partition. So when you are calculating the number of cells, you need to skip over counting static columns. A simple formula is

Number of Cell = Rows * (Total Columns – Total PK – Static Columns) + Total Static Columns

Let's look at an example.

```
CREATE TABLE data_modeling.cust_by_ticker_s (
    custno int,
```

```
    ticker text,
    company text static,
    name text static,
    qty int,
    PRIMARY KEY (custno, ticker)
) WITH CLUSTERING ORDER BY (ticker ASC)
```

In the above table, the total number of columns are 5. The number of primary key columns (*custno, ticker*) are 2. The number of static columns are 2. If we have to calculate the number of cells for this tables when it has 1000 rows (one partition for *custno*), use below formula.

The number of cells is equal to = (Number of rows) * (number of columns – number of primary key columns – number of static columns) + number of static columns.

The number of cells is equal to = 1000 * (5 – 2 – 2) + 2 = 1002.

Calculating Partition Size

To calculate the partition size, we need to know the data type of each column. Below output shows a few data types and the number of bytes it occupies. Refer to online documentation for all other datatypes and correct bytes for your version.

Data Type		Number of Bytes
ascii		No.of Char * 1 byte/char
bigint	8	bytes
counter	8	bytes
date	4	bytes
double	8	bytes
float	4	bytes
inet	4	bytes (IPv4) or 16 bytes (IPV6)
int	4	bytes
smallint	2	bytes
text		No.of Char * (No.of bytes/Char for the language)

time	8	bytes
timestamp	8	bytes
timeuuid	16	bytes
tinyint	1	byte
uuid	16	bytes

To calculate the partition size, use the below general formula. Note that this is an approximation size and this formula is more for Cassandra version < 3.0. For accurate size calculation, please refer to online documentation.

$$TB = PK + S + r * (cc + ac) + nc * 8$$

TB = Total Bytes

PK = Size of all partition key columns

S = Total size of all static columns

r = Number of rows (this should be same as above in Calculating Partition Cells)

cc = Total size of all clustering columns

ac = Total size of all other columns excluding partition, clustering, static columns

nc = Number of Cells in the partition from above Calculating Partition Cells.

8 = This is the size of timestamp which is written for each cell. In version 3.0 and above, it can be stored only once per row. But for simplicity, we are counting this towards all cells.

Let's calculate the partition size for *cust_by_ticker_s*.

TB = 4 (*custno* int) + (40+40) (avg for *name*+avg for *company*) * 1000 (8 (avg for *ticker*) + 4 (*qty* int) + 1002 * 8

Total Bytes = 4 + 80 * 1000 (8 +4) + 1002 * 8 = 20,100

Calculating the partition size will give you an approximate size which can be further used in calculating table size, heap requirement.

Data Duplication

During RDBMS only days, we were using very slow computers. The hard disk capacity was limited, memory was limited, and CPU speed was slow. The benefit of normalization was less data duplication on disks, thus less disk I/O and we needed less disk space. Data normalizing made sense with the technology available at the time. In Sybase (ASE), the difference between char(n) and varchar(n) made a big difference when it came to designing the tables. All CHAR values were blank padded to the max length, whereas in VARCHAR, no blanks were padded. The reason was to store the data compactly so that performance will be better. The main reason was, disk I/O, CPU speed was slow, and on top of it, memory was limited. The bottom line is, normalization made sense those days (and it still makes sense today when it comes to RDBMS).

Cassandra's problem in normalizing the table is that there are no joins. SELECT query does not allow you to join tables. In a distributed database like Cassandra, providing join capability will be very expensive as it involves hundreds of nodes, and data transfer between the nodes consume more network bandwidth. Since you cannot join tables, you need to duplicate your data based on your query patterns. When you duplicate the data, it's the application's responsibility to maintain the data consistency between duplicated tables.

As a data modeler, you must know how much data you are duplicating. Based on the expected number of rows in each table, we will know the approximate data size for the cluster. For example, say you need to build a cluster to store 5 TB of data. This information is crucial to DBA's and the architects to size the cluster. If you decide to have 3 replicas, that means the requirement of data goes from 5 TB to 15 TB. Note that setting replication factor is not considered as data duplication. For high-availability replication is needed.

Static Columns

In Cassandra, we de-normalize data so that we can get a good read performance. De-normalizing the tables increases the disk space requirements. As a data modeler, it's important to know how static columns stored internally. As you read in partition size estimation, static columns are stored only once per partition. Static columns provide benefits when the table is de-normalized with one-to-many relations. Following are some advantages.

1. INSERT operation becomes simpler.
2. Number of UPDATE operations is reduced to maintain the data consistency.
3. Static columns reduce the table size thus increasing read performance.

Cassandra Admin DBA Guide

Figure 5.5: Non static & Static column table

Consider the above use case — table *'customer'* stores customer data & table *'ticker'* stores stock ticker details. There is a many-to-many relation between *customer* to the *ticker*, which means customers can own multiple tickers and tickers can have multiple stockholders (customer). *Figure 5.5* displays *customer->ticker* as 1-n relation in this example. Table *cust_by_ticker* is a de-normalized table, which duplicates and stores customer name, email data from the *customer* table.

We will review the advantages of having a static column vs. non-static column when you duplicate the data. For our test case, we will perform the following DML and evaluate the results.

1. Insert data into the *cust_by_ticker* table.
2. Update customer name and email to keep the data consistency with *customer* table.

Test case 1 – without static column.

In our first test case, we will create the table *cust_by_ticker* <u>without</u> static columns.

```
CREATE TABLE data_modeling.cust_by_ticker (
    custno      int,
    ticker      text,
    email       text,
    name        text,
    qty         int,
    PRIMARY KEY (custno, ticker)
);

INSERT INTO cust_by_ticker(custno,ticker,name,email,qty)
VALUES (100,'AMZN','Dhinakaran G','dg_email',1000);

INSERT INTO cust_by_ticker(custno,ticker,name,email,qty)
VALUES (100,'BABA','Dhinakaran G','dg_email',2000);

INSERT INTO cust_by_ticker(custno,ticker,name,email,qty)
VALUES (200,'FB','Vahe A','va_email',5000);

INSERT INTO cust_by_ticker(custno,ticker,name,email,qty)
VALUES (200,'NFLX','Vahe A','va_email',200);

INSERT INTO cust_by_ticker(custno,ticker,name,email,qty)
VALUES (300,'BAC','Manjunath S','ms_email',3300);
INSERT INTO cust_by_ticker(custno,ticker,name,email,qty)
VALUES (300,'NFLX','Manjunath S','ms_email',100);
```

```
INSERT INTO cust_by_ticker(custno,ticker,name,email,qty)
VALUES (300,'AAPL','Manjunath S','ms_email',100);

cqlsh:data_modeling> SELECT * FROM cust_by_ticker;
```

```
custno | ticker | email     | name         | qty
--------+--------+-----------+--------------+------
   200 |     FB | va_email  |       Vahe A | 5000
   200 |   NFLX | va_email  |       Vahe A |  200
   100 |   AMZN | dg_email  | Dhinakaran G | 1000
   100 |   BABA | dg_email  | Dhinakaran G | 2000
   300 |   AAPL | ms_email  |  Manjunath S |  100
   300 |    BAC | ms_email  |  Manjunath S | 3300
   300 |   NFLX | ms_email  |  Manjunath S |  100

(7 rows)
cqlsh:data_modeling>
```

In the above output, we created the table without static columns and inserted data for 3 customers who are following some tickers. When we added the data rows, for a given customer, *name* and *email* information is duplicated in each row during insertion.

We will do two types of updates — first update of the *qty* and second update of the *name* for the customer.

First update case, update *qty* for given *custno* and *ticker*. As you see in the below output, this is a simple update and relatively easy as column '*qty*' is stored within the clustering key.

```
cqlsh:data_modeling> SELECT * FROM cust_by_ticker WHERE custno=100;

custno | ticker | email     | name         | qty
--------+--------+-----------+--------------+------
   100 |   AMZN | dg_email  | Dhinakaran G | 1000
   100 |   BABA | dg_email  | Dhinakaran G | 2000

(2 rows)
cqlsh:data_modeling> UPDATE cust_by_ticker
                     SET qty=2000
                     WHERE custno=100 AND ticker='AMZN';
cqlsh:data_modeling> SELECT * FROM cust_by_ticker WHERE custno=100;
```

```
custno | ticker | email     | name          | qty
--------+--------+-----------+---------------+------
   100 |   AMZN | dg_email  | Dhinakaran G  | 2000
   100 |   BABA | dg_email  | Dhinakaran G  | 2000

(2 rows)
```

Second update case, update name for a given *custno*. Column *'name'* is stored within the clustering key, whereas it was supposed to be stored within the partition key. If we change the name of the customer in table *'customer'*, we need to update all the de-normalized tables which store *custno* and *name*, which include this table *cust_by_ticker*. Since it is stored within the clustering key level, we don't have any other option but run multiple updates for each ticker for a given *'custno'*. Let's update *custno* = 300 in this example.

```
cqlsh:data_modeling> SELECT * FROM cust_by_ticker
                     WHERE custno=300;

custno | ticker | email     | name          | qty
--------+--------+-----------+---------------+------
   300 |   AAPL | ms_email  | Manjunath S   | 100
   300 |    BAC | ms_email  | Manjunath S   | 3300
   300 |   NFLX | ms_email  | Manjunath S   | 100

(3 rows)

UPDATE cust_by_ticker SET name='Manju'
WHERE custno=300 AND ticker='AAPL';

UPDATE cust_by_ticker SET name='Manju'
WHERE custno=300 AND ticker='BAC';

UPDATE cust_by_ticker SET name='Manju'
WHERE custno=300 AND ticker='NFLX';
```

```
cqlsh:data_modeling> SELECT * FROM cust_by_ticker WHERE custno=300;

 custno | ticker | email     | name  | qty
--------+--------+-----------+-------+------
    300 |   AAPL | ms_email  | Manju |  100
    300 |    BAC | ms_email  | Manju | 3300
    300 |   NFLX | ms_email  | Manju |  100

(3 rows)
cqlsh:data_modeling>
```

If partition key *custno* = 300 has 1000 tickers in this table, we need to issue 1000 separate UPDATE statements to update all the rows, which is not a good scenario for the development team as well as for the performance of the cluster. Now you must be wondering why not update the name with only partition key as one update? Since the column *'name'* is a regular column and not a static column, Cassandra needs a full primary key in WHERE clause to update the row. If you give just partition key, the statement fails.

```
cqlsh:data_modeling> SELECT * FROM cust_by_ticker
                     WHERE custno=300;

 custno | ticker | email     | name  | qty
--------+--------+-----------+-------+------
    300 |   AAPL | ms_email  | Manju |  100
    300 |    BAC | ms_email  | Manju | 3300
    300 |   NFLX | ms_email  | Manju |  100

(3 rows)
cqlsh:data_modeling> UPDATE cust_by_ticker SET name='Manju S'
                     WHERE custno=300;
InvalidRequest: Error from server: code=2200 [Invalid query]
message="Some clustering keys are missing: ticker"
cqlsh:data_modeling>
```

Let's review how Cassandra stores the data internally when the column is NOT defined as static.

Data directory for cust_by_ticker is
$CASSANDRA_HOME/data/data/data_modeling/**cust_by_ticker-**
a9359a4014fb11e99a0371719c65b92a

$CASSANDRA_HOME/tools/bin/sstabledump -d mc-1-big-Data.db

[200]@0 Row[info=[ts=1547152926236511]]: FB | [email=va_email ts=1547152926236511],
[name=Vahe A ts=1547152926236511], [qty=5000 ts=1547152926236511]
[200]@51 Row[info=[ts=1547152926295054]]: NFLX | [email=va_email ts=1547152926295054],
[name=Vahe A ts=1547152926295054], [qty=200 ts=1547152926295054]

[100]@87 Row[info=[ts=1547152926143307]]: AMZN | [email=dg_email ts=1547152926143307],
[name=Dhinakaran G ts=1547152926143307], [qty=2000 ts=1547152990324541]
[100]@148 Row[info=[ts=1547152926195511]]: BABA | [email=dg_email ts=1547152926195511],
[name=Dhinakaran G ts=1547152926195511], [qty=2000 ts=1547152926195511]

[300]@190 Row[info=[ts=1547152926467863]]: AAPL | [email=**ms_email**
ts=1547152926467863], [name=**Manju** ts=1547326874017307],
[qty=100 ts=1547152926467863]
[300]@248 Row[info=[ts=1547152926344302]]: BAC | [email=**ms_email**
ts=1547152926344302], [name=**Manju** ts=1547326874145626], [qty=3300
ts=1547152926344302]
[300]@287 Row[info=[ts=1547152926392581]]: NFLX | [email=**ms_email**
ts=1547152926392581], [name=**Manju** ts=1547326874214405],
[qty=100 ts=1547152926392581]

Above output is from *sstabledump* run in data directory for *cust_by_ticker* table. Option -d output the data as CQL row per line internal representation. Above output has been modified for readability by adding an extra line for after each partition. As you see here, the column *'name'* & *'email'* stored within the clustering column, and the duplicated value stored and repeated for each row within each partition (*custno*).

Test case 2 – with static column.

In our second test case, we will create the table cust_by_ticker_s with static columns. Table cust_by_ticker_s is precisely the same as cust_by_ticker in test case 1; the only difference is that the columns 'name' & 'email' defined as static. We will perform similar insert and update on this table to see how defining columns to static will impact the INSERT, UPDATE and size of the table.

```
CREATE TABLE data_modeling.cust_by_ticker_s
        (    custno      int,
             ticker      text,
             name        text static,
             email       text static,
             qty         int,
             PRIMARY KEY (custno,ticker)
        );

INSERT INTO cust_by_ticker_s(custno,name,email)
VALUES (100,'Dhinakaran G','dg_email');

INSERT INTO cust_by_ticker_s(custno,name,email)
VALUES (200,'Vahe A','va_email');

INSERT INTO cust_by_ticker_s(custno,name,email)
VALUES (300,'Manjunath S','ms_email');

cqlsh:data_modeling> SELECT * FROM cust_by_ticker_s;

 custno | ticker | email    | name          | qty
--------+--------+----------+---------------+------
    200 |   null | va_email |        Vahe A | null
    100 |   null | dg_email | Dhinakaran G  | null
    300 |   null | ms_email |  Manjunath S  | null

(3 rows)
cqlsh:data_modeling>
```

As you see in the above output, we have created the same table with the same primary key. The only difference is that we have defined the columns *'name'* and *'email'* as static. In earlier example when the column not defined as static, the data stored at a clustering column level. A static column resides at a higher level within the partition key (In this case it is *custno*), which make INSERTs easier. Since *'name'* and *'email'* stored at the partition level, you can INSERT the row without the clustering key and the columns which are not static. You insert the rows in two steps.

1. Insert rows with the partition key and static columns.
2. Insert rows which are at clustering key level. In this example, value for column *ticker* and *qty* along partition key, *custno*.

The beauty of this feature is when you INSERT values for clustering keys and non-static columns, based on the partition key, the static columns values are inherited automatically at the clustering key level.

```
cqlsh:data_modeling> SELECT * FROM data_modeling.cust_by_ticker_s;

 custno | ticker | email    | name         | qty
--------+--------+----------+--------------+------
    200 |   null | va_email |       Vahe A | null
    100 |   null | dg_email | Dhinakaran G | null
    300 |   null | ms_email |  Manjunath S | null

(3 rows)
INSERT INTO cust_by_ticker_s(custno,ticker,qty) VALUES (100,'AMZN',1000);
INSERT INTO cust_by_ticker_s(custno,ticker,qty) VALUES (100,'BABA',2000);
cqlsh:data_modeling> SELECT * FROM data_modeling.cust_by_ticker_s;

 custno | ticker | email    | name         | qty
--------+--------+----------+--------------+------
    200 |   null | va_email |       Vahe A | null
    100 |   AMZN | dg_email | Dhinakaran G | 1000
    100 |   BABA | dg_email | Dhinakaran G | 2000
```

```
    300 |     null |   ms_email |    Manjunath S |  null
```

(4 rows)

As you see in the above output, both INSERTs included only partition key (*custno*), clustering key (*ticker*) and non-static columns (*qty*). Static columns *'name'* & *'email'* are not part of the INSERT statement. Now insert rest of the rows.

```
cqlsh:data_modeling> SELECT * FROM data_modeling.cust_by_ticker_s;

 custno | ticker | email     | name          | qty
--------+--------+-----------+---------------+------
    200 |   null |  va_email |        Vahe A |  null
    100 |   AMZN |  dg_email |  Dhinakaran G | 1000
    100 |   BABA |  dg_email |  Dhinakaran G | 2000
    300 |   null |  ms_email |    Manjunath S |  null

(4 rows)
```

INSERT INTO cust_by_ticker_s(custno,ticker,qty) VALUES (200,'FB',5000);
INSERT INTO cust_by_ticker_s(custno,ticker,qty) VALUES (200,'NFLX',200);
INSERT INTO cust_by_ticker_s(custno,ticker,qty) VALUES (300,'AAPL',100);
INSERT INTO cust_by_ticker_s(custno,ticker,qty) VALUES (300,'BAC',3300);
INSERT INTO cust_by_ticker_s(custno,ticker,qty) VALUES (300,'NFLX',100);

```
cqlsh:data_modeling> SELECT * FROM data_modeling.cust_by_ticker_s;

 custno | ticker | email     | name          | qty
--------+--------+-----------+---------------+------
    200 |     FB |  va_email |        Vahe A | 5000
    200 |   NFLX |  va_email |        Vahe A |  200
    100 |   AMZN |  dg_email |  Dhinakaran G | 1000
    100 |   BABA |  dg_email |  Dhinakaran G | 2000
    300 |   AAPL |  ms_email |    Manjunath S |  100
```

```
    300 |      BAC |  ms_email |  Manjunath S |  3300
    300 |     NFLX |  ms_email |  Manjunath S |  100

(7 rows)
cqlsh:data_modeling>
```

When partition key dependent columns defined as static, you don't need to run multiple updates to have consistency in the data. In our earlier example, where columns were not static, we ran the UPDATE for each ticker as shown below.

```
UPDATE cust_by_ticker SET name='Manjunath' WHERE custno=300 AND ticker='AAPL';
UPDATE cust_by_ticker SET name='Manjunath' WHERE custno=300 AND ticker='BAC';
UPDATE cust_by_ticker SET name='Manjunath' WHERE custno=300 AND ticker='NFLX';
```

If partition key custno=300 owns 1000 tickers, you need to run 1000 updates without static columns! Defining these columns static makes the updates easy. We need to issue only one UPDATE at partition key level, as shown in below output.

```
cqlsh:data_modeling> SELECT * FROM cust_by_ticker_s WHERE custno=300;
 custno | ticker | email     | name         | qty
--------+--------+-----------+--------------+------
    300 |   AAPL |  ms_email |  Manjunath S |  100
    300 |    BAC |  ms_email |  Manjunath S |  3300
    300 |   NFLX |  ms_email |  Manjunath S |  100

(3 rows)

UPDATE cust_by_ticker_s SET name='Manju' WHERE custno=300;

cqlsh:data_modeling> SELECT * FROM cust_by_ticker_s
                WHERE custno=300;

 custno | ticker | email     | name   | qty
--------+--------+-----------+--------+------
```

```
    300 |    AAPL | ms_email | Manju |   100
    300 |     BAC | ms_email | Manju |  3300
    300 |    NFLX | ms_email | Manju |   100

(3 rows)
cqlsh:data_modeling>
```

Let's review how Cassandra stores the data internally when the column is defined as static.

Run sstabledump in data directory

$CASSANDRA_HOME/data/data/data_modeling/
cust_by_ticker_s-9da00a7016af11e99a0371719c65b92a

$CASSANDRA_HOME/tools/bin/sstabledump -d mc-1-big-Data.db

[200]@0 Row[info=[ts=-9223372036854775808]]: **STATIC** | [email=va_email
ts=1547328059100148], [name=Vahe A ts=1547328059100148]
[200]@0 Row[info=[ts=1547330339074405]]: FB | [qty=5000 ts=1547330339074405]
[200]@63 Row[info=[ts=1547330339100927]]: NFLX | [qty=200 ts=1547330339100927]

[100]@83 Row[info=[ts=-9223372036854775808]]: **STATIC** | [email=dg_email
ts=1547328059035555], **[name=Dhinakaran G** ts=1547328059035555]
[100]@83 Row[info=[ts=1547328313401221]]: AMZN | [qty=1000 ts=1547328313401221]
[100]@149 Row[info=[ts=1547328314664337]]: BABA | [qty=2000 ts=1547328314664337]

[300]@168 Row[info=[ts=-9223372036854775808]]: **STATIC** | [email=ms_email
ts=1547328060774777], **[name=Manju** ts=1547328060774777]
[300]@168 Row[info=[ts=1547330339142602]]: AAPL | [qty=100 ts=1547330339142602]
[300]@238 Row[info=[ts=1547330339175793]]: BAC | [qty=3300 ts=1547330339175793]
[300]@256 Row[info=[ts=1547330339263087]]: NFLX | [qty=100 ts=1547330339263087]

Above sstabledump output shows, column 'name' & 'email' stored at the partition level only once. This saves a lot of disk space and reduces partition size.

Static columns are an easy way of sharing the same data across the same data partition, but it has some restrictions.

- A table without clustering columns cannot have static columns. In a table without clustering columns, every partition will have only one row.

- Only non primary key columns can be defined as static.

Column name size

We all want to give descriptive names for our tables and columns. One thing you should pay attention to is the column length in your table definition. Cassandra stores each column name and its value repeatedly in each row. When we define long column names, we use a lot of memory, during read and in row cache and in heap. Compression on the disk mitigates the disk space issue, but it all adds up during read and write. For example, look at the table creation below.

```
CREATE TABLE data_modeling.table_with_long_column_name
(
    custno                                          int,
    name_of_the_customer                            text,
    is_this_customer_currently_active_values_Y_or_N   text,
    PRIMARY KEY (custno)
);

INSERT INTO data_modeling.table_with_long_column_name
(custno,name_of_the_customer,is_this_customer_currently_active_values_Y_or_N)
VALUES (100,'Name A','Y');

INSERT INTO data_modeling.table_with_long_column_name
(custno,name_of_the_customer,is_this_customer_currently_active_values_Y_or_N)
VALUES (200,'Name B','N');

cqlsh:data_modeling> SELECT * FROM table_with_long_column_name;
```

```
custno | is_this_customer_currently_active_values_y_or_n | name_of_the_customer
--------+------------------------------------------------------+----------------------
   200 |                                                  N |        Name B
   100 |                                                  Y |        Name A

(2 rows)
cqlsh:data_modeling>
```

Now flush the SSTable and do a *sstabledump* to inspect the disk representation of the data.

Run sstabledump in directory

$CASSANDRA_HOME/data/data/data_modeling/
table_with_long_column_name-e153085016f311e9a7e5c9baef8ac57f

$CASSANDRA_HOME/tools/bin/sstabledump -d mc-1-big-Data.db

[200]@0 Row[info=[ts=1547357256415327]]: | [**is_this_customer_currently_active_values_y_
or_n**=N ts=1547357256415327], [name_of_the_customer=Name B ts=1547357256415327]

[100]@37 Row[info=[ts=1547357248349217]]: | [**is_this_customer_currently_active_values_y_
or_n**=Y ts=1547357248349217], [name_of_the_customer=Name A ts=1547357248349217]

We have dumped the SSTable to show the internal storage of the table and its values. As shown in the above output, the long column name repeated and stored for each row. Cassandra does have good compression to store data, but still, you should consider limiting the length of the column names. In a future version, this may be taken care of and not going to be an issue.

It is a good idea to club together columns that are read together and store as a single column in JSON format if your use case allows.

Tombstones

Tombstones are deletion markers written when data gets deleted. Each delete writes a record with a local delete time. The deleted data goes through Cassandra's write path and stored in SSTable. The tombstones are removed from the SSTable as part of Cassandra's normal compaction process. The compaction process drops the tombstones only after local_delete_time + gc_grace_seconds defined for that table. The default value for 'gc_grace_seconds' is 864000 seconds, which is ten days. The 'gc_grace_seconds' is configurable at the table level.

A quick look at tombstone in SSTable with JSON dump.

```
cassandra@cqlsh> CREATE TABLE data_modeling.tombstone
                (
                        custcode int,
                        bcode     int,
                        cmt       text,
                        PRIMARY KEY (custcode, bcode)
                ) ;
cassandra@cqlsh> INSERT INTO tombstone(custcode,bcode,cmt) VALUES (1,1,'one');
cassandra@cqlsh> INSERT INTO tombstone(custcode,bcode,cmt) VALUES (2,2,'two');
cassandra@cqlsh> DELETE FROM data_modeling.tombstone WHERE custcode=2;
cassandra@cqlsh> SELECT * FROM tombstone;

 custcode | bcode | cmt
-------------+----------+-----
        1 |       1 | one

(1 rows)
cassandra@cqlsh>
```

sstabledump of the SSTable after a nodetool flush

```
sstabledump -t mc-1-big-Data.db
[
  {
    "partition" : {
      "key" : [ "1" ],
      "position" : 0
    },
    "rows" : [
      {
        "type" : "row",
        "position" : 18,
        "clustering" : [ "1" ],
        "liveness_info" : { "tstamp" : "1555111780823055" },
        "cells" : [
          { "name" : "cmt", "value" : "one" }
        ]
      }
    ]
  },
  {
    "partition" : {
      "key" : [ "2" ],
      "position" : 33,
      "deletion_info" : { "marked_deleted" : "1555111792200120", "local_delete_time" :
"1555111792" }
    }
  }
]
```

Once the data deleted, you have to deal with it for 10 days. To understand this clearly, say you have a table in which you have inserted 20 million rows and deleted 19 million rows. These 19 million tombstoned rows will occupy your SSTable's for *gc_grace_seconds* time. If you are running a SELECT query on this table within the *gc_grace_seconds* time, you probably will be reading part of this 19 million deleted rows, which may cause read performance issues.

So, are tombstones bad? Do we need to avoid deleting the data? Absolutely No. In a distributed database like Cassandra, writing tombstone allows it to give high write throughput. But as a data modeler, you need to carefully review your tables and especially how the data gets inserted, updated, and deleted to avoid any performance issues due to tombstones. Many times, a lack of understanding of tombstones can cause production issues. When this happens, going back and fixing the code, business logic or data modeling can become a headache, expensive and even could affect the business.

Tombstones take up space and increase the storage requirement. Most of the production clusters configured with multiple data centers and at least 3 replicas per data center. Now you can imagine the amount of storage the tombstones going to occupy! Secondly, querying these tables with a large number of tombstones affects the performance and even may exhaust the server heap and CPU. These points are essential if tombstones are generated unnecessarily due to bad data modeling.

From a data modeling point of view, we need to pay attention to those tables which are de-normalized (index tables) for fast query performance and how we have defined the primary key for those tables. For any data duplications that we do, we need to handle the data consistency across index tables, and this requires an update or delete followed by the insert to maintain that consistency. As a data modeler, we need to know how many of such UPDATEs expected on the base table which result in a DELETE (tombstone) on index table? Because based on the data modeling, more the update, it will generate more tombstones.

Let's look at an example below. You have a *transaction* table in which transaction goes through several status changes before the *status* become 'cancel' or 'fill'. You have a requirement to run a report to provide details about all transactions for given *status*. A custom secondary index table (we will refer them as *index tables*) *tran_by_status* created for the same purpose, but it is a regular table. When we de-normalize tables like this, manually we need to maintain data consistency between these two tables.

Cassandra Admin DBA Guide

transactions		
custno	int	PK
tran_no	int	C
status	text	
...		

tran_by_status		
status	text	PK
custno	int	C
tran_no	int	C
...		

tombstone consideration.

INSERT Operation

INSERT INTO transactions (custno,tran_no,status..) VALUES (1,2,"open")
INSERT INTO tran_by_status(status,custno,tran_no) VALUES ("open",1,2)

UPDATE Operation

UPDATE transactions SET status="fill" WHERE custno=1 AND tran_no=2

INSERT INTO tran_by_status(status,custno,tran_no) VALUES ("fill",1,2)

DELETE FROM tran_by_status
WHERE status="open" AND custno=1 AND tran_no=2

Figure 5.6 : Tombstone creation through custom secondary index table.

To INSERT a new transaction, we need to perform 2 INSERTS. First, insert on transactions table. Second insert on the *tran_by_status* table. Inserting data in these two tables have no issues.

Now we will review how UPDATE works. As per use case, the *transactions.status* goes through many stages before it is finally updated with *status* = 'fill' or 'cancel'. Each time the *transactions.status* changes, we need to UPDATE both tables to keep it in synchronization. The update on *transactions* is simple, as shown in *Figure 5.6*. A simple UPDATE updates the *status* from 'open' to 'fill'. Now you need to update *tran_by_status.status* table with the same value to keep the data in synchronization. But you cannot UPDATE the *status* column on *tran_by_status* as it is partition key. In Cassandra, you cannot update the primary key columns. To keep the data consistency, you need to INSERT a row with new *status*='fill' and DELETE the row with earlier *status*='open'. Each update of *transaction.status* will generate a tombstone in the *tran_by_status* table.

Just for a theoretical discussion, let's say that on an average each transaction goes through 9 status updates of the row. This type UPDATE is just fine for transactions table. But in the *tran_by_status* table, you are generating approximately 90% tombstones, which is occupying the storage for 10 days (*gc_grace_seconds*). If the tombstone count is more than *tombstone_failure_threshold* (default to 100,000), your query will abort.

In one of the client place, a new feature was rolled out with new tables. New functionality has updates which were similar to the updates like *'status'*. These changes never tested in a lower environment with production size volume. When the code went into production, the number of tombstones increased in multiple folds. The new functionality was not only affected, but queries started failing due to tombstones crossing the threshold of *tombstone_failure_threshold*.

Based on the use case and requirement, we duplicate data by creating index tables, but we need to pay attention to tombstones and wide partitions it can generate. You might think, instead of index tables, you will create a materialized view to handle such use case. You will face a similar issue in this case as well.

Let's take a similar example using the materialized view. We have created a transaction table. Instead of creating an index table, we will create a materialized view on the transaction table. Materialized views don't need manual data synchronization. These views are actual table maintained automatically by Cassandra. Data modification on the base table automatically updates all the underlying dependent view tables. In this example, any INSERT/UPDATE/DELETE on the *transaction* table automatically updates the underlying view table *tran_by_status*.

```
CREATE TABLE data_modeling.transaction (
        custno      int,
        tran_no     int,
        ticker      text,
        qty         int,
        status      text,
        PRIMARY KEY (custno,tran_no)
);


CREATE MATERIALIZED VIEW data_modeling.tran_by_status
AS
SELECT * FROM data_modeling.transaction
WHERE status   IS NOT NULL
AND    custno   IS NOT NULL
AND    tran_no IS NOT NULL
PRIMARY KEY(status,custno,tran_no)
WITH comment = 'transactions by status';
```

Let's INSERT 3 rows in the *transaction* table, and you can see that 3 rows are INSERTED in *tran_by_status* automatically by Cassandra.

```
cqlsh:data_modeling> SELECT * FROM transaction;

 custno | tran_no | qty | status | ticker
--------+---------+-----+--------+--------

(0 rows)
cqlsh:data_modeling> SELECT * FROM tran_by_status;

 status | custno | tran_no | qty | ticker
--------+--------+---------+-----+--------

(0 rows)

INSERT INTO transaction (custno,tran_no,ticker,qty,status)
VALUES (1,100,'AMZN',100,'open');

INSERT INTO transaction (custno,tran_no,ticker,qty,status)
VALUES (2,101,'FB',200,'open');

INSERT INTO transaction (custno,tran_no,ticker,qty,status)
VALUES (1,103,'BAC',500,'fill');

cqlsh:data_modeling> SELECT * FROM transaction;

 custno | tran_no | qty | status | ticker
--------+---------+-----+--------+--------
      1 |     100 | 100 |   open |   AMZN
      1 |     103 | 500 |   fill |    BAC
      2 |     101 | 200 |   open |     FB

(3 rows)
cqlsh:data_modeling> SELECT * FROM tran_by_status;
```

```
 status | custno | tran_no | qty | ticker
--------+--------+---------+-----+--------
   open |      1 |     100 | 100 |    AMZN
   open |      2 |     101 | 200 |      FB
   fill |      1 |     103 | 500 |     BAC

(3 rows)
cqlsh:data_modeling>
```

Below output is *sstabledump* output for both the tables.

sstabledump of transaction

[1]@0 Row[info=[ts=1547360432559337]]: 100 | [qty=100 ts=1547360432559337], [status=open ts=1547360432559337], [ticker=AMZN ts=1547360432559337]
[1]@44 Row[info=[ts=1547360434041691]]: 103 | [qty=500 ts=1547360434041691], [status=fill ts=1547360434041691], [ticker=BAC ts=1547360434041691]

[2]@72 Row[info=[ts=1547360432604505]]: 101 | [qty=200 ts=1547360432604505], [status=open ts=1547360432604505], [ticker=FB ts=1547360432604505]

sstabledump of tran_by_status (MATERIALIZED VIEW)

[open]@0 Row[info=[ts=1547360432559337]]: 1, 100 | [qty=100 ts=1547360432559337], [ticker=AMZN ts=1547360432559337]
[open]@42 Row[info=[ts=1547360432604505]]: 2, 101 | [qty=200 ts=1547360432604505], [ticker=FB ts=1547360432604505]

[fill]@67 Row[info=[ts=1547360434041691]]: 1, 103 | [qty=500 ts=1547360434041691], [ticker=BAC ts=1547360434041691]

Now, let's UPDATE *transaction* table and set the status to a new value.

UPDATE transaction SET status='cancel' WHERE custno=1 AND tran_no=100;

The above query updates the *'status'* column in the base table *transaction* and doesn't generate any tombstone in this table. However, in the view table *tran_by_status*, the *'status'* column is part of the primary key and when the status changes, the partition key changes as well. To maintain the consistency of the data in view table with the base table *transaction*, Cassandra needs to delete the row from the existing partition and insert a new one into the new partition. Let's view the *sstabledump* after this UPDATE in the base table *transaction*.

sstabledump of *transaction*

[1]@0 Row[info=[ts=1547360432559337]]: **100** | [qty=100 ts=1547360432559337],
[**status=cancel** ts=1547361089696931], [ticker=AMZN ts=1547360432559337]
[1]@51 Row[info=[ts=1547360434041691]]: 103 | [qty=500 ts=1547360434041691], [status=fill
ts=1547360434041691], [ticker=BAC ts=1547360434041691]

[2]@79 Row[info=[ts=1547360432604505]]: 101 | [qty=200 ts=1547360432604505],
[status=open ts=1547360432604505], [ticker=FB ts=1547360432604505]

sstabledump *of tran_by_status* (MATERIALIZED VIEW)

[open]@0 Row[info=[ts=-9223372036854775808] **del=deletedAt**=1547360432559337, **localDeleti
on**=1547361089(shadowable)]: 1, **100** |
[open]@34 Row[info=[ts=1547360432604505]]: 2, 101 | [qty=200 ts=1547360432604505],
[ticker=FB ts=1547360432604505]

[cancel]@59 Row[info=[ts=1547361089696931]]: 1, **100** | [qty=100 ts=1547360432559337],
[ticker=AMZN ts=1547360432559337]

[fill]@110 Row[info=[ts=1547360434041691]]: 1, 103 | [qty=500 ts=1547360434041691],
[ticker=BAC ts=1547360434041691]

As you can see, *tran_by_status* has a tombstone marked as deleted. The reason why data modeler needs to pay attention is, if tables/views designed without giving a thought, there could be significant performance issues.

```
UPDATE transaction SET status='reopen'      WHERE custno=1 AND tran_no=100;
UPDATE transaction SET status='processing'  WHERE custno=1 AND tran_no=100;
UPDATE transaction SET status='partial'     WHERE custno=1 AND tran_no=100;
UPDATE transaction SET status='fill'        WHERE custno=1 AND tran_no=100;
```

To review further, say this one particular row goes thru multiple updates with the 'status' column as listed in the above output. For each UPDATE on the transaction table, there is one tombstone generated in the tran_by_status table, as listed in the sstabledump output below. The row with del=deletedAt=<timestamp> is a tombstone.

```
sstabledump of tran_by_status (MATERIALIZED VIEW)

[open]@0 Row[info=[ts=-9223372036854775808] del=deletedAt=1547360432559337, localDeleti
on=1547361089(shadowable) ]: 1, 100 |
[open]@34 Row[info=[ts=1547360432604505] ]: 2, 101 | [qty=200 ts=1547360432604505],
[ticker=FB ts=1547360432604505]

[cancel]@59 Row[info=[ts=-9223372036854775808] del=deletedAt=1547361089696931, localDel
etion=1547361641(shadowable) ]: 1, 100 |

[partial]@101 Row[info=[ts=-9223372036854775808] del=deletedAt=1547361674557859, localD
eletion=1547361684(shadowable) ]: 1, 100 |

[reopen]@144 Row[info=[ts=-9223372036854775808] del=deletedAt=1547361641562293, localD
eletion=1547361663(shadowable) ]: 1, 100 |

[fill]@186 Row[info=[ts=1547361684874469] ]: 1, 100 | [qty=100 ts=1547360432559337],
[ticker=AMZN ts=1547360432559337]
[fill]@234 Row[info=[ts=1547360434041691] ]: 1, 103 | [qty=500 ts=1547360434041691],
[ticker=BAC ts=1547360434041691]

[processing]@260 Row[info=[ts=-9223372036854775808] del=deletedAt=1547361663531489, lo
calDeletion=1547361674(shadowable) ]: 1, 100 |
```

In conclusion, tombstone generation is normal. But you have to pay attention to your data modeling and materialized view creation. You need to be thoughtful when designing primary key for index table and views. Note that, tombstones are not generated only by DELETEs; they could be coming from UPDATE or even INSERT. Cassandra does not store null values, and updating or inserting 'null' values will also create tombstones.

Time-to-Live (TTL)

Traditional RDBMS always has a problem of purging the old data. As the data increase in the table, the queries start running slow, especially if the queries doing a table scan without a proper index. Cassandra has an optional Time-to-Live feature, which can expire and delete data after a certain period.

When designing your tables, consider using TTL for certain tables based on the purge requirement. You always set TTL in seconds. Data expires and marked as tombstone once it exceeds the TTL period. TTL can be set while creating the table or by altering the table using 'default_time_to_live' property.

Note that when you alter the table to change this property, existing data will not be affected by the new value. For example, if you set TTL to 3 months and inserted a lot of data and later if you decide to increase this to 6 months, the old data will be still deleted after 3 months. Only new data inserted after ALTER TABLE will be marked for deletion after 6 months.

Example

```
CREATE TABLE data_modeling.TTLexample ( id int, name text, PRIMARY KEY (id) )
WITH default_time_to_live=300;
```

The table TTLexample is created with a TTL of 5 minutes, which is 300 seconds. Any row inserted in this table will be automatically deleted after 300 seconds and will become a tombstone.

You can also override the TTL for each INSERT or UPDATE using the TTL command shown below.

127

```
INSERT INTO TTLexample (id,name) VALUES (2,'test') USING TTL 600;
```

As a data modeler decide on the proper TTL upfront and Know how much data will be purged from the tables and be aware of the tombstones.

Secondary Index / ALLOW FILTERING

In traditional RDBMS, creating an index is a common practice. If there is any query performance issue, instead of looking at the application code, purging unwanted data, both developer and DBA tend to create an index, which solves the immediate performance issue. Creating an index is required in some cases, but it's not always recommended. I have seen tables with more number of indexes than actual columns in it.

Cassandra also allows you to create secondary indexes on the table. In Cassandra, you can retrieve data using partition key, secondary index or by ALLOW FILTERING.

```
cqlsh:data_modeling> SELECT * FROM customer;

 custno | loginname | name    | phone     | state
--------+-----------+---------+-----------+-------
    500 |     mike1 | Michael | 123-4567 |    DE
    200 |  warren_2 |  Warren | 321-6789 |    NY
    100 |  bill_001 |    Bill | 123-4567 |    NJ
    400 |     mark9 |    Mark | 876-9876 |    PA
    300 |    jeff00 |    Jeff | 123-9876 |    NJ

(5 rows)
cqlsh:data_modeling> SELECT * FROM customer WHERE state='NJ';
InvalidRequest: Error from server: code=2200 [Invalid query]
message="Cannot execute this query as it might involve data filtering and
thus may have unpredictable performance. If you want to execute this query
despite the performance unpredictability, use ALLOW FILTERING"
```

As you see *'state'* is not a partition key and Cassandra throws an error when you use that in a WHERE clause. The reason behind the error is, in Cassandra, you cannot query on a column without including partition keys in WHERE clause. If you do not include partition key in the WHERE clause, there is no way for Cassandra to know which node to go for retrieving the data. To retrieve the data, you need to use ALOW FILTERING clause or create an index on *'state'* column.

```
cqlsh:data_modeling> SELECT * FROM customer
                 WHERE state='NJ' ALLOW FILTERING;

 custno | loginname | name | phone     | state
--------+-----------+------+-----------+-------
    100 |  bill_001 | Bill | 123-4567  |    NJ
    300 |    jeff00 | Jeff | 123-9876  |    NJ

(2 rows)
```

When you use ALLOW FILTERING, Cassandra retrieves all the rows and apply the filters and returns the matching row.

When you use ALLOW FILTERING, Cassandra returns the matching rows by retrieving all the rows and applying the filters on it. In this case, it retrieves 5 rows and after filtering returns 2 rows. ALLOW FILTERING can be used on small tables without a performance issue. For example, if your table has 2 million rows and over 90-95% data returns with ALLOW FILTERING, we can still consider it as an efficient query. On the other hand, if the query returns a few hundred rows, it is inefficient. In this case, it is better to create a secondary index on that column.

```
cqlsh:data_modeling> SELECT * FROM customer WHERE state='NJ';
InvalidRequest: Error from server: code=2200 [Invalid query] message="Cannot execute this query
as it might involve data filtering and thus may have unpredictable performance. If you want to
execute this query despite the performance unpredictability, use ALLOW FILTERING"
cqlsh:data_modeling>
cqlsh:data_modeling> CREATE INDEX cutomer_state_idx ON customer(state);
cqlsh:data_modeling> SELECT * FROM customer WHERE state='NJ';
```

```
custno | loginname | name | phone     | state
--------+-----------+------+-----------+-------
   100 |   bill_001 | Bill | 123-4567 |    NJ
   300 |     jeff00 | Jeff | 123-9876 |    NJ
```

(2 rows)

Once you create index, you can retrieve the data without the ALLOW FILTERING clause.

If the index works this well, why not go ahead and create indexes on the columns where it is required? Why do we need to duplicate data or create custom secondary index tables? Creating an index comes with a cost. Internally Cassandra stores Indexes as hidden tables, with the indexed column as the partition key. If you consider the above customer table, both the base table and index will look like in the below output.

```
CREATE TABLE customer (
    custno      bigint,
    loginname text,
    name        text,
    phone       text,
    state       text,
    PRIMARY KEY(custno)
);


CREATE TABLE customer_state (
    state   text,
    custno  bigint,
    PRIMARY KEY( (state), custno)
);
```

The difference between the secondary index, *customer_state*, and regular Cassandra table is how the data distributed in the cluster. Index data will not be distributed using the cluster-wide partitioner. The index data is co-located with the source data on the same node. Confused? Let's look at an example of the *customer* table and its data. Say we have a 4 node cluster and *customer* table has 5 rows, as listed above. Let's see how the data stored on the cluster for the base table customer and its secondary index *customer_state*.

Node	customer (not all columns are included)	customer_state
node1	{100, "bill_001", "NJ" } {500, "mike1", "DE" }	{ "NJ", 100 } { "DE",500 }
node2	{200, "warren_2", "NY" }	{ "NY", 200}
node3	{300, "jeff00", "NJ" }	{ "NJ", 300}
node4	{400, "mark9", "PA" }	{ "PA", 400}

Figure 5.7: Table and Secondary index data distribution

Figure 5.7 shows the distribution of the data for the table and the secondary index. For the customer table, the partitions are distributed by hashing the custno. In our example, based on the hashed token, data is distributed and stored on the 4 nodes as shown above.

Secondary index data is not distributed by hashing the partition key. If the index data stored like a regular table, it will create wide partition and hotspots. If that was the case, assume that there are 1 million rows in *customer* table out of which 90% are from NJ (*state*='NJ'). In that case, 900,000 *customer_state* data will reside on a single node. For this reason, secondary indexes are not distributed like a regular table.

Secondary indexes index the data held by that node. The downside to such a design is that when we search for a column with a particular value, the coordinator node needs to forward the query to all nodes because coordinator node does not know in which node to look for the data. This makes the search with this method unscalable. If you add a partition key in the where clause along with the indexed column, then secondary index search will be efficient. Any query that does not specify a partition key with secondary index lookup can be avoided to enable your cluster scalable.

When you run index lookup query, every node is queried, and each node does one index lookup plus one lookup for the data. If you run a query with state='NJ', it does one index lookup on each node, and it does a lookup of customer table using partition key 'custno' (in our example, it's on node1 & node3). Cardinality is very important for secondary index. A general rule of thumb is to use a secondary index with low cardinality. Low-cardinality refers to a column with few unique values. A low-cardinality example is the value of column 'state'. If we have 100 million customer rows, there will be a maximum of 50 unique values of the state. Now take an example of high-cardinality. If you have to create an index on customer email address, the chances are that you will have 100 million unique email address. So in this case, it's high-cardinality, and it is not recommended. So how do you solve looking up a customer with email? In this case, it would be ideal to create another index table customer_email with partition key as ((email), custno). You can look up 'custno' using email, which will be a quick single partition scan and another quick single partition scan using 'custno'.

SASI Index

SASI (acronym of SSTable-Attached Secondary Indexing) is an alternate to Cassandras secondary index which supports more sophisticated search queries such as Wildcard (LIKE operator using PREFIX, CONTAINS, and SPARSE) search in text values, range query and AND or OR combinations. SASI uses significantly less resource like memory, disk, and CPU.

SASI attaches to each SSTable its immutable index file and also attaches an index to each memtable. During compaction, the SASI index files also compacted together to create new index files. If you decide to use SASI in production, keep in mind that SASI does impact your compaction, repair and write throughput. It is expected because SASI index files follow SSTable life-cycle.

Example:

```
cassandra@cqlsh:data_modeling> SELECT * FROM customer;

 custno | loginname |  name   |  phone   | state
--------+-----------+---------+----------+-------
    400 |     mark9 |    Mark | 876-9876 |    PA
    500 |     mike1 | Michael | 123-4567 |    DE
    300 |    jeff00 |    Jeff | 123-9876 |    NJ
    100 |  bill_001 |    Bill | 123-4567 |    NJ
    200 |  warren_2 |  Warren | 321-6789 |    NY

(5 rows)
```

```
cassandra@cqlsh:data_modeling> select * from customer1 WHERE name like '%M%';
InvalidRequest: Error from server: code=2200 [Invalid query] message="LIKE restriction is only
supported on properly indexed columns. name LIKE '%M%' is not valid."
SyntaxException: line 1:0 no viable alternative at input ';' ([;])
cassandra@cqlsh:data_modeling> CREATE CUSTOM INDEX idx1 ON
                              data_modeling.customer(name) USING 'org.apache.cassandra.
index.sasi.SASIIndex' WITH OPTIONS = {'mode': 'CONTAINS'};
cassandra@cqlsh:data_modeling>
cassandra@cqlsh:data_modeling> SELECT * FROM customer WHERE name LIKE '%M%';
```

custno	loginname	name	phone	state
400	mark9	**Mark**	876-9876	PA
500	mike1	**Michael**	123-4567	DE

(2 rows)

SASI Index SSTable files listed below

```
$ cd $CASSANDRA_HOME/data/data/data_modeling
$ ls -l customer-ded102705dee11e9bd2753cd4263aa3f
total 72
drwxrwxr-x 3 cassandra cassandra   4096 Apr 13 09:23 backups
-rw-rw-r-- 1 cassandra cassandra     43 Apr 13 09:23 mc-1-big-CompressionInfo.db
-rw-rw-r-- 1 cassandra cassandra    203 Apr 13 09:23 mc-1-big-Data.db
-rw-rw-r-- 1 cassandra cassandra     10 Apr 13 09:23 mc-1-big-Digest.crc32
-rw-rw-r-- 1 cassandra cassandra     24 Apr 13 09:23 mc-1-big-Filter.db
-rw-rw-r-- 1 cassandra cassandra     62 Apr 13 09:23 mc-1-big-Index.db
-rw-rw-r-- 1 cassandra cassandra  12312 Apr 13 11:11 mc-1-big-SI_idx1.db
-rw-rw-r-- 1 cassandra cassandra   4764 Apr 13 09:23 mc-1-big-Statistics.db
-rw-rw-r-- 1 cassandra cassandra     68 Apr 13 09:23 mc-1-big-Summary.db
-rw-rw-r-- 1 cassandra cassandra     92 Apr 13 09:23 mc-1-big-TOC.txt
$
```

Keyspace separation

Many application needs to ingest a lot of temporary data for intermediate processing. In this use case, data is inserted and truncated very frequently in the staging tables. I think for almost all use cases, truncate is safer than dropping and recreating the staging table each time. As Cassandra is a distributed database, drop and recreate table needs to reach all nodes to avoid any schema disagreements. In the earlier version of Cassandra, there have been issues with dropping and recreating tables which used to bring the ghost data back. Also, keep in mind that undelaying directories are not removed when you drop the table. It is best practice to set *auto_snapshot* = true for production clusters. When *auto_snapshot* is set to true, truncate table will take a snapshot of the table, which is going to occupy the disk space. You need to make sure to clean up these snapshots periodically. Currently, *auto_snapshot* is configurable at the cluster level, and maybe in the future, it will be changed to keyspace level.

Cassandra data model consists of keyspaces at the highest level, and within keyspaces, the tables are defined. Replication factor is set at the keyspace level, which you can configure to span across data centers. When designing keyspaces and tables, it is a good idea to create individual keyspaces per application. It is also essential to create the staging tables in a separate keyspace if your use case permits.

Data modeling does not stop at the table and index creation. You need separate keyspaces for your use cases. Let's review a simple hypothetical example.

Consider following example. We have created a ***ClientInfo*** keyspace, which is replicated to several datacenters as listed below.

```
CREATE KEYSPACE ClientInfo WITH REPLICATION = {
  'class' : 'NetworkTopologyStrategy',
  'NewYork_DC' : '3' ,
  'PA_DC': '3',
  'London_DC': '3',
   'NJ_DC': '2'
};
```

```
CREATE TABLE ClientInfo.client_transactions_staging (...);
CREATE TABLE ClientInfo.client_transactions (...);
CREATE TABLE ClientInfo.europe_clients(...);
```

We have created a table *client_transactions_staging*, in which a large amount of data is ingested from NJ_DC several times a day. Once the data is processed, it is inserted into the *client_transactions* table, and *client_transactions_staging* table is truncated.

The issue with keeping the *client_transactions_staging* table in *ClientInfo* keyspace is,

1. Temporary ingested data is replicated to all datacenters, which is not required.
2. It's additional network traffic consuming the network bandwidth.
3. It occupies extra disk space on the other datacenter, and also we need to clean up the frequently truncated snapshots on all the datacenters.
4. It generates additional writes on all the datacenters due to replication & repairs.

To fix this design issue, we need to move this table to a separate keyspace with a replication factor set to only NJ_DC. So if NJ_DC is down, your ingestion of data will fail? Yes, correct. In this case, you can add another additional datacenter NewYork_DC to it. But it will be much better than replicating to all datacenters.

```
CREATE KEYSPACE ks_staging WITH REPLICATION = {
 'class' : 'NetworkTopologyStrategy',
  'NJ_DC': '3'
 };

CREATE TABLE ks_staging.client_transactions_staging (...);
```

Now we will take a look at the table europe_clients. This table is replicated to all the datacenters, and it's a non-issue. Say due to some European policy changes; now you need to restrict the data in this table to only London_DC. In this case, we can separate such tables/ data beforehand by creating a separate keyspace and table as below.

```
CREATE KEYSPACE UKClientInfo WITH REPLICATION = {
 'class' : 'NetworkTopologyStrategy',
```

```
'London_DC': '3'
};

CREATE TABLE UKClientInfo.europe_clients(...);
```

If we separated this table into *UKClientInfo* keyspace at the design time, the keyspace replication can be altered to implement this mandatory policy changes without major code changes.

Before Policy change:

```
CREATE KEYSPACE UKClientInfo WITH REPLICATION = {
  'class' : 'NetworkTopologyStrategy',
  'NewYork_DC' : '3' ,
  'PA_DC': '3',
  'London_DC': '3',
   'NJ_DC': '2'
};

CREATE TABLE UKClientInfo.europe_clients(...);

Policy Change:

ALTER KEYSPACE UKClientInfo WITH REPLICATION = {
  'class' : 'NetworkTopologyStrategy',
  'London_DC': '3'
};
```

Keyspace separation is purely a use case related configurations which everyone can give a thought before designing, which could save some development cycles later on.

∗　∗　∗

CHAPTER 6

Security

I n recent years a growing number of companies have adopted Cassandra. These organizations need scalable, highly available and secure databases such as Cassandra. When it comes to securing Cassandra, we will go through detailed information and actual setup on below topics.

- Database authentication and authorization
- JMX access
- Encryption
- Auditing

Database Authentication and Authorization

Cassandra out-of-the-box installation comes with *AllowAllAuthenticator*, which perform no checks on who connects to the database. This allows any client on your network to connect to the database.

Authentication is validating user connection to the database. Authorization is keyspace and table level permission granted for the roles (users).

In below output, we will see that out-of-the-box Cassandra does not need a user id to login to the database. This is due to *authenticator* is set to *AllowAllAuthenticator* in *cassandra.yaml* file.

```
$ $CASSANDRA_HOME/bin/cqlsh  192.168.1.87
Connected to testclust at 192.168.1.87:9042.
```

```
[cqlsh 5.0.1 | Cassandra 3.10 | CQL spec 3.4.4 | Native protocol v4]
Use HELP for help.
cqlsh> desc keyspaces;

system_traces  system_schema  system_auth  system  system_distributed

cqlsh> exit

$ egrep "authenticator:|authorizer:|role_manager:" cassandra.yaml
authenticator: AllowAllAuthenticator
authorizer: AllowAllAuthorizer
role_manager: CassandraRoleManager
# internode_authenticator: org.apache.cassandra.auth.AllowAllInternodeAuthenticator
$
```

Enable Authentication

Authentication is pluggable in Cassandra, and this is configurable in *cassandra.yaml*. By default, the configuration is set to "authenticator: AllowAllAuthenticator". The '*AllowAllAuthenticator*', performs no checks. To enable authentication, modify *cassandra.yaml* file and update "Authenticator: PasswordAuthenticator" and restart the Cassandra.

Once Authentication is enabled, Cassandra expects user id and password for connecting to the database. As we can see in the below output, without supplying user and password, it does not connect.

```
$ $CASSANDRA_HOME/bin/cqlsh 192.168.1.87
Connection error: ('Unable to connect to any servers', {'192.168.1.87':
AuthenticationFailed('Remote end requires authentication.',)})
$
```

When we enable authentication, by default, Cassandra will create a role 'cassandra' with the same password. We can view all the roles (users) from the *system_auth.roles* table as listed in the below output.

```
$ $CASSANDRA_HOME/bin/cqlsh -u cassandra -p cassandra 192.168.1.87
Connected to testclust at 192.168.1.87:9042.
[cqlsh 5.0.1 | Cassandra 3.10 | CQL spec 3.4.4 | Native protocol v4]
Use HELP for help.
cassandra@cqlsh> use system_auth;
cassandra@cqlsh:system_auth> SELECT * FROM roles;
role | can_login | is_superuser | member_of | salted_hash
---------------+-------------+------------------+-----------------+------------------------------
cassandra | True | True | null | $2a$10$rAsOIGrritWN[..]
(1 rows)
cassandra@cqlsh:system_auth>
```

Default role 'cassandra'

When we enable authentication, Cassandra creates a default role 'cassandra' with password 'cassandra' as a super user. Since everyone knows the default role and password, it is highly recommended to create a new role with superuser and disable 'cassandra' role or change the password for 'cassandra' right away.

We will change the 'cassandra' password to 'cassandra1' and we will create a new role 'dba' with superuser role as listed in below output.

```
cassandra@cqlsh:system_auth> SELECT * FROM roles;


 role       | can_login | is_superuser | member_of | salted_hash
-----------+-----------+--------------+-----------+--------------------
 cassandra |      True |         True |      null | $2a$10$rAsOIGrritWN..

(1 rows)
cassandra@cqlsh:system_auth> CREATE ROLE dba
                             WITH SUPERUSER = true
                             AND LOGIN = true AND PASSWORD = 'dba1';
cassandra@cqlsh:system_auth> ALTER ROLE cassandra
                             WITH PASSWORD = 'cassandra1';
```

```
cassandra@cqlsh:system_auth> SELECT * FROM roles;

 role      | can_login | is_superuser | member_of | salted_hash
-----------+-----------+--------------+-----------+--------------------
--
       dba |      True |         True |      null | $2a$10$BsQZOgkkUz..
 cassandra |      True |         True |      null | $2a$10$SWls8sjD...
(2 rows)
cassandra@cqlsh:system_auth> list roles;

 role      | super | login | options
-----------+-------+-------+---------
 cassandra |  True |  True |        {}
       dba |  True |  True |        {}

(2 rows)
cassandra@cqlsh:system_auth>
```

Enable Authorization

Authorization is pluggable in Cassandra and this configurable in *cassandra.yaml*. By default, the configuration is set to "authorizer: AllowAllAuthorizer", which by default grants all permissions to all roles. No production or pre-production cluster should be running without authentication and authorization. Cassandra has role based access control (RBAC) and using this we can configure proper access profile and schema access limitations.

To enable authorization, modify *cassandra.yaml* file and update "**authorizer: Cassandra Authorizer**" and restart Cassandra on the node.

Once authorization is enabled, create proper access profile for your cluster. Few recommendations are

1. Create an alternate superuser role and make sure it is working.

2. Change password for default 'cassandra' role or disable this role.
3. Do not give direct object access to any individual roles.

Cassandra has a powerful and flexible role-based access control (RBAC). You can have a simple approach to managing permissions by creating high-level roles which we can think as of group and grant permissions to these roles. Once we have bundled together with the required permissions on these roles, they can be granted to the individual user/roles. This approach greatly simplifies permission management and helps DBA's/administrators.

For example, say you have two keyspaces, *customer* and *transactions*. We may create the roles as below.

Create high-level roles, which we can think as groups. Note that these are created with LOGIN = false. We are creating these high-level roles as a place holder for all the permissions. These are not created for logging in to the database. Role names are self-explanatory. Note that, only 'operation_dba' is created with SUPERUSER = true.

```
CREATE ROLE 'operation_dba' WITH SUPERUSER = true AND LOGIN = false;
CREATE ROLE 'customer_admin' WITH PASSWORD = 'xyz' AND LOGIN = false;
CREATE ROLE 'transaction_admin' WITH PASSWORD = 'xyz' AND LOGIN = false;
CREATE ROLE 'read_only' WITH LOGIN = false;
```

GRANT ALL Permissions to operation_dba role.

```
GRANT ALL PERMISSIONS on ALL KEYSPACES to 'operation_dba';
GRANT ALL PERMISSIONS on ALL FUNCTIONS to 'operation_dba';
GRANT ALL PERMISSIONS on ALL ROLES to 'operation_dba';
```

Grant SELECT, CREATE & MODIFY to customer_admin on *customer* keyspace.

```
GRANT SELECT ON KEYSPACE customer TO 'customer_admin';
GRANT CREATE ON KEYSPACE customer TO 'customer_admin';
GRANT MODIFY ON KEYSPACE customer TO 'customer_admin';
```

Grant SELECT, CREATE & MODIFY to transaction_admin on transactions keyspace.

```
GRANT SELECT ON KEYSPACE transactions TO 'transaction_admin';
GRANT CREATE ON KEYSPACE transactions TO 'transaction_admin';
GRANT MODIFY ON KEYSPACE transactions TO 'transaction_admin';
```

We are creating *read_only* role across all the keyspaces. So grant SELECT on all keyspaces to *read_only* role.

```
GRANT SELECT ON ALL KEYSPACES TO 'read_only';
```

Create below individual roles for Cassandra DBA's. Note that these roles are created with LOGIN=true.

```
CREATE ROLE prasad WITH PASSWORD = 'abc' AND LOGIN = true;
CREATE ROLE victor WITH PASSWORD = 'xyz' AND LOGIN = true;
```

Since 'prasad' & 'victor' are DBA's, all we need to do is grant 'operation_dba' role to these individual roles created above. This simplifies role and permission management for DBA's.

```
GRANT 'operation_dba' TO prasad;
GRANT 'operation_dba' TO victor;
```

Now both prasad & victor get all the permissions of 'operation_dba', as listed below.

```
cassandra@cqlsh> list all permissions of victor;

 role           | username       | resource         | permission
----------------+----------------+------------------+------------
 operation_dba  | operation_dba  | <all keyspaces>  |    CREATE
 operation_dba  | operation_dba  | <all keyspaces>  |     ALTER
 operation_dba  | operation_dba  | <all keyspaces>  |      DROP
 operation_dba  | operation_dba  | <all keyspaces>  |    SELECT
 operation_dba  | operation_dba  | <all keyspaces>  |    MODIFY
 operation_dba  | operation_dba  | <all keyspaces>  | AUTHORIZE
 operation_dba  | operation_dba  | <all functions>  |    CREATE
 operation_dba  | operation_dba  | <all functions>  |     ALTER
```

```
operation_dba | operation_dba | <all functions> |    DROP
operation_dba | operation_dba | <all functions> | AUTHORIZE
operation_dba | operation_dba | <all functions> |  EXECUTE
operation_dba | operation_dba |    <all roles>  |   CREATE
operation_dba | operation_dba |    <all roles>  |    ALTER
operation_dba | operation_dba |    <all roles>  |    DROP
operation_dba | operation_dba |    <all roles>  | AUTHORIZE
operation_dba | operation_dba |    <all roles>  | DESCRIBE

(16 rows)
cassandra@cqlsh>
```

Create below individual roles for *customer* keyspace admin and grant the customer_admin role.

```
CREATE ROLE vahe WITH PASSWORD = 'xyz' AND LOGIN = true;
CREATE ROLE imran WITH PASSWORD = 'xyz' AND LOGIN = true;
GRANT 'customer_admin' TO vahe;
GRANT 'customer_admin' TO imran;
```

Similarly create below individual roles for *transactions* keyspace admin and grant them transaction_admin role.

```
CREATE ROLE rick WITH PASSWORD = 'xyz' AND LOGIN = true;
CREATE ROLE paul WITH PASSWORD = 'xyz' AND LOGIN = true;
GRANT 'transaction_admin' TO rick;
GRANT 'transaction_admin' TO paul;
```

Create below individual roles who can be admin for both customer and transactions keyspace.

```
CREATE ROLE kate WITH PASSWORD = 'xyz' AND LOGIN = true;
CREATE ROLE peter WITH PASSWORD = 'xyz' AND LOGIN = true;
```

Grant both admin roles to the individual roles created above

```
GRANT 'transaction_admin' TO kate;
GRANT 'customer_admin' TO kate;
GRANT 'transaction_admin' TO peter;
GRANT 'customer_admin' TO peter;
```

When you give both 'transaction_admin' & 'customer_admin' roles, peter & kate, both will inherit all the permissions as listed below.

```
cassandra@cqlsh> list all permissions of kate;

role              | username          | resource                  | permission
------------------+-------------------+---------------------------+-----------
   customer_admin |    customer_admin |     <keyspace customer>   |     CREATE
   customer_admin |    customer_admin |     <keyspace customer>   |     SELECT
   customer_admin |    customer_admin |     <keyspace customer>   |     MODIFY
transaction_admin | transaction_admin | <keyspace transactions>   |     CREATE
transaction_admin | transaction_admin | <keyspace transactions>   |     SELECT
transaction_admin | transaction_admin | <keyspace transactions>   |     MODIFY

(6 rows)
cassandra@cqlsh>
```

Create below individual roles or reporting id roles, which allows the read only permission across all the keyspaces. Grant them 'read_only' role.

```
CREATE ROLE mike WITH PASSWORD = 'xyz' AND LOGIN = true;
CREATE ROLE joe WITH PASSWORD = 'xyz' AND LOGIN = true;
CREATE ROLE reporting WITH PASSWORD = 'xyz' AND LOGIN = true;
```

```
GRANT 'read_only' TO mike;
GRANT 'read_only' TO joe;
GRANT 'read_only' TO reporting;
```

You can view all roles by command "list roles" or by below select statement. The column 'member_of' in the *system_auth.roles* table records the what other roles it is member of.

```
cassandra@cqlsh> list roles;

 role               | super | login | options
--------------------+-------+-------+---------
          cassandra |  True |  True |       {}
     customer_admin | False | False |       {}
                dba |  True |  True |       {}
              imran | False |  True |       {}
                joe | False |  True |       {}
               kate | False |  True |       {}
               mike | False |  True |       {}
      operation_dba |  True | False |       {}
               paul | False |  True |       {}
              peter | False |  True |       {}
             prasad | False |  True |       {}
          read_only | False | False |       {}
          reporting | False |  True |       {}
               rick | False |  True |       {}
  transaction_admin | False | False |       {}
               vahe | False |  True |       {}
             victor | False |  True |       {}

(17 rows)
cassandra@cqlsh> SELECT role,member_of FROM system_auth.roles;

 role               | member_of
--------------------+------------------------------------------
             victor |                        {'operation_dba'}
  transaction_admin |                                     null
     customer_admin |                                     null
      operation_dba |                                     null
               kate | {'customer_admin', 'transaction_admin'}
```

```
           dba |                                            null
           joe |                                   {'read_only'}
        prasad |                               {'operation_dba'}
         peter | {'customer_admin', 'transaction_admin'}
     reporting |                                   {'read_only'}
     cassandra |                                            null
          mike |                                   {'read_only'}
          vahe |                               {'customer_admin'}
          paul |                            {'transaction_admin'}
     read_only |                                            null
         imran |                               {'customer_admin'}
          rick |                            {'transaction_admin'}


(17 rows)
```

JMX Access

Apache Cassandra exposes many metrics and commands over JMX. Cassandra nodes in the cluster exposes a JMX interface on default port 7199 to which a client can connect and query for objects called MBeans. The "*nodetool*" command-line utility communicates with JMX to perform its tasks. By default, JMX security is disabled and accessible only from *localhost* without authentication. This means anyone with the Cassandra id access to the host can run any *nodetool* commands. Commands such as

nodetool removenode
nodetool decommission
nodetool clearsnapshots

These above commands can harm if it is run by someone who is not Cassandra admin. Configuring JMX authentication can be done using local password by access file settings in *cassandra-env.sh*.

Follow these steps to enable authentication for *nodetool* and JMX.

Step 1: Modify $CASSANDRA_HOME/conf/*cassandra-env.sh* file update below lines. You are enabling JMX by setting authenticate=true and creating a password file in /etc/cassandra.

JVM_OPTS="$JVM_OPTS -Dcom.sun.management.jmxremote.authenticate=true"
JVM_OPTS="$JVM_OPTS -Dcom.sun.management.jmxremote.password.file=
/etc/cassandra/jmxremote.password"

Step 2: Update */etc/cassandra/jmxremote.password* file and add user id and password. Change the ownership of the file and make it read only

```
$ sudo vi /etc/cassandra/jmxremote.password
$ ls -l /etc/cassandra/
total 4
-rw-r-—r-- 1 root root 30 Dec 29 2018 jmxremote.password
$ cat /etc/cassandra/jmxremote.password
dba dba1
cassandra cassandra
$ sudo chown cassandra:cassandra /etc/cassandra/jmxremote.password
$ sudo chmod 400 /etc/cassandra/jmxremote.password
$ ls -l /etc/cassandra/
total 4
-r-------- 1 cassandra cassandra 44 Dec 29 2018 jmxremote.password
```

Step 3: Add cassandra with readwrite permission to jmxremote.access file. This file is under $JAVA_HOME/jre/lib/management/. if you are using JDK, its under $JAVA_HOME/lib/management/

```
$ cat $JAVA_HOME/jre/lib/management/jmxremote.access | tail -6

monitorRole readonly
cassandra readwrite
controlRole readwrite \
create javax.management.monitor.*,javax.management.timer.* \
unregister
```

Step 4: Restart Cassandra on the node.

Once we setup JMX authentication, we need to provide the user id and password configured under /etc/cassandra/jmxremote.password. If we do not provide the password, *nodetool* will fail with the error messages as listed in the below output

```
$ $CASSANDRA_HOME/bin/nodetool status
nodetool: Failed to connect to '127.0.0.1:7199' - SecurityException: 'Authentication failed! Credentials required'.

$ $CASSANDRA_HOME/bin/nodetool -u dba status
Password:
Datacenter: dc
==============
Status=Up/Down
|/ State=Normal/Leaving/Joining/Moving
--   Address      Load      Tokens  Owns (effective)  Host ID                               Rack
UN  192.168.1.87 216.76 KiB   3        100.0%          f5b07323-214f-4a78-8640-c3ed1b61c15d  rack1
$
```

Encryption using SSL

Apache Cassandra provides following SSL encryption.

Node-to-node encryption	Internode or node-to-node encryption is used to secure data between the nodes in the cluster.
Client-to-node encryption	Client-to-node encryption is used to secure data between client to server.

When we talk about security in Cassandra, we enabled authentication and authorization so that data access can be secured. Also, we enabled JMX authentication, which restricts *nodetool* access to only certain users. To secure the data completely, we need to encrypt the data at the storage level, secure it when client accesses it and when data transferred from node to node. When data travel across the network, it could be accessed by someone who is not authorized to see the data. If data includes personal information such as SSN, date of birth, etc. you want to make sure that the data encrypted.

To configure node-to-node and client-to-node encryption, SSL certificates must be generated first. To generate the certificate, we will use **openssl** and **keytool** commands. To validate the certificates, we need to generate a self-signed Certificate Authority (CA).

Let's setup node-to-node and client-to-node on a two node cluster. We have a two node cluster 'sslCluster' on hosts ssl1 & ssl2.

```
ssl$ $CASSANDRA_HOME/bin/nodetool status
Datacenter: datcenter1
======================
Status=Up/Down
|/ State=Normal/Leaving/Joining/Moving
--   Address        Load         Tokens  Owns (effective)  Host ID                                Rack
UN  192.168.1.27  151.74 KiB  2       29.9%             cee0734f-fbf1-4fd2-94b4-a3df3994e48c   rack1
UN  192.168.1.28  185.19 KiB  2       70.1%             c9cc9b8e-1329-423d-a32b-94cda6a0142d  rack1

ssl$
ssl$ $CASSANDRA_HOME/bin/nodetool describecluster
Cluster Information:
    Name: sslCluster
    Snitch: org.apache.cassandra.locator.DynamicEndpointSnitch
    Partitioner: org.apache.cassandra.dht.Murmur3Partitioner
    Schema versions:
        3a7ee577-df1b-3a62-9f9d-421e78205784: [192.168.1.27, 192.168.1.28]

ssl$
```

Install JCE files

To use enterprise strength encryption, you need to install the Java Cryptography Extension (JCE). The default JCE strength policy file provided by Oracle Java implementation has an upper limit of maximum key sizes up to 128. Cassandra may complain if you try to use 256-bit encryption Without JCE.

Install JCE with below command

```
ssl1 $ sudo apt-get install oracle-java8-unlimited-jce-policy
```

Setup node-to-node encryption

First step is creating certificates. We will walk through step by step in creating certificates.

STEP 1: Create root CA and key & Verify

To create root CA use openssl command and below cluster.conf file.

Content of cluster.conf file

```
[ req ]
distinguished_name = req_distinguished_name
prompt = no
output_password = rootpass
default_bits = 2048
[ req_distinguished_name ]
C          =          US
ST         =          NJ
L          =          southbrunswick
O          =          CADG
OU         =          sslcluster
CN         =          sslclusterCA
```

We will use below passwords for entire setup.

Root key   : rootpass
Truststore : tstorepass
Keystore   : mykeypass

```
ssl$ openssl req -config cluster.conf
        -new -x509 -nodes
        -subj "/C=US/ST=NJ/L=southbrunswick/O=CADG/OU=sslcluster/CN=sslclusterCA"
        -keyout sslcluster.key
        -out sslcluster_rootCa.crt
        -days 500
Generating a 2048 bit RSA private key
................................................+++
......................+++
writing new private key to 'sslcluster.key'
-----
ssl$
```

This will create key file and root CA certificate as listed below

```
ssl$ ls -lrt
total 12
-rw-rw-r-- 1 cassandra cassandra 216 Dec 27 21:45 cluster.conf
-rw-rw-r-- 1 cassandra cassandra 1704 Dec 27 22:09 sslcluster.key
-rw-rw-r-- 1 cassandra cassandra 1220 Dec 27 22:09 sslcluster_rootCa.crt
ssl$
```

Content of the certificate file can be viewed by cat.

```
ssl$ cat sslcluster_rootCa.crt
-----BEGIN CERTIFICATE-----
MIIDWDCCAkACCQDZSVwm2WIEpTANBgkqhkiG9w0BAQUFADBuMQswCQYDVQQGEwJV
UzELMAkGA1UECBMCTkoxFzAVBgNVBAcTDnNvdXRoYnJ1bnN3aWNrMQ0wCwYDVQQK
EwRDQURHMRMwEQYDVQQLEwpzc2xjbHVzdGVyMRUwEwYDVQQDEwxzc2xjbHVzdGVy
Q0EwHhcNMTgxMjI4MDMwOTU2WhcNMjAwNTExMDMwOTU2WjBuMQswCQYDVQQGEwJV
UzELMAkGA1UECBMCTkoxFzAVBgNVBAcTDnNvdXRoYnJ1bnN3aWNrMQ0wCwYDVQQK
EwRDQURHMRMwEQYDVQQLEwpzc2xjbHVzdGVyMRUwEwYDVQQDEwxzc2xjbHVzdGVy
Q0EwggEiMA0GCSqGSIb3DQEBAQUAA4IBDwAwggEKAoIBAQDHnuDfQayYKA59Xwl1
HZtxU87KASOUpcxMod9b4+3oDnqWF7ynPqwL8GdJNQkDqg1RXQi7QbxVbG9mCYKT
ZXrwkvZlbBn3/MUDOg4RGXwuYxmakVyBcrLqbxao8q0VcdPUnY3SZRsVFX680xao
```

```
JHMzellsjofmA6ik6wxS6brYl2MeWRyEQgORGFTHmzvQG+NW6Cdk+y8KqGsEx6Kq
10vckY5+YCcTs7RL0IHlIKG+pCKgyzy8i/SiPTZuofEIfjKYQNaNwrVWWmIQwkU9
q6kyBXEv3JPcn09MgYEg8+uViwhQhBlri0KVo8kFM0pUQGf8QDp18oHdV5eY4iaX
3Xa5AgMBAAEwDQYJKoZIhvcNAQEFBQADggEBABuoh7NsmkufrY3CR+2uCHU9H8TM
VWoA3gOqIpfo/cIE+faYEpbZDWI0mtRyP9vMMBJ2RWx12vAogh15ziCY37TGf4g6
3hoFaHEOorOCeBUXlWmU5hqm+Va44DnjWKeZC9rPpV2CyhYhHpqFXrVyt10v/N/n
k8tCELrCR1PJulDlNGmlmYGcYgmIcMcfp9VpNyubLc+yBHmJif+vZtgWwDtkMYhP
llWKPXGdcf5wYnfLXYDTcXfpR40Z+CXS7zMSszm6h2ewYhBfoDqvxPfb2n3eisnQ
r2L3Q0QL170mXNBJ4c0xJexil3w8OXDqXT6evb4RiIfib+YxjGUA4uGz6Wc=
-----END CERTIFICATE-----
ssl$
```

Verify the sslcluster_rootCa.crt certificate. When creating the CA, we gave validity as 500 days. This is verified in the validity section.

```
ssl$ openssl x509
      -in sslcluster_rootCa.crt
      -text -noout
Certificate:
    Data:
        Version: 1 (0x0)
        Serial Number: 15657146901455832229 (0xd9495c26d96204a5)
    Signature Algorithm: sha1WithRSAEncryption
        Issuer: C=US, ST=NJ, L=southbrunswick, O=CADG, OU=sslcluster,
CN=sslclusterCA
        Validity
            Not Before: Dec 28 03:09:56 2018 GMT
            Not After : May 11 03:09:56 2020 GMT
        Subject: C=US, ST=NJ, L=southbrunswick, O=CADG, OU=sslcluster,
CN=sslclusterCA
        Subject Public Key Info:
            Public Key Algorithm: rsaEncryption
                Public-Key: (2048 bit)
                Modulus:
                    00:c7:9e:e0:df:41:ac:98:28:0e:7d:5f:0d:75:1d:
```

```
                    9b:71:53:ce:ca:01:23:94:a5:cc:4c:a1:df:5b:e3:
                    ed:e8:0e:7a:96:17:bc:a7:3e:ac:0b:f0:67:49:35:
                    09:03:aa:0d:51:5d:08:bb:41:bc:55:6c:6f:66:09:
                    82:93:65:7a:f0:92:f6:75:6c:19:f7:fc:c5:03:3a:
                    0e:11:19:7c:2e:63:19:9a:91:5c:81:72:b2:ea:6f:
                    16:a8:f2:ad:15:71:d3:d4:9d:8d:d2:65:1b:15:15:
                    7e:bc:d3:16:a8:24:73:33:7a:59:6c:8e:87:e6:03:
                    a8:a4:eb:0c:52:e9:ba:d8:97:63:1e:59:1c:84:42:
                    03:91:18:54:c7:9b:3b:d0:1b:e3:56:e8:27:64:fb:
                    2f:0a:a8:6b:04:c7:a2:aa:d7:4b:dc:91:8e:7e:60:
                    27:13:b3:b4:4b:d0:81:f5:20:a1:be:a4:22:a0:cb:
                    3c:bc:8b:f4:a2:3d:36:6e:a1:f1:08:7e:32:98:40:
                    d6:8d:c2:b5:56:5a:62:10:c2:45:3d:ab:a9:32:05:
                    71:2f:dc:93:dc:9f:4f:4c:81:81:20:f3:eb:95:8b:
                    08:50:84:1d:6b:8b:42:95:a3:c9:05:33:4a:54:40:
                    67:fc:40:3a:75:f2:81:dd:57:97:98:e2:26:97:dd:
                    76:b9
                Exponent: 65537 (0x10001)
        Signature Algorithm: sha1WithRSAEncryption
            1b:a8:87:b3:6c:9a:4b:9f:ad:8d:c2:47:ed:ae:08:75:3d:1f:
            c4:cc:55:6a:00:de:03:aa:22:97:e8:fd:c2:04:f9:f6:98:12:
            96:d9:0d:62:34:9a:d4:72:3f:db:cc:30:12:76:45:6c:75:da:
            f0:28:82:1d:79:ce:20:98:df:b4:c6:7f:88:3a:de:1a:05:68:
            71:0e:a2:b3:82:78:15:17:95:69:94:e6:1a:a6:f9:56:b8:e0:
            39:e3:58:a7:99:0b:da:cf:a5:5d:82:ca:16:21:1e:9a:85:5e:
            b5:72:b7:5d:2f:fc:df:e7:93:cb:42:10:ba:c2:47:53:c9:ba:
            50:e5:34:69:a5:99:81:9c:62:09:88:70:c7:1f:a7:d5:69:37:
            2b:9b:2d:cf:b2:04:79:89:89:ff:af:66:d8:16:c0:3b:64:31:
            88:4f:d6:55:8a:3d:71:9d:71:fe:70:62:77:cb:5d:80:d3:71:
            77:e9:47:8d:19:f8:25:d2:ef:33:12:b3:39:ba:87:67:b0:62:
            10:5f:a0:3a:af:c4:f7:db:da:7d:de:8a:c9:d0:af:62:f7:43:
            44:0b:d7:bd:26:5c:d0:49:e1:cd:31:25:ec:62:97:7c:3c:39:
            70:ea:5d:3e:9e:bd:be:11:88:87:e2:6f:e6:31:8c:65:00:e2:
            e1:b3:e9:67
ssl$
```

STEP 2: Create truststore & Verify

A server truststore can be used to establish trust between all the nodes of the cluster.

```
ssl$ keytool -importcert
        -keystore sslcluster_truststore.jks
        -alias rootca
        -file sslcluster_rootCa.crt
        -keypass rootpass
        -storepass tstorepass
        -noprompt
Certificate was added to keystore
```

This creates truststore file as listed below

```
ssl$ ls -lrt
total 16
-rw-rw-r-- 1 cassandra cassandra   216  Dec 27 21:45 cluster.conf
-rw-rw-r-- 1 cassandra cassandra  1704  Dec 27 22:09 sslcluster.key
-rw-rw-r-- 1 cassandra cassandra  1220  Dec 27 22:09 sslcluster_rootCa.crt
-rw-rw-r-- 1 cassandra cassandra   923  Dec 27 22:25 sslcluster_truststore.jks
ssl$
```

Verify the truststore file using keytool list command

```
ssl$ keytool -list
        -keystore sslcluster_truststore.jks
        -storepass tstorepass

Keystore type: jks
Keystore provider: SUN

Your keystore contains 1 entry
```

```
rootca, Dec 27, 2018, trustedCertEntry,
Certificate fingerprint (SHA1): 6E:82:EC:35:59:B6:EF:74:DC:47:3E:CB:5E:0A:3E:0B:24:F8:7C:80
ssl$
```

STEP 3: Create keystore and generate public/private key pair & Verify

```
ssl$ keytool -genkeypair
        -keyalg RSA
        -alias sslcluster_node
        -keystore sslcluster_keystore.jks
        -storepass mykeypass
        -keypass mykeypass
        -validity 500
        -keysize 2048
        -dname "CN=sslclusterCA, OU=sslcluster, O=CADG, C=US"
ssl$
```

This will generate the keystore file sslcluster_keystore.jks.

```
ssl$ ls -lrt
total 20
-rw-rw-r-- 1 cassandra cassandra    216  Dec 27 21:45 cluster.conf
-rw-rw-r-- 1 cassandra cassandra   1704  Dec 27 22:09 sslcluster.key
-rw-rw-r-- 1 cassandra cassandra   1220  Dec 27 22:09 sslcluster_rootCa.crt
-rw-rw-r-- 1 cassandra cassandra    923  Dec 27 22:25 sslcluster_truststore.jks
-rw-rw-r-- 1 cassandra cassandra   2181  Dec 27 22:40 sslcluster_keystore.jks
ssl$
```

Repeat this command for each node to generate a separate keystore file for each node. We can generate these keystore files on a single node and later distribute it to individual nodes. For example, we are generating the certificates for two node cluster, on host ssl1 (192.168.1.27) and ssl2 (192.168.1.28). In the above command we need to substitute **-keystore sslcluster_ssl1.jks** or **-keystore sslcluster_192.168.1.27.jks** and **-alias ssl1_192.168.1.27** to generate keystore file for ssl1 hostname and similarly for ssl2 hostname.

Generating keystore file for each individual nodes becomes a big maintenance task. If you have a 100 nodes cluster, you need to generate 100 keystore files. Instead of generating keystore for each node, we could generate one keystore for a node and distribute the same keystore on all the nodes. This is the reason we did give **-alias sslcluster_node** and **-keystore sslcluster_keystore.jks** as generic name. This makes maintenance easier. If you are adding 10 nodes to the cluster, you don't need to generate a keystore for each of them. Using one generic keystore will keep certification expiry for all the nodes same.

If your shop does not like the idea of having one generic certificate, then you can go with individual node certificates.

Verify the certificate.

```
ssl$ keytool -list
        -keystore sslcluster_keystore.jks
        -storepass mykeypass

Keystore type: jks
Keystore provider: SUN

Your keystore contains 1 entry

sslcluster_node, Dec 27, 2018, PrivateKeyEntry,
Certificate fingerprint (SHA1): C5:0F:69:32:8B:40:1D:76:BD:AD:B0:92:F7:8A:F1:CA:6B:73:DB:A5

ssl$
```

Step 4: Export certificate signing request (CSR) and Sign node certificate with sslcluster_ rootCa.crt

Once the sslcluster_keystore.jks (key and certificate) is generated, a certificate signing request (CSR) is exported. The CSR will be signed with the sslcluster_rootCa.crt certificate to verify that the node's certificate is trusted.

```
ssl$ keytool -certreq
        -keystore sslcluster_keystore.jks
        -alias sslcluster_node
        -file sslcluster_node.csr
        -keypass mykeypass
        -storepass mykeypass
        -dname "CN=sslclusterCA, OU=sslcluster, O=CADG, C=US"
ssl$
```

CSR file is generated.

```
ssl$ ls -lrt
total 24
-rw-rw-r-- 1 cassandra cassandra    216  Dec 27 21:45 cluster.conf
-rw-rw-r-- 1 cassandra cassandra   1704  Dec 27 22:09 sslcluster.key
-rw-rw-r-- 1 cassandra cassandra   1220  Dec 27 22:09 sslcluster_rootCa.crt
-rw-rw-r-- 1 cassandra cassandra    923  Dec 27 22:25 sslcluster_truststore.jks
-rw-rw-r-- 1 cassandra cassandra   2181  Dec 27 22:40 sslcluster_keystore.jks
-rw-rw-r-- 1 cassandra cassandra   1047  Dec 27 22:53 sslcluster_node.csr
ssl$
```

Now sign the node certificate with root CA. For this sslcluster_node.csr is used as input & signed with the sslcluster_rootCa.crt certificate and a signed node certificate sslcluster_node. crt_signed is created

```
ssl$ openssl x509
        -req
        -CA sslcluster_rootCa.crt
        -CAkey sslcluster.key
        -in sslcluster_node.csr
        -out sslcluster_node.crt_signed
        -days 500 -CAcreateserial
        -passin pass:rootpass
        Signature ok
        subject=/C=US/O=CADG/OU=sslcluster/CN=sslclusterCA
```

```
        Getting CA Private Key
ssl$
```

Signed certificate file is generated.

```
ssl$ ls -lrt
total 32
-rw-rw-r-- 1 cassandra cassandra    216  Dec 27 21:45 cluster.conf
-rw-rw-r-- 1 cassandra cassandra   1704  Dec 27 22:09 sslcluster.key
-rw-rw-r-- 1 cassandra cassandra   1220  Dec 27 22:09 sslcluster_rootCa.crt
-rw-rw-r-- 1 cassandra cassandra    923  Dec 27 22:25 sslcluster_truststore.jks
-rw-rw-r-- 1 cassandra cassandra   2181  Dec 27 22:40 sslcluster_keystore.jks
-rw-rw-r-- 1 cassandra cassandra   1047  Dec 27 22:53 sslcluster_node.csr
-rw-rw-r-- 1 cassandra cassandra     17  Dec 27 22:59 sslcluster_rootCa.srl
-rw-rw-r-- 1 cassandra cassandra   1168  Dec 27 22:59 sslcluster_node.crt_signed
ssl$
```

Verify the signed certificate by running openssl

```
ssl$ openssl verify -CAfile sslcluster_rootCa.crt sslcluster_node.crt_signed
sslcluster_node.crt_signed: OK
ssl$
```

Step 5: Import sslcluster_rootCa.crt certificate into node's keystore sslcluster_keystore.jks

```
ssl$ keytool -importcert
        -keystore sslcluster_keystore.jks
        -alias rootca
        -file sslcluster_rootCa.crt
        -noprompt
        -keypass mykeypass
        -storepass mykeypass
Certificate was added to keystore


ssl$
```

Step 6: Import node's signed certificate sslcluster_node.crt_signed into node keystore sslcluster_keystore.jks

```
ssl$ keytool -importcert
        -keystore sslcluster_keystore.jks
        -alias sslcluster_node
        -noprompt
        -file sslcluster_node.crt_signed
        -keypass mykeypass
        -storepass mykeypass
Certificate reply was installed in keystore
ssl$
```

Verify keystore sslcluster_keystore.jks

```
ssl$ keytool -list -keystore sslcluster_keystore.jks -storepass mykeypass
Keystore type: jks
Keystore provider: SUN

Your keystore contains 2 entries

rootca, Dec 27, 2018, trustedCertEntry,
Certificate fingerprint (SHA1): 6E:82:EC:35:59:B6:EF:74:DC:47:3E:CB:5E:0A:3E:0B:24:F8:7C:80
sslcluster_node, Dec 27, 2018, PrivateKeyEntry,
Certificate fingerprint (SHA1): 02:47:AB:68:C8:2C:C5:20:21:38:EE:5F:DE:53:3B:A0:43:B8:A7:04

ssl$
```

Step 7: Copy the certificates to all nodes and update *cassandra.yaml*

Once you have certificates ready, we need to copy these certificates on each node and modify the *cassandra.yaml* with below settings. We have copied the keystore and truststore files on /usr/local/cssandra/ssl folder on both nodes (hostname ssl1 and ssl2)

```
server_encryption_options:
  internode_encryption: all
  keystore: /usr/local/cassandra/ssl/sslcluster_keystore.jks
  keystore_password: mykeypass
  truststore: /usr/local/cassandra/ssl/sslcluster_truststore.jks
  truststore_password: tstorepass
  # More advanced defaults below:
  protocol: TLS
  algorithm: SunX509
  store_type: JKS
  cipher_suites: [TLS_RSA_WITH_AES_128_CBC_SHA,TLS_RSA_WITH_AES_256_CBC_SHA,TLS_
DHE_RSA_WITH_AES_128_CBC_SHA,TLS_DHE_RSA_WITH_AES_256_CBC_SHA,TLS_ECDHE_RSA_
WITH_AES_128_CBC_SHA,TLS_ECDHE_RSA_WITH_AES_256_CBC_SHA]
  require_client_auth: true
  # require_endpoint_verification: false
```

Step 8: Restart cassandra

Once the files are copied to all the nodes and *cassandra.yaml* changes are done and verified, we need to do a rolling restart of Cassandra on each node. If you are using *GossipingPropertyFileSnitch*, do a rolling restart of nodes by RACK wise within a datacenter. You will see below message in the system.log.

```
ssl$ grep "Starting Encrypted Messaging Service on SSL" $CASSANDRA_HOME/logs/system.log
INFO [main] 2018-12-28 00:06:52,891 MessagingService.java:687 - Starting Encrypted Messaging
Service on SSL port 7001
ssl$

ss2$ grep "Starting Encrypted Messaging Service on SSL" $CASSANDRA_HOME/logs/system.log
INFO [main] 2018-12-28 00:06:55,666 MessagingService.java:687 - Starting Encrypted Messaging
Service on SSL port 7001
```

Setup client-to-node encryption

Encryption between client and node protects the data in flight by establishing a secure channel between the client and coordinator node. The steps to generate certificates are the same as node-to-node but with a different naming convention. In the below section all steps are listed below without any explanation.

We will use the same cluster.conf file to generate root CA.

```
cassandra@ssl1:/usr/local/cassandra/ssl$ cat cluster.conf
[ req ]
distinguished_name = req_distinguished_name
prompt = no
output_password = rootpass
default_bits = 2048
[ req_distinguished_name ]
C          =         US
ST         =         NJ
L          =         southbrunswick
O          =         CADG
OU         =         sslcluster
CN         =         sslclusterCA
cassandra@ssl1:/usr/local/cassandra/ssl$
```

Step 1: Create root CA and key & Verify

```
ssl$ openssl req
        -config cluster.conf
        -new -x509 -nodes
        -subj "/C=US/ST=NJ/L=southbrunswick/O=CADG/OU=sslcluster/CN=sslclusterCA"
        -keyout sslcluster_client.key
        -out sslcluster_rootCa_client.crt
        -days 500
```

Verify.

```
ssl$ openssl x509 -in sslcluster_rootCa_client.crt -text - noout
```

Step 2: Create truststore & Verify

```
ssl$ keytool -importcert
        -keystore sslcluster_truststore_client.jks
        -alias rootca
        -file sslcluster_rootCa_client.crt
        -keypass rootpass
        -storepass tstorepass
        -noprompt
```

Verify

```
ssl$ keytool -list -keystore sslcluster_truststore_client.jks -storepass tstorepass
```

Step 3: Create keystore and generate public/private key pair & Verify

```
ssl$ keytool -genkeypair
        -keyalg RSA
        -alias sslcluster_client
        -keystore sslcluster_keystore_client.jks
        -storepass mykeypass
        -keypass mykeypass
        -validity 500
        -keysize 2048
        -dname "CN=sslclusterCA, OU=sslcluster_client, O=CADG, C=US"
```

Verify

```
ssl$ keytool -list -keystore sslcluster_keystore_client.jks -storepass mykeypass
```

Step 4: Export certificate signing request (CSR) and Sign node certificate with sslcluster_rootCa.crt

```
ssl$ keytool -certreq
        -keystore sslcluster_keystore_client.jks
        -alias sslcluster_client
        -file sslcluster_client.csr
        -keypass mykeypass
        -storepass mykeypass
        -dname "CN=sslclusterCA, OU=sslcluster_client, O=CADG, C=US"
```

```
ssl$ openssl x509
        -req
        -CA sslcluster_rootCa_client.crt
        -CAkey sslcluster_client.key
        -in sslcluster_client.csr
        -out sslcluster_client.crt_signed
        -days 500
        -CAcreateserial
        -passin pass:rootpass
```

Verify the signed certificate by running openssl

```
ssl$ openssl verify -CAfile sslcluster_rootCa_client.crt sslcluster_client.crt_signed
```

Step 5: Import sslcluster_rootCa_client.crt certificate into node's keystore sslcluster_keystore_client.jks

```
ssl$ keytool -importcert
        -keystore sslcluster_keystore_client.jks
        -alias rootca
        -file sslcluster_rootCa_client.crt
        -noprompt
        -keypass mykeypass
        -storepass mykeypass
```

Step 6: Import node's signed certificate sslcluster_node.crt_signed into node keystore sslcluster_keystore.jks

```
ssl$ keytool -importcert
        -keystore sslcluster_keystore_client.jks
        -alias sslcluster_client
        -noprompt
        -file sslcluster_client.crt_signed
        -keypass mykeypass
        -storepass mykeypass
```

Verify keystore sslcluster_keystore.jks

```
ssl$ keytool -list -keystore sslcluster_keystore_client.jks -storepass mykeypass
```

Step 7: Generate pem key to use with cqlsh

```
ssl$ keytool -exportcert
        -alias rootca
        -keypass mykeypass
        -keystore sslcluster_truststore_client.jks
        -storepass tstorepass
        -rfc
        -file sslcluster_cqlsh.pem
Certificate stored in file <sslcluster_cqlsh.pem>
```

List all file generated for client-to-node encryption

```
ssl$ ls -lrt | grep client
-rw-rw-r-- 1 cassandra cassandra  1708  Dec 28 10:23 sslcluster_client.key
-rw-rw-r-- 1 cassandra cassandra  1220  Dec 28 10:23 sslcluster_rootCa_client.crt
-rw-rw-r-- 1 cassandra cassandra   923  Dec 28 10:25 sslcluster_truststore_client.jks
-rw-rw-r-- 1 cassandra cassandra  1059  Dec 28 10:27 sslcluster_client.csr
```

```
-rw-rw-r-- 1 cassandra cassandra    17  Dec 28 10:28 sslcluster_rootCa_client.srl
-rw-rw-r-- 1 cassandra cassandra  1180  Dec 28 10:28 sslcluster_client.crt_signed
-rw-rw-r-- 1 cassandra cassandra  3955  Dec 28 10:36 sslcluster_keystore_client.jks
ssl$
ssl$ ls -lrt | grep cqlsh
-rw-rw-r-- 1 cassandra cassandra  1237  Dec 28 10:41 sslcluster_cqlsh.pem
ssl$
```

Step 8: Copy the certificates to all nodes and update *cassandra.yaml*

Once you have all the client-to-node certificates ready, we need to copy these certificates on each node and modify the *cassandra.yaml* with below settings. We have copied the keystore and truststore files on /usr/local/cssandra/ssl folder on both nodes (hostname ssl1 and ssl2)

```
# enable or disable client/server encryption.
client_encryption_options:
   enabled: true
   # If enabled and optional is set to true encrypted and unencrypted connections are handled.
   optional: false
   keystore: /usr/local/cassandra/ssl/sslcluster_keystore_client.jks
   keystore_password: mykeypass
   truststore: /usr/local/cassandra/ssl/sslcluster_truststore_client.jks
   truststore_password: tstorepass
   # More advanced defaults below:
   protocol: TLS
   algorithm: SunX509
   store_type: JKS
   cipher_suites: [TLS_RSA_WITH_AES_128_CBC_SHA,TLS_RSA_WITH_AES_256_CBC_SHA,TLS_
DHE_RSA_WITH_AES_128_CBC_SHA,TLS_DHE_RSA_WITH_AES_256_CBC_SHA,TLS_ECDHE_RSA_
WITH_AES_128_CBC_SHA,TLS_ECDHE_RSA_WITH_AES_256_CBC_SHA]
```

Step 8: Restart Cassandra

Do a rolling restart of Cassandra on all the node datacenter wise and RACK wise.

Step 9: Verification

```
ssl$ grep native_transport_port cassandra.yaml
native_transport_port: 9042
# standard native_transport_port.
# Enabling client encryption and keeping native_transport_port_ssl disabled will use encryption
# for native_transport_port. Setting native_transport_port_ssl to a different value
# from native_transport_port will use encryption for native_transport_port_ssl while
# keeping native_transport_port unencrypted.
# native_transport_port_ssl: 9142
ssl$
```

When you enable client-to-node encryption, it will encrypt all traffic on *native_transport_port*, by default it is 9042. If we need both encrypted and unencrypted traffic, we must enable *native_transport_port_ssl* port. By default, it is set to 9142 and it is commented.

Now if you run cqlsh, it will give you error

```
ssl$ $CASSANDRA_HOME/bin/cqlsh -u cassandra -p cassandra
Connection error: ('Unable to connect to any servers', {'192.168.1.27':
ConnectionShutdown('Connection <AsyncoreConnection(48714576) 192.168.1.27:9042 (closed)>
is already closed',)})
```

You need to use "—ssl" option with cqlsh

```
ssl$ $CASSANDRA_HOME/bin/cqlsh -u cassandra -p cassandra --ssl
Connected to sslCluster at 192.168.1.27:9042.
[cqlsh 5.0.1 | Cassandra 3.10 | CQL spec 3.4.4 | Native protocol v4]
Use HELP for help.
cassandra@cqlsh>
```

For ssl to work with cqlsh, you need to update cqlshrc file and update [ssl] section as listed below. Note that we have configured the key generated in Step 7 to use with cqlsh.

```
ssl$ cat ~/.cassandra/cqlshrc
[connection]
hostname = 192.168.1.27
port = 9042
factory = cqlshlib.ssl.ssl_transport_factory

[ssl]
certfile = /usr/local/cassandra/ssl/sslcluster_cqlsh.pem
validate = true ## Optional, true by default
ssl$
```

Auditing

Many companies today have internal security policies and mandate that require the auditing on all databases to capture certain activities like

- DDL changes
- Truncate table
- Authentication changes such as create user (role), drop user (role), grant and revoke of object level permissions
- DML such as INSERT or DELETE on certain sensitive data

Current version of Apache Cassandra does not support the auditing yet. If you are using DataStax Enterprise Cassandra (DSE), it supports database auditing on the cluster.

In DSE version of Cassandra, database activity can be captured into a log file or a table. You can enable audit logging by editing *audit_logging_options* in *dse.yaml* file.

```
audit_logging_options:
    enabled: true
    logger: CassandraAuditWriter
    retention_time: 12
```

Above settings enable the auditing and logging to a table. *CassandraAuditWriter* record all the database activities on the local nodes to the *dse_audit.audit_log* table. You can ALTER KEYSPACE *dse_audit* to NetworkTopologyStrategy and set the RF for each datacenter where auditing is enabled.

You can exclude or include event categories such as

- QUERY   (SELECT, SOLR_QUERY)
- DML   (INSERT,BATCH,TRUNCATE,UPDATE,DELETE etc)
- DDL   (CREATE/DROP keyspace/table/index/view etc)
- DCL   (CREATE ROLE/DROP ROLE/GRANT/REVOKE etc)
- AUTH   (LOGIN/LOGIN FAILURE etc)
- ERROR
- UNKNOWN

Auditing can be enabled on specific nodes, entire datacenter or entire cluster. For logging you can apply role filtering. For more details, refer documentation on www.datastax.com

✶ ✶ ✶

CHAPTER 7

Cassandra Node Management—Single Token

In this chapter, we will look at Cassandra node management to keep the cluster running and scalable. As a Cassandra admin, you need to make sure cluster size and throughput are optimal, and disk space is sufficient and can support the growth. Adding nodes or adding a datacenter are straightforward tasks but need to be appropriately planned. Similarly scaling down by removing nodes and decommissioning a datacenter also need to be appropriately planned.

Node management tasks are slightly different between the single token cluster and vnode cluster. In this chapter, we will go through details on setting up a single token cluster, adding a node, replacing a dead node, removing a node, and decommissioning a node.

Clone the Machine

As you have seen in the Installation chapter, we have created a node "cc1" and installed Cassandra on it. Once you install Cassandra, make sure it is working. For this chapter and the next few chapters, we need to create four to six nodes. Instead of spending a lot of time on creating additional nodes, you can clone the cc1 node as four new hosts. To create new clones, open VirtualBox and click on "cc1" and under "Machine" select "Clone" and repeat the process to create four new clones by the names host1, host2, host3, and host4. Once you create clones, update */etc/hosts* and */etc/hostname* to update the hostnames. Note down the IP address for each node by running ipconfig.

For this entire chapter, we will use the below four nodes with their respective IP addresses.

Hostname	IP Address
host1	192.168.1.32
host2	192.168.1.30
host3	192.168.1.31
host4	192.168.1.33

Reset the node

One of the steps in preparing a node is to reset it. Reset node means, remove any existing data from the node and reset it. In your shop, if you are re-provisioning a host from one environment to another, you need to make sure to clean up the data directory before you add it to any cluster.

So if you read a step that says reset the node, it means remove existing data. Reset node includes the below steps.

```
cassandra@host1:/usr/local/cassandra/data$ cd $CASSANDRA_HOME/data
cassandra@host1:/usr/local/cassandra/data$ ls -l
total 16
drwxrwxr-x 2 cassandra cassandra 4096 Jan 23 20:54 commitlog
drwxrwxr-x 8 cassandra cassandra 4096 Jan 23 21:06 data
drwxrwxr-x 2 cassandra cassandra 4096 Jan 23 21:14 hints
drwxrwxr-x 2 cassandra cassandra 4096 Jan 28 20:54 saved_caches
cassandra@host1:/usr/local/cassandra/data$rm -R data
cassandra@host1:/usr/local/cassandra/data$rm -R saved_caches/
cassandra@host1:/usr/local/cassandra/data$rm -R commitlog/
cassandra@host1:/usr/local/cassandra/data$rm -R hints/
```

Single Token Two-Node cluster

We will build a two-node cluster using host1 and host2, making host1 as a seed node.

On host1 (192.168.1.32) *cassandra.yaml* file have following configuration.

cluster_name: 'singletoken'
- seeds: "192.168.1.32"
listen_address: 192.168.1.32
broadcast_address: 192.168.1.32
rpc_address: 192.168.1.32
#num_tokens: 4
partitioner: org.apache.cassandra.dht.Murmur3Partitioner
initial_token: -9223372036854775808

On host2 (192.168.1.30) *cassandra.yaml* file have following configuration.

cluster_name: 'singletoken'
- seeds: "192.168.1.32"
listen_address: 192.168.1.30
broadcast_address: 192.168.1.30
rpc_address: 192.168.1.30
#num_tokens: 4
partitioner: org.apache.cassandra.dht.Murmur3Partitioner
initial_token: 0

For Murmur3Partitioner when using two nodes, the token calculator gives the above two initial tokens. Since this is not a vnode, we have commented out num_token. As you can see, both the nodes have the seed IP of host1, which is 192.168.1.32; cluster_name is self-explanatory.

Reset the node and start Cassandra on host1 first, followed by on host2. You will have a two-node cluster up and running.

Few things to observe from the system.log on host1:

"data," "commitlog," "saved_caches," and "hints" folders were created in $CASSANDRA_HOME/data.

In the below output, *nodetool status* shows all the nodes in the cluster and their status. Also it does show the data load on each node.

The *nodetool ring* shows almost similar information, and it shows the actual tokens. Since this is a single token cluster, you will see only one range of token for host1 and host2. If it is vnode, based on num_token configuration, you will see "num_token" number of ranges for that given node.

```
cassandra@host1:~$ nodetool status
Datacenter: NewYork_DC
=======================
Status=Up/Down
|/ State=Normal/Leaving/Joining/Moving
--  Address       Load      Tokens  Owns (effective) Host ID                               Rack
UN  192.168.1.30  92.8 KiB  1       100.0%           88e61bce-9e1b-4805-b5eb-919377ae5b82  rack1
UN  192.168.1.32  65.23 KiB 1       100.0%           2677450d-70b7-4bb6-b95c-17e700739a70  rack1


cassandra@host1:~$ nodetool ring


Datacenter: NewYork_DC
==========
Address        Rack    Status  State    Load       Owns      Token
                                                                       0
192.168.1.32   rack1   Up      Normal   65.23 KiB  100.00%   -9223372036854775808
192.168.1.30   rack1   Up      Normal   92.8 KiB   100.00%   0


cassandra@host1:~$
```

The *nodetool describecluster* shows cluster information, snitch, partitioner, and schema versions. You need to pay attention to schema versions. In a large cluster, when you run this command, all nodes should be at the same schema version.

```
cassandra@host1:~$ nodetool describecluster
Cluster Information:
    Name: singletoken
```

```
    Snitch: org.apache.cassandra.locator.DynamicEndpointSnitch
    Partitioner: org.apache.cassandra.dht.Murmur3Partitioner
    Schema versions:
        86afa796-d883-3932-aa73-6b017cef0d19: [192.168.1.30, 192.168.1.32]
cassandra@host1:~$
```

Create Table and Insert Data

Now we have a two-node single token cluster. Let's create a keyspace and table and insert a large amount of data. The reason for creating a table and adding the data is so that we can see the distribution and streaming of data as we add nodes and decommission the nodes.

We will create a keyspace "node_mgmt" and tables city and code.

```
cassandra@host1:~$ cqlsh -u cassandra -pcassandra 192.168.1.32
Connected to singletoken at 192.168.1.32:9042.
[cqlsh 5.0.1 | Cassandra 3.10 | CQL spec 3.4.4 | Native protocol v4]
Use HELP for help.
cassandra@cqlsh> CREATE KEYSPACE node_mgmt WITH
                    replication={'class':'SimpleStrategy','replication_factor':1};
cassandra@cqlsh> CREATE TABLE node_mgmt.city
  (
    id      int,
    city    text,
    comment text,
    PRIMARY KEY (id,city)
  );
cassandra@cqlsh> CREATE TABLE node_mgmt.code
  (
    id      int,
    comment text,
    PRIMARY KEY (id)
  );
```

```
cassandra@cqlsh> desc keyspaces;

node_mgmt system_schema system_auth system system_distributed system_traces

cassandra@cqlsh>
```

To insert a large amount of data, you can write a simple script to generate a large text file, which can be imported into these tables.

Insert Data into Table "city."

Create a file "city" and enter the details you want to.

```
cassandra@host1:/usr/local/cassandra$ cat city
NewYork
SouthBrunswick
Princeton
Plainsboro
Edison
Monroe
Philadelphia
```

Create a shell script which will generate a large text file.

```
cassandra@host1:/usr/local/cassandra$ cat createcity.sh
i=1
while [ $i -lt 120000 ];
do
 for city in `cat city`
  do
    echo $i,$city,"$i We are inserting large text so that it will occupy more space.( Cassandra
Admin DBA Guide)"
  done
```

```
  i=$((i + 1))
done;
```

Content of the text file created for importing.

```
cassandra@host1:/usr/local/cassandra$ ./createcity.sh > /tmp/city.txt
cassandra@host1:/usr/local/cassandra$ head /tmp/city.txt
1,NewYork,1 We are ... will occupy more space.( Cassandra Admin DBA Guide)
1,SouthBrunswick,1 We are ... will occupy more space.( Cassandra Admin DBA Guide)
1,Princeton,1 We are ... will occupy more space.( Cassandra Admin DBA Guide)
1,Plainsboro,1 We are ... will occupy more space.( Cassandra Admin DBA Guide)
1,Edison,1 We are ... will occupy more space.( Cassandra Admin DBA Guide)
1,Monroe,1 We are ... will occupy more space.( Cassandra Admin DBA Guide)
1,Philadelphia,1 We are ... will occupy more space.( Cassandra Admin DBA Guide)
```

Now login to cqlsh and import the data into node_mgmt.city table.

```
cassandra@cqlsh:node_mgmt> COPY node_mgmt.city FROM '/tmp/city.txt';
Using 1 child processes

Starting copy of node_mgmt.city with columns [id, city, comment].
Processed: 839993 rows; Rate: 1698 rows/s; Avg. rate: 2217 rows/s
839993 rows imported from 1 files in 6 minutes and 18.892 seconds (0 skipped).
cassandra@cqlsh:node_mgmt>
```

Insert Data into Table "code."

```
cassandra@host1:/usr/local/cassandra$ cat create_code.sh
i=1
while [ $i -lt 1000 ];
do
  echo $i,"code $i "
  i=$((i + 1))
done;
```

```
cassandra@host1:/usr/local/cassandra$ ./create_code.sh > /tmp/code.txt
cassandra@host1:/usr/local/cassandra$ head /tmp/code.txt
1,code 1
2,code 2
3,code 3
4,code 4

cassandra@host1:/usr/local/cassandra/data$ $CASSANDRA_HOME/bin/cqlsh -u cassandra -pcas-
sandra 192.168.1.32
Connected to singletoken at 192.168.1.32:9042.
[cqlsh 5.0.1 | Cassandra 3.10 | CQL spec 3.4.4 | Native protocol v4]
Use HELP for help.
cassandra@cqlsh> use node_mgmt ;
cassandra@cqlsh:node_mgmt> COPY node_mgmt.code FROM '/tmp/code.txt';
Using 1 child processes

Starting copy of node_mgmt.code with columns [id, comment].
Processed: 999 rows; Rate:    437 rows/s; Avg. rate:    802 rows/s
999 rows imported from 1 files in 1.246 seconds (0 skipped).
```

As you import the file, you will see the data space increased on both the nodes. The following is the *du* output before and after importing the file on host1.

```
cassandra@host1:/usr/local/cassandra/data/data$ pwd
/usr/local/cassandra/data/data
cassandra@host1:/usr/local/cassandra/data/data$ du -sch *
28K     node_mgmt        <- before INSERT data
556K    system
72K     system_auth
28K     system_distributed
592K    system_schema
20K     system_traces
1.3M    total
```

```
cassandra@host1:/usr/local/cassandra/data/data$ pwd
/usr/local/cassandra/data/data
cassandra@host1:/usr/local/cassandra/data/data$ du -sch *
4.8M      node_mgmt        <- after INSERT data
556K      system
72K       system_auth
28K       system_distributed
592K      system_schema
20K       system_traces
6.1M      total
```

You can see the data distribution and the load on both the nodes by running *nodetool ring* command. In the output below, ownership is at 50 percent, and data is about 4.5 MB on each node.

```
cassandra@host1:~$ nodetool ring

Datacenter: NewYork_DC
==========
Address         Rack    Status  State   Load     Owns      Token
                                                            0
192.168.1.32  rack1    Up     Normal   4.8 MiB   50.00%    -9223372036854775808
192.168.1.30  rack1    Up     Normal  4.45 MiB   50.00%    0

cassandra@host1:~$
```

Add Third Node to the Cluster

Now that we have a two-node single token cluster running, we will add a third node to this cluster. To prepare the third node host3, first reset the node.

On host3 (192.168.1.31) Cassandra.yaml file have following configuration.

cluster_name: 'singletoken'

- seeds: "192.168.1.32"

listen_address: 192.168.1.31

broadcast_address: 192.168.1.31

rpc_address: 192.168.1.31

#num_tokens: 4

partitioner: org.apache.cassandra.dht.Murmur3Partitioner

initial_token: **3074457345618258602**

auto_bootstrap: true

As you can see, we have kept the seed node as host1 IP, which is 192.168.1.32; initial_token is calculatedusingthewebsitehttps://www.geroba.com/cassandra/cassandra-token-calculator/.

Single Token values for 3 node Murmur3Partitioner

-9223372036854775808

-3074457345618258603

3074457345618258602

We have updated host3 initial_token as 3074457345618258602. We need to go back and update the initial_token value for host2 as -3074457345618258603. Initial_token for host1 remains the same after recalculation. So we don't need to change for host1.

Once you reset the node and updated all configuration on host3, start Cassandra on it. Once host3 (192.168.1.31) joins the cluster, you will see that token for host2 has not changed yet. Also you see that, ownership of data is not equal.

```
cassandra@host1:~$ nodetool ring

Datacenter: NewYork_DC
==========
```

Address	Rack	Status	State	Load	Owns	Token
						3074457345618258602
192.168.1.32	rack1	Up	Normal	4.82 MiB	33.33%	-9223372036854775808

```
192.168.1.30  rack1    Up     Normal    4.46 MiB    50.00%      0
192.168.1.31  rack1    Up     Normal    78.17 KiB   16.67%      3074457345618258602

cassandra@host1:~$
```

After host3 joins the cluster, host2 still owns the data from token range, which is owned by host3. To rebalance the data, we need to run *nodetool move* command. We need to give new token for host2. This command moves host2 from earlier token of "0" to "-3074457345618258603". Make sure to run this command on "host2", which is important.

```
cassandra@host2:/usr/local/cassandra$ nodetool move -3074457345618258603
cassandra@host2:/usr/local/cassandra$
```

When you execute this command on host2, you could see the following messages in host2 Cassandra logs.

```
INFO [RMI TCP Connection(2)-127.0.0.1] 2018-10-27 22:30:32,551 StorageService.java:1435 -
MOVING: Moving /192.168.1.30 from 0 to -3074457345618258603.
INFO [RMI TCP Connection(2)-127.0.0.1] 2018-10-27 22:31:03,819 StorageService.java:1435 -
MOVING: fetching new ranges and streaming old ranges
INFO [RMI TCP Connection(2)-127.0.0.1] 2018-10-27 22:31:03,866 StreamResultFuture.java:90 -
[Stream #835d3b70-da59-11e8-a84f-076dede16ee7] Executing streaming plan for Relocation
INFO [StreamConnectionEstablisher:1] 2018-10-27 22:31:03,909 StreamSession.java:266 - [Stream
#835d3b70-da59-11e8-a84f-076dede16ee7] Starting streaming to /192.168.1.31
INFO [StreamConnectionEstablisher:1] 2018-10-27 22:31:03,968 StreamResultFuture.java:173
- [Stream #835d3b70-da59-11e8-a84f-076dede16ee7 ID#0] Prepare completed. Receiving 0
files(0.000KiB), sending 4 files(1.333MiB)
```

Once the data is streamed to host3, you will see the ownership is equally distributed among the three nodes.

```
cassandra@host2:/usr/local/cassandra$ nodetool ring

Datacenter: NewYork_DC
==========
```

Address	Rack	Status	State	Load	Owns	Token
						3074457345618258602
192.168.1.32	rack1	Up	Normal	4.82 MiB	33.33%	-9223372036854775808
192.168.1.30	rack1	Up	Normal	4.85 MiB	33.33%	-3074457345618258603
192.168.1.31	rack1	Up	Normal	1.67 MiB	33.33%	3074457345618258602

cassandra@host2:/usr/local/cassandra$

Keyspace *node_mgmt* has been created with replication_factor as 1. This means there is only one primary copy stored on one node. Due to this reason, you see ownership as 33 percent on each node.

For a given keyspace.table and partition key, *nodetool getendpoints* can display the data location and number of replicas. Since we have replication_factor = 1, any given row can be available only on one node. Let's check a few random partition keys from *node_mgmt.code* table.

```
cassandra@host1:~$ nodetool getendpoints node_mgmt code 200
192.168.1.31
cassandra@host1:~$ nodetool getendpoints node_mgmt code 300
192.168.1.32
cassandra@host1:~$ nodetool getendpoints node_mgmt code 500
192.168.1.30
cassandra@host1:~$ nodetool getendpoints node_mgmt code 4500
192.168.1.31
cassandra@host1:~$
```

Note that in code table, id = 4500 does not exist. But nodetool endpoints hash the key and give the token range that is owned by node host3, which is 192.168.1.31.

Now let's increase the replication_factor to 2 by altering the keyspace.

```
cassandra@cqlsh> SELECT keyspace_name,replication
                FROM system_schema.keyspaces WHERE keyspace_name='node_mgmt';
```

```
 keyspace_name | replication
-----------------+---------------------------------------------------------------
   node_mgmt | {'class': 'org.apache.cassandra.locator.SimpleStrategy', 'replication_factor': '1'}

(1 rows)
cassandra@cqlsh> ALTER KEYSPACE node_mgmt
                 WITH replication = {'class': 'SimpleStrategy', 'replication_factor': '2'};
cassandra@cqlsh> SELECT keyspace_name,replication
                 FROM system_schema.keyspaces WHERE keyspace_name='node_mgmt';

 keyspace_name | replication
---------------+---------------------------------------------------------------
   node_mgmt | {'class': 'org.apache.cassandra.locator.SimpleStrategy', 'replication_factor': '2'}

(1 rows)
```

Once you increase the replication_factor from 1 to 2, the ownership increases from 33.3 percent to 66.67 percent.

```
cassandra@host1:~$ nodetool ring

Datacenter: NewYork_DC
==========
Address        Rack    Status  State    Load      Owns      Token
                                                            3074457345618258602
192.168.1.32   rack1   Up      Normal   4.81 MiB  66.67%    -9223372036854775808
192.168.1.30   rack1   Up      Normal   4.87 MiB  66.67%    -3074457345618258603
192.168.1.31   rack1   Up      Normal   1.67 MiB  66.67%    3074457345618258602

cassandra@host1:~$
```

Now if you run the same *nodetool getendpoints*, you see that the row ownership exists on 2 nodes, primary and second replica.

```
cassandra@host1:~$ nodetool getendpoints node_mgmt code 200
192.168.1.31
192.168.1.32
cassandra@host1:~$ nodetool getendpoints node_mgmt code 300
192.168.1.32
192.168.1.30
cassandra@host1:~$ nodetool getendpoints node_mgmt code 500
192.168.1.30
192.168.1.31
```

Altering keyspace to increase replication_factor from 1 to 2 does not insert the data into the second replica. You can check this by running du -sch *. You need to run the repair on each node. Cassandra accomplishes anti-entropy repair using Merkle trees. Anti-entropy is a process of comparing the data of all replicas and updating each replica to the newest data.

For example, id = 200 from node_mgmt.code generates a token that falls in a range, which is owned by host3 (192.168.1.31). In the ring, the next node is host1 (192.168.1.32), which is the second replica for all the ranges of host3. Similarly, host3 (192.168.1.31) is second replica for host2(192.168.1.30).

```
cassandra@cqlsh> SELECT id,token(id) FROM node_mgmt.code WHERE id=200;
id | system.token(id)
-----+--------------------
200 | 1543354510515183773 <- This token owned by host3(192.168.1.31)
(1 rows)
cassandra@host1:~$ nodetool getendpoints node_mgmt code 200
192.168.1.31 <- host3
192.168.1.32 <- host1 (replica for host3)
```

Run repairs on each host with the below command. The output of repairs on one host is listed below. When you run the repair on host3, repair process streams all the data to its replica node, which is host1. Make a note that, this statement is valid for a single token cluster and not for vnode. Also in this case, we have *replication_factor* as 2, means each node will have an only second replica. After repairs run on all nodes, you would see the disk space increase by one-third of the data.

```
cassandra@host3:/usr/local/cassandra/conf$ nodetool repair -pr
[2018-10-27 23:21:14,669] Replication factor is 1. No repair is needed for keyspace 'system_auth'
[2018-10-27 23:21:14,826] Starting repair command #2 (86bcb5f0-da60-11e8-b6bc-
297365b556d7), repairing keyspace node_mgmt with repair options (parallelism: parallel, primary
range: true, incremental: true, job threads: 1, ColumnFamilies: [], dataCenters: [], hosts: [], # of
ranges: 1, pull repair: false)
[2018-10-27 23:21:35,505] Repair session 86cfa1b0-da60-11e8-b6bc-297365b556d7 for range [(-
3074457345618258603,3074457345618258602]] finished (progress: 100%)
[2018-10-27 23:21:36,522] Repair completed successfully
[2018-10-27 23:21:36,580] Repair command #2 finished in 21 seconds
[2018-10-27 23:21:36,892] Starting repair command #3 (93f4f520-da60-11e8-b6bc-
297365b556d7), repairing keyspace system_traces with repair options (parallelism: parallel,
primary range: true, incremental: true, job threads: 1, ColumnFamilies: [], dataCenters: [], hosts:
[], # of ranges: 1, pull repair: false)
[2018-10-27 23:21:37,383] Repair session 9406a860-da60-11e8-b6bc-297365b556d7 for range
[(-3074457345618258603,3074457345618258602]] finished (progress: 100%)
[2018-10-27 23:21:37,617] Repair completed successfully
[2018-10-27 23:21:37,671] Repair command #3 finished in 0 seconds
cassandra@host3:/usr/local/cassandra/conf$
```

Once repairs are completed, each node will be populated with the secondary replica data, which reflect in the Load section of the *nodetool ring* output.

```
cassandra@host1:~$ nodetool ring

Datacenter: NewYork_DC
==========
Address        Rack   Status State    Load      Owns      Token
                                                          3074457345618258602
192.168.1.32   rack1  Up     Normal   6.7 MiB   66.67%    -9223372036854775808
192.168.1.30   rack1  Up     Normal   8.38 MiB  66.67%    -3074457345618258603
192.168.1.31   rack1  Up     Normal   6.69 MiB  66.67%    3074457345618258602

cassandra@host1:~$
```

Replacing a Dead Node in a Single Token Cluster

In a distributed database like Cassandra, you need to deal with hardware situations like node crashes, disks going bad, network card issues, and many more situations. If you can bring up the same node within three hours, you may not need to replace that node. But for any reason, if it cannot be brought back up immediately, you need to replace that node.

Why three hours?

The following is the default hint configuration in *cassandra.yaml* file.

```
# this defines the maximum amount of time a dead host will have hints
# created until it has been seen alive and gone down again.
max_hint_window_in_ms: 10800000 # 3 hours
```

If the node is up within three hours, all the hints will be applied, and data will be in synch. After three hours, hints will not be stored, and the data can be stale. Hopefully, your application is not using read with consistency ONE. If they are, in such situations, you read stale data and return the wrong results.

If the downtime for the machine is more than three hours, you have the option of removing the node or replacing it with another node. In this section, we will discuss the steps needed to replace a dead node.

1. Confirm that the node is dead by checking *nodetool ring* or *status* command.
2. On replacement machine, make sure Cassandra is installed and *cassandra.yaml* file matches all the configuration in the dead node. In most of the shops, few spare nodes are always ready with similar configurations. You need to make sure to reset the node (if this is used earlier, remove files from the data, commitlog, saved_cache and hint folders).
3. Make sure *auto_bootstrap* is set to *true*. If *auto_bootstrap* is missing in *cassandra.yaml* file, it automatically defaults to true.
4. In the replacement machine, set the *initial_token* to dead machines *initial_token* - 1 value.

5. Start Cassandra on replacement machine by adding -Dcassandra.replace_address = <dead_node_address> in *jvm.options* and monitor bootstrapping.
6. Run *nodetool removenode* to remove the dead node.
7. You need to run repair to make sure the new node is fully consistent.

From our example, let's shut down host3. We will see that 192.168.1.31 is down.

```
cassandra@host1:~$ nodetool ring

Datacenter: NewYork_DC
==========
Address        Rack    Status  State   Load      Owns     Token
                                                           3074457345618258602
192.168.1.32   rack1   Up      Normal  6.69 MiB  66.67%   -9223372036854775808
192.168.1.30   rack1   Up      Normal  8.41 MiB  66.67%   -3074457345618258603
192.168.1.31   rack1   Down    Normal  6.69 MiB  66.67%   3074457345618258602
cassandra@host1:~$
```

When this node is down, we will write some data using host1 (192.168.1.32). In this case, host1 acts as a coordinator, and any data it can't write to host3, which is down, it will store a hint locally.

```
cassandra@host1:~$ cqlsh -u cassandra -pcassandra 192.168.1.32
Connected to singletoken at 192.168.1.32:9042.
[cqlsh 5.0.1 | Cassandra 3.10 | CQL spec 3.4.4 | Native protocol v4]
Use HELP for help.
cassandra@cqlsh> COPY node_mgmt.code FROM '/tmp/code2.txt';
Using 1 child processes

Starting copy of node_mgmt.code with columns [id, comment].
Processed: 495 rows; Rate:    217 rows/s; Avg. rate:    368 rows/s
495 rows imported from 1 files in 1.346 seconds (0 skipped).
cassandra@cqlsh>
```

```
cassandra@host1:/usr/local/cassandra/data$ pwd
/usr/local/cassandra/data
cassandra@host1:/usr/local/cassandra/data$ ls -l hints/
total 28
-rw-rw-r-- 1 cassandra cassandra 26522 Oct 27 23:49 61aecd3e-ef96-4cbe-858d-5a7a8e-
c36e70-1540698586583-1.hints          ← hints file on host1
cassandra@host1:/usr/local/cassandra/data$
```

In the above output, you see that host3 (192.168.1.31) is dead and down. On host1, we did insert (imported via copy) data into *node_mgmt.code* table. Since host3 is down, it created hint files.

We will replace host3 (192.168.1.31) with host4 (192.168.1.33). For this we need to modify *jvm.options* on host4 and add below line. We are indicating here, host4 (192.168.1.33) will be replacing host3 (192.168.1.31).

```
-Dcassandra.replace_address=192.168.1.31
```

Once the node is up on host4 (192.168.1.33), we will see that a new node has taken over the dead hosts token range.

```
cassandra@host1:~$ nodetool ring

Datacenter: NewYork_DC
==========
```

Address	Rack	Status	State	Load	Owns	Token
						3074457345618258602
192.168.1.32	rack1	Up	Normal	6.72 MiB	33.33%	-9223372036854775808
192.168.1.30	rack1	Up	Normal	8.41 MiB	66.67%	-3074457345618258603
192.168.1.33	rack1	**Up**	Normal	3.43 MiB	66.67%	**3074457345618258601**
192.168.1.31	rack1	**Down**	Normal	6.69 MiB	33.33%	**3074457345618258602**

```
cassandra@host1:~$
cassandra@host1:~$ nodetool status
```

```
Datacenter: NewYork_DC
=======================
Status=Up/Down
|/ State=Normal/Leaving/Joining/Moving
--  Address        Load    Tokens Owns   Host ID                                Rack
UN  192.168.1.30  8.43 MiB   1    66.7%  88e61bce-9e1b-4805-b5eb-919377ae5b82  rack1
DN  192.168.1.31  6.69 MiB   1    33.3%  61aecd3e-ef96-4cbe-858d-5a7a8ec36e70  rack1
UN  192.168.1.32  6.72 MiB   1    33.3%  2677450d-70b7-4bb6-b95c-17e700739a70  rack1
UN  192.168.1.33  3.43 MiB   1    66.7%  b752f5ea-95d2-43c7-9ef2-490a4d89777d  rack1


cassandra@host1:~$
```

Our next step is to run nodetool remove command and pass the Host ID of the removed node. In this case it will be **61aecd3e-ef96-4cbe-858d-5a7a8ec36e70** for host3.

```
cassandra@host1 $ nodetool removenode 61aecd3e-ef96-4cbe-858d-5a7a8ec36e70
cassandra@host1 $ nodetool ring

Datacenter: NewYork_DC
==========
Address        Rack    Status  State    Load      Owns      Token
                                                            3074457345618258601
192.168.1.32  rack1   Up      Normal  6.71 MiB  66.67%    -9223372036854775808
192.168.1.30  rack1   Up      Normal  8.43 MiB  66.67%    -3074457345618258603
192.168.1.33  rack1   Up      Normal  6.66 MiB  66.67%    3074457345618258601
←host4

cassandra@host1:/usr/local/cassandra/data$ pwd
/usr/local/cassandra/data
cassandra@host1:/usr/local/cassandra/datals -l hints/
total 0  ← hints applied
cassandra@host1:/usr/local/cassandra/data$
```

Once the replacement node host4 (192.168.1.33) is up, it assumes the token range of host3 (192.168.1.31).

Decommission Node

Decommissioning a node means you are removing a live node. Why do you want to decommission a live node? There are varied reasons.

You always will have more than one environment to do proper testing of all the procedures, load testing and functional testing. As part of maintaining all environments, you will be decommissioning and moving around the nodes from one environment to another.

You may want to reduce capacity by decommissioning a few nodes or you may want to decommission the entire datacenter.

You may need to do hardware maintenance such as adding memory or fixing disks on the machine.

Below is the procedure to decommission a node in a single token cluster.

1. Check the status of the node by running *nodetool status* or *ring*. Make sure the node you want to decommission is up and running.
2. Recalculate the tokens, and adjust your tokens on remaining nodes to evenly distribute the data across the cluster.
3. Login to the node you want to decommission, and run *nodetool describecluster* as a best practice to make sure you are on the right cluster. You may want to run "hostname" or ipconfig to double check you are logged in on the right node. Then run *nodetool decommission*
4. Once you decommission, this will assign the token ranges the decommissioned node was responsible for, to other nodes in the datacenter and replicate the appropriate data in those nodes. If you have a keyspace with *replication_factor* = 1, you don't need to worry about the data sitting on this node. Decommission process replicates this data to the other node.
5. Once a node leaves the cluster, you can restart Cassandra nodes in the datacenter that got the new tokens. Make sure you update the *initial_token* before restarting Cassandra. Based on how you recalculated the token, run *nodetool move* command.

Let's decommission host4 (192.168.1.33) as an example. To demonstrate data is streamed after decommissioning of the node for keyspace with replication_factor = 1, we will create a new keyspace and table and insert some data. In the below output, we have created keyspace repfactor1 with RF=1 and created table kode and inserted data into it.

```
cassandra@host1: $ cqlsh -u cassandra -pcassandra 192.168.1.32
Connected to singletoken at 192.168.1.32:9042.
[cqlsh 5.0.1 | Cassandra 3.10 | CQL spec 3.4.4 | Native protocol v4]
Use HELP for help.
cassandra@cqlsh> CREATE KEYSPACE repfactor1
                WITH replication = {'class': 'SimpleStrategy', 'replication_factor': '1'};
cassandra@cqlsh> CREATE TABLE repfactor1.kode ( id int PRIMARY KEY,comment text);
cassandra@cqlsh> COPY repfactor1.kode  FROM '/tmp/code.txt';
Using 1 child processes

Starting copy of repfactor1.kode with columns [id, comment].
Processed: 999 rows; Rate:    268 rows/s; Avg. rate:    508 rows/s
999 rows imported from 1 files in 1.966 seconds (0 skipped).
cassandra@cqlsh>
```

The below output shows ownership of token for keyspace repfactor1 and getendpoints for three records in repfactor1.kode, which are located on three different nodes.

```
cassandra@host1:$ nodetool status repfactor1
Datacenter: NewYork_DC
=======================
Status=Up/Down
|/ State=Normal/Leaving/Joining/Moving
-- Address       Load      Tokens  Owns     Host ID                                 Rack
UN 192.168.1.30  8.43  MiB  1       33.3%     88e61bce-9e1b-4805-b5eb-919377ae5b82  rack1
UN 192.168.1.32  6.74  MiB  1       33.3%     2677450d-70b7-4bb6-b95c-17e700739a70  rack1
UN 192.168.1.33  6.69  MiB  1       33.3%     b752f5ea-95d2-43c7-9ef2-490a4d89777d  rack1
```

```
cassandra@host1:$
cassandra@host1:$ nodetool getendpoints repfactor1 kode 200
192.168.1.33
cassandra@host1:$ nodetool getendpoints repfactor1 kode 300
192.168.1.32
cassandra@host1:$ nodetool getendpoints repfactor1 kode 500
192.168.1.30
cassandra@host1:$
```

Before decommissioning host4 (192.1681.33), make sure to check you are on the right cluster and right host.

```
cassandra@host4:~$ nodetool describecluster
Cluster Information:
    Name: singletoken
    Snitch: org.apache.cassandra.locator.DynamicEndpointSnitch
    Partitioner: org.apache.cassandra.dht.Murmur3Partitioner
    Schema versions:
        d3e7f630-cf67-3b5c-a64f-4faa102d8a61: [192.168.1.30, 192.168.1.32, 192.168.1.33]
cassandra@host4:~$ nodetool decommission
cassandra@host4:~$
```

While decommissioning, *nodetool netstats* on host4 will show all the streaming activity and the mode as LEAVING. When decommission is completed, the mode shows as DECOMMISSIONED.

The below output shows nodetool status output for keyspace repfactor1 before and after decommission. As you can see, after decommission of host4 (192.168.1.33), the token ownership shows 2/3rd.

```
cassandra@host1:$ nodetool status repfactor1
Datacenter: NewYork_DC
=======================
Status=Up/Down
|/ State=Normal/Leaving/Joining/Moving
--  Address       Load      Tokens  Owns(effective)  Host ID                                Rack
```

```
UN  192.168.1.30  8.43 MiB  1      33.3%           88e61bce-9e1b-4805-b5eb-919377ae5b82  rack1
UN  192.168.1.32  6.74 MiB  1      33.3%           2677450d-70b7-4bb6-b95c-17e700739a70  rack1
UN  192.168.1.33  6.69 MiB  1      33.3%           b752f5ea-95d2-43c7-9ef2-490a4d89777d   rack1


cassandra@host1:$ nodetool status repfactor1
Datacenter: NewYork_DC
========================
Status=Up/Down
|/ State=Normal/Leaving/Joining/Moving
--   Address       Load     Tokens  Owns(effective) Host ID                                      Rack
UN  192.168.1.30  11.73 MiB  1      33.3%           88e61bce-9e1b-4805-b5eb-919377ae5b82  rack1
UN  192.168.1.32  10.07 MiB  1      66.7%           2677450d-70b7-4bb6-b95c-17e700739a70  rack1
```

Also you can see that getendpoints for the kode partition key now return host1 and host2.

```
cassandra@host1:/usr/local/cassandra/data$ nodetool getendpoints repfactor1 kode 200
192.168.1.32
cassandra@host1:/usr/local/cassandra/data$ nodetool getendpoints repfactor1 kode 300
192.168.1.32
cassandra@host1:/usr/local/cassandra/data$ nodetool getendpoints repfactor1 kode 500
192.168.1.30
cassandra@host1:/usr/local/cassandra/data$
```

Once streaming is over and the node is decommissioned, based on how you recalculated the tokens, run nodetool move command. In our example, after decommission we have 2 node cluster. We recalculated the token for 2 node cluster and got token as -9223372036854775808 and 0. Since host1 has already configured with initial_token as -9223372036854775808, we need to update initial_token as 0 for host2 (192.168.30). After restarting the node with "0" as initial_token, we did a nodetool move as below. As you can see, the ownership before and after is back to normal.

```
cassandra@host2:~$ nodetool ring repfactor1

Datacenter: NewYork_DC
==========
```

Address	Rack	Status	State	Load	Owns	Token
						-3074457345618258603
192.168.1.32	rack1	Up	Normal	10.08 MiB	66.67%	-9223372036854775808
192.168.1.30	rack1	Up	Normal	11.69 MiB	33.33%	-3074457345618258603

```
cassandra@host2:~$ nodetool move 0
cassandra@host2:~$ nodetool ring repfactor1
```

Datacenter: NewYork_DC
==========

Address	Rack	Status	State	Load	Owns	Token
						0
192.168.1.32	rack1	Up	Normal	10.08 MiB	50.00%	-9223372036854775808
192.168.1.30	rack1	Up	Normal	11.7 MiB	50.00%	0

```
cassandra@host2:~$
```

Decommission by Mistake

Oops! Say by mistake you decommissioned host4 (192.168.1.33). As soon as decommissioning is over, data on host4 is streamed to remaining nodes (in our case host1 and host2). But your action was an accident, and you want to bring this node back into the cluster. If you start Cassandra on host4, it will not join the cluster. When you decommission the node, other nodes remember the decommissioned Host ID of host4 (in our case it was b752f5ea-95d2-43c7-9ef2-490a4d89777d), and will refuse to talk. On the host4 log, you will get the following message:

```
ERROR [main] 2018-10-28 01:14:58,028 CassandraDaemon.java:752 - Fatal configuration error org.
apache.cassandra.exceptions.ConfigurationException: This node was decommissioned and will not
rejoin the ring unless cassandra.override_decommission = true has been set, or all existing data is
removed and the node is bootstrapped again.
```

As you see from the error message, you have two options.

1. Clear all the data and start Cassandra. This will generate a new Host ID.
2. Start Cassandra with -D Cassandra.override_decommision = true. In this case, the node will rejoin with the same Host ID.

You may need to move the token once the decommissioned node rejoins the cluster. In our case, you need to run move on host2, as it was moved to 0 after decommission.

On host2 - $CASSANDRA_HOME/bin/*nodetool move* -3074457345618258603

When this happens, data on host1 and host2, which were originally owned by host4, will not be deleted automatically. You need to run *nodetool cleanup* on host1 and host2 to clear the data. Run repair to make sure data is in sync on all nodes.

Clean way to handle this is by adding the node procedure.

Remove Node

When a node is down, we cannot use *nodetool decommission*. When a node is down due to a hardware issue, use the *nodetool removenode* command. In a single token cluster, before removing the node, adjust the tokens. This will assign the token ranges of the old node being decommissioned to other nodes and stream the appropriate data from other replicas.

To remove a node, run *nodetool status* and note the Host ID that is down.

```
cassandra@host1:~$ nodetool ring

Datacenter: NewYork_DC
==========
```

Address	Rac	Status	State	Load	Owns	Token
						3074457345618258602
192.168.1.32	rack1	Up	Normal	6.72 MiB	66.67%	-9223372036854775808
192.168.1.30	rack1	Up	Normal	8.41 MiB	66.67%	-3074457345618258603
192.168.1.31	rack1	Down	Normal	6.69 MiB	66.67%	3074457345618258602

```
cassandra@host1:~$ nodetool status
Datacenter: NewYork_DC
========================
Status=Up/Down
|/ State=Normal/Leaving/Joining/Moving
--   Address       Load      Tokens   Owns(effective) Host ID                                 Rack
UN   192.168.1.30  8.43 MiB  1        66.7%           88e61bce-9e1b-4805-b5eb-919377ae5b82    rack1
DN   192.168.1.31  6.69 MiB  1        66.7%           61aecd3e-ef96-4cbe-858d-5a7a8ec36e70    rack1
UN   192.168.1.32  6.72 MiB  1        66.7%           2677450d-70b7-4bb6-b95c-17e700739a70    rack1
```

In the above output, node 192.168.1.31 is down, which needs to be removed. Use the Host Id of the downed node to remove it. The *nodetool removenode* <Host ID> needs to be issued from any node in the cluster, and *nodetool removenode status* will give you the status of the removal process.

```
cassandra@host1:$ nodetool removenode 61aecd3e-ef96-4cbe-858d-5a7a8ec36e70
cassandra@host1:$ nodetool ring

Datacenter: NewYork_DC
==========
Address        Rack    Status  State   Load      Owns       Token
                                                             -3074457345618258603
192.168.1.32   rack1   Up      Normal  6.71 MiB  100.00%    -9223372036854775808
192.168.1.30   rack1   Up      Normal  8.43 MiB  100.00%    -3074457345618258603

cassandra@host2:$ nodetool move 0
cassandra@host1:$ nodetool ring

Datacenter: NewYork_DC
==========
Address        Rack    Status State   Load      Owns       Token
                                                            0
192.168.1.32   rack1   Up     Normal  6.71 MiB  100.00%    -9223372036854775808
192.168.1.30   rack1   Up     Normal  8.43 MiB  100.00%    0
```

In the above output, nodetool removenode is run to remove the downed node. Once it is removed, the token for 192.168.1.30 (host2) does not change. Run nodetool move token to 0 to adjust the tokens in the ring. You might have the question, "Why Owns changed from 66.67 percent to 100 percent after removing the node?" We had only one keyspace with replication factor = 2. Since the third node was removed from the cluster, 'Owns' became 100 percent.

CHAPTER 8

Cassandra Node Management—vnode

In this chapter, we will look at Cassandra node management using vnode, and we will go through details on setting up the vnode cluster, adding a node(s), replacing a dead node, removing a node, and decommissioning a node. Working with a vnode cluster is much simpler than a single token cluster, as you don't need to change the token ranges manually.

For this entire chapter, we will use these 4 nodes.

Hostname	IP Address
host1	192.168.1.32
host2	192.168.1.30
host3	192.168.1.31
host4	192.168.1.33

Two-Node vnode Cluster

We will build a two-node vnode cluster using host1 and host2, making host1 as a seed node. For this build, we will set *num_tokens* to 2. Note that *initial_token* has been commented out for vnode setup.

On host1 (192.168.1.32) *cassandra.yaml* file have the following configuration.

cluster_name: 'vnodecluster'
- seeds: "192.168.1.32"
listen_address: 192.168.1.32
broadcast_address: 192.168.1.32
rpc_address: 192.168.1.32
num_tokens: 2
partitioner: org.apache.cassandra.dht.Murmur3Partitioner
#initial_token: -9223372036854775808

On host2 (192.168.1.30) *cassandra.yaml* file have the following configuration.

cluster_name: ' vnodecluster '
- seeds: "192.168.1.32"
listen_address: 192.168.1.30
broadcast_address: 192.168.1.30
rpc_address: 192.168.1.30
num_tokens: 2
partitioner: org.apache.cassandra.dht.Murmur3Partitioner
#initial_token: 0

Reset the node and start Cassandra on host1 first, followed by on host2. You will have a two-node cluster up and running.

In the below output, *nodetool status* shows all the nodes in the cluster and their status. The 'Token' output shows as 2, as we set *num_tokens* as 2.

The nodetool ring two token ranges for host1 (192.168.1.32) and two token ranges for host2 (192.168.1.30). If you configure *num_token* as 16, you would see 16 token ranges for each host.

```
cassandra@host1:~$ nodetool status
Datacenter: NewYork_DC
======================
Status=Up/Down
|/ State=Normal/Leaving/Joining/Moving
```

```
--   Address        Load     Tokens  Owns(effective) Host ID                                          Rack
UN  192.168.1.30  96.68 KiB  2     100.0%          681b5c33-2229-47e4-b550-3385288d0c5a rack1
UN  192.168.1.32  77.23 KiB  2     100.0%          d68756be-3c24-4147-a801-686dc628ccf6   rack1


cassandra@host1:~$ nodetool ring


Datacenter: NewYork_DC

==========

Address        Rack    Status  State    Load       Owns         Token
                                                                 8245570350364163195
192.168.1.30  rack1   Up      Normal   96.68 KiB  100.00%      -2170975102946717593
192.168.1.32  rack1   Up      Normal   77.23 KiB  100.00%      -1704036680756789190
192.168.1.32  rack1   Up      Normal   77.23 KiB  100.00%      4893218769933209714
192.168.1.30  rack1   Up      Normal   96.68 KiB  100.00%      8245570350364163195


cassandra@host1:~$
```

As mentioned in the previous chapter, create keyspace *node_mgmt* and *city* table, and insert a large amount of data.

Add Node to the Cluster or Bootstrapping

Adding nodes in a single token cluster requires token calculation and balancing the cluster. Virtual nodes simplify the task of adding new nodes to the cluster. Rebalancing of the cluster is not necessary, as nodes joining the cluster take ownership for an even portion of the data.

Bootstrapping is a process when a new node joins the cluster and gets the data streamed from other nodes in the cluster. The new node joining the cluster should be an empty node without any data. When a new node bootstraps into the cluster, the following operations happen.

1. The new node gossips with the seed node to understand the ring and token ownership of other nodes and to ensure schema agreement.
2. The new node transitions its status to UJ for Up and Joining.
3. Token range calculation happens for the assignment for the new node.

4. The current owner of those ranges starts streaming the data to the new node. This can be monitored by *nodetool netstats*.

5. Once streaming is completed, it transitions its status to UN.

In a single token cluster, since each node is responsible for one large continuous range of token, bootstrapping takes a little longer time. In virtual nodes, since many smaller range tokens are spread over the cluster, more nodes will stream the data. This allows faster streaming and rebuilding of the new node.

For adding a new node, the following is the procedure:

1. Install the same version of Cassandra on the node. Reset the host— means clear all data, commit_logs, hints, saved_caches directory. Deleting old data is very important, as most of the times the nodes we want to add to a cluster may have been used earlier in a different environment and may contain data.

2. Set the following properties in *cassandra.yaml* file on the node you are adding to the cluster. In our case, we are adding host3 (192.168.1.31).

   cluster_name: 'vnodecluster'
   - seeds: "192.168.1.32"
   listen_address: 192.168.1.31
   broadcast_address: 192.168.1.31
   rpc_address: 192.168.1.31
   num_tokens: 2
   partitioner: org.apache.cassandra.dht.Murmur3Partitioner
   auto_bootstrap: true
   #initial_token: -9223372036854775808

   Name of the *cluster_name* should match with existing cluster name. Copy the list of seed nodes from existing nodes of the cluster. Update appropriate IP address for *listen_address*, *broadcast_address*, and *rpc_address* on the new node; in our case its 192.168.1.31. Make sure to set *num_tokens* value same as the other hosts in the datacenter. Best practice is to have same *num_tokens* values across the datacenter. Make sure to use the same partitioner. Make sure you set the right values in *cassandra-rackdc.properties* or *cassandra-topology.properties* based on the snitch you use. In this example, we are using *cassandra-rackdc.properties* with datacenter as NewYork_DC.

Set *auto_bootstrap* to "true." This is not listed in the original *cassandra.yaml* file, and by default it's "true." If it exists in the *cassandra.yaml* file and is set to "false," update it to "true." Also make sure the IP address of the new node is not part of the seeds list. The new node will not bootstrap and join the cluster if it's part of the seeds list.

3. Start Cassandra on the new node.

As soon as Cassandra starts, you will see the node Up and Joining (status = UJ). You will see the following information in system.log.

> WARN [main] 2018-10-28 22:05:07,313 SystemKeyspace.java:1082 - No host ID found, created **c3b3fe2a-baac-4825-843b-a3c7d66f100e** (Note: This should happen exactly once per node).
> INFO [main] 2018-10-28 22:05:10,468 StorageService.java:818 - Starting up server gossip
> INFO [main] 2018-10-28 22:05:15,324 StorageService.java:1435 - JOINING: waiting for ring information
> INFO [InternalResponseStage:1] 2018-10-28 22:05:28,558 ColumnFamilyStore.java:406 - Initializing **node_mgmt.city**
> INFO [main] 2018-10-28 22:05:30,829 StorageService.java:1435 - JOINING: waiting for schema information to complete
> INFO [main] 2018-10-28 22:05:33,851 StorageService.java:1435 - JOINING: waiting for pending range calculation
> INFO [main] 2018-10-28 22:05:33,852 StorageService.java:1435 - JOINING: calculation complete, ready to bootstrap
> INFO [main] 2018-10-28 22:05:33,858 StorageService.java:1435 - JOINING: getting bootstrap token
>
> INFO [main] 2018-10-28 22:06:04,376 StorageService.java:1435 - JOINING: Starting to bootstrap...
> INFO [STREAM-IN-/**192.168.1.30**:7000] 2018-10-28 22:06:06,420 StreamResultFuture. java:173 - [Stream #30cb9e80-db1f-11e8-b323-495f071ce1fe ID#0] Prepare completed. **Receiving 4 files(6.119MiB),** sending 0 files(0.000KiB)

INFO [STREAM-IN-/**192.168.1.32**:7000] 2018-10-28 22:06:07,343 StreamResultFuture.
java:187 - [Stream #30cb9e80-db1f-11e8-b323-495f071ce1fe] Session with /192.168.1.32
is complete
INFO [StreamReceiveTask:1] 2018-10-28 22:06:49,909 StorageService.java:1491 -
Bootstrap completed! for the tokens **[-2923522239997868538, -6090611633803484029]**
INFO [main] 2018-10-28 22:06:50,452 StorageService.java:1435 - JOINING: Finish joining
ring

In the above output, you can see some important information like

a) Host ID created for the new cluster. This can be displayed by *nodetool status*.

```
cassandra@host3:$ nodetool status
Datacenter: NewYork_DC
=====================
Status=Up/Down
|/ State=Normal/Leaving/Joining/Moving
--  Address      Load      Tokens  Owns       Host ID                                Rack
                                   (effective)
UN  192.168.1.31  7.24 MiB  2      39.5%      c3b3fe2a-baac-4825-843b-a3c7d66f100e   rack1
UN  192.168.1.30  11.37 MiB 2      22.3%      681b5c33-2229-47e4-b550-3385288d0c5a   rack1
UN  192.168.1.32  6.63 MiB  2      38.3%      d68756be-3c24-4147-a801-686dc628ccf6   rack1
cassandra@host3:$
```

b) Streaming from host1 (192.168.1.32) and host2 (192.168.1.30). This can be viewed by **nodetool netstats** during bootstrapping.

```
cassandra@host3: $ nodetool netstats
Mode: JOINING
Bootstrap 30cb9e80-db1f-11e8-b323-495f071ce1fe
    /192.168.1.30
        Receiving 4 files, 6416081 bytes total. Already received 0 files, 58878 bytes total
            node_mgmt/city 58878/486577 bytes(12%) received from idx:0/192.168.1.30
    /192.168.1.32
```

```
Read Repair Statistics:
Attempted: 0
Mismatch (Blocking): 0
Mismatch (Background): 0
Pool Name          Active  Pending   Completed  Dropped
Large messages      n/a     0          0         0
Small messages      n/a     0          6         0
Gossip messages     n/a     0          272       0
```

c) You see that token range [-2923522239997868538, -6090611633803484029] was assigned to host3 after bootstrap from system.log message. This can be viewed in nodetool ring output.

```
cassandra@host3:$ nodetool ring

Datacenter: NewYork_DC
==========
Address        Rack    Status  State   Load       Owns     Token
                                                            8245570350364163195
192.168.1.31   rack1   Up      Normal  7.32 MiB   39.45%   -6090611633803484029
192.168.1.31   rack1   Up      Normal  7.32 MiB   39.45%   -2923522239997868538
192.168.1.30   rack1   Up      Normal  11.37 MiB  22.25%   -2170975102946717593
192.168.1.32   rack1   Up      Normal  6.63 MiB   38.30%   -1704036680756789190
192.168.1.32   rack1   Up      Normal  6.63 MiB   38.30%   4893218769933209714
192.168.1.30   rack1   Up      Normal  11.37 MiB  22.25%   8245570350364163195

cassandra@host3:$
```

4. Run *nodetool cleanup* on all existing nodes to remove the data belonging to those ranges that are assigned and streamed to the new node. Suggested best practice is to run *nodetool cleanup* one node at a time. The cleanup can be scheduled to run at off hours unless you are running low on disk space on those nodes. As you can see from the below output, data size on host2:*node_mgmt* keyspace has dropped from 12 MB to 4.2 MB after cleanup. By default, when data is streamed from one node to another, the node which no more owns that token range, but existing data is not removed for

performance issue. If you are seeing that adding new nodes did not reduce the disk usage on the old nodes, it means you forgot to run cleanup.

```
cassandra@host2:/usr/local/cassandra/data/data$ pwd
/usr/local/cassandra/data/data
cassandra@host2:/usr/local/cassandra/data/data$ du -sch *
12M    node_mgmt
448K   system
36K    system_auth
28K    system_distributed
556K   system_schema
20K    system_traces
13M    total
cassandra@host2:/usr/local/cassandra/data/data$ nodetool cleanup
cassandra@host2:/usr/local/cassandra/data/data$ du -sch *
4.2M   node_mgmt
448K   system
36K    system_auth
28K    system_distributed
556K   system_schema
20K    system_traces
5.3M   total

cassandra@host2:/usr/local/cassandra/data/data$
```

Adding Multiple Nodes

When a node is bootstrapped, Cassandra takes two minutes to ensure the range of the new node to be known to all nodes. If you are adding multiple nodes to the cluster, it may introduce consistency issues, as data may get streamed from any replicas, including new nodes. It is always recommended that you add one node at a time and wait for the node to bootstrap and join completely before you add the next node.

But this may not be efficient in some shops, and you may want to add nodes simultaneously (two minutes apart from each bootstrap).

In this case, start each node with **consistent.rangemovement** property turned off. In package installation you can set this in *cassandra-env.sh* or *jvm.options*.

JVM_OPTS="$JVM_OPTS -Dcassandra.consistent.rangemovement=false

Or you can start Cassandra with this option like

$CASSANDRA_HOME/ bin/cassandra -Dcassandra.consistent.rangemovement=false

After node is bootstrapped, you can remove this option from the *cassandra-env.sh* or *jvm. options* file.

Bootstrap Seed Node

If the node you are adding is a seed node, you cannot update the "seeds" in *cassandra.yaml* and bootstrap it. It will not join the cluster. What you need to do is, add it as a regular node, and once it bootstraps and joins the cluster, you can promote it as a seed node. To promote that as seed node, follow the below procedure.

1. Stop Cassandra on the new node.
2. Update *cassandra.yaml* file, and update the nodes' IP address in the seed provider list.
3. Make the same change on all other nodes in the cluster.
4. Start Cassandra on the new node.
5. Do a rolling restart of the cluster.

Replacing a Dead Node in the Cluster

Replacing a dead node in the cluster is very simple. Note that before bringing host3 down to simulate the dead node, the replication factor for keyspace node_mgmt has increased to 2 from 1. If RF = 1 and you have a dead node, it means no other node has that data, and they can't stream.

Following is the procedure.

1. Find the node that is down by running nodetool status.

```
cassandra@host1:~$ nodetool status
Datacenter: NewYork_DC
=======================
Status=Up/Down
|/ State=Normal/Leaving/Joining/Moving
--  Address       Load       Tokens  Owns      Host ID                                    Rack
                                      (effective)
DN  192.168.1.31 10.65 MiB  2        57.6%     c3b3fe2a-baac-4825-843b-a3c7d66f100e   rack1
UN  192.168.1.30 18.35 MiB  2        100.0%    681b5c33-2229-47e4-b550-3385288d0c5a rack1
UN  192.168.1.32  7.86 MiB  2        42.4%     d68756be-3c24-4147-a801-686dc628ccf6   rack1

cassandra@host1:~$
```

2. If the dead node is a seed node, update all the nodes in the cluster, and remove the IP address of the dead node, and restart the nodes.
3. Make sure new replacement node has Cassandra installed, and reset the node by clearing all the data.
4. Verify the replacement node to make sure the below settings match the node that is dead. A dead node may be not accessible, but mostly the configuration of all the nodes in a datacenter will have the same configuration. So in that case, you can compare and update the replacement node with the existing node.

   Update *seeds, cluster_name, endpoint_snitch, num_tokens, listen_address, rpc_address, broadcast_rpc_address* in *cassandra.yaml*
   If you are using *GossipingPropertyFileSnitch*, make sure to update the **dc** and **rack** in *cassandra-rackdc.properties* file.
   Set the *auto_bootstrap* value to true.

5. On the replacement node (host4 in our case) *cassandra-env.sh* file or *jvm.options* file, add or update the below line

    In jvm.options
    # To replace a node that has died, restart a new node in its place specifying the address of the
    # dead node. The new node must not have any data in its data directory, that is, it must be in the
    # same state as before bootstrapping.
    -Dcassandra.replace_address=192.168.1.31
    Or in Cassandra-env.sh
    JVM_OPTS="$JVM_OPTS -Dcassandra.replace_address=192.168.1.31"

6. Start Cassandra on the replacement node. The replicas of the token range owned by the dead nodes will start streaming the data to the new replacement node. In our case, the new node is 192.1.168.34. You can see the streaming on those nodes by running nodetool netstats.

7.

```
cassandra@host4:$ nodetool netstats
Mode: JOINING
Bootstrap 617d8170-db28-11e8-9ddd-df1e5794fb02
    /192.168.1.30
        Receiving 3 files, 9422527 bytes total. Already received 0 files, 795073 bytes total
            node_mgmt/city 795073/9420769 bytes(8%) received from idx:0/192.168.1.30
Read Repair Statistics:
Attempted: 0
Mismatch (Blocking): 0
Mismatch (Background): 0
```

Pool Name	Active	Pending	Completed	Dropped
Large messages	n/a	1	0	0
Small messages	n/a	1	6	0
Gossip messages	n/a	1	414	0

Also you see information message in system.log of changing ownership of dead node 192.168.1.31 to new node 192.168.1.33.

INFO [main] 2018-10-28 23:11:21,082 StorageService.java:1435 - JOINING: Replacing a node with token(s): [-2923522239997868538, -6090611633803484029]
INFO [main] 2018-10-28 23:11:21,532 StorageService.java:1435 - JOINING: sleeping 30000 ms for pending range setup
WARN [PendingRangeCalculator:1] 2018-10-28 23:11:21,601 TokenMetadata.java:215 - Token -2923522239997868538 changing ownership from /192.168.1.31 to /192.168.1.33
WARN [PendingRangeCalculator:1] 2018-10-28 23:11:21,605 TokenMetadata.java:215 - Token -6090611633803484029 changing ownership from /192.168.1.31 to /192.168.1.33
WARN [PendingRangeCalculator:1] 2018-10-28 23:11:21,665 TokenMetadata.java:215 - Token -2923522239997868538 changing ownership from /192.168.1.31 to /192.168.1.33
WARN [PendingRangeCalculator:1] 2018-10-28 23:11:21,669 TokenMetadata.java:215 - Token -6090611633803484029 changing ownership from /192.168.1.31 to /192.168.1.33
WARN [PendingRangeCalculator:1] 2018-10-28 23:11:21,686 TokenMetadata.java:215 - Token -2923522239997868538 changing ownership from /192.168.1.31 to /192.168.1.33
WARN [PendingRangeCalculator:1] 2018-10-28 23:11:21,692 TokenMetadata.java:215 - Token -6090611633803484029 changing ownership from /192.168.1.31 to /192.168.1.33
WARN [PendingRangeCalculator:1] 2018-10-28 23:11:21,723 TokenMetadata.java:215 - Token -2923522239997868538 changing ownership from /192.168.1.31 to /192.168.1.33
WARN [PendingRangeCalculator:1] 2018-10-28 23:11:21,727 TokenMetadata.java:215 - Token -6090611633803484029 changing ownership from /192.168.1.31 to /192.168.1.33
INFO [main] 2018-10-28 23:11:51,544 StorageService.java:1435 - JOINING: Starting to bootstrap...
WARN [main] 2018-10-28 23:11:51,587 TokenMetadata.java:215 - Token -2923522239997868538 changing ownership from /192.168.1.31 to /192.168.1.33
WARN [main] 2018-10-28 23:11:51,593 TokenMetadata.java:215 - Token -6090611633803484029 changing ownership from /192.168.1.31 to /192.168.1.33
WARN [main] 2018-10-28 23:11:51,671 TokenMetadata.java:215 - Token -2923522239997868538 changing ownership from /192.168.1.31 to /192.168.1.33
WARN [main] 2018-10-28 23:11:51,694 TokenMetadata.java:215 - Token -6090611633803484029 changing ownership from /192.168.1.31 to /192.168.1.33

8. Once node joins the cluster, you can verify that it has replaced the old node. Also you will notice that the new node (192.168.1.33) has taken over the range owned by dead node (192.168.1.31). In the below output, you see that *nodetool status* before replacement and after replacement and also the token range for the new bootstrapped node.

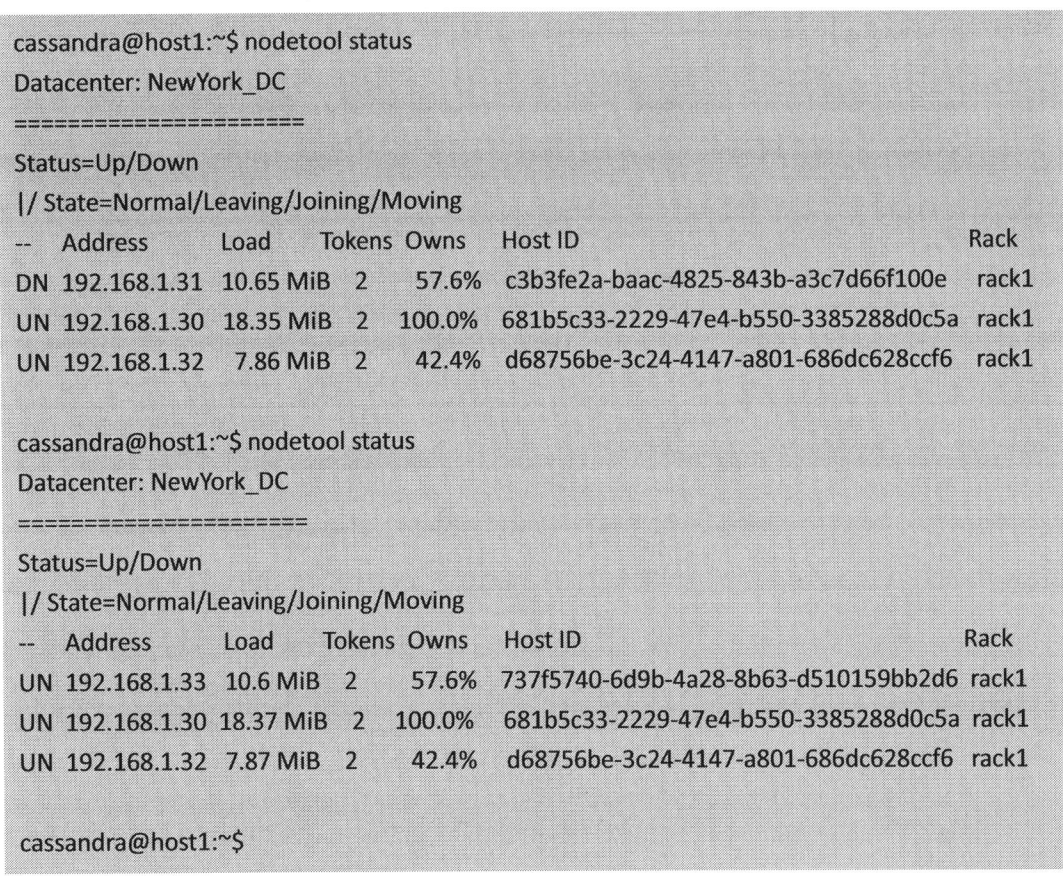

```
cassandra@host1:~$ nodetool status
Datacenter: NewYork_DC
=======================
Status=Up/Down
|/ State=Normal/Leaving/Joining/Moving
--  Address        Load       Tokens  Owns    Host ID                               Rack
DN  192.168.1.31  10.65 MiB  2       57.6%   c3b3fe2a-baac-4825-843b-a3c7d66f100e  rack1
UN  192.168.1.30  18.35 MiB  2       100.0%  681b5c33-2229-47e4-b550-3385288d0c5a  rack1
UN  192.168.1.32   7.86 MiB  2       42.4%   d68756be-3c24-4147-a801-686dc628ccf6  rack1


cassandra@host1:~$ nodetool status
Datacenter: NewYork_DC
=======================
Status=Up/Down
|/ State=Normal/Leaving/Joining/Moving
--  Address        Load       Tokens  Owns    Host ID                               Rack
UN  192.168.1.33  10.6 MiB   2       57.6%   737f5740-6d9b-4a28-8b63-d510159bb2d6  rack1
UN  192.168.1.30  18.37 MiB  2       100.0%  681b5c33-2229-47e4-b550-3385288d0c5a  rack1
UN  192.168.1.32   7.87 MiB  2       42.4%   d68756be-3c24-4147-a801-686dc628ccf6  rack1


cassandra@host1:~$
```

Remove Node

To remove a node, run *nodetool status* to check if the node you want to remove is up or down. If the node is up and running, follow the below procedure to decommission the node.

If the node is down, use *nodetool removenode* command. If *nodetool removenode* fails, run *nodetool assassinate* <ip address> command.

Decommission Node

Decommissioning of a node can be done only if it is up and running. Login to the node you want to decommission and run

nodetool decommission

The procedures to decommission a node or remove a node (downed node) are simple. But what you need to consider is the cluster setup, replication factor, and how consistency is used in your application. This is very critical when it comes to reducing the size of the cluster.

For example, say you have an eighteen-node cluster with two datacenters configured as in *Figure 8.1*.

Cassandra Admin DBA Guide

cassandra-rackdc.properties

node1 : dc=USWEST, rack=rack1   node10 : dc=USEAST, rack=rack1
node2 : dc=USWEST, rack=rack2   node11 : dc=USEAST, rack=rack2
node3 : dc=USWEST, rack=rack3   node12 : dc=USEAST, rack=rack3

node4 : dc=USWEST, rack=rack1   node13 : dc=USEAST, rack=rack1
node5 :dc=USWEST, rack=rack2   node14 : dc=USEAST, rack=rack2
node6 : dc=USWEST, rack=rack3   node15 : dc=USEAST, rack=rack3

node7 : dc=USWEST, rack=rack1   node16 : dc=USEAST, rack=rack1
node8 : dc=USWEST, rack=rack2   node17 : dc=USEAST, rack=rack2
node9 : dc=USWEST, rack=rack3   node18 : dc=USEAST, rack=rack3

Figure 8.1: 18 node cluster with two datacenters.

In *Figure 8.1*, the cluster is configured to have two datacenters — each datacenter with nine nodes and three racks. Normally, in a configuration like this, the replication factor is always configured as three, so that you can have more control over where the data is written. Now if you decide to decommission node5 from USWEST datacenter, it could pose some problems. By decommissioning node5, now you are left with only two nodes in USWEST.rack2 i.e node2 and node8. If one of the nodes (node2 or node8 – rack2) is down or going through a heavy load and not accessible, your LOCAL_QUORUM or EACH_QUORUM for read or write will fail, causing application outage.

CHAPTER 9

Cassandra Multi-datacenter

Cassandra cluster is made up of one or more datacenters. A datacenter is a group of nodes and can be seen as a concept of real datacenters. You usually create a Cassandra datacenter based on the location of the physical datacenters. But you can also create virtual datacenters where all the nodes belong to the same physical datacenters. All this is done by configuration, which we will go through later in this chapter.

For example, below is a Cassandra cluster of thirty-six nodes with four datacenters.

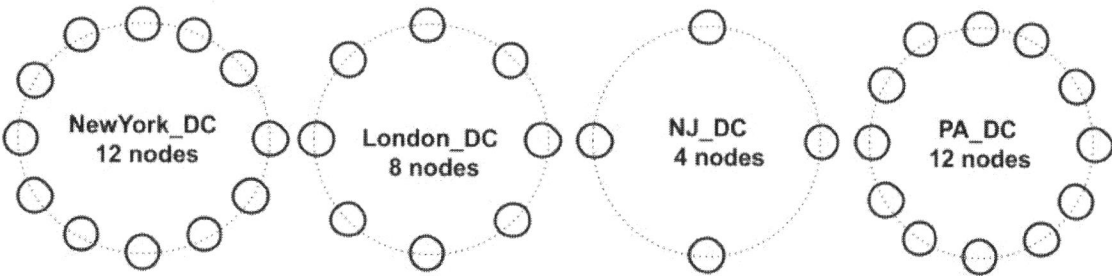

Figure 9.1: Multi-datacenter.

Use Case

Why create multiple datacenters? Cassandra's replication supports multiple datacenters and cloud availability zones. Replication is easy to set up and modify. The combination of multi-datacenters and replication has many use cases.

Disaster Recovery

Multiple datacenters and cloud availability zones ensure constant uptime for application. Setting up multiple datacenters makes sure that even if you lose one entire datacenter, applications can connect to a datacenter that is up. Applications can be designed to route requests to the appropriate datacenter based on availability.

In Figure 9.1, NewYork_DC and PA_DC Cassandra nodes are in different physical datacenters, and one of them can be used as a disaster recovery datacenter.

Geographic Location

In certain situations, data need to be available and stored in different geographic locations. This way, an application or user can read or write data in a datacenter from the same region for faster read & write performance. For example, from the above picture, applications or users from London can read or write to London_DC instead of NewYork_DC, which can add additional latency.

Another use case for a geographic location would be to store certain data locally in that country. There are emerging legal and trade trend in which you need to store data locally in that country. Cassandra can be configured easily to store certain data locally to satisfy the legal restrictions from that country.

For example, reference to *Figure 9.1*, you can create a keyspace to store certain tables only in London_DC.

Example of Keyspace creation.

```
CREATE KEYSPACE UKClientInfo WITH REPLICATION = {
'class' : 'NetworkTopologyStrategy',
'London_DC': '3'
};
```

Live Backup Datacenter

The replication strategy can be configured to have an entire datacenter as a live backup, in case of disaster. For example, NJ_DC can be configured as a live backup datacenter with *replication_factor*=2. So in this case, none of your read or write goes to NJ_DC.

Example of Keyspace creation.

```
CREATE KEYSPACE ClientInfo WITH REPLICATION = {
        'class' : 'NetworkTopologyStrategy',
        'NewYork_DC' : '3' ,
        'PA_DC': '3',
        'London_DC': '3',
        'NJ_DC': '2'
};
```

Workload Separation

Datacenters can be built to separate workload. For example, you can run analytics on one datacenter whereas reporting on another datacenter.

There are certain use cases where data is injected into the cluster for temporary processing purpose. Once the data is processed and inserted into another table, the temporary data gets truncated. Refer "Keyspace Separation" in *Chapter 5, Cassandra Data Modeling*.

Multi datacenter hosts

For this entire chapter, we will use the following six nodes and in detail learn on below topics.

- Build a single datacenter, NewYork_DC using 3-nodes.
- Create keyspace, table and set replication.
- Add a 3-node new datacenter, NJ_DC, to existing cluster and alter the replication.
- Decommission the entire datacenter, NJ_DC.

hostname	IP Address	seed	cassandra-rackdc.properties
host1	192.168.1.32	Yes	dc=NewYork_DC rack=rack1
host2	192.168.1.30	No	dc=NewYork_DC rack=rack1
host3	192.168.1.31	No	dc=NewYork_DC rack=rack1
host4	192.168.1.33	Yes	dc=NJ_DC rack=rack1
host5	192.168.1.82	No	dc=NJ_DC rack=rack1
host6	192.168.1.83	No	dc=NJ_DC rack=rack1

Figure 9.2: Hosts and IP addresses.

Start New Single Datacenter Cluster

First, we will set up a three-node cluster. We will use host1, host2, and host3 to setup the cluster by making host1 as a seed node.

Once a three-node cluster with a single datacenter, NewYork_DC, is up and running, we will create a keyspace and create some data.

We will add host4, host5, and host6 as a second datacenter to this existing cluster. We will go through all the steps to set up a multi-datacenter cluster.

Start NewYork_DC

Make sure to reset the node on host1, host2, and host3. Refer "Reset Node" in *Chapter 7, "Cassandra Node Management—Single Token"*.

Set $CASSANDRA_HOME/conf/*cassandra-rackdc.properties* values as shown in *Figure 9.2*. We will build both datacenters, NewYork_DC and NJ_DC with only one RACK - rack1.

Set the below configuration in *cassandra.yaml* on host1, host2, and host3.

```
cluster_name: 'multidc'
- seeds: "192.168.1.32"
partitioner: org.apache.cassandra.dht.Murmur3Partitioner
endpoint_snitch: GossipingPropertyFileSnitch
num_tokens: 3
listen_address: <ip of the host>
rpc_address: <ip of the host>
```

Start Cassandra on host1. As this is the seed node, we need to start this node first.

Start Cassandra on host2 and host3. Now cluster 'multidc' is up and running with three nodes.

```
cassandra@host1:~$ nodetool status
Datacenter: NewYork_DC
======================
Status=Up/Down
|/ State=Normal/Leaving/Joining/Moving
--  Address        Load        Tokens  Owns        Host ID                               Rack
                                       (effective)
UN  192.168.1.31   78.39 KiB   3       58.4%       1151d63b-9fa2-4eb3-a708-abe910d7e275  rack1
UN  192.168.1.30   131.04 KiB  3       84.1%       b24abb0d-a30a-457a-93ce-4d6e7ad666e9  rack1
UN  192.168.1.32   124.41 KiB  3       57.6%       10ecaf81-844c-4065-b302-7d5ca4305055  rack1
cassandra@host1:~$
```

Once a single datacenter cluster is up and running, create below keyspace and table. We are creating the keyspace with 'SimpleStrategy' strategy and 1 replica.

```
CREATE KEYSPACE node_mgmt
WITH  replication = { 'class':'SimpleStrategy', 'replication_factor':1 };

CREATE TABLE node_mgmt.city
  (
    id    int,
    city   text,
    comment text,
    PRIMARY KEY (id,city)
  );
```

You can view the current replication setup for all keyspaces by running below query. As you can see from the output, all the keyspaces are created with *'SimpleStrategy'*. For a multi-datacenter setup, this needs to be modified to *"NetworkTopologyStrategy'*. *'NetworkTopologyStrategy'* is highly recommended for most deployments because it is much easier to expand to multiple datacenters when required.

```
cassandra@cqlsh> select keyspace_name,replication from system_schema.keyspaces ;

 keyspace_name    | replication
------------------------+-----------------------------------------------------------------------------------
      system_auth | {'class': 'org.apache.cassandra.locator.SimpleStrategy', 'replication_factor': '1'}
     system_schema |                         {'class': 'org.apache.cassandra.locator.LocalStrategy'}
        node_mgmt | {'class': 'org.apache.cassandra.locator.SimpleStrategy', 'replication_factor': '1'}
system_distributed | {'class': 'org.apache.cassandra.locator.SimpleStrategy', 'replication_factor': '3'}
            system |                         {'class': 'org.apache.cassandra.locator.LocalStrategy'}
    system_traces | {'class': 'org.apache.cassandra.locator.SimpleStrategy', 'replication_factor': '2'}

(6 rows)
```

Now insert data into *city* table by copying about a million rows. The reason we are creating the data is so that when we add a second datacenter to the existing cluster, you can see streaming happening. Insert data as discussed in the earlier *Chapter 7, "Cassandra Node Management—Single Token"*.

```
cassandra@cqlsh> COPY node_mgmt.city FROM '/tmp/city.txt';
Using 1 child processes

Starting copy of node_mgmt.city with columns [id, city, comment].
1079991 rows imported from 1 files in 9 minutes and 42.993 seconds (0 skipped).
cassandra@cqlsh>
```

Add datacenter to existing cluster.

We have an existing cluster "multidc" with single datacenter "NewYork_DC." We will follow the below procedure to add a new datacenter "NJ_DC" to the existing cluster.

Step 1: Make sure that host4, host5, and host6 have the same version of Cassandra installed. Make sure to reset the node.

Step 2: Set $CASSANDRA_HOME/conf/*cassandra-rackdc.properties* values as shown in *Figure 9.2*.

Step 3: On host4, host5, and host6, edit *cassandra.yaml* file and update with the following configuration values.

```
cluster_name: 'multidc'
- seeds: "192.168.1.32"
partitioner: org.apache.cassandra.dht.Murmur3Partitioner
endpoint_snitch: GossipingPropertyFileSnitch
num_tokens: 3
listen_address: <ip of the host>
rpc_address: <ip of the host>
```

We are matching *endpoint_snitch*, *seeds*, *cluster_name* from one of the existing node from NewYork_DC hosts. For adding the new datacenter, *cassandra-rackdc.properties* values are important for these nodes. As you see in *Figure 9.2*, these are set to

dc=NJ_DC
rack=rack1

Step 4: Make sure *auto_bootstrap* is set to *'false'*.

If this entry is missing in *cassandra.yaml* file, it defaults to 'true'. So add it. Setting this value to *'false'* prevents the node from getting the data from other nodes. We will be using *nodetool rebuild* command to get the data from the existing datacenter, which is NewYork_DC.

Step 5: Before we start any Cassandra node in the new NJ_DC datacenter, make sure that any clients that connect to the cluster will not auto-discover these new nodes. Since there is no bootstrap phase for these nodes, it means they are up and online instantly with no data. We need to wait until the rebuild is run on all nodes before any clients can discover these nodes.

If your application is using consistency level QUORUM or EACH_QUORUM for writes and reads, check to make sure that the newly added datacenter meets all the requirements for this multi-datacenter setup. Consider using LOCAL_QUORUM if your use case allows for a multi-datacenter setup.

Step 5: Start all Cassandra nodes in the new datacenter. In our case it's host4, host5, and host6.

```
cassandra@host1:~$ nodetool status
Datacenter: NJ_DC
==================
Status=Up/Down
|/ State=Normal/Leaving/Joining/Moving
--  Address        Load       Tokens  Owns        Host ID                                Rack
                                       (effective)
UN  192.168.1.33  106.85 KiB  3       11.5%       02e60819-b00e-4221-8c28-a75fc4ffd546   rack1
UN  192.168.1.82  24.26 KiB   3       10.7%       31c467d3-236f-4538-936c-82598377a853   rack1
```

```
UN 192.168.1.83   19.54 KiB   3      23.5%        b00313b2-2daf-4c39-bc65-5595463e198c  rack1
Datacenter: NewYork_DC
=====================
Status=Up/Down
|/ State=Normal/Leaving/Joining/Moving
--   Address       Load     Tokens  Owns      Host ID                                    Rack
                                    (effective)
UN 192.168.1.31   1.77 MiB   3      6.0%        1151d63b-9fa2-4eb3-a708-abe910d7e275   rack1
UN 192.168.1.30   4.5 MiB    3      31.6%       b24abb0d-a30a-457a-93ce-4d6e7ad666e9  rack1
UN 192.168.1.32   4.46 MiB   3      16.7%       10ecaf81-844c-4065-b302-7d5ca4305055   rack1
```

Step 6: Alter replication topology and *replication_factor*.

A replication strategy determines the nodes where replicas are placed. The total number of replicas across the cluster is referred to as the replication factor, which is configured for each datacenter. A replication factor of 2 means two copies of the data, where each copy is on a different node within that datacenter. Once all nodes are up and running, alter the keyspaces to change the replication strategy from *SimpleStrategy* to *NetworkTopologyStrategy,* and extend on to the new datacenter NJ_DC with replication factor as 1. If you forgot to alter the replication, the rebuild would not populate data in the new datacenter.

You also have to alter the system keyspaces *system_distributed*, *system_auth*, and *system_traces* to rebuild to work.

```
ALTER KEYSPACE node_mgmt WITH
replication = {'class':'NetworkTopologyStrategy','NewYork_DC' : 1, 'NJ_DC':1};

ALTER KEYSPACE system_auth WITH
replication = {'class':'NetworkTopologyStrategy','NewYork_DC' : 1, 'NJ_DC':1};

ALTER KEYSPACE system_distributed WITH
replication= {'class':'NetworkTopologyStrategy','NewYork_DC' : 1, 'NJ_DC':1};

ALTER KEYSPACE system_traces WITH
replication= {'class':'NetworkTopologyStrategy','NewYork_DC' : 1, 'NJ_DC':1};
```

```
SELECT replication FROM system_schema.keyspaces WHERE keyspace_name='node_mgmt' ;

replication
---------------------------------------------------------------------------------------------------
{'NJ_DC': '1', 'NewYork_DC': '1', 'class': 'org.apache.cassandra.locator.NetworkTopologyStrategy'}

Run SELECT keyspace,replication FROM system_schema.keyspaces; to display for all kespaces.
```

Step 7: Run *nodetool rebuild*

The *nodetool rebuild* is similar to the bootstrapping process, mainly used when you are adding a new datacenter. We added the new datacenter nodes by setting *auto_bootstrap*=false. All NJ_DC datacenters live nodes are empty at this moment. This command rebuilds a node's data by streaming data from other nodes in the cluster; in our case, we will be rebuilding the NJ_DC nodes by NewYork_DC nodes. Run the following command on host4, host5, and host6.

```
cassandra@host4:~$ $CASSANDRA_HOME/bin/nodetool rebuild -- NewYork_DC
```

You are rebuilding all keyspaces, tables from NewYork_DC. This will start streaming data from nodes in NewYork_DC. You will see a rebuild message in system.log like below. You can see in system.log the streaming sessions with host1, host2, and host3.

```
INFO  [RMI TCP Connection(2)-127.0.0.1] 2018-10-26 17:41:46,951 StorageService.java:1168 -
rebuild from dc: NewYork_DC, (All keyspaces), (All tokens)
INFO  [RMI TCP Connection(2)-127.0.0.1] 2018-10-26 17:41:47,397 StreamResultFuture.java:90 -
[Stream #f03ba620-d967-11e8-8a67-a1ca380a0681] Executing streaming plan for Rebuild
INFO  [StreamConnectionEstablisher:1] 2018-10-26 17:41:47,587 StreamCoordinator.java:264
- [Stream #f03ba620-d967-11e8-8a67-a1ca380a0681, ID#0] Beginning stream session with
/192.168.1.31
INFO  [StreamConnectionEstablisher:1] 2018-10-26 17:41:47,640 StreamCoordinator.java:264
- [Stream #f03ba620-d967-11e8-8a67-a1ca380a0681, ID#0] Beginning stream session with
/192.168.1.30
```

```
INFO [StreamConnectionEstablisher:1] 2018-10-26 17:41:47,705 StreamCoordinator.java:264
- [Stream #f03ba620-d967-11e8-8a67-a1ca380a0681, ID#0] Beginning stream session with
/192.168.1.32
[...]
INFO [StreamReceiveTask:1] 2018-10-26 17:42:02,928 StreamResultFuture.java:187 - [Stream
#f03ba620-d967-11e8-8a67-a1ca380a0681] Session with /192.168.1.31 is complete
INFO [StreamReceiveTask:1] 2018-10-26 17:42:04,566 StreamResultFuture.java:187 - [Stream
#f03ba620-d967-11e8-8a67-a1ca380a0681] Session with /192.168.1.32 is complete
INFO [StreamReceiveTask:1] 2018-10-26 17:42:07,502 StreamResultFuture.java:187 - [Stream
#f03ba620-d967-11e8-8a67-a1ca380a0681] Session with /192.168.1.30 is complete
INFO [StreamReceiveTask:1] 2018-10-26 17:42:07,578 StreamResultFuture.java:219 - [Stream
#f03ba620-d967-11e8-8a67-a1ca380a0681] All sessions completed
```

If you get an error like below, it means you have forgotten to alter one of the system's keyspace replication_factor. Alter the keyspace replication factor to expand on NJ_DC, and rerun the rebuild command. If rebuild fails, you can always restart it.

```
cassandra@host4:~$ nodetool rebuild -- NewYork_DC
nodetool: Unable to find sufficient sources for streaming range (-3074457345618258603,3074457
345618258601] in keyspace system_traces
```

You can rebuild on more than one node in parallel. Make sure that your cluster can handle the network pressure and disk I/O. In a running production cluster with 300–500 GB data per node, this may take a few hours based on your network bandwidth and current load on the cluster. To speed up the rebuild process, you can increase the compaction throughput.

Run below command to get current throughput and set the new throughput.

```
#get current compaction throughput for the node
$nodetool getcompactionthroughput

#set compaction throughput to 32 MB. It's always in MB
$nodetool setcompactionthroughput 32
```

It is recommended to run this operation during a quiet time. Note that, if you forgot to mention -- <source DC> in the rebuild, it might appear that the rebuild has run, but you won't see any data. Check the $CASSANDRA_HOME/data/data directory to verify.

Run *nodetool netstats* to monitor streaming activity. In the below output, you can see rebuild is running on host5 and host6.

```
cassandra@host1:~$ $CASSANDRA_HOME/bin/nodetool netstats
Mode: NORMAL
Rebuild b4437280-d96a-11e8-a420-5333b5c2db0e
  /192.168.1.82
     Sending 3 files, 1626156 bytes total. Already sent 2 files, 1457555 bytes total
        /usr/local/apache-cassandra-3.10/data/data/node_mgmt/city-95ab-
d2c0d93511e8a51ae59d1b0ded96/mc-6-big-Data.db 285485/285485 bytes(100%) sent to
idx:0/192.168.1.82
        /usr/local/apache-cassandra-3.10/data/data/node_mgmt/city-95ab-
d2c0d93511e8a51ae59d1b0ded96/mc-5-big-Data.db 1172070/1172070 bytes(100%) sent to
idx:0/192.168.1.82
Rebuild b40aaf40-d96a-11e8-aa50-9f90be2e92e2
  /192.168.1.83
     Sending 3 files, 2160951 bytes total. Already sent 3 files, 2160951 bytes total
        /usr/local/apache-cassandra-3.10/data/data/node_mgmt/city-95ab-
d2c0d93511e8a51ae59d1b0ded96/mc-6-big-Data.db 382945/382945 bytes(100%) sent to
idx:0/192.168.1.83
        /usr/local/apache-cassandra-3.10/data/data/node_mgmt/city-95ab-
d2c0d93511e8a51ae59d1b0ded96/mc-7-big-Data.db 226032/226032 bytes(100%) sent to
idx:0/192.168.1.83
        /usr/local/apache-cassandra-3.10/data/data/node_mgmt/city-95ab-
d2c0d93511e8a51ae59d1b0ded96/mc-5-big-Data.db 1551974/1551974 bytes(100%) sent to
idx:0/192.168.1.83
Read Repair Statistics:
Attempted: 0
Mismatch (Blocking): 0
Mismatch (Background): 0
Pool Name              Active  Pending   Completed  Dropped
```

Large messages	n/a	0	0	0
Small messages	n/a	0	104	0
Gossip messages	n/a	0	117152	0

Decommissioning Datacenter NJ_DC

Decommission of a datacenter should be a planned event. Care must be taken before decommissioning a datacenter from the production cluster. Follow the below procedure to decommission datacenter NJ_DC from "multidc" cluster.

Step 1: Make sure all the nodes are up in the cluster, especially the datacenter you want to decommission. Run *nodetool status* to check this information.

Step 2: Make sure there is no read or write traffic on the datacenter you want to decommission. One way to check is to run *netstat -an | grep 9042 | grep ESTABLISHED* on all the nodes in the datacenter. In our case, run on host4, host5, and host6, which are configured as NJ_DC.

9042 is the native port configured in *cassandra.yaml*.

cassandra@host3:/usr/local/cassandra$ grep 9042 conf/*cassandra.yaml*

native_transport_port: 9042

As an example below, we could see a connection (cqlsh) on host4.

```
cassandra@host4:~$ netstat -an | grep 9042
tcp    0    0 192.168.1.33:9042     0.0.0.0:*          LISTEN
tcp    0    0 192.168.1.33:9042     192.168.1.33:49918    ESTABLISHED
tcp    0    0 192.168.1.33:9042     192.168.1.33:49919    ESTABLISHED
tcp    0    0 192.168.1.33:49918    192.168.1.33:9042     ESTABLISHED
tcp    0    0 192.168.1.33:49919    192.168.1.33:9042     ESTABLISHED
```

Step 3: Any data updated with the latest timestamp on the decommissioning cluster needs to be propagated to every datacenter. To make sure of this, run a full repair. The repair will make all the data consistent across the cluster.

Step 4: Alter all keyspaces to remove replication for the decommissioned datacenter. Take a full schema backup before you disable replication.

```
ALTER KEYSPACE node_mgmt WITH
replication = {'class':'NetworkTopologyStrategy','NewYork_DC' : 1};

ALTER KEYSPACE system_auth WITH
replication={ 'class':'NetworkTopologyStrategy','NewYork_DC' : 1};

ALTER KEYSPACE system_distributed WITH
replication={ 'class':'NetworkTopologyStrategy','NewYork_DC' : 1};

ALTER KEYSPACE system_traces WITH
replication= {'class':'NetworkTopologyStrategy','NewYork_DC' : 1};

SELECT keyspace_name,replication FROM system_schema.keyspaces ;

 keyspace_name     | replication
-------------------------+-----------------------------------------------------------------------------------------
system_auth|{'NewYork_DC': '1', 'class': 'org.apache.cassandra.locator.NetworkTopologyStrategy'}
system_schema|{'class': 'org.apache.cassandra.locator.LocalStrategy'}
node_mgmt|{'NewYork_DC': '1', 'class': 'org.apache.cassandra.locator.NetworkTopologyStrategy'}
system_distributed|{'NewYork_DC':'1', 'class':'org.apache.cassandra.locator.NetworkTopologyStrategy'}
system |{'class': 'org.apache.cassandra.locator.LocalStrategy'}
system_traces |{'NewYork_DC': '1', 'class':'org.apache.cassandra.locator.
NetworkTopologyStrategy'}

(6 rows)
```

In SELECT * FROM system_schema.keyspaces; output: you should not see any keyspace replicating to NJ_DC datacenter.

Step 5: Start decommissioning each node in the datacenter—in our case, host4, host5, and host6.

```
Run
$CASSANDRA_HOME/bin/nodetool decommission.
```

You will see following INFO messages in the system.log.

```
INFO [RMI TCP Connection(8)-127.0.0.1] 2018-10-26 18:44:48,115 StorageService.java:1435 -
LEAVING: sleeping 30000 ms for batch processing and pending range setup
INFO [RMI TCP Connection(8)-127.0.0.1] 2018-10-26 18:45:18,211 StorageService.java:1435 -
LEAVING: replaying batch log and streaming data to other nodes
INFO [RMI TCP Connection(8)-127.0.0.1] 2018-10-26 18:45:18,241 StreamResultFuture.java:90 -
[Stream #cfe75910-d970-11e8-8a67-a1ca380a0681] Executing streaming plan for Unbootstrap
INFO [HintsDispatcher:2] 2018-10-26 18:45:18,386 HintsDispatchExecutor.java:152 - Transferring
all hints to 31c467d3-236f-4538-936c-82598377a853
INFO [RMI TCP Connection(8)-127.0.0.1] 2018-10-26 18:45:18,815 StorageService.java:2505 -
Removing tokens [-4043924615920211521, -7458695136978899856, -8888314017202525064]
for /192.168.1.33
INFO [RMI TCP Connection(8)-127.0.0.1] 2018-10-26 18:45:19,328 StorageService.java:3938 -
Announcing that I have left the ring for 30000ms
INFO [RMI TCP Connection(8)-127.0.0.1] 2018-10-26 18:45:50,113 StorageService.java:1435
– DECOMMISSIONED
```

Step 6: If you are using *PropertyFileSnitch* as *endpoint_snitch*, you need to do additional steps.

Once all the nodes are decommissioned, wait for seventy-two hours, and then you need to update $CASSANDRA_HOME/conf/*cassandra-topology.properties* on all the nodes in the cluster and remove the entries for nodes belonging to the datacenter being decommissioned. In our case, you need to update all nodes in NewYork_DC (host1, host2, and host3) and remove entries for NJ_DC (host4, host5, and host6) nodes.

If you remove the entries too soon, problems may result. Use **nodetool gossipinfo** to check the gossip status.

Get a downtime, and do a rolling restart of all the nodes in all other datacenters, one at a time. Best practice is to perform this rolling restart one datacenter at a time.

But since we are using *endpoint_sntich* as *GossipingPropertyFileSnitch*, we don't need to run this step. When using *GossipingPropertyFileSnitch*, $CASSANDRA_HOME/conf/*cassandra-rackdc. properties* file does not contain any IP address of other hosts; therefore, you don't need this step.

Single Token Multi-Datacenter Setup

If you are building a single token multi-datacenter, you need to avoid token collisions. For a single token cluster, you comment out *num_token* (which is used only for virtual node), and you provide *initial_token* value for the node. In the entire cluster, whether it's single datacenter or multi-datacenter, no two nodes can have the same *initial_token*. If two or more nodes have the same *initial_token*, it is called collision. So it's important to review the *initial_token* for each node when you add a new datacenter to the cluster. *Figure 9.3* shows a wrong setup of token for the cluster with three datacenters; all three have the same *initial_token* configured for Murmur3Partitioner.

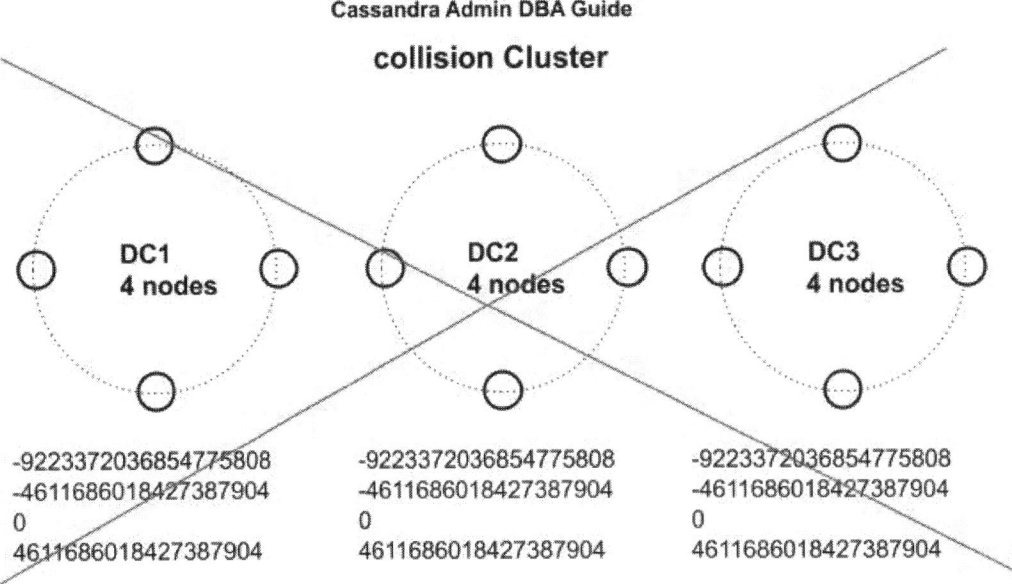

Figure 9.3: Single token datacenter (collision).

Note that every datacenter will be having an entire token range (in this example, it's Murmur3Partitioner), but you need to configure token offset for each datacenter so that tokens will not collide. In Figure 9.4 below, we have configured three datacenters with four nodes each. As you see, each token of the node in DC2 is offset by 40 with DC1. Similarly, each token of the node in DC3 is offset by 40 with DC2.

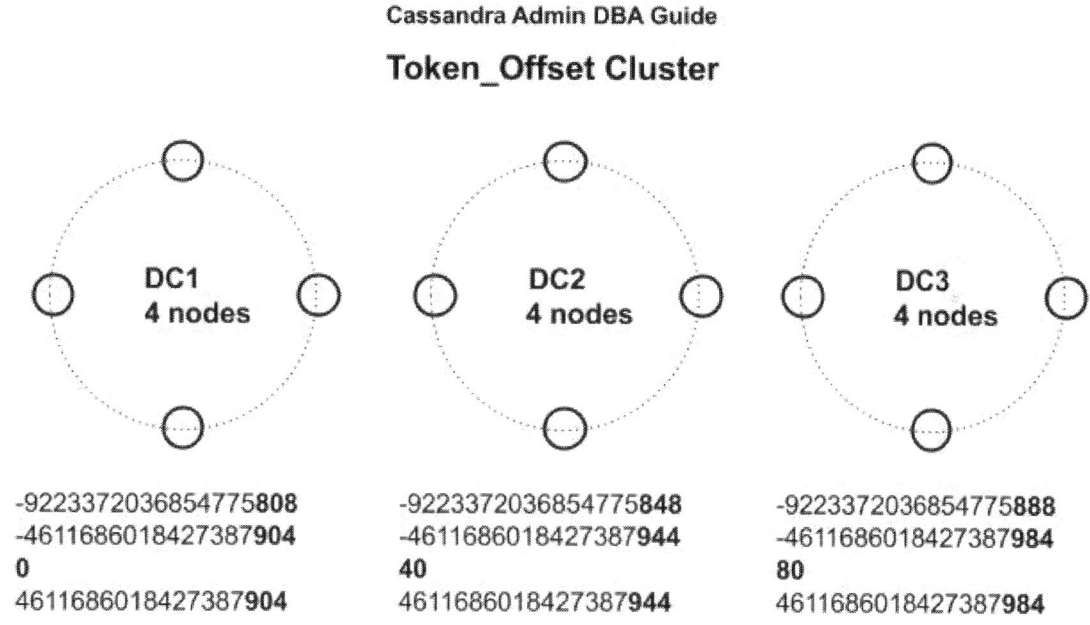

Figure 9.4: Single token datacenter (offset).

Multi-Datacenter and Consistency Level

As you have read, you have many use cases to go for multi-datacenter configuration. Either you are going to build an application around your existing multi-datacenter, or you are adding new datacenter for an existing application. You must review how the replication is set up and what consistency level (CL) you are using in your application. Your CL will decide which nodes across all the datacenters it will involve for the execution of the query.

For example, say you have written your application with CL QUORUM with three replicas in a single datacenter. Now you decide to add a second datacenter to the cluster and configure three replicas on it too. Everything will be fine, but your entire application might get into trouble if one entire datacenter needs to be taken out for maintenance. How? With a single datacenter, as long as your read/write is successful on two replica nodes, your query will be successful. But as soon as you add a second datacenter, now QUORUM needs four replica nodes to respond for your query to be successful. If your second datacenter is out for maintenance, your application will stop working.

If your use case allows, use LOCAL_QUORUM instead of QUORUM or EACH_QUORUM. In the above example, if you add second DC2 and third DC3, your application continues to work if you are using LOCAL_QUORUM. Ideally, you should be able to configure your entire application to point to a single datacenter.

Synchronous and Asynchronous

How is your application written? If you are using local CL, it means all replication and updates are happening asynchronously. For example, if you use LOCAL_QUORUM to write to DC1, the write is completed, and an acknowledgment is sent back even before another datacenter acknowledges the write. So it will be asynchronous and will be eventually consistent.

If you use QUORUM or EACH_QUORUM, it will be synchronous. Choose the CL carefully in this case. If you are using QUORUM, you need to build a cluster with very low network latencies between all datacenters. High network latencies between datacenters will cause performance degradation and even time-outs. If you are using EACH_QUORUM, it means, as the name says, QUORUM needs to be satisfied in each datacenter. This means you cannot take out one datacenter out for any maintenance.

What is the difference between QUORUM and EACH_QUORUM? For example, assuming RF = 3 in three datacenters DC1, DC2, and DC3, if you are performing a write, the following writes can be considered as successful.

EACH_QUORUM : DC1: node1/node3, DC2:node2/node5, DC3:node1/node4

QUORUM : DC1:node1/node2/node3, DC2:node2/node5

In above example, nodes are selected randomly for illustration purposes. As you see, for EACH_QUORUM, write needs to succeed on *two nodes from **each** datacenter*. If one of the datacenters is out for maintenance, your application fails.

For QUORUM, write needs to succeed on any five nodes from three datacenters. In this case it succeeded on five nodes from DC1 and DC2. So QUORUM will succeed even if you take entire DC3 for maintenance.

Replication Factor

Whenever you add a new datacenter or decommission a datacenter or increase or decrease capacity of any datacenter, you must be very careful, and you need to review CL and replication factor for your keyspaces. Also, you have to be very careful whenever you increase or decrease the replication factor of any keyspace.

Best Practices

If you are setting multi-datacenter, make sure to have at least two nodes in each datacenter as seed nodes.

If you are using vnode, make sure to have the same *num_token* for all nodes in a datacenter and also preferably the same *num_token* across all datacenters. If you are running heterogeneous hardware, then you can set up different *num_token* based on the capacity of the node. Note that setting different *num_token* will distribute the data unevenly. Setting *num_token* very high could cause some performance issue. Ideally set *num_token* to 16 or 32 in a production environment instead of 256. Do load tests with different *num_token* values for your use case before making a decision.

One of the use cases for multi-datacenter setup is the geographic location for your applications and reports. It's best practice to point your applications and reports to the nearest local datacenter to reduce the latency. For example, take a look at *Figure 9.1* above. You can set up a replication factor as

```
CREATE KEYSPACE ClientInfo WITH REPLICATION = {
  'class' : 'NetworkTopologyStrategy',
  'NewYork_DC' : '3' ,
  'PA_DC': '3',
  'London_DC': '3',
   'NJ_DC': '2'
};
```

If you read/write at LOCAL_QUORUM, it will make it strongly consistent and asynchronous. You can check your use case and avoid using QUORUM. Using QUORUM could give a slow performance as it will add additional latency between New York and London. In this case, clients in London can connect locally to London_DC.

Run repairs without -pr within *gc_grace_seconds*. If you are using DataStax Enterprise product, you can opt for OpsCenter repairs.

As explained above, avoid using EACH_QUORUM in a multi-datacenter setup unless use case demands. Using EACH_QUORUM can cause application outage if a datacenter has to be taken down for maintenance or it goes down.

CHAPTER 10

Cassandra Architecture II

I n chapter 2, we went through the basic architecture of Cassandra, learning gossip protocol, data partitioning, replication, consistency, and a few other topics. In this chapter, we will dive little deep into Cassandras read and write path, compactions & repairs. All these topics play a vital role in Cassandra and need detailed explanation.

Write and Read Path

It is essential to understand how 'write path' and 'read path' works to manage and administer Cassandra. As a Cassandra DBA, knowing the internals will help you better architect the cluster in the area of consistency, replication and data modeling

In this section, we will focus on just one node of the cluster and will try to understand the 'write path' and 'read path'. Also, we will review configurations mapped to the 'write path' and 'read path' and how to tune them where necessary.

Most RDBMS architected around making the database read fast at the expense of the writes. In RDBMS, writes are expensive as data needs to be written at a particular location and it has to update all the indexes. If you have constraints such as primary key, foreign key and column level constraints, writes have to read the data which will increase the latency. All these disks seek are random disk reads. If you are using rotational disks, then this disk i/o will take additional time and further slow down the writes.

Cassandra has the best architecture and the simplest way of writing the data, which makes it best suited for write-heavy workloads. Cassandra does not have table-level constraints. Cassandra uses a log-structured storage engine, which avoids random disk reads. Any write coming in is appended only to CommitLog. This write-friendly architecture makes the read a little more expensive and complicated. Bu the SSTable architecture and compactions make it a little easier, which we will see later in this chapter.

Write Path

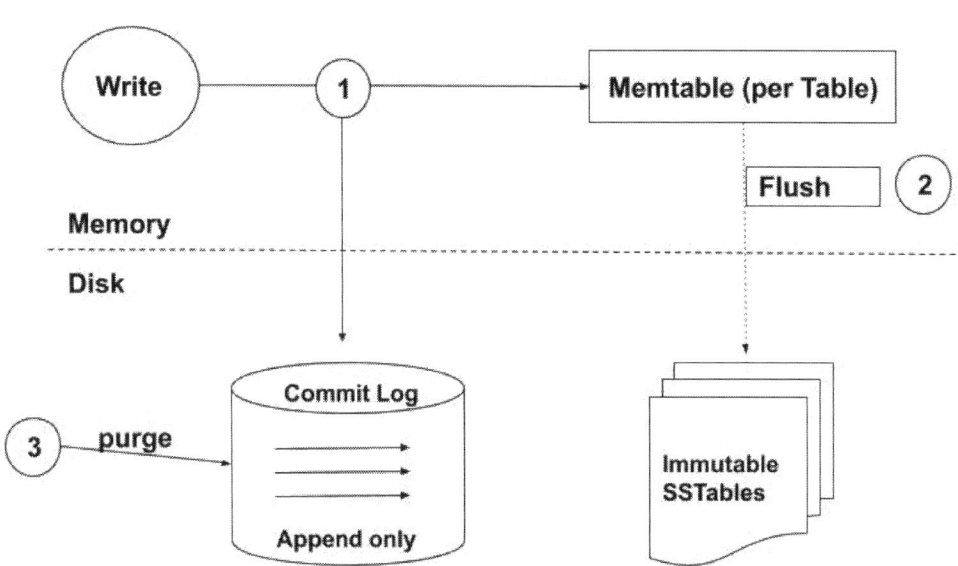

Figure 10.1: Cassandra Write Path.

1. When a write occurs, first it writes to the memtable (memory structure per table) and CommitLog (append only) on disks, and then it acknowledges the write.
2. When CommitLog reaches its maximum size or the memtable surpasses its threshold, the cleanup process flushes the largest memtable to the disk as a SSTable.

3. When the memtable is flushed to the disk, the corresponding data in CommitLog gets purged.

Let's briefly discuss and understand the components in the 'write path'.

CommitLog

CommitLog is a transactional recovery log in case the node goes down. This can be compared to redo logs in Oracle or syslogs in Sybase ASE. Write operation gets written to CommitLog first, and then it gets updated in the memtable. This is an append-only log and provides durable writes. This means multiple updates of the same row on a table are appended with a timestamp and not overwritten. All these are sequential append updates without a random disk search. That's the reason writes are very fast in Cassandra. The primary purpose of CommitLog is to store all the data that has not been written to an SSTable.

In RDBMS, writes are written to a particular location, and this requires the disk head to move randomly. RDBMS is designed to read efficiently at the expense of writes. Cassandra writes are fast, as it does not need to seek a specific location on the disk to write. Insert, update, or even deletion of a row is always an append-only write to the commit log as shown below in *Figure10.2*. And its sequential write.

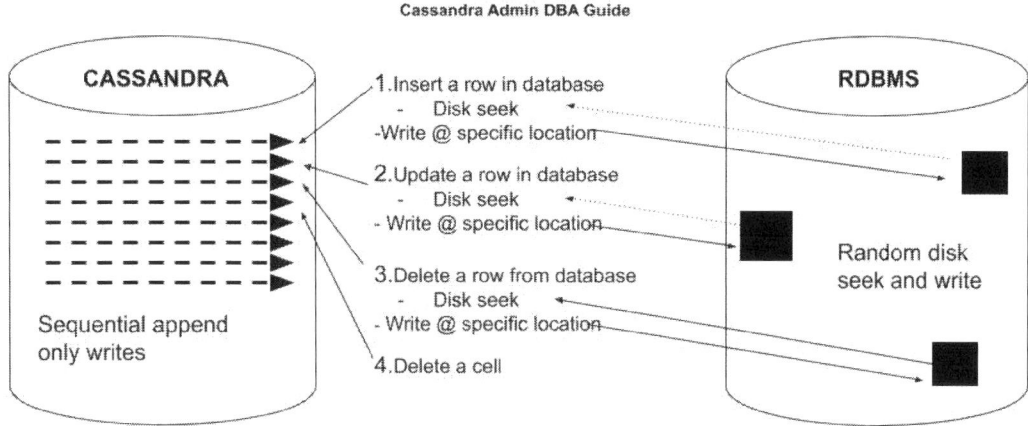

Figure 10.2: Writes in Cassandra vs RDBMS

The primary purpose of the CommitLog is the recovery of the data which is not yet written to the SSTable. The CommitLog will hold a replay of any transactions that were in memory when the node stopped. If a node crashes and comes back online, CommitLog will be replayed, and the memtables will be rebuilt. If you are restarting any Cassandra node for maintenance, you can run *nodetool drain or nodetool flush*, which flushes all memtables to the disk, thus, shortening recovery on startup by replaying CommitLogs.

We say that writes are durable because those are written to disk first, in this case, written to CommitLog first, before an acknowledgment is sent to the client. But CommitLog is not immediately synced to the disk for performance reasons. The 'commitlog_sync', which controls how the CommitLog is synced. It may be either "periodic" or "batch". The default is "periodic" with following settings for *commitlog_sync* and is configurable in *cassandra.yaml* file.

commitlog_sync: periodic

commitlog_sync_period_in_ms: 10000

As per default settings, commit log is synced to the disk every ten seconds. If there is a failure, you lose up to ten seconds of data. But you don't need to worry, as most Cassandra setup will have a replication factor of 3. You need to have a failure on multiple nodes within the same ten seconds to have any chance of data loss.

If this risk is not acceptable, you can use the batch mode for CommitLog. In batch mode, writes will not be acknowledged to the client until CommitLog has been synced to the disk. Check the default value for the version you are using by checking the parameter *commitlog_sync_batch_window_in_ms*. If you are configuring *commitlog_sync* to 'batch', you will be adding additional write latency of 'commitlog_sync_batch_window_in_ms' milliseconds as configured in *cassandra.yaml*.

If you are using spinning disks on your node, make sure to configure CommitLogs on a separate physical disk. If you configure your data and CommitLog on the same physical disk, you will be giving a mixed workload to the disk and losing clean, sequential writes, because the disk head will be wasting its time in moving between reading/writing SSTables and writing CommitLog. If you are using SSD, it will be OK to configure both data and CommitLog on the same disk.

Memtable

The memtable is a memory cache just like buffer cache in Oracle or "default" or named caches in ASE Sybase. Memtable is write-back data cache, in-memory structure for every CQL table and its indexes. The memtable stores writes in sorted order by row key. Unlike CommitLog, there is no duplicate data stored in the memtable. Any update to the data is overwritten in the memtable, whereas updated data in CommitLog is appended. Figure 10.3, shows how writes stored in both CommitLog and the memtable. Note that there are no duplicates in memtable and it is sorted by row key.

Write Operation	In Commit log	In memtable
INSERT cust(id,name) values (100,"X-corp")	{100,"X-corp"}	{100,"X-corp"}
INSERT cust(id,name) values (20,"Y-corp")	{100,"X-corp"} {20,"Y-corp"}	{20,"Y-corp"} {100,"X-corp"}
UPDATE cust set name="Z-corp" WHERE id=20	{100,"X-corp"} {20,"Y-corp"} {20,"Z-corp"}	{20,"Z-corp"} {100,"X-corp"}
DELETE cust WHERE id=20	{100,"X-corp"} {20,"Y-corp"} {20,"Z-corp"} {20,"Z-corp"}-deleted	{20,"Z-corp"}-deleted {100,"X-corp"}

Figure 10.3: Writes in CommitLog and the memtable.

Memtable is flushed when the number of objects stored in it reaches the threshold. Memtables are sorted key structure, and when they are flushed to the disk as SSTables, they are written sequentially.

SSTable

SSTables are sorted string tables. They are actual data files and stored in the data directory, which configured in *cassandra.yaml*.

data_file_directories: $CASSANDRA_HOME/data/data

SSTables are immutable (i.e., once the data is flushed from the memtable and written to an SSTable, it is not updated again). If an existing row is updated in the memtable and when flushed, the new version of the row is saved in a new SSTable with a new timestamp. As a result of memtable flush, more SSTables are created for a given table. As the number of SSTables increase, it becomes expensive to read the data, as it has to read all the SSTables and merge the result based on the timestamp. Imagine that you need to read 100 SSTables to retrieve a single partition! Don't worry. These SSTables are periodically compacted, which is called compaction. Compaction operation merges multiple SSTables into one single SSTable.

For better understanding, let's see how multiple SSTables gets created. This is an example for one table on a single node cluster.

Write Operation followed by flush	SSTable List	Content in the each SSTable
INSERT cust(id,name) values (100,"X-corp"); INSERT cust(id,name) values (200,"Y-corp");	SSTable-1-Data.db	{100,"X-corp"}, timestamp=13 {200,"Y-corp"}, timestamp=17
UPDATE cust set name="Z-corp" where id=200; INSERT cust(id,name) values (300,'A-corp');	SSTable-2-Data.db	{200,"Z-corp"}, timestamp=22 {300,"A-corp"}, timestamp=27
INSERT cust(id,name) values (600,'D-corp'); INSERT cust(id,name) values (500,'C-corp'); INSERT cust(id,name) values (400,'B-corp'); DELETE cust where id=100;	SSTable-3-Data.db	{100,"X-corp"} deleted, timestamp=40 {400,"B-corp"}, timestamp=32 {500,"C-corp"}, timestamp=33 {600,"D-corp"}, timestamp=36

Figure 10.4: nodetool flush and SSTable.

As you can see, each flush creates a new SSTable with sorted data from the memtable. In *Figure 10.4*, the 3rd SSTable data is sorted on the partition key 'id', irrespective of the order in which rows were inserted or deleted. As data get updated and memtable flush creates new SSTables, the data belong to the same partition will exist in multiple SSTables.

When we talk about SSTables, actually it's not just one file; it's a set of following files.

```
host1:/usr/local/cassandra/data/data/demo/test-631288a0e55511e8be1e4fa05a863635$ ls -l
total 40
drwxrwxr-x 2 cassandra cassandra  4096  Nov 10 20:59 backups
-rw-rw-r-- 1 cassandra cassandra    43  Nov 10 21:00 mc-1-big-CompressionInfo.db
-rw-rw-r-- 1 cassandra cassandra    89  Nov 10 21:00 mc-1-big-Data.db
-rw-rw-r-- 1 cassandra cassandra    10  Nov 10 21:00 mc-1-big-Digest.crc32
-rw-rw-r-- 1 cassandra cassandra    16  Nov 10 21:00 mc-1-big-Filter.db
-rw-rw-r-- 1 cassandra cassandra    24  Nov 10 21:00 mc-1-big-Index.db
-rw-rw-r-- 1 cassandra cassandra  4662  Nov 10 21:00 mc-1-big-Statistics.db
-rw-rw-r-- 1 cassandra cassandra    56  Nov 10 21:00 mc-1-big-Summary.db
-rw-rw-r-- 1 cassandra cassandra    92  Nov 10 21:00 mc-1-big-TOC.txt
@host1:/usr/local/cassandra/data/data/demo/test-631288a0e55511e8be1e4fa05a863635$
```

CompressionInfo.db – Metadata for Data file compression algorithm.

Data.db – This is the actual SSTable which contains the data.

Filter.db – Bloom filter to validate if row exits which optimize reads

Index.db – Stores primary index data

Statistics.db – Stores statistics for the SSTable

Summary.db – Stores summary data for the primary index file

TOC.txt – Stores all component list for the SSTable

Read Path

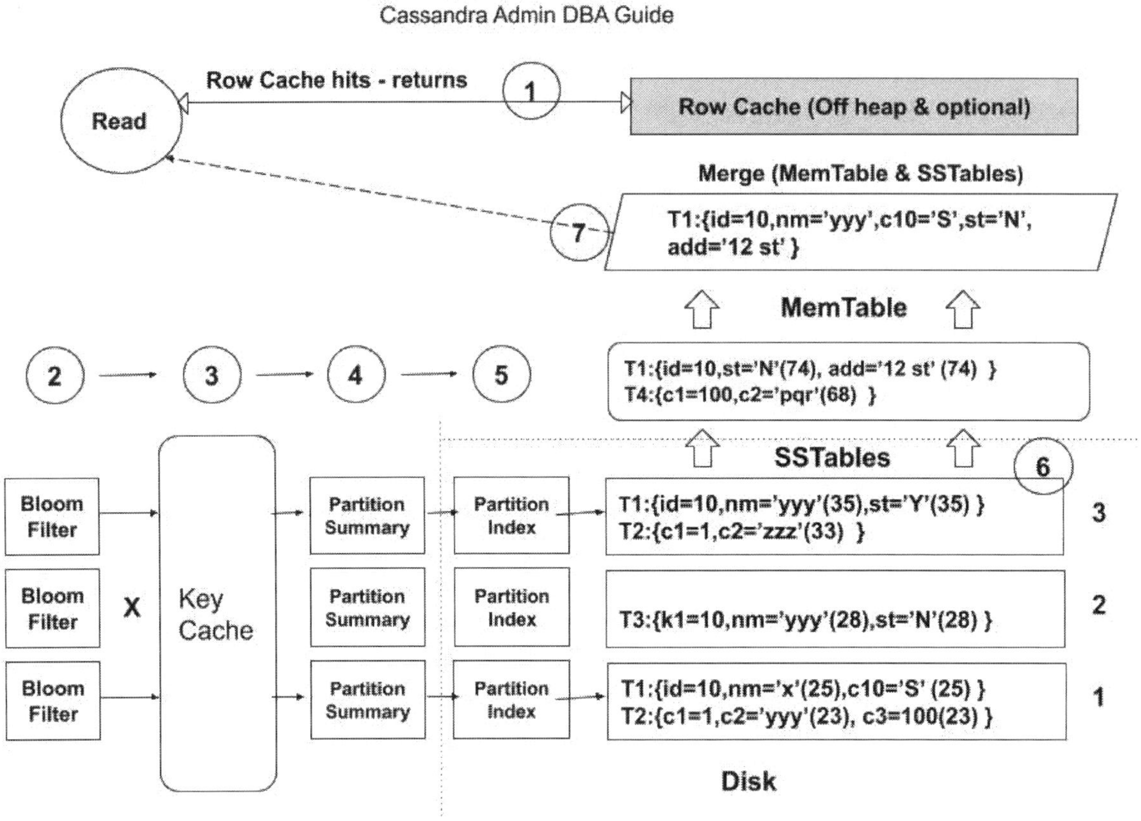

Cassandra Admin DBA Guide

Figure 10.5: Read path.

RDBMS is designed to read efficiently at the expense of writes. Cassandra is designed to write fast at the expense of reads. It's not a significant expense, but compare to write; reads are a little more complicated. When data is written, we need to remember four main things:

1. Cassandra writes are sequential in CommitLog and memtables are sorted by the key.
2. When memtables are flushed, each flush creates a new SSTable, which is immutable, and the data in it is in sorted order.
3. Compaction process merges several SSTables into one.
4. An entire row can be spread across one or many SSTables and memtables.

Now let's discuss how Cassandra reads data for a given key in a table on one node. For understanding purpose, *Figure 10.5* has some dummy data in it.

Step 1: Row cache

When a read request finds the row in Row Cache, it returns immediately, which is the fastest response we can get. In case the entire partition is not in Row Cache, or there is no data found in Row Cache, Cassandra has to go through the next steps to read the whole data from the memtable and SSTables. If there is a Row Cache hit, it can save a minimum of two physical reads.

Row Cache is just like buffer cache in Oracle or "default" or named caches in ASE Sybase. Typically, reads are faster when requested data is available in the memory. By default, row cache is disabled, because mostly, frequently read data is cached by OS cache, and enabling row cache will result in double caching.

```
# Default is 0 to disable saving the row cache.
row_cache_save_period: 0
# Default value is 0 to disable row caching.
row_cache_size_in_mb: 0
```

Row Cache uses off-heap memory, which relieves garbage collection pressure in the JVM. The Row Cache size is configurable in *cassandra.yaml* as shown above. When enabled, it saves the merged result from the memtable and SSTables, and it maintains the cache in LRU (least recently used) mode. Note that when a write happens to the row, which is cached, it invalidates that row in the Row Cache and flushes it out. That row needs to be reread, to be cached again in Row Cache. If you have enabled Row Cache and you update the row frequently, then Row cache will not be beneficial for you.

Step 2: Bloom Filter

When the desired partition data is not found in the Row Cache, then Cassandra first checks the Bloom Filter. Imagine there are ten SSTables and only two SSTables have the requested partition key. If there is no Bloom Filter, you may need to do a minimum of ten disks seeks to check if the partition key exists in those ten SSTables! Cassandra uses Bloom Filter to determine if the SSTable has requested the partition key. Another way of explaining, Bloom Filters can tell us the partition key we are looking for does not exist in that SSTable. In *Figure 10.5*, if we are reading partition key id = 10 from table T1, Bloom Filter tells us, "Don't check SSTable2, as it does not exist." The advantage here is that read process does not even need to seek this SSTable. Bloom Filter never results in a false negative—that is, it never says that the partition key is not there when it is. But Bloom Filter may result in false positives—that is, it may say that the partition key does exist in an SSTable, but it may not exist. In the example above, key id = 10 from table T1 does exist in SSTable 1 and 3.

In the SSTable list, Filter.db is Bloom Filter associated with that particular SSTable. The same copy is loaded in off-heap memory for performance purpose.

Step 3: Key Cache

When Bloom Filter says data may exist in some SSTables, the read process accesses Key Cache. Key Cache stores a list of partition keys and specific disk offset information in the SSTable. This allows the read process to skip over partition summary and partition index and directly jump to compression offset map in the SSTable, saving, at the minimum, one disk seek.

Key Cache is configurable by *key_cache_size_in_mb* and plays a very important role in read performance. You can check the Key Cache statistics by running *nodetool info*.

A sample line of Key Cache from *nodetool info* is listed below. As you see, a hit rate of 0.98 is a good value.

Key Cache : entries 49, size 4.59 KiB, capacity 16 MiB, 2820 hits, 2878 requests, **0.980 recent hit rate**, 14400 save period in seconds

If a partition key is not found in the Key Cache, then the partition summary is searched. If you see the hit rate at a lower percent, review the *nodetool info* output and configure more memory for the Key Cache.

Step 4: Partition Summary

If the partition key does not exist in the Key Cache, the read process seeks the key in the partition summary, which is an off-heap memory structure. Partition summary stores the sampling of the partition index. It's an index on the index. Partition summary samples every "min_index_interval"[th] key from partition index. The read process finds the range of the key in partition summary and jumps to the approximate location in the partition index. Thus, it saves additional disk seek of partition index, which is on disk.

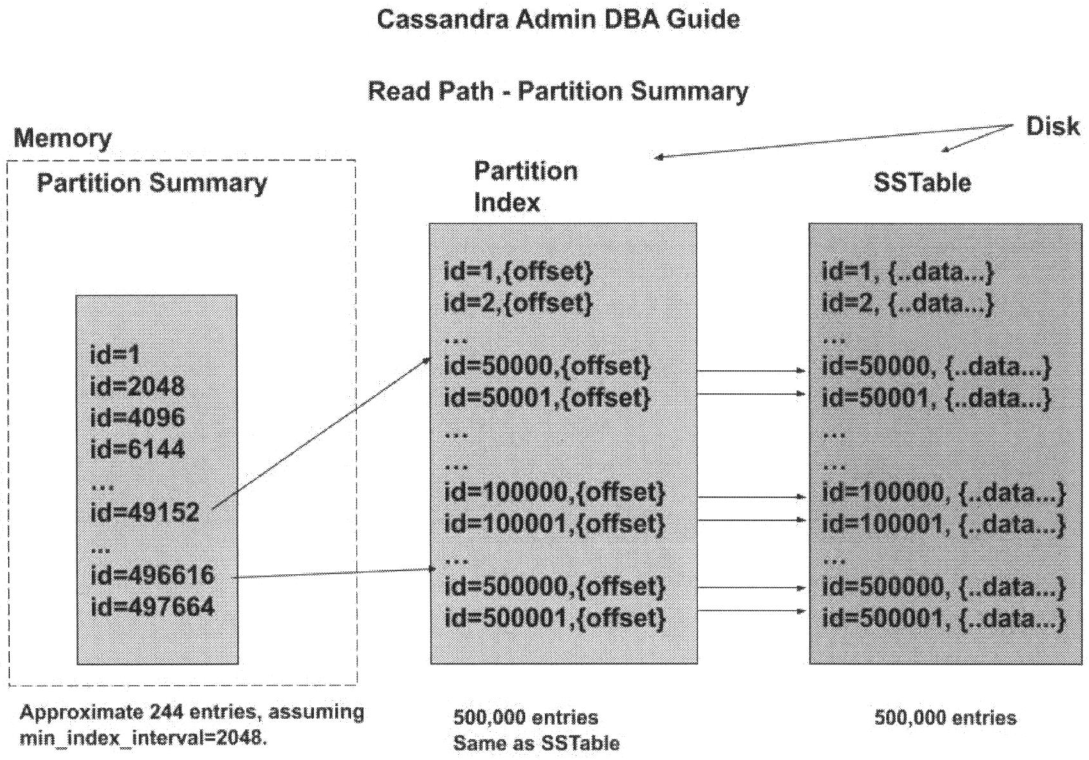

Figure 10.6: Partition Summary.

As shown in *Figure 10.6*, say SSTable1 has 500,001 rows with key id = 1 to 500,001, partition index will also have these 500,001 keys. Partition Summary will be in-memory sampling from partition index with an approximate location in the index. In this case, partition summary will have 244 entries based on *min_index_interval* = 2048. The sampling can be configured with table properties *min_index_interval* and *max_index_interval*. If there is memory pressure, Cassandra decreases the partition summary density for the cold SSTable to *max_index_interval*.

Step 5: Partition Index

Partition Index resides on the disk along with the actual SSTable and stores all the keys present in the SSTable and their offset in the SSTable. This same offset is stored in Key Cache. If Key Cache does not have the partition key information, then the read process reads the partition summary and partition index to retrieve the offset location of the data in the SSTable. At this time, this information added to the Key Cache. This way, any future read can have a Key Cache hit and save disk seek on partition index.

Step 6: SSTable

Once the data is read from each SSTable, based on the time stamp of each column value, the row data is prepared to be merged with memtable.

As you can see from figure 10.5, key id = 10 from table T1 is found in two SSTables: 1 and 3.

Step 7: Merge memtable and SSTable

Assuming client requested data from table T1 where id = 10, the entire row for table T1 with id = 10 returned from merging memtable and SSTables. Table T1 row with id = 10 is found in two SSTables, as listed below.

```
T1:{id=10,nm='yyy',c10='S',st='N', add='12 st' } ← Merged data
T1:{id=10,st='N'(74), add='12 st' (74)} ← memtable
T1:{id=10,nm='yyy'(35),st='Y'(35) }       ← SSTable3
T1:{id=10,nm='x'(25),c10='S' (25) }       ← SSTable1
```

Column *nm*='yyy' is taken from SSTable 3 as the timestamp of 35 is > 25 from SSTable 1

Column *c10*='S' is taken from SSTable 1 as that is the only entry found in SSTables and mem Table.

Column *St*='N' & *add*='12 St' is taken from Mem Table as it's the latest timestamp of 74, which is not flushed yet to any SSTable.

Compaction

Compaction operation in Cassandra merges multiple SSTables into one single SSTable. When a read request reaches a node, it may be required to read multiple SSTables to read a specific partition and return the data. The more SSTables it has to read, the more latency and the read operation will become expensive. Let's take a hypothetical example below.

```
INSERT INTO tblA ( ......) - 1,000 rows
DELETE 250 rows (which generates 25% tombstones)
UPDATE remaining 750 rows multiple times
nodetool flush
```

The above CQL, followed by a *nodetool flush* will create an SSTable on each node on the cluster. Now if you repeat this one hundred times, you will end up with one hundred SSTables on each node, **assuming there is no compaction**. Can you imagine how a Cassandra read will perform to retrieve the data? It has to read all one hundred SSTables, discard 25% of the tombstones and get 75% of the rows by merging a hundred SSTables. The same read operation will happen on each node on the cluster, and a final merge will be done. That's the reason we have compactions.

Compaction process regularly merge multiple SSTable and write to a single SSTable thus it improves the read performance.

What Does Compaction Do?

Compaction

1. merges partition keys and all columns from multiple SSTable and creates a new SSTable
2. removes tombstones if their *gc_grace_seconds* are over
3. rebuilds the partition index and partition summary for the new SSTable
4. removes the old SSTables.

Compaction is a very I/O intensive operation, as it has to read multiple SSTables from the disk and merge them to write to a new SSTable. Since the SSTables are immutable and sorted on the key, compaction does not need to load the entire SSTables into memory for merging. Since it is sorted, it does streaming merge sort of these SSTables efficiently to create the new SSTable.

Compaction is triggered whenever

1. Whenever memtable flush happens, it creates an SSTable
2. When a new SSTable is created, and the number of SSTables for that table on the node meets the *min_threshold*.
3. When you bootstrap the node or rebuild the node, steaming of data creates a SSTable which may trigger compaction
4. The repair process creates an SSTable, which may trigger compaction.

In version 3.10, Cassandra offers three types of compactions.

Size-Tiered Compaction Strategy

Size-tiered compaction strategy (STCS) triggers minor compaction when the number of SSTables meets the min_threshold, which is, by default, four. This means whenever there are four SSTables of the same size; it triggers minor compaction.

The min_threshold can be changed by ALTER TABLE command.

```
ALTER TABLE ks.table WITH compaction = {
    'class' : 'SizeTieredCompactionStrategy', 'min_threshold' : 6
};
```

This strategy has several size tiers, and it is controlled by compaction sub-property *bucket_low* (default 0.5) and *bucket_high* (default 1.5). During compaction, SSTable size within (avg size * *bucket_low*) and (avg size * *bucket_high*) are compacted together. The reason these tiers are created is so that similar size SSTables can get compacted together efficiently through streaming merge join.

For example, if there are four 100 MB SSTables, those will fall into a tier 50MB >= to =< 150 MB. These 4 SSTables will be compacted and become one SSTable of a size equivalent to about 400 MB.

[100 MB] [100 MB] [100 MB] [100 MB] SSTables -> compacted to a 400 MB SSTable.

This 400 MB SSTable is placed into a tier of 200 MB to 600 MB based on default *bucket_low* and *bucket_high* as calculated below.

400 * 0.5 (bucket_low) >= to <= 400 * 1.5 (bucket_high) = (Tier 200 MB >= to <= 600 MB)

Now during the next flush, say another SSTable is created with a size of 100 MB. Since this falls outside the 200–600 MB tier, there is a new tier created with 50–150 MB based on *bucket low*_and *bucket_high*. When three more SSTables are flushed of sizes between 50–150 MB, those four will be compacted to form another big SSTable of size around 400 MB. This SSTable will be placed into the earlier tier of 200–600 MB. This process continues, and it creates larger SSTables. When there are four SSTables in this tier of 200–600 MB, it compacts them into one large SSTable of size around 1600 MB.

[400 MB] [400 MB] [400 MB] [400 MB] SSTables -> compacts to a 1600 MB SSTable.

In STCS, you may end up with a large number of SSTables of various sizes. When this happens, your frequently updated partition may be spread across several SSTables. This may lead to inconsistent read latency.

STCS is suitable for write-heavy use cases, and it is the default compaction strategy for the table. It may require 50% of disk space to be free to run compaction.

Minor compactions are triggered automatically based on the thresholds. You can manually initiate major compaction by the "nodetool compact" command. Be aware that this is not recommended in a production environment — major compaction compacts all SSTables into a single large SSTable. If you have one very large SSTable, it may not trigger minor compactions, as it will wait on four similar size SSTables. In this case, you may use sstablesplit. Refer "sstablesplit" in Chapter 12, Cassandra Utilities.

Leveled Compaction Strategy

Leveled compaction strategy (LCS) was introduced to address some of its shortcomings of STCS. STCS is suitable for write-heavy use cases, whereas LCS is suitable for read-heavy use cases. LCS comes with a price of 2× I/O on compaction. If your table is write heavy, don't use LCS strategy.

LCS creates a small size SSTable based on the sstable_size_in_mb option, which is set to 160 MB by default. Note that this setting is not in *cassandra.yaml* file.

This can be set using ALTER TABLE as given below.

```
ALTER TABLE ks.table WITH  compaction = {
     'class' : 'LeveledCompactionStrategy', 'sstable_size_in_mb' : 100
};
```

Any new SSTable created are set at level 0. Only at level 0, the SSTable can be the size of less than 160 MB. Minor exceptions where it can be a little larger to make sure the last written partition is complete. At level 0, SSTables can overlap the token range.

During level 0 compaction, it will select all the SSTables that are overlapping as well as all overlapping SSTables from level 1. A maximum of 32 SSTables from level 0 and ten from level 1 are considered for this compaction. All these SSTables will be compacted and written to multiple level 1 SSTables with a maximum size of 160 MB each, which is configurable as shown above. The same process continues from level 1 to level 2 with 10× the size of the previous level.

As SSTables are compacted to the next level, from level 0 and above, the overlap is removed. There is no overlap of tokens in level 1 and up. As level 1 SSTables are written from compactions, it keeps calculating the total size of level 1 SSTables with the level's capacity. This is called a compaction score. Level 1 SSTable capacity is 1.6 GB with the default *sstble_size_in_mb* as 160 MB. So when level 1 size exceeds 1.6 GB, up-level compactions starts from level 1 to level 2.

LCS requires more disk I/O, and due to this, it could start falling behind on compacting level 0. In level 0, partition could be overlapped in multiple SSTables, and thus, read could start hitting many SSTables at level 0, which could increase read latency. To reduce this bottleneck, LCS switches to STCS at level 0. Before any compactions trigger from level 1 to level n, it always checks to see if level 0 compactions are falling behind. It does this by checking if there are more than 32 SSTables at level 0.

In LCS, during compaction from one level to the next level, partition keys are sorted and stored in one SSTable. So if you are querying a partition, it will reside in only one SSTable per level (except L0). This means reads are faster because it has to seek fewer SSTables and less disk I/O.

LCS is the best fit where you need consistent read performance with higher read-to-write ratio.

LCS requires less disk space for compactions compared to STCS. Since LCS compacts frequently, it needs more I/O compared to STCS. Due to this reason, it's not suitable for heavy write use cases. Since it requires more I/O, don't use LCS where the node does not have enough I/O bandwidth such as SAN, rotating disks, NFS, or non-SSD disks.

Don't use LCS where you have wide partitions exceeding 160 MB.

Time Window Compaction Strategy

Time window compaction strategy (TWCS) has been designed for time-series data. Tables need to be configured with a time window. At the end of the time window, it compacts all the SSTables using STCS strategy. TWCS works well with write-once rows with a TTL (Time-To-Live). When rows are updated or explicitly deleted, it will not go well with TWCS. If all rows are written with the same TTL, the entire SSTable will contain 100% tombstone. The benefit of TWCS is that based on the configurable window size, it separates data on the disk and allows fully expired SSTables to drop efficiently when TTL is set properly.

Below is an example: table *demo.twc* has been created with a twenty-four-hour TTL and one-hour compaction window. Every hour, all the SSTables in that hour window are compacted into a one larger SSTable.

compaction_window_unit takes value of "MINUTES", "HOURS" or "DAYS"

```
CREATE TABLE demo.twc (
    id int,
    datavalue int,
    notes text,
    PRIMARY KEY (id, datavalue)
) WITH gc_grace_seconds = 600
    AND default_time_to_live = 86400
    AND compaction = {  'compaction_window_size': '60',
                        'compaction_window_unit': 'MINUTES',
    'class': 'org.apache.cassandra.db.compaction.TimeWindowCompactionStrategy'
};
```

TWCS compacts all SSTables that fall into the time window into a single SSTable. Once the major compaction for a time window is completed, as in the above case, no further compaction of the data will ever occur.

Tombstone Compaction

Deleting data in a distributed database like Cassandra is difficult and challenging if it is not designed correctly. In this type of design, you cannot locate a piece of data and delete it. Cassandra is designed for fast writes with the design of immutable SSTables. In Cassandra deleting the data is designed to improve performance. Tombstones are "delete" marker and written to immutable SSTables as an indicator of data deletion. These deletes are actually, a write which goes through Cassandra's write path. This means Cassandra read path has to compensate for the fast writes of tombstones.

To ensure availability and partition tolerance, Cassandra replicates data. Multiple copies of the data are stored on different nodes and datacenters, based on the configuration of the replication factor at the keyspace level. This helps prevent data loss. When we delete data, Cassandra writes tombstone, and this tombstone replicates to all the replica nodes and datacenters. In a distributed database like Cassandra, nodes may be down, and there could be network issues, disk issues, and the chances are that tombstones which are written have not reached all the replicas; thus, the unresponsive node contains the pre-deleted version of the data. Before downed node recovers, If the tombstone marker is compacted and removed from the rest of the nodes, downed node does not know that the data has been deleted. When this downed node recovers, since it did not get the tombstone, it still has pre-deleted data on just this node. When this data is accessed, Cassandra propagates this to other replicas as read repair. This is called zombie rows or data. To prevent these zombies from appearing due to a downed replica, Cassandra gives a grace period for each tombstone. This helps prevent incorrect data from reappearing, as the grace period gives downed nodes time to recover and receive the tombstone marker via hinted handoff or repair. By default, the grace period is set to 864,000 seconds (ten days) via property *gc_grace_seconds*. When *nodetool repair* is run on the downed node when it recovers, the data will become consistent, and it will receive the tombstone. The repair process replicates the tombstone marker to this node before *gc_grace_seconds*. In short, once you delete data, the deleted data with tombstone marker remains in the SSTable until *gc_gace_seconds* have passed

As you delete data, it will not be removed immediately from the SSTables. If any replica does not get a write of that tombstone, it is not aware of that delete. This could happen when a node is down and recovers without hints, and you have still not run the repair on it. At this state, if you run a SELECT or UPDATE with consistency as ANY or ONE, and for any reason, if the coordinator node chooses this particular replica, the data becomes inconsistent. Since the node does not have the tombstone, the zombie data is returned or updated with the new time stamp. This is the reason you must pay attention to your consistency when you read or write data. How this scenario plays out when you use QUORUM instead of ANY or ONE consistency? When you run the SELECT or UPDATE with QUORUM or LOCAL_QUORUM on this downed node, the coordinator node runs anti-entropy repair, and the downed node will receive the latest tombstone marker, instead of bringing the zombie data to live.

Read "How deleted data can reappear?" in *Chapter 2 Basic Cassandra Architecture.*

It is normal to have tombstones in the database when you delete or TTL the data. The compaction process removes these tombstones once they pass *gc_grace_seconds* after local delete time. This is the reason you run repairs within *gc_grace_seconds* on all the nodes so that tombstones can be propagated to all replicas. The presence of tombstones in SSTables does affect the read performance. So care must be taken in your design and process not to generate tombstones when it's not necessary. Tombstones can take up a lot of space and impact the read performance. This can be dealt with aggressive compaction strategy, and the good thing is we can adjust many of the properties at the table level.

There are three tombstone compaction properties you can set based on your use case.

- *tombstone_threshold* is the percent of tombstones that can be evicted from the SSTable. If the ratio of these in the SSTable exceeds this limit, Cassandra starts compaction on that table alone and purge the tombstones. By default, this value is 0.2, which is 20%.
- *tombstone_compaction_interval* is the number of seconds after which the SSTable is created before Cassandra can trigger single SSTable tombstone compaction when it exceeds the *tombstone_threshold* percent.
- *unchecked_tombstone_compaction*, when set to true, will trigger single SSTable compaction every *tombstone_compaction_interval* as soon as tombstone percent in that SSTable exceeds *tombstone_threshold*. Note that, when it is set to 'true', tombstone compaction happens without pre-checking the eligibility of the table. Use this with care based on your use case.

Let's see an example code of setting this compaction.

```
cassandra@cqlsh:demo> desc table test;
CREATE TABLE demo.test (
    id int PRIMARY KEY,
    city text,
    status text
) WITH bloom_filter_fp_chance = 0.01
    AND caching = {'keys': 'ALL', 'rows_per_partition': 'NONE'}
    AND comment = ''
    AND compaction = {'class': 'org.apache.cassandra.db.compaction.
SizeTieredCompactionStrategy', 'max_threshold': '32', 'min_threshold': '4'}
    AND compression = {'chunk_length_in_kb': '64', 'class': 'org.apache.cassandra.io.compress.
LZ4Compressor'}
    AND crc_check_chance = 1.0
    AND dclocal_read_repair_chance = 0.1
    AND default_time_to_live = 0
    AND gc_grace_seconds = 864000
    AND max_index_interval = 2048
    AND memtable_flush_period_in_ms = 0
    AND min_index_interval = 128
```

```
AND read_repair_chance = 0.0
AND speculative_retry = '99PERCENTILE';
```

Now alter this table, and set the tombstone compaction properties. We will set the threshold to 10% instead of the default 20% and tombstone compaction interval to six hundred seconds, and set unchecked to true.

```
ALTER TABLE demo.test WITH compaction = {
 'class':'org.apache.cassandra.db.compaction.SizeTieredCompactionStrategy',
 'tombstone_compaction_interval': '600',
 'tombstone_threshold': '0.1',
 'unchecked_tombstone_compaction': 'true'
};

cassandra@cqlsh:demo> desc table test;

CREATE TABLE demo.test (
    id int PRIMARY KEY,
    city text,
    status text
) WITH bloom_filter_fp_chance = 0.01
    AND caching = {'keys': 'ALL', 'rows_per_partition': 'NONE'}
    AND comment = ''
    AND compaction = {'class': 'org.apache.cassandra.db.compaction.SizeTieredCompactionStrategy',
'max_threshold': '32', 'min_threshold': '4', 'tombstone_compaction_interval': '600', 'tombstone_
threshold': '0.1', 'unchecked_tombstone_compaction': 'true'}
    AND compression = {'chunk_length_in_kb': '64', 'class': 'org.apache.cassandra.io.compress.
LZ4Compressor'}
    AND crc_check_chance = 1.0
    AND dclocal_read_repair_chance = 0.1
    AND default_time_to_live = 0
    AND gc_grace_seconds = 864000
    AND max_index_interval = 2048
    AND memtable_flush_period_in_ms = 0
    AND min_index_interval = 128
```

```
    AND read_repair_chance = 0.0
    AND speculative_retry = '99PERCENTILE';
 cassandra@cqlsh:demo>
```

If you are running a one node cluster (which is odd) or a very small cluster, you can adjust *gc_grace_seconds* to a very low value to purge the tombstone faster so that you will not fill up the disk space. In below example, we are setting this to two minutes (compare to the default 864,000 seconds which is ten days). In this case, make sure you use very strong consistency for all your reads and writes.

```
 cassandra@cqlsh:demo> ALTER TABLE demo.test WITH gc_grace_seconds = 120;
```

Regular Delete versus TTL Delete

There is a big difference between regular tombstone generated by DELETE and a TTL-generated tombstone. In case of a DELETE, the tombstone marker has to be written to each replica, which is asynchronous. If any replica node is down and misses the tombstone marker, it may generate a zombie when it recovers. When you write data with TTL, the expiration is written along with the data. This means that if that node goes down and recovers, it will still carry the expiration date and time and generate that tombstone. With TTL delete, you don't need to worry about if the zombie data is generated and also you don't need to worry about running repairs on the node if they go down and then recover.

DELETE generates tombstone

Note that if you DELETE a row that does not exist, it generates a tombstone, and it has to go through compaction process. Unlike in RDBMS, it does not give any messages like '*0 rows deleted*' or '*0 rows affected*'. A quick example below: Create a table and delete three rows that do not exist in the empty table.

```
 ccassandra@cqlsh:demo> CREATE TABLE demo.tombstone_test (id int PRIMARY KEY,name text);
 cassandra@cqlsh:demo> SELECT * FROM demo.tombstone_test ;
```

```
id | name
----+------

(0 rows)
cassandra@cqlsh:demo> DELETE FROM demo.tombstone_test WHERE id=1;
cassandra@cqlsh:demo> DELETE FROM demo.tombstone_test WHERE id=2;
cassandra@cqlsh:demo> DELETE FROM demo.tombstone_test WHERE id=3;
cassandra@cqlsh:demo>
```

Now run *nodetool flush* and run *sstabledump*. Output shows three tombstones generated due to DELETE on data, which does not exist.

```
cassandra@host1:$ $CASSANDRA_HOME/bin/nodetool flush
cassandra@host1:/usr/local/cassandra/data/data/demo/tombstone_test-
55e78da0eaec11e8a943d330b5c3dec0$ ls -lrt
total 40
drwxrwxr-x 2 cassandra cassandra  4096 Nov 17 23:42 backups
-rw-rw-r-- 1 cassandra cassandra    16 Nov 17 23:43 mc-1-big-Filter.db
-rw-rw-r-- 1 cassandra cassandra    56 Nov 17 23:43 mc-1-big-Summary.db
-rw-rw-r-- 1 cassandra cassandra    24 Nov 17 23:43 mc-1-big-Index.db
-rw-rw-r-- 1 cassandra cassandra    60 Nov 17 23:43 mc-1-big-Data.db
-rw-rw-r-- 1 cassandra cassandra  4619 Nov 17 23:43 mc-1-big-Statistics.db
-rw-rw-r-- 1 cassandra cassandra    10 Nov 17 23:43 mc-1-big-Digest.crc32
-rw-rw-r-- 1 cassandra cassandra    43 Nov 17 23:43 mc-1-big-CompressionInfo.db
-rw-rw-r-- 1 cassandra cassandra    92 Nov 17 23:43 mc-1-big-TOC.txt

cassandra@host1:/usr/local/cassandra/data/data/demo/tombstone_test-55e78da0eae-
c11e8a943d330b5c3dec0$ sstabledump -d mc-1-big-Data.db
[1]@0 deletedAt=1542516153569559, localDeletion=1542516153
[2]@19 deletedAt=1542516157083925, localDeletion=1542516157
[3]@38 deletedAt=1542516160057917, localDeletion=1542516160
cassandra@host1:/usr/local/cassandra/data/data/demo/
tombstone_test-55e78da0eaec11e8a943d330b5c3dec0$
```

Compaction Process Example

Here is an example of the actual compaction process. In this example, you will see how STCS compaction happens when four SSTables are flushed. After each flush and compaction, run the *sstabledump* to see how the data is stored internally. Finally, you will see the tombstone stored in the SSTable. For this, let's create a table and insert and update data and run *nodetool flush* to create SSTable.

First SSTable flush

```
cassandra@cqlsh> CREATE KEYSPACE demo WITH
                 replication = { 'class':'SimpleStrategy','replication_factor':1};
cassandra@cqlsh> create table demo.test(id int primary key, city text,status text);
cassandra@cqlsh> insert into demo.test(id,city,status) values (1,'New York','A');
cassandra@cqlsh> insert into demo.test(id,city,status) values (2,'London','A');
cassandra@cqlsh> insert into demo.test(id,city,status) values (3,'Tokyo','N');
```

Run *nodetool flush* to create first SSTable.

```
cassandra@host1:/usr/local/cassandra/data/data/demo/test-
631288a0e55511e8be1e4fa05a863635$ $CASSANDRA_HOME/bin/nodetool flush
cassandra@host1:/usr/local/cassandra/data/data/demo/test-631288a0e55511e8be1e4f-
a05a863635$ ls -l
total 40
drwxrwxr-x 2 cassandra cassandra   4096 Nov 10 20:59 backups
-rw-rw-r-- 1 cassandra cassandra     43 Nov 10 21:00 mc-1-big-CompressionInfo.db
-rw-rw-r-- 1 cassandra cassandra     89 Nov 10 21:00 mc-1-big-Data.db
-rw-rw-r-- 1 cassandra cassandra     10 Nov 10 21:00 mc-1-big-Digest.crc32
-rw-rw-r-- 1 cassandra cassandra     16 Nov 10 21:00 mc-1-big-Filter.db
-rw-rw-r-- 1 cassandra cassandra     24 Nov 10 21:00 mc-1-big-Index.db
-rw-rw-r-- 1 cassandra cassandra   4662 Nov 10 21:00 mc-1-big-Statistics.db
-rw-rw-r-- 1 cassandra cassandra     56 Nov 10 21:00 mc-1-big-Summary.db
-rw-rw-r-- 1 cassandra cassandra     92 Nov 10 21:00 mc-1-big-TOC.txt
cassandra@host1:/usr/local/cassandra/data/data/demo/
test-631288a0e55511e8be1e4fa05a863635$
```

Now run *sstabledump* to view the data in the SSTable mc-1-big-Data.db.

```
ccassandra@host1:/usr/local/cassandra/data/data/demo/test-631288a0e55511e8be1e4f-
a05a863635$ $CASSANDRA_HOME/tools/bin/sstabledump -d mc-1-big-Data.db

[1]@0 Row[info=[ts=1541901556122756] ]: | [city=New York ts=1541901556122756], [status=A
ts=1541901556122756]

[2]@36 Row[info=[ts=1541901562552706] ]: | [city=London ts=1541901562552706], [status=A
ts=1541901562552706]

[3]@73 Row[info=[ts=1541901569003528] ]: | [city=Tokyo ts=1541901569003528], [status=N
ts=1541901569003528]
cassandra@host1:/usr/local/cassandra/data/data/demo/
test-631288a0e55511e8be1e4fa05a863635$
```

Second SSTable flush

Now run the update, delete, and insert statements to modify the data and run again *nodetool flush*, which creates the second SSTable. For shorter output, data directory folder has been removed from the output for the next few examples.

```
cassandra@cqlsh> update demo.test set city='Boston' where id=1;
cassandra@cqlsh> update demo.test set status='X' where id=2;
cassandra@cqlsh> delete status from demo.test where id=3 ;
cassandra@cqlsh> insert into demo.test(id,city,status) values (4,'BigCity','A');

cassandra@host1:/usr/local/cassandra$ $CASSANDRA_HOME/bin/nodetool flush

cassandra@host1: $ $CASSANDRA_HOME/tools/bin/sstabledump -d mc-2-big-Data.db

[1]@0 Row[info=[ts=-9223372036854775808] ]: | [city=Boston ts=1541901767461503]

[2]@32 Row[info=[ts=-9223372036854775808] ]: | [status=X ts=1541901777512372]
```

```
[4]@62 Row[info=[ts=1541901790057441] ]: | [city=BigCity ts=1541901790057441], [status=A
ts=1541901790057441]

[3]@100 Row[info=[ts=-9223372036854775808] ]: | [status=<tombstone>
ts=1541901783694931 ldt=1541901783]

cassandra@host1: $
```

Few observations.

a) *ts* represents the time stamp the statement ran.
b) Deleting of status column (for id = 3) has generated a cell **tombstone**.
c) Value for city = 'Tokyo' for id=3 does not appear in this SSTable. Since only status column for id = 3 has been deleted, only that cell tombstone with time stamp is stored in the SSTable. This means that if you run "SELECT * from demo.test where id=3," then the read path will scan both mc-1-big-Data.db and mc-2-big-Data.db and merge the results from two SSTables and return the result with status as "null." The reason is *ts* = 1541901569003528 for status = *N* is older than *ts* = 1541901783694931 for status = <tombstone>.

Third SSTable flush

Now run few more updates and deletes. Run *nodetool flush* to create the thrird SSTable.

```
cassandra@cqlsh> update demo.test set city='Washington' where id=1;
cassandra@cqlsh> update demo.test set city='New York' where id=1;
cassandra@cqlsh> update demo.test set city='Paris' where id=2;
cassandra@cqlsh> delete from demo.test where id=4;

cassandra@host1: $CASSANDRA_HOME/bin/nodetool flush

assandra@host1: $ $CASSANDRA_HOME/tools/bin/sstabledump -d mc-3-big-Data.db
[1]@0 Row[info=[ts=-9223372036854775808] ]: | [city=New York ts=1541902053338307]
```

```
[2]@36 Row[info=[ts=-9223372036854775808] ]: | [city=Paris ts=1541902060799765]
[4]@69 deletedAt=1541902077083706, localDeletion=1541902077
cassandra@host1:$
```

Few observations.

    a) The delete statement (for id = 4) has generated a full row tombstone.

    b) There were two updates run for id = 1, but you see only one row in the SSTable. The reason is that when the row is updated with "New York" value, it overwrote the value in memtable, and thus, *nodetool flush* generated only one entry.

    c) You don't see the row for id = 3. The reason is since the data for id = 3 has not been modified, it does not exist in this SSTable.

Now if you run select * with id=1, the read path has to read all three SSTables to retrieve the correct value. This can be checked with "tracing on." Note that in the below output of tracing shows that the read path has to read three SSTables and merge and display the row. The below output has been edited to remove the time stamp, source_elapsed and client columns for readability.

```
cassandra@host1:$ cqlsh -u cassandra -pcassandra 192.168.1.54
Connected to CADG_cluster at 192.168.1.54:9042.
[cqlsh 5.0.1 | Cassandra 3.10 | CQL spec 3.4.4 | Native protocol v4]
Use HELP for help.
cassandra@cqlsh> tracing on;
Now Tracing is enabled
cassandra@cqlsh> SELECT * FROM demo.test WHERE id=1;

 id | city     | status
----+----------+--------
  1 | New York |      A

(1 rows)


Tracing session: 3f5a2d30-e557-11e8-be1e-4fa05a863635
```

```
activity
-------------------------------------------------------------------
                                              Execute CQL3 query
Parsing SELECT * FROM demo.test WHERE id=1; [Native-Transport-Requests-1]
                       Preparing statement [Native-Transport-Requests-1]
                Executing single-partition query on test [ReadStage-2]
                        Acquiring sstable references [ReadStage-2]
                          Merging memtable contents [ReadStage-2]
                       Merging data from sstable 3 [ReadStage-2]
          Partition index with 0 entries found for sstable 3 [ReadStage-2]
                       Merging data from sstable 2 [ReadStage-2]
          Partition index with 0 entries found for sstable 2 [ReadStage-2]
                       Merging data from sstable 1 [ReadStage-2]
          Partition index with 0 entries found for sstable 1 [ReadStage-2]
                   Read 1 live and 0 tombstone cells [ReadStage-2]
                                              Request complete
cassandra@cqlsh>
```

Now run a single row update and run *nodetool flush* again to generate the fourth SSTable. This should trigger compaction and compact all the SSTables into a fifth SSTable.

```
cassandra@host1:$ sstabledump -d mc-5-big-Data.db
[1]@0 Row[info=[ts=1541901556122756] ]: | [city=New York ts=1541902053338307], [status=A ts=1541901556122756]
[2]@41 Row[info=[ts=1541901562552706] ]: | [city=Paris ts=1541902060799765], [status=X ts=1541901777512372]
[4]@86 deletedAt=1541902077083706, localDeletion=1541902077
[3]@105 Row[info=[ts=1541901569003528] ]: | [city=Tokyo ts=1541901569003528], [status=y ts=1541902748494676]
cassandra@host1: $
```

Few observations.

a) The compaction process compacted all four SSTables into a fifth SSTable mc-5-big-Data.db.

b) "delete from demo.test where id=4;" has generated tombstone. This tombstone still exists in the SSTable until the gc_grace_seconds are over from its time of deletion.

If you run select on the table again with tracing on, you would see that the read path has to read only one SSTable.

```
cassandra@cqlsh> tracing on;
Now Tracing is enabled
cassandra@cqlsh> SELECT * FROM demo.test WHERE id=1;

 id | city      | status
----+-----------+--------
  1 | New York  |      A

(1 rows)

Tracing session: 6204bac0-e558-11e8-be1e-4fa05a863635

 activity
---------------------------------------------------------------------------
                                                        Execute CQL3 query
  Parsing SELECT * FROM demo.test WHERE id=1; [Native-Transport-Requests-1]
                          Preparing statement [Native-Transport-Requests-1]
              Executing single-partition query on test [ReadStage-2]
                        Acquiring sstable references [ReadStage-2]
                          Merging memtable contents [ReadStage-2]
                     Merging data from sstable 5 [ReadStage-2]
                       Key cache hit for sstable 5 [ReadStage-2]
                 Read 1 live and 0 tombstone cells [ReadStage-2]
                                                          Request complete
cassandra@cqlsh>
```

When you run a TRACING ON, you will see the msg saying "Tracing session: 6204bac0-e558-11e8-be1e-4fa05a863635." The tracing sessions are recorded in two tables, *events* and *sessions* in keyspace *system_traces*. You can query these two tables to find the same output and query in those tables.

Repairs

Cassandra is a distributed system with eventual consistency architecture. This means the data you update may not be matching on all the nodes and all the datacenters based on the consistency you use. When we mention "repair" in Cassandra, it does not mean we will be repairing the data which corrupted. All it means is this: synchronize data across all replicas.

Why Repair?

Cassandra is an eventually consistent database in which the repair mechanism is very critical to keep all the replicas in synchronization. Data in a replica can become inconsistent due to the distributed nature of the database. When a node is unreachable or down, it needs eventually updated with the data it missed. Hinted handoff repairs the missing data within 3 hours, but it's not guaranteed. Network issue can cause message drops which can cause data inconsistency. If not repaired, it can eventually result in data loss and queries may return wrong results. To keep all the replicas in sync, we need to run the repair service.

How Anti-entropy Repair Works?

Anti-entropy is a process in Cassandra that compares the data of all replicas, and if there is a difference, it updates each replica to the newest version. When you think about repairs in Cassandra, don't think in terms of the underlying data in a table. Yes, it synchronizes all the underlying data in each table, but mainly it works on token ranges. The repair-initiating node builds a Merkel tree for each replica and compares the differences. If any difference is detected, then it will stream only inconsistent data.

In *Figure 10.7*, you would see the Merkel tree generated for two replicas. The picture and hash representation are for understanding only. For simplicity, we have shown just a depth of two levels, which is a leaf, and ideally, it represents partition in that range. The root hash represents the data in that token range. As you can see, at leaf level in replica B, hash "H-E" differs from hash "H-C" from replica A. Once the Merkel tree is generated, the comparison begins at the top. The trees are compared recursively starting at the root hash. If there is no difference detected in the root hash, it means no repair is needed. If there is a difference, then the left child hashes are compared followed by the right child hashes. This comparison continues until all the token ranges that differ between the two trees are calculated. When it finds the point where it differs, the leaves below that Merkel tree data will be replaced with new data. This is when part of the SSTable is streamed. In *Figure 10.7*, "H-CD" and "H-ED" hashes are different, and only that data is fixed and streamed. The branch "H-AB" will not be repaired as there is no difference.

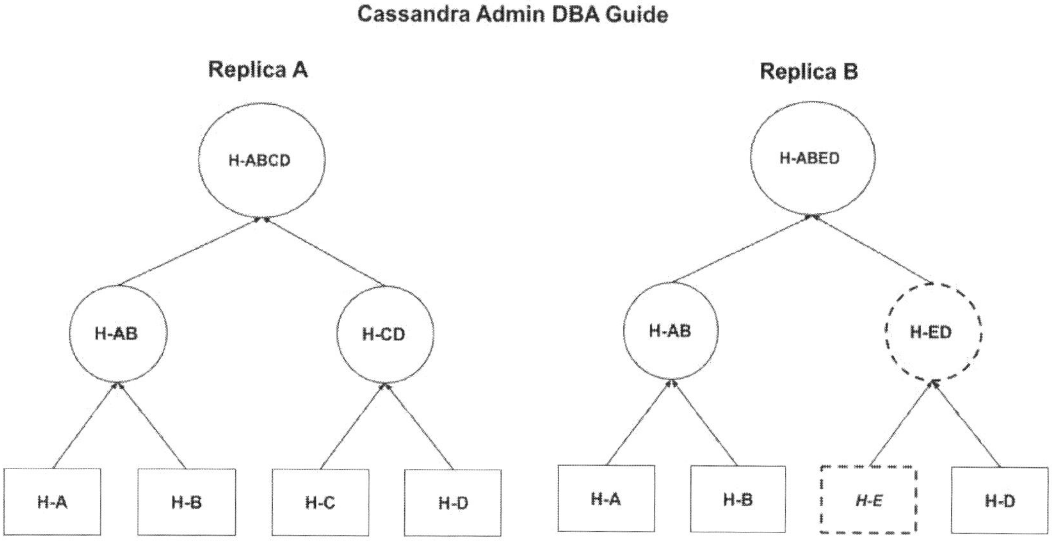

Cassandra Admin DBA Guide

Figure 10.7: Merkel tree.

The Merkel tree provides an efficient way to find the differences in replicas and reduces the amount of data read and transfer over the network for comparison. Think about data size in the above picture with leaf level at 2 GB. The coordinator replica nodes have to read about 16 GB of data and transfer over the network to find out only 2 GB of data is different. Hashing the data and sending hash value over the network is very efficient.

Repair Types

There are two types of repairs: incremental repairs and full repairs. In Cassandra 3.1, the incremental repair is the default repair type.

Full repairs initiate repairs of every token range owned by the node.

Incremental repairs only repair data that's been written after previous full or incremental repair. As the name suggests, repairs are done incrementally. When running incremental repairs, once some data is repaired, it will mark *repaired* and *unrepaired* data separately. This process of separating repaired and unrepaired data is called anti-compaction. At the end of the repair session, the SSTable is split into repaired and unrepaired. Repaired SSTable is marked by a setting "repairedAt" with a time stamp. When you run repair next time, during Merkel tree calculation, which is called validation compaction, the repair process will skip these SSTables that are marked "repairedAt" time stamp greater than 0.

nodetool repair

Use the "*nodetool repair*" command to initiate repairs. This command comes with many options, and it is essential to understand how these options work. To check existing repair options, run

nodetool help repair

Let's take an example of nine nodes single token cluster with a replication factor of three. Assume entire token range for the cluster is from 1–900. Now if you look at *Figure 10.8*, you will see how each node owns the token ranges. For example, node1 owns primary token range 1–100, and its second replica is on node2, and the third replica is on node3.

Node	Primary Token Range	Second Replica Tokens	Third Replica Tokens
node1	**1–100**	801–900	701–800
node2	101–200	**1–100**	801–900
node3	**201–300**	101–200	**1–100**
node4	**301–400**	**201–300**	101–200
node5	**401–500**	**301–400**	**201–300**
node6	501–600	**401–500**	**301–400**
node7	601–700	501–600	**401–500**
node8	701–800	601–700	501–600
node9	801–900	701–800	601–700

Figure 10.8: Repair tokens.

When you run *nodetool repair* on a node, it initiates the repair on that node and based on the repair options; it repairs certain ranges. If you run with full option, it repairs every token range owned by that node. For example, if you run full repair (i.e., *"nodetool repair -full"* on node5), here's what happens:

From Figure 10.8, node5 owns three token ranges. Its primary token range is 401–500. It holds second replica for node4, so it owns the second replica token range from 301 to 400. It holds third replica for node3, so it owns the third replica token range from 201 to 300. Similarly, the secondary replica for node5 is node6, and the third replica for node5 is node7.

It repairs the range 201-300 by comparing node3 <-> node5, node4 <-> node5 and node3 <-> node4.

Similarly the range 301-400 by comparing node4 <-> node6, node5 <-> node6 and node4 <-> node5.

Similarly the range 401-500 by comparing node5 <-> node7, node6 <-> node7 and node5 <-> node6.

Running *"nodetool repair -full"* on node5, there will be five nodes repairing data with each other. If you run full repair like this on all the nodes of the cluster, you are duplicating the repairs unnecessarily and wasting resources.

This is where the option "-pr" comes in handy; "-pr" option repairs only the primary partition range of the node. When you mention the "-pr" option with "nodetool repair" command, it repairs only the primary range owned by the node. This means, if you take above example and run "nodetool repair -pr" on node5, it initiates repair only on its primary range of 401–500 and repairs node6 and node7, as they own the token range 401–500. When you use "-pr," you need to run a repair with this option on every node in every datacenter of the cluster. If you use "-pr" on just one node, or just on one data center, you will only repair a subset of the data on those nodes.

When to Run Repair?

Run repairs daily. Run full repairs weekly or monthly and incremental repairs daily. Your goal is to run repairs on every node in the cluster once within the *gc_grace_seconds* setting, which is, by default, ten days. Running repair within the *gc_grace_seconds* is because tombstones can be synchronized to all the replicas. If you are using Datastax OpsCenter, you can run repairs from OpsCenter

Repairs are CPU, network, and I/O intensive. So run repairs when the cluster is in low-usage hours. Based on your use case, you may want to set up streaming and compaction throughput to proper configuration to speed up the repairs. This is critically important if your use case is write heavy.

Run repairs at these times:

1. Occasionally when a node becomes unresponsive due to hardware issues, network issues, or just too busy due to GC pauses. When you bring back the node, run a manual repair. It seems that hinted handoff eliminates the need of manual repairs, but repairs are required, as loss of hints, which are not applied yet due to the coordinator being down or the node being down little over *max_hint_window_in_ms*.
2. Your node is down for an extended period and you bootstrapped the node.
3. You modified and increased the replication factor for one or more keyspaces.
4. You restored snapshot for a given table or keyspace.
5. You truncated a table and restored it using COPY command.

CHAPTER 11

Backup and Restore

T he reasons we take backups is, to restore the data if needed. Cassandra is a distributed database running on multiple nodes across multiple datacenters. In many traditional RDBMSs, which are mostly running on only one physical box, you need to take backups on only one host. Whereas in Cassandra, it involves taking the backup of data files on all the nodes of the cluster, or at least one entire datacenter. In a multi-datacenter cluster, if all the keyspaces are replicated on all datacenters, you can take the backup of only one datacenter. If a particular keyspace is not replicated to all datacenters, make sure to take the backup of the datacenter where that keyspace is replicated.

Why Backup?

All businesses need to have a disaster recovery plan. Regardless of how small or large a cluster may be, data is vital to run your business. The loss of data, which can happen due to many reasons, can end up costing you a lot of money. Data loss and your application downtime can also cause damage to your business reputation and drive away customers, which could result in a huge business loss.

Data loss can happen due to system crash, disk or storage issue, human error, or even natural disaster. The truth is that this happens when it's least expected. So the preparation is essential.

- The data might be lost due to a hardware issue.
- A human error that could potentially run a TRUNCATE table or INSERT/UPDATE/DELETE data, which can overwrite existing data by mistake.
- A human error that could wipe out data from *$CASSANDRA_HOME/data/ data* with "rm -R *"! You wanted to remove data from a few hosts in

development cluster, but by mistake, you provided production host list for this command.

- You might lose an entire datacenter due to a natural disaster.

Once data is lost, there will be no time to think about what to do next. How fast can the recovery be made will be the next question?

If you design your cluster correctly, you can prevent recovery in certain scenarios. Following are some best practices you can follow while creating your cluster.

Set up your cluster with more than one datacenter. If one datacenter goes down or multiple nodes are down in one datacenter, you can still fall back to the second datacenter. In this case, you may not need recovery.

Make sure to set up proper replication factors for your keyspaces to avoid any data loss due to system crash or disk issues. Setting RF < 3 is not recommended for production clusters.

Data loss due to TRUNCATE table can't be avoided, as Cassandra replicates the TRUNCATE throughout the cluster. But you can set up appropriate permissions to prevent a human error

When we talk about backup, the cost of backup always comes in the picture. There are many different backup solutions you can opt for, including the third-party vendor. For this chapter, we will cover backup and restore using *nodetool snapshots* and *sstableloader*.

Environment for this chapter

For this entire chapter, we will use the below five hosts and following two clusters listed below.

Hostname	IP Address
host1	192.168.1.32
host2	192.168.1.30
host3	192.168.1.31
host4	192.168.1.33
host5	192.168.1.82

Cluster : 'backup_cluster'

```
cassandra@host1:/usr/local/cassandra$ $CASSANDRA_HOME/bin/nodetool describecluster
Cluster Information:
    Name: backup_cluster
    Snitch: org.apache.cassandra.locator.DynamicEndpointSnitch
    Partitioner: org.apache.cassandra.dht.Murmur3Partitioner
    Schema versions:
        ca383af7-0fbd-3aaa-9e68-bd5f26a8a917: [192.168.1.32, 192.168.1.30, 192.168.1.31]
```

Cluster : 'restoreclust'

```
cassandra@host4:~$ $CASSANDRA_HOME/bin/nodetool describecluster
Cluster Information:
    Name: restoreclust
    Snitch: org.apache.cassandra.locator.DynamicEndpointSnitch
    Partitioner: org.apache.cassandra.dht.Murmur3Partitioner
    Schema versions:
        86afa796-d883-3932-aa73-6b017cef0d19: [192.168.1.33, 192.168.1.82]
```

Cassandra Data Directory

Before we look into backup, let us see how the Cassandra data files are stored. $CASSANDRA_HOME/conf/*cassandra.yaml* file contains below configuration.

```
# If not set, the default directory is $CASSANDRA_HOME/data/data.
# data_file_directories:
# - /var/lib/cassandra/data
```

In our case, *$CASSANDRA_HOME/data/data* contains all the data files for Cassandra on that node. For this entire chapter, we will use *node_mgmt.code* keyspace and table to perform a backup and restore.

```
cassandra@host1:~$ $CASSANDRA_HOME/bin/cqlsh -u cassandra -pcassandra 192.168.1.32
Connected to backup_cluster at 192.168.1.32:9042.
[cqlsh 5.0.1 | Cassandra 3.10 | CQL spec 3.4.4 | Native protocol v4]
Use HELP for help.
cassandra@cqlsh> DESC keyspaces;
node_mgmt system_schema system_auth system system_distributed system_traces

cassandra@cqlsh> USE node_mgmt ;
cassandra@cqlsh:node_mgmt> DESC tables;
city    code
cassandra@cqlsh:node_mgmt>
```

Directory structure for 'node_mgmt' keyspace on one node of the cluster.

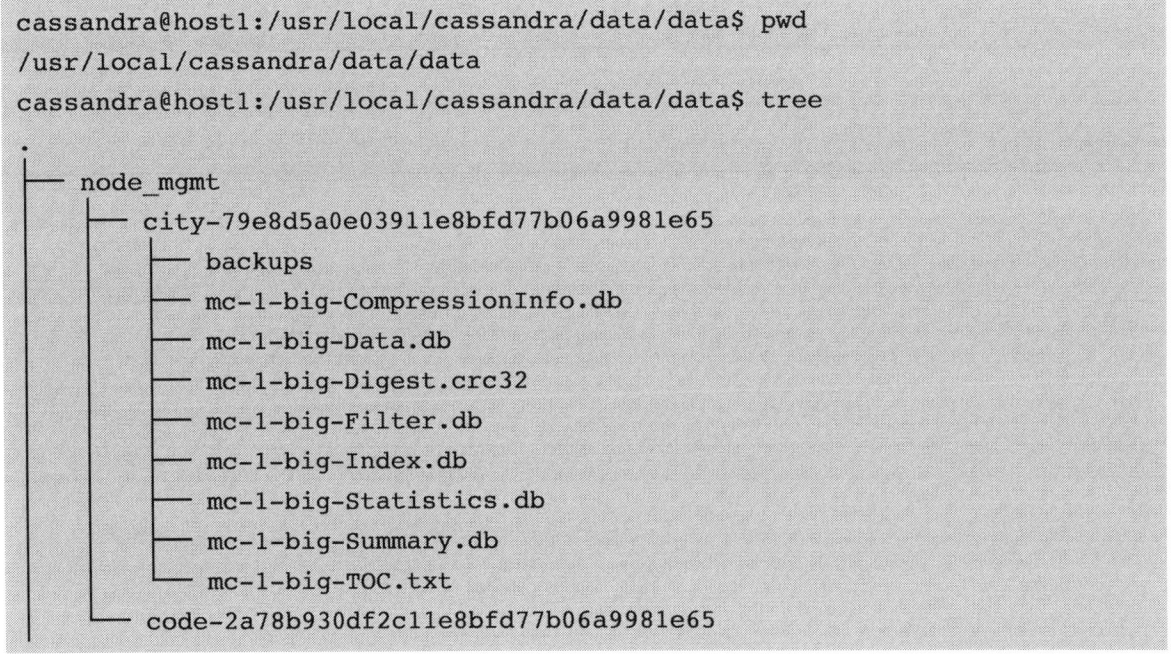

```
cassandra@host1:/usr/local/cassandra/data/data$ pwd
/usr/local/cassandra/data/data
cassandra@host1:/usr/local/cassandra/data/data$ tree

.
├── node_mgmt
│   ├── city-79e8d5a0e03911e8bfd77b06a9981e65
│   │   ├── backups
│   │   ├── mc-1-big-CompressionInfo.db
│   │   ├── mc-1-big-Data.db
│   │   ├── mc-1-big-Digest.crc32
│   │   ├── mc-1-big-Filter.db
│   │   ├── mc-1-big-Index.db
│   │   ├── mc-1-big-Statistics.db
│   │   ├── mc-1-big-Summary.db
│   │   └── mc-1-big-TOC.txt
│   └── code-2a78b930df2c11e8bfd77b06a9981e65
```

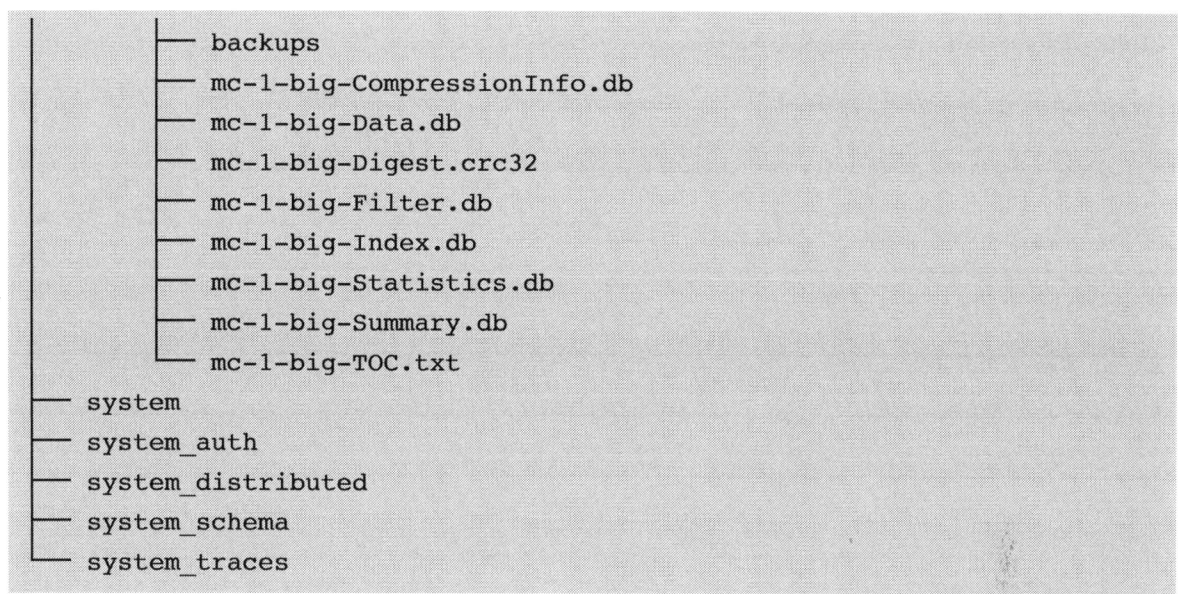

```
          backups
          mc-1-big-CompressionInfo.db
          mc-1-big-Data.db
          mc-1-big-Digest.crc32
          mc-1-big-Filter.db
          mc-1-big-Index.db
          mc-1-big-Statistics.db
          mc-1-big-Summary.db
          mc-1-big-TOC.txt
  system
  system_auth
  system_distributed
  system_schema
  system_traces
```

Cassandra keeps its data in SSTable files. SSTables files are stored in the keyspace directory within the *$CASSANDRA_HOME/data/data* directory path specified by the *"data_file_directories"* parameter in the *cassandra.yaml* file as in the above output. Some output has been removed to accommodate all the keyspaces in the picture.

Backup

In Cassandra, you can take two types of backups.

1. Snapshot backup
2. Incremental backup

Snapshot Backup

The "nodetool snapshot" command takes a snapshot of the data on that node. You need to run this command on all the nodes in the cluster or at least one entire datacenter. This can be run in parallel on all the nodes or you can take the snapshot backup, one node at a time.

You can take a snapshot of all keyspaces or certain keyspaces or a single table in a keyspace. Refer to the complete syntax of the *nodetool snapshot* for detailed usage. Below are some of the examples of using '*nodetool snapshot*'. Note that, these commands take snapshot on one node only. You need to run the same command on all the nodes in the cluster.

Takes snapshot of all keyspaces and tables.
nodetool snapshot

Takes snapshot of keyspace node_mgmt.
nodetool snapshot node_mgmt

Takes snapshot of keyspace node_mgmt and name the snapshot using -t option.
nodetool snapshot -t 2018_Nov_4_before_chages node_mgmt

Takes snapshot of table *code* in keyspace *node_mgmt*.
nodetool snapshot --table code node_mgmt

The snapshot directory is <Cassandra data directory>/*keyspace_name/table_name–UUID/* snapshots/<epoch time>/snapshot_name>. If you do not give *-t* <snapshot_name>, *nodetool* will create a directory with epoch time. Best practice is to give *-t* when you run *nodetool snapshot*. This way it is easy to manage the directory and maintain snapshots.

Let's take a snapshot backup on cluster "backup_cluster" and also we will review the directory structure of the snapshot.

In the below output, we have taken a snapshot of keyspace node_mgmt and named it as "2018_Nov_4_before_changes". We used "for" loop to take the snapshot on all the nodes in backup_cluster.

```
cassandra@host1: $ for host in `cat backup_cluster.hosts`;
do
    echo "$host";
    echo "-------";
    ssh $host /<path>/nodetool snapshot -t 2018_Nov_4_before_chages node_mgmt;
done
```

```
host1
-------
Requested creating snapshot(s) for [node_mgmt] with snapshot name [2018_Nov_4_before_cha-
ges] and options {skipFlush=false}
Snapshot directory: 2018_Nov_4_before_chages
host2
-------
Requested creating snapshot(s) for [node_mgmt] with snapshot name [2018_Nov_4_before_cha-
ges] and options {skipFlush=false}
Snapshot directory: 2018_Nov_4_before_chages
host3
-------
Requested creating snapshot(s) for [node_mgmt] with snapshot name [2018_Nov_4_before_cha-
ges] and options {skipFlush=false}
Snapshot directory: 2018_Nov_4_before_chages
```

Run *nodetool listsnapshots* to view the snapshots on the node.

```
cassandra@host1:~$ nodetool listsnapshots
Snapshot Details:
Snapshot name        Keyspace name Column family name True size Size on disk
2018_Nov_4_before_chages node_mgmt    code          4.83 KiB    5.67 KiB
2018_Nov_4_before_chages node_mgmt    city          27.3 KiB    28.2 KiB

Total TrueDiskSpaceUsed: 32.13 KiB
cassandra@host1:~$
```

Now run *nodetool snapshot* for the *node_mgmt.city* table, without naming the snapshot. This created a snapshot directory with the current epoch timing of 1541355034212, which is GMT: Sunday, November 4, 2018, 6:10:34.212 PM.

```
cassandra@host1:~$ nodetool snapshot --table city node_mgmt
Requested creating snapshot(s) for [node_mgmt] with snapshot name [1541355034212]    and
options {skipFlush=false}
Snapshot directory: 1541355034212
```

```
cassandra@host1:~$ nodetool listsnapshots
Snapshot Details:
Snapshot name          Keyspace name Column family name True size Size on disk
2018_Nov_4_before_chages node_mgmt    code            4.83 KiB   5.67 KiB
2018_Nov_4_before_chages node_mgmt    city            27.3 KiB   28.2 KiB
1541355034212            node_mgmt    city            27.3 KiB   28.2 KiB


Total TrueDiskSpaceUsed: 59.42 KiB
cassandra@host1:~$
```

Directory structure of keyspace *node_mgmt* after these snapshots looks like this on host1. As you can see, since we ran snapshot on only "*city*" table without -*t* option, you don't see that snapshot directory on "*code*" table

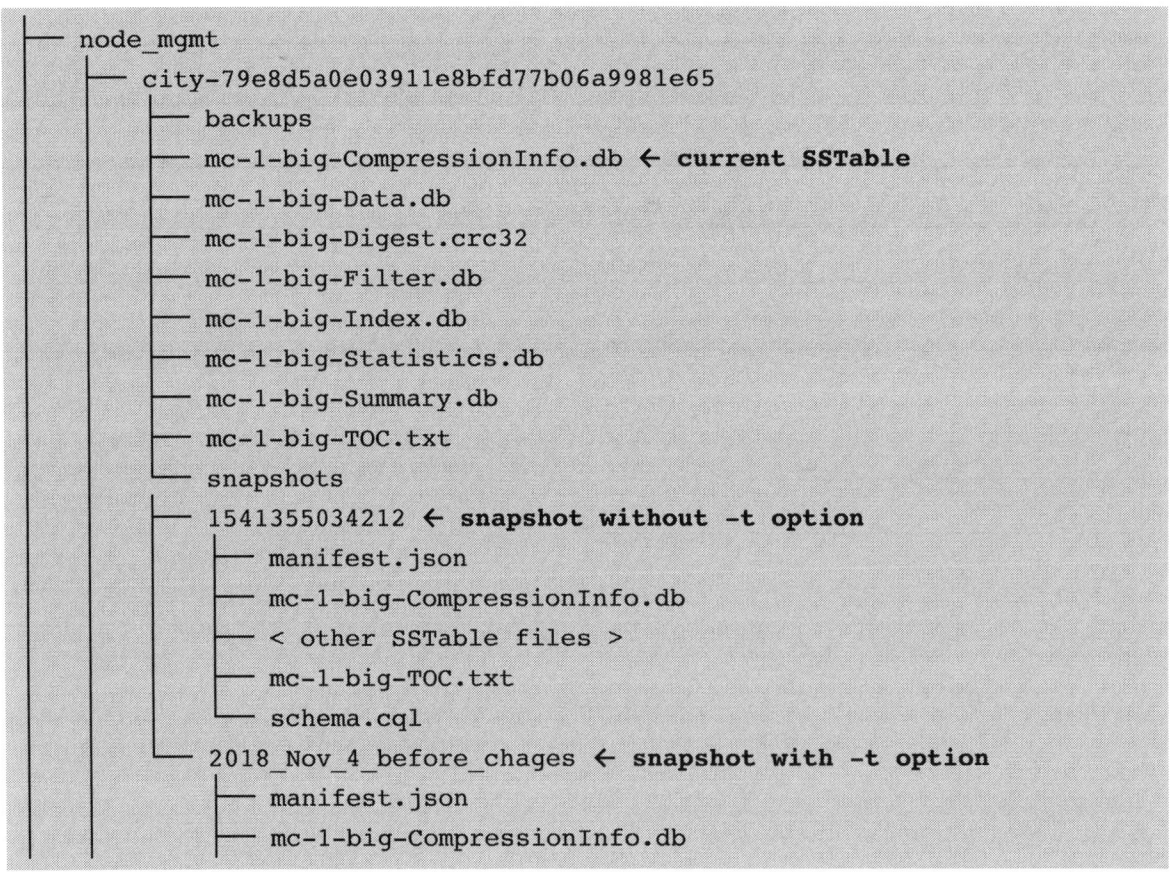

272

```
              ├── < other SSTable files >
              ├── mc-1-big-TOC.txt
              └── schema.cql
      └── code-2a78b930df2c11e8bfd77b06a9981e65
   ├── backups
   ├── mc-1-big-CompressionInfo.db ← current SSTable
   ├── mc-1-big-Data.db
   ├── mc-1-big-Digest.crc32
   ├── mc-1-big-Filter.db
   ├── mc-1-big-Index.db
   ├── mc-1-big-Statistics.db
   ├── mc-1-big-Summary.db
   ├── mc-1-big-TOC.txt
   └── snapshots
       └── 2018_Nov_4_before_chages ← snapshot with -t option
           ├── manifest.json
           ├── mc-1-big-CompressionInfo.db
           ├── < other SSTable files >
           ├── mc-1-big-TOC.txt
           └── schema.cql
```

When you run *nodetool snapshot*, it does the following:

- Flushes memtables to the disk as SSTables.
- Based on the command option such as *-t*, it creates a folder under "*snapshots*" for each table.
- It creates a hard link to all SSTables in the snapshots folder. These hard links stay under the same data directory.

If you see the above output, Folder "city-79e8d5a0e03911e8bfd77b06a9981e65" contains actual SSTables. Since we took two different snapshots, those two folders, snapshots/1541355034212 and snapshots/2018_Nov_4_before_chages are created with a hard link for each file into files under "city-79e8d5a0e03911e8bfd77b06a9981e65."

Hard links are created using the "ln" command internally, which creates a link to the original files. It does not copy the SSTables but establishes a link. That's the reason, running *nodetool snapshot* is faster. It does not copy or duplicate any data. It quickly creates a link. You can run "find -type f -links +1|grep mc-1-big-Data.db" command to see all the hard links for an existing file like in the below output.

```
cassandra@host1: $ pwd
/usr/local/cassandra/data/data/node_mgmt/city-79e8d5a0e03911e8bfd77b06a9981e65
Cassandra@host1$ ls -l
total 60
drwxrwxr-x  2 cassandra cassandra   4096 Nov  4 08:56  backups
-rw-rw-r--  3 cassandra cassandra     67 Nov  4 08:59  mc-1-big-CompressionInfo.db
-rw-rw-r--  3 cassandra cassandra  18844 Nov  4 08:59  mc-1-big-Data.db
-rw-rw-r--  3 cassandra cassandra      8 Nov  4 08:59  mc-1-big-Digest.crc32
-rw-rw-r--  3 cassandra cassandra    384 Nov  4 08:59  mc-1-big-Filter.db
-rw-rw-r--  3 cassandra cassandra   2939 Nov  4 08:59  mc-1-big-Index.db
-rw-rw-r--  3 cassandra cassandra   5529 Nov  4 08:59  mc-1-big-Statistics.db
-rw-rw-r--  3 cassandra cassandra     88 Nov  4 08:59  mc-1-big-Summary.db
-rw-rw-r--  3 cassandra cassandra     92 Nov  4 08:59  mc-1-big-TOC.txt
drwxrwxr-x 4 cassandra cassandra   4096 Nov  4 13:10   snapshots
cassandra@host1: $
cassandra@host1: $ find -type f -links +1|grep mc-1-big-Data.db
./snapshots/1541355034212/mc-1-big-Data.db
./snapshots/2018_Nov_4_before_chages/mc-1-big-Data.db
./mc-1-big-Data.db
cassandra@host1: $
```

It is essential to know that creating snapshots means creating hard links to the SSTables. These files cannot be deleted unless you remove these snapshots (i.e., remove hard links). If you do not remove snapshots, disk space usage will go up, and it could affect the compactions and even lead to nodes going down if the disk is full.

Remove Snapshot

When you take a snapshot, it occupies disk space, which is not deleted automatically. The *nodetool clearsnapshot* command, removes all the snapshots on the node. To remove specific snapshots on the node, run *nodetool clearsnapshot -t <snapshot_name>*.

In the below output, you see that *clearsnapshot* removed the entire directory structure of "snapshots" for both city and code table. The below output has been edited to remove the list of folder and files under all system keyspaces to shorten the output.

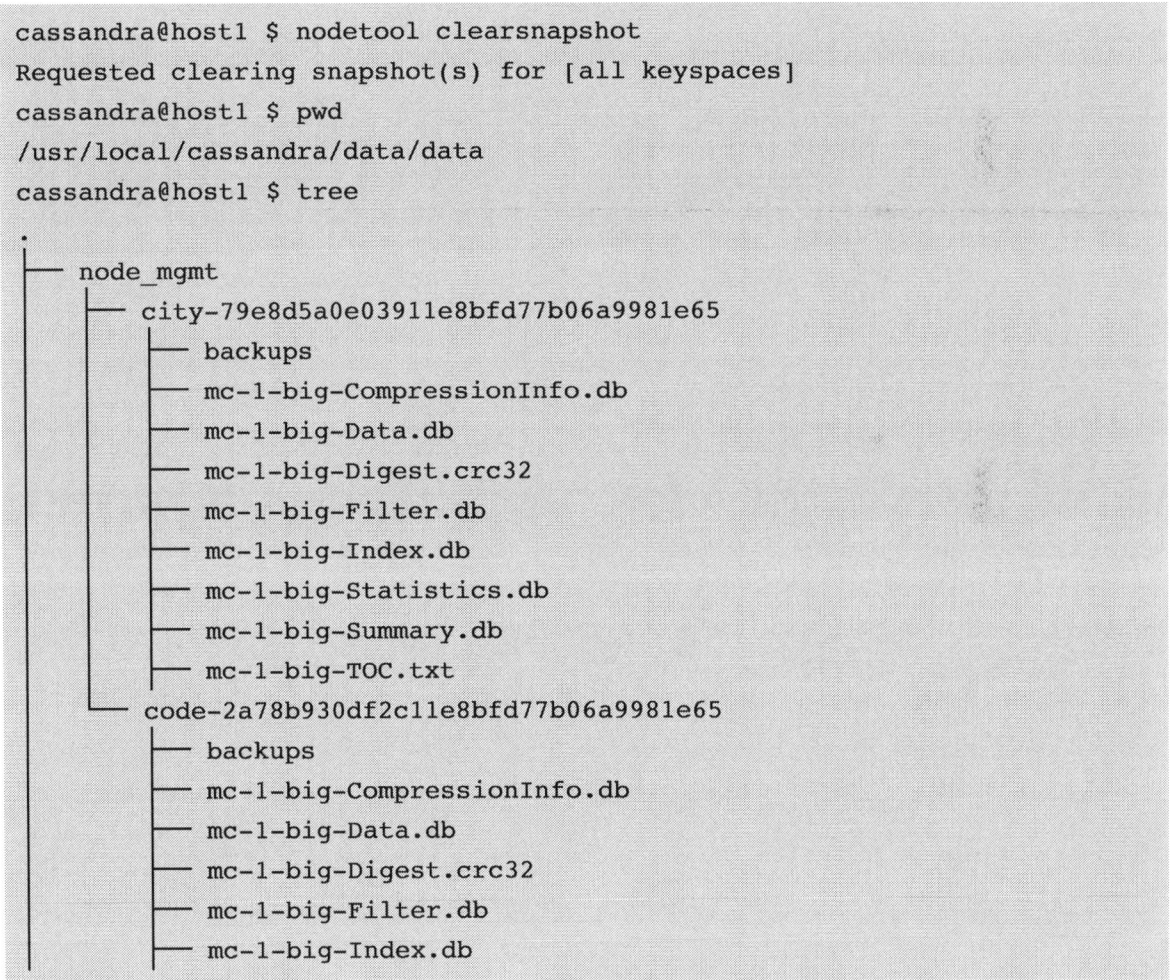

```
cassandra@host1 $ nodetool clearsnapshot
Requested clearing snapshot(s) for [all keyspaces]
cassandra@host1 $ pwd
/usr/local/cassandra/data/data
cassandra@host1 $ tree
.
├── node_mgmt
│   ├── city-79e8d5a0e03911e8bfd77b06a9981e65
│   │   ├── backups
│   │   ├── mc-1-big-CompressionInfo.db
│   │   ├── mc-1-big-Data.db
│   │   ├── mc-1-big-Digest.crc32
│   │   ├── mc-1-big-Filter.db
│   │   ├── mc-1-big-Index.db
│   │   ├── mc-1-big-Statistics.db
│   │   ├── mc-1-big-Summary.db
│   │   └── mc-1-big-TOC.txt
│   └── code-2a78b930df2c11e8bfd77b06a9981e65
│       ├── backups
│       ├── mc-1-big-CompressionInfo.db
│       ├── mc-1-big-Data.db
│       ├── mc-1-big-Digest.crc32
│       ├── mc-1-big-Filter.db
│       ├── mc-1-big-Index.db
```

```
        ├── mc-1-big-Statistics.db
        ├── mc-1-big-Summary.db
        ├── mc-1-big-TOC.txt
├── system
├── system_auth
├── system_distributed
├── system_schema
└── system_traces
```

Incremental Backup

Cassandra also provides incremental backups. By default, incremental backup is disabled. This can be enabled by setting *incremental_backups* to *true* in *cassandra.yaml file*. When this option is enabled, Cassandra creates a hard link to each new SSTable (flushed from memtable) to a backup's directory under the keyspace data directory –

<data directory>/<keyspace>/<table_xxx>/backups.

These hard-linked new SSTables are dependent on the last snapshot backup. Restoring just these files will not be enough.

The *nodetool* command can be used to dynamically enable or disable incremental backups. Note that this will not update the *cassandra.yaml* file and reset *incremental_backups* value.

nodetool enablebackup Enable incremental backup
nodetool disablebackup Disable incremental backup

In the case of incremental backups, less disk space is required because it only contains links to the new SSTable files generated since the last full snapshot. Since Cassandra does not automatically remove the backup files, you need to monitor and remove these files regularly.

auto_snapshot

Note that if you set *auto_snapshot* to true in *cassandra.yaml*, truncate table or drop table will take a snapshot of the table before truncate/drop operation. Like any other snapshot, these are not automatically removed. You need to run *nodetool clearsnapshot* or manually remove them to clear the disk space.

If you have a use case where you need to truncate a table many times a day and reload the data, make sure to pay attention to disk space and remove these snapshots. The best practice is to set *auto_snapshot* = 'false' in a lower environment and set to 'true' on production. If you set to 'true' in production, make sure your use case does not require you to truncate the table many times a day. Also, note that this option is at the node level. In the current version, you cannot set this at the table level or keyspace level. I hope in future this can be set at the keyspace level.

Restore

Restoring backup files in Cassandra is not complicated. All you need is the SSTables taken from the snapshot or incremental backup. There can be many reasons you want to restore the data; few are listed below.

- Truncated table: Numerous times the human error is the reason you may want to restore the data. The DBA or the user is not aware that they are connected to a production cluster and run a truncate table. It is important to review the access and have the best practice of having different passwords for production and nonproduction clusters (Refer to the "Operational" topic in *Chapter 13, Best Practices*).
- You want to restore the production data to a lower environment.
- You want to restore a table's data in a new table.

If you are from a traditional RDBMS background, restoring a complete database (ASE Sybase & SQL Server) or Schema (Oracle) is, in a way, simple. You use the LOAD DATABASE or RMAN to load all the tables. But restoring complete keyspace involves restoring each table on every node in the cluster.

There are two ways you can restore data, nodetool refresh, and sstableloader.

277

Restore Using nodetool

For restoring an entire keyspace, you need to restore each table on each node. Cassandra can restore a table when the table exists. If the table does not exist, you must create the it first. Here are the steps.

1. If schema exists, truncate the table.
2. Copy all the SSTables to <Cassandra data directory>/keyspace_name/table_name–UUID/ folder. Make sure to copy the SSTables to the most recent folder. If you drop table/ create the table multiple times, the data directory may contain multiple table_name-UUID folders, which you forgot to remove. For example, the below output shows the column *id* for *node_mgmt.code* with the matching directory in $CASSANDRA_HOME/ data/data.

```
cassandra@host1:/usr/local/cassandra/data/data/node_mgmt$ pwd
/usr/local/cassandra/data/data/node_mgmt
cassandra@host1:/usr/local/cassandra/data/data/node_mgmt$ ls -l
total 8
drwxrwxr-x 3 cassandra cassandra 4096 Nov  4 18:40 city-79e8d5a0e03911e8bfd77b06a9981e65
drwxrwxr-x 3 cassandra cassandra 4096 Nov  4 18:40 code-2a78b930df2c11e8bfd77b06a9981e65

cassandra@host1: $ $CASSANDRA_HOME/bin/cqlsh -u cassandra -pcassandra 192.168.1.32
Connected to backup_cluster at 192.168.1.32:9042.
[cqlsh 5.0.1 | Cassandra 3.10 | CQL spec 3.4.4 | Native protocol v4]
Use HELP for help.
cassandra@cqlsh> SELECT  keyspace_name,table_name,id
                 FROM    system_schema.tables
                 WHERE   keyspace_name='node_mgmt';


 keyspace_name | table_name | id
---------------+------------+-------------------------------------
    node_mgmt  |       city | 79e8d5a0-e039-11e8-bfd7-7b06a9981e65
    node_mgmt  |       code | 2a78b930-df2c-11e8-bfd7-7b06a9981e65
```

```
(2 rows)
cassandra@cqlsh>
```

If you drop a table, Cassandra does not clean up and remove the folder. It needs to done manually. If you create the same table name again, it will create a different ID. This is the reason why when you restore a table; you need to copy the SSTables to the right directory. Look at the below example. Table "*xyz*" created, dropped, and created again. The directory with the first id "1b4613d0-e090-11e8-b0d6-d1a3870f4bd8" is not dropped.

```
cassandra@cqlsh> CREATE TABLE node_mgmt.xyz( id int , nm text, primary key(id));
cassandra@cqlsh> SELECT keyspace_name, table_name,id
                FROM system_schema.tables
                WHERE keyspace_name='node_mgmt';

 keyspace_name | table_name | id
---------------+------------+-------------------------------------
     node_mgmt |       city | 79e8d5a0-e039-11e8-bfd7-7b06a9981e65
     node_mgmt |       code | 2a78b930-df2c-11e8-bfd7-7b06a9981e65
     node_mgmt |        xyz | 1b4613d0-e090-11e8-b0d6-d1a3870f4bd8

(3 rows)
cassandra@cqlsh> DROP TABLE node_mgmt.xyz ;
cassandra@cqlsh> CREATE TABLE node_mgmt.xyz( id int , nm text, primary key(id));
cassandra@cqlsh> SELECT keyspace_name, table_name,id
                FROM system_schema.tables
                WHERE keyspace_name='node_mgmt';

 keyspace_name | table_name | id
---------------+------------+-------------------------------------
     node_mgmt |       city | 79e8d5a0-e039-11e8-bfd7-7b06a9981e65
     node_mgmt |       code | 2a78b930-df2c-11e8-bfd7-7b06a9981e65
     node_mgmt |        xyz | 2c2ba390-e090-11e8-b0d6-d1a3870f4bd8

(3 rows)
cassandra@host1:/usr/local/cassandra/data/data/node_mgmt$ pwd
```

```
/usr/local/cassandra/data/data/node_mgmt
cassandra@host1:/usr/local/cassandra/data/data/node_mgmt$ ls -lrt
total 16
drwxrwxr-x 3 cassandra cassandra  4096  Nov  4 18:40
code-2a78b930df2c11e8bfd77b06a9981e65
drwxrwxr-x 3 cassandra cassandra  4096  Nov  4 18:40  city-79e8d5a0e03911e8bfd77b06a9981e65
drwxrwxr-x 4 cassandra cassandra  4096  Nov  4 19:17  xyz-1b4613d0e09011e8b0d6d1a3870f4bd8
drwxrwxr-x 3 cassandra cassandra  4096  Nov  4 19:17  xyz-2c2ba390e09011e8b0d6d1a3870f4bd8
cassandra@host1:/usr/local/cassandra/data/data/node_mgmt$
```

3. Run *nodetool refresh*.
4. Once refresh is done on all nodes, run repair on that keyspace.table on all nodes.

If you have a sixteen-node cluster, you need to do this on each node. Make sure to copy the correct backup (if it is moved away from snapshots folder) of SSTables to correct nodes. If you are restoring from an earlier snapshot, it's easy to copy the files.

from <Cassandra data directory>/*keyspace_name*/*table_name–UUID*/snapshots/<name>

to <Cassandra data directory>/*keyspace_name*/*table_name–UUID*/

Let's see an example of restoring a snapshot for one single table "node_mgmt.code." Before proceeding with restore, let's see how the table data is spread across the cluster. The output below shows node_mgmt.code table has fifteen rows, which is spread across three nodes.

```
cassandra@cqlsh> select * from node_mgmt.code ;

 id | comment
----+----------
  5 |   code 5
 10 |  code 10
 13 |  code 13
 11 |  code 11
  1 |   code 1
  8 |   code 8
```

```
    2 |   code  2
    4 |   code  4
   15 |  code  15
    7 |   code  7
    6 |   code  6
    9 |   code  9
   14 |  code  14
   12 |  code  12
    3 |   code  3

(15 rows)
cassandra@cqlsh>
```

Let's see how many SSTable "node_mgmt.code" table has on each node. Let's review this with a for loop.

```
cassandra@host1:/usr/local/cassandra$ for host in `cat backup_cluster.hosts`;
do
    echo $host;
    echo "";
    ssh $host ls -l $CASSANDRA_HOME/data/data/node_mgmt/code-2a78b930df2c11e8bfd77b06
a9981e65/*big-Data.db;
done

host1
-rw-rw-r-- 1 cassandra cassandra 77 Nov  3 23:20 /usr/local/cassandra/data/data/node_mgmt/
code-2a78b930df2c11e8bfd77b06a9981e65/mc-1-big-Data.db

host2
-rw-rw-r-- 2 cassandra cassandra 60 Nov  3 23:20 /usr/local/cassandra/data/data/node_mgmt/
code-2a78b930df2c11e8bfd77b06a9981e65/mc-1-big-Data.db

host3
```

```
-rw-rw-r-- 2 cassandra cassandra 126 Nov  3 23:20 /usr/local/cassandra/data/data/node_mgmt/
code-2a78b930df2c11e8bfd77b06a9981e65/mc-1-big-Data.db
cassandra@host1:/usr/local/cassandra$
```

Each node has only one SSTable for *code* table. We will run one more *for* loop to check the distribution of the primary key partition ID across three nodes using *sstabledump*.

```
cassandra@host1:$ for host in `cat backup_cluster.hosts`;
do
  echo $host;
  echo "";
  ssh $host $CASSANDRA_HOME/tools/bin/sstabledump -d $CASSANDRA_HOME/data/data/
node_mgmt/code-2a78b930df2c11e8bfd77b06a9981e65/mc-1-big-Data.db;
done

host1

[7]@0 Row[info=[ts=1541301187723463] ]: | [comment=code 7  ts=1541301187723463]
[6]@32 Row[info=[ts=1541301187723463] ]: | [comment=code 6  ts=1541301187723463]
[9]@64 Row[info=[ts=1541301187723463] ]: | [comment=code 9  ts=1541301187723463]
[14]@96 Row[info=[ts=1541301187723463] ]: | [comment=code 14  ts=1541301187723463]

host2

[11]@0 Row[info=[ts=1541301187725588] ]: | [comment=code 11  ts=1541301187725588]
[1]@33 Row[info=[ts=1541301187725588] ]: | [comment=code 1  ts=1541301187725588]
host3

[5]@0 Row[info=[ts=1541301187721763] ]: | [comment=code 5  ts=1541301187721763]
[10]@32 Row[info=[ts=1541301187721763] ]: | [comment=code 10  ts=1541301187721763]
[13]@65 Row[info=[ts=1541301187721763] ]: | [comment=code 13  ts=1541301187721763]
[8]@98 Row[info=[ts=1541301187721763] ]: | [comment=code 8  ts=1541301187721763]
[2]@130 Row[info=[ts=1541301187721763] ]: | [comment=code 2  ts=1541301187721763]
[4]@162 Row[info=[ts=1541301187721763] ]: | [comment=code 4  ts=1541301187721763]
[15]@194 Row[info=[ts=1541301187721763] ]: | [comment=code 15  ts=1541301187721763]
```

```
[12]@227 Row[info=[ts=1541301187721763] ]: | [comment=code 12 ts=1541301187721763]
[3]@260 Row[info=[ts=1541301187721763] ]: | [comment=code 3 ts=1541301187721763]
cassandra@host1: $
```

As you can see from the above output, "*node_mgmt.code*" table's fifteen rows, which are spread across three nodes: host1 has 4 rows, host2 has 2 rows, and host3 has remaining 9 rows. Below output shows directory of *node_mgmt.code* table on host1. It has one set of SSTables and there are no snapshot backups.

```
cassandra@host1:/usr/local/cassandra/data/data/node_mgmt/code-2a78b930df-
2c11e8bfd77b06a9981e65$ tree
.
├── backups
├── mc-1-big-CompressionInfo.db
├── mc-1-big-Data.db
├── mc-1-big-Digest.crc32
├── mc-1-big-Filter.db
├── mc-1-big-Index.db
├── mc-1-big-Statistics.db
├── mc-1-big-Summary.db
└── mc-1-big-TOC.txt

1 directory, 8 files
```

Now run TRUNCATE node_mgmt.code. Since *auto_snapshot* is set to 'true', Cassandra will take a snapshot backup before it truncates the table, and all the SSTables are moved under folder "truncated-999999999999-code." We will use this snapshot to restore the table in the next step.

```
cassandra@host1:~$ $CASSANDRA_HOME/bin/cqlsh -u cassandra -pcassandra 192.168.1.32
Connected to backup_cluster at 192.168.1.32:9042.
[cqlsh 5.0.1 | Cassandra 3.10 | CQL spec 3.4.4 | Native protocol v4]
Use HELP for help.
cassandra@cqlsh> TRUNCATE node_mgmt.code ;
cassandra@cqlsh> SELECT * FROM node_mgmt.code ;
```

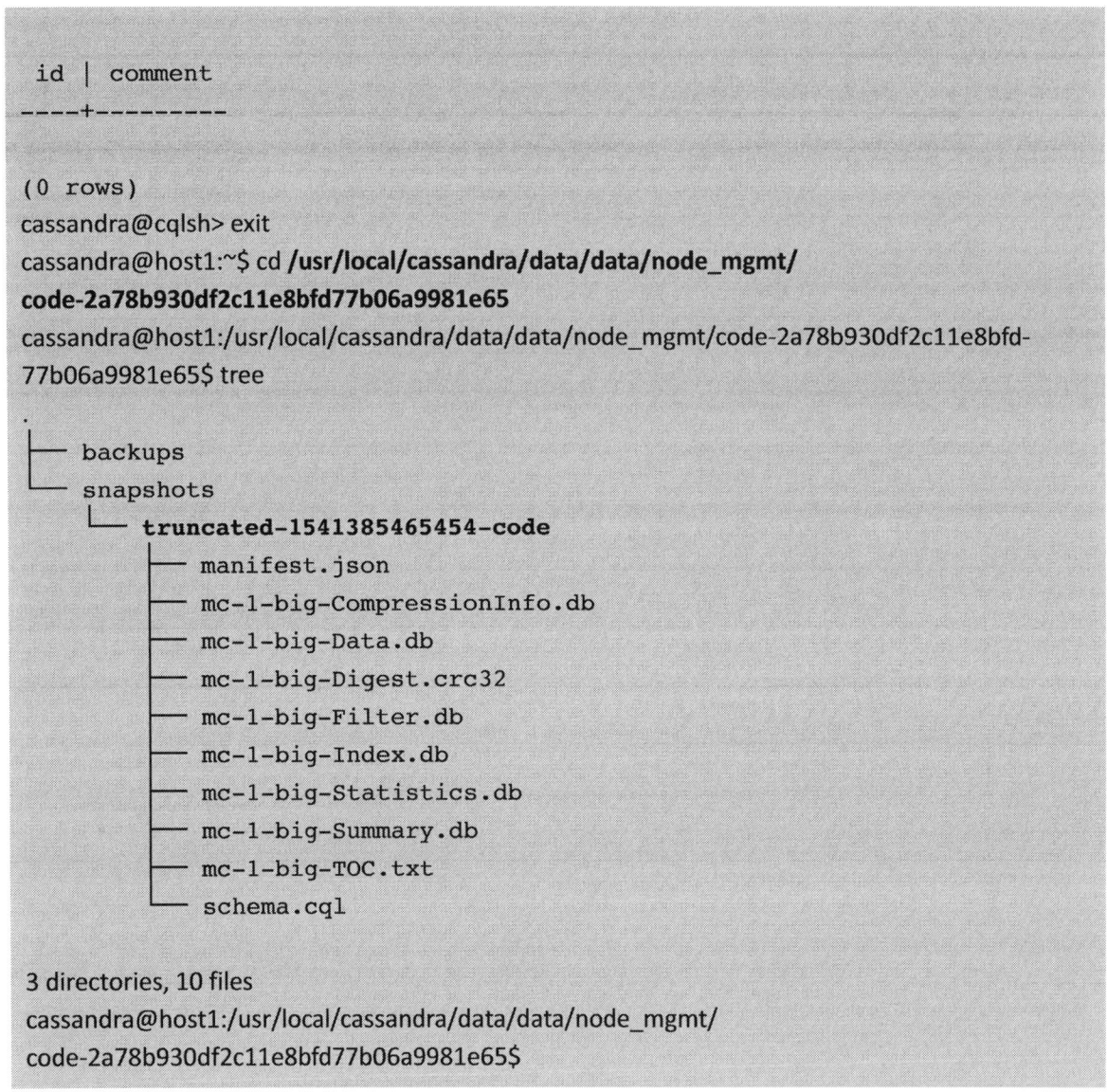

```
 id | comment
----+---------

(0 rows)
cassandra@cqlsh> exit
cassandra@host1:~$ cd /usr/local/cassandra/data/data/node_mgmt/
code-2a78b930df2c11e8bfd77b06a9981e65
cassandra@host1:/usr/local/cassandra/data/data/node_mgmt/code-2a78b930df2c11e8bfd-
77b06a9981e65$ tree
.
├── backups
└── snapshots
    └── truncated-1541385465454-code
        ├── manifest.json
        ├── mc-1-big-CompressionInfo.db
        ├── mc-1-big-Data.db
        ├── mc-1-big-Digest.crc32
        ├── mc-1-big-Filter.db
        ├── mc-1-big-Index.db
        ├── mc-1-big-Statistics.db
        ├── mc-1-big-Summary.db
        ├── mc-1-big-TOC.txt
        └── schema.cql

3 directories, 10 files
cassandra@host1:/usr/local/cassandra/data/data/node_mgmt/
code-2a78b930df2c11e8bfd77b06a9981e65$
```

Now that table is truncated, and there are zero rows in the table *code*; we will restore the data from the truncated snapshots.

```
cassandra@host1:/usr/local/cassandra/data/data/node_mgmt/code-
2a78b930df2c11e8bfd77b06a9981e65$ ls -l
total 8
```

```
drwxrwxr-x 2 cassandra cassandra 4096 Nov  3 01:49 backups
drwxrwxr-x 3 cassandra cassandra 4096 Nov  4 21:37 snapshots

cassandra@host1:/usr/local/cassandra/data/data/node_mgmt/code-
2a78b930df2c11e8bfd77b06a9981e65$ mv snapshots/truncated-1541385465454-code/* .
cassandra@host1:/usr/local/cassandra/data/data/node_mgmt/code-
2a78b930df2c11e8bfd77b06a9981e65$ ls -l
total 52
drwxrwxr-x 2 cassandra cassandra    4096 Nov  3 01:49  backups
-rw-rw-r-- 1 cassandra cassandra      31 Nov  4 21:37  manifest.json
-rw-rw-r-- 1 cassandra cassandra      43 Nov  3 23:20  mc-1-big-CompressionInfo.db
-rw-rw-r-- 1 cassandra cassandra      77 Nov  3 23:20  mc-1-big-Data.db
-rw-rw-r-- 1 cassandra cassandra      10 Nov  3 23:20  mc-1-big-Digest.crc32
-rw-rw-r-- 1 cassandra cassandra      16 Nov  3 23:20  mc-1-big-Filter.db
-rw-rw-r-- 1 cassandra cassandra      32 Nov  3 23:20  mc-1-big-Index.db
-rw-rw-r-- 1 cassandra cassandra    4621 Nov  3 23:20  mc-1-big-Statistics.db
-rw-rw-r-- 1 cassandra cassandra      56 Nov  3 23:20  mc-1-big-Summary.db
-rw-rw-r-- 1 cassandra cassandra      92 Nov  3 23:20  mc-1-big-TOC.txt
-rw-rw-r-- 1 cassandra cassandra     831 Nov  4 21:37  schema.cql
drwxrwxr-x 3 cassandra cassandra    4096 Nov  4 21:37  snapshots

cassandra@host1:/usr/local/cassandra/data/data/node_mgmt/code-2a78b930df2c11e8bfd-
77b06a9981e65$ ls -l snapshots/truncated-1541385465454-code/
total 0
cassandra@host1:/usr/local/cassandra/data/data/node_mgmt/
code-2a78b930df2c11e8bfd77b06a9981e65$
```

In the above output, we moved the SSTables from the truncated snapshot folder to *node_ mgmt.code* tables data directory. Copying SSTables to the data directory will not bring back the data right away. We need to run *nodetool refresh* command to restore the data. The *nodetool refresh* command loads the newly placed SSTables into memory. You need to provide keyspace and table name as an input for this command.

```
cassandra@host1:~$ $CASSANDRA_HOME/bin/nodetool refresh node_mgmt code
cassandra@host1:~$
```

When you run the command, you will see the below information messages in the system.log.

```
INFO  [RMI TCP Connection(26)-127.0.0.1] 2018-11-04 21:52:30,605 ColumnFamilyStore.java:712
- Loading new SSTables for node_mgmt/code...

INFO  [RMI TCP Connection(26)-127.0.0.1] 2018-11-04 21:52:30,634 ColumnFamilyStore.
java:759 - Renaming new SSTable /usr/local/apache-cassandra-3.10/data/data/node_mgmt/code-
2a78b930df2c11e8bfd77b06a9981e65/mc-1-big to /usr/local/apache-cassandra-3.10/data/data/
node_mgmt/code-2a78b930df2c11e8bfd77b06a9981e65/mc-2-big

INFO  [RMI TCP Connection(26)-127.0.0.1] 2018-11-04 21:52:30,657 ColumnFamilyStore.
java:781 - Loading new SSTables and building secondary indexes for node_mgmt/code:
[BigTableReader(path='/usr/local/apache-cassandra-3.10/data/data/node_mgmt/code-
2a78b930df2c11e8bfd77b06a9981e65/mc-2-big-Data.db')]

INFO  [RMI TCP Connection(26)-127.0.0.1] 2018-11-04 21:52:30,663 ColumnFamilyStore.java:789
- Done loading load new SSTables for node_mgmt/code
```

Now cqlsh and run SELECT on the table to view the data.

```
cassandra@host1:~$ $CASSANDRA_HOME/bin/cqlsh -u cassandra -pcassandra 192.168.1.32
Connected to backup_cluster at 192.168.1.32:9042.
[cqlsh 5.0.1 | Cassandra 3.10 | CQL spec 3.4.4 | Native protocol v4]
Use HELP for help.
cassandra@cqlsh> SELECT * FROM node_mgmt.code ;

 id | comment
----+----------
  7 |   code 7
  6 |   code 6
  9 |   code 9
 14 |  code 14

(4 rows)
cassandra@cqlsh>
```

Surprised! We do see only four rows! What was the issue? Why did the restore not restore all fifteen rows? The reason is that fifteen rows are spread across three nodes across the cluster and we did restore on only one node (i.e., host1). As you see in the earlier *sstabledump* output, host1 SSTables had only four rows, which were restored.

You need to repeat the same restore process on the rest of the nodes (host2 and host3) in the cluster to complete the full restore.

Restore Using sstableloader

Another option to restore a table is to use *sstableloader* utility. Also called as Cassandra bulk loader, it can load existing SSTables into the same or different cluster. This can be used to load or restore data into another cluster with a different number of nodes and replication factor. It streams the data in the SSTable into a live cluster.

Follow the below steps to load the SSTables:

1. On the target cluster, create the necessary table if it does not exist. Note that, if the table exists, you don't have to truncate the table if you want to add the data. If necessary, truncate the table.
2. Create a directory where you want to copy the SSTables for loading. Note that for the source folder from where the SSTables will be loaded, the paths must end with / [keyspace_name]/[table_name]. This is the format *sstableloader* uses for parsing. If this does not match exactly in the schema, the load will fail.
3. Run *sstableloader* -d <node ip> <SSTables directory>/[keyspace_name]/[table_name].
4. Restore *node_mgmt.code* table on a different cluster.

We will restore the table *node_mgmt.code* from cluster "*backup_cluster*" to cluster "*restoreclust*". On the target cluster, keyspace and table names need not be the same. We will copy the SSTables from host1, host2, and host3 to host4 under /tmp. As *sstableloader* expects paths to the SSTable to be ended with /[keyspace_name]/[table_name], files are copied accordingly. Note that on the target cluster – "*restoreclust*", we have created the client.*kode* table with the same schema as the *node_mgmt.code* table on the source cluster.

```
cassandra@host4:~$ ls -lrt /tmp/host1/client/kode
total 36
-rw-rw-r-- 1 cassandra cassandra      43 Nov  5 21:16  mc-1-big-CompressionInfo.db
-rw-rw-r-- 1 cassandra cassandra      77 Nov  5 21:16  mc-1-big-Data.db
-rw-rw-r-- 1 cassandra cassandra      10 Nov  5 21:16  mc-1-big-Digest.crc32
-rw-rw-r-- 1 cassandra cassandra      16 Nov  5 21:16  mc-1-big-Filter.db
-rw-rw-r-- 1 cassandra cassandra      32 Nov  5 21:16  mc-1-big-Index.db
-rw-rw-r-- 1 cassandra cassandra    4621 Nov  5 21:16  mc-1-big-Statistics.db
-rw-rw-r-- 1 cassandra cassandra      56 Nov  5 21:16  mc-1-big-Summary.db
-rw-rw-r-- 1 cassandra cassandra      92 Nov  5 21:16  mc-1-big-TOC.txt
cassandra@host4:~$ ls -lrt /tmp/host2/client/kode
total 36
-rw-rw-r-- 1 cassandra cassandra      43 Nov  5 21:15  mc-1-big-CompressionInfo.db
-rw-rw-r-- 1 cassandra cassandra      60 Nov  5 21:15  mc-1-big-Data.db
-rw-rw-r-- 1 cassandra cassandra      16 Nov  5 21:15  mc-1-big-Filter.db
-rw-rw-r-- 1 cassandra cassandra      10 Nov  5 21:15  mc-1-big-Digest.crc32
-rw-rw-r-- 1 cassandra cassandra      16 Nov  5 21:15  mc-1-big-Index.db
-rw-rw-r-- 1 cassandra cassandra    4613 Nov  5 21:15  mc-1-big-Statistics.db
-rw-rw-r-- 1 cassandra cassandra      56 Nov  5 21:15  mc-1-big-Summary.db
-rw-rw-r-- 1 cassandra cassandra      92 Nov  5 21:15  mc-1-big-TOC.txt
cassandra@host4:~$ ls -lrt /tmp/host3/client/kode
total 36
-rw-rw-r-- 1 cassandra cassandra      43 Nov  5 21:17  mc-1-big-CompressionInfo.db
-rw-rw-r-- 1 cassandra cassandra     126 Nov  5 21:17  mc-1-big-Data.db
-rw-rw-r-- 1 cassandra cassandra      10 Nov  5 21:17  mc-1-big-Digest.crc32
-rw-rw-r-- 1 cassandra cassandra      77 Nov  5 21:17  mc-1-big-Index.db
-rw-rw-r-- 1 cassandra cassandra      24 Nov  5 21:17  mc-1-big-Filter.db
-rw-rw-r-- 1 cassandra cassandra    4638 Nov  5 21:17  mc-1-big-Statistics.db
-rw-rw-r-- 1 cassandra cassandra      92 Nov  5 21:17  mc-1-big-TOC.txt
-rw-rw-r-- 1 cassandra cassandra      56 Nov  5 21:17  mc-1-big-Summary.db
cassandra@host4:~$
```

After *scp,* the files to host4, create keyspace *client* and table *kode* on target "restoreclust" cluster. The keyspace and table names are different than from the "backup_cluster."

```
cassandra@host4:~$ $CASSANDRA_HOME/bin/nodetool describecluster
Cluster Information:
    Name: restoreclust
    Snitch: org.apache.cassandra.locator.DynamicEndpointSnitch
    Partitioner: org.apache.cassandra.dht.Murmur3Partitioner
    Schema versions:
        86afa796-d883-3932-aa73-6b017cef0d19: [192.168.1.33, 192.168.1.82]

cassandra@host4:~$ $CASSANDRA_HOME/bin/cqlsh -u cassandra -pcassandra 192.168.1.33
Connected to restoreclust at 192.168.1.33:9042.
[cqlsh 5.0.1 | Cassandra 3.10 | CQL spec 3.4.4 | Native protocol v4]
Use HELP for help.
cassandra@cqlsh> CREATE KEYSPACE client
                WITH replication={'class':'SimpleStrategy','replication_factor':1};
cassandra@cqlsh> CREATE TABLE client.kode (id int PRIMARY KEY,comment text);
cassandra@cqlsh> SELECT * FROM client.kode ;

 id | comment
----+---------


(0 rows)
cassandra@cqlsh>
```

For restoring, the output below shows the target directory created with matching keyspace and table name, and we have copied the necessary SSTable file(s) to host4. We need to run *sstableloader* by passing the directory name as an argument to stream the data.

```
cassandra@host4: $ pwd
/tmp/host1/client/kode
cassandra@host4: $ ls -lrt
total 36
-rw-rw-r-- 1 cassandra cassandra    43 Nov  5 21:16  mc-1-big-CompressionInfo.db
-rw-rw-r-- 1 cassandra cassandra    77 Nov  5 21:16  mc-1-big-Data.db
-rw-rw-r-- 1 cassandra cassandra    10 Nov  5 21:16  mc-1-big-Digest.crc32
-rw-rw-r-- 1 cassandra cassandra    16 Nov  5 21:16  mc-1-big-Filter.db
```

```
-rw-rw-r-- 1 cassandra cassandra     32 Nov  5 21:16  mc-1-big-Index.db
-rw-rw-r-- 1 cassandra cassandra  4621 Nov  5 21:16  mc-1-big-Statistics.db
-rw-rw-r-- 1 cassandra cassandra     56 Nov  5 21:16  mc-1-big-Summary.db
-rw-rw-r-- 1 cassandra cassandra     92 Nov  5 21:16  mc-1-big-TOC.txt
cassandra@host4: $
cassandra@host4: $ sstableloader -d 192.168.1.33 /tmp/host1/client/kode
Established connection to initial hosts
Opening sstables and calculating sections to stream
Streaming relevant part of /tmp/host1/client/kode/mc-1-big-Data.db to [/192.168.1.33,
/192.168.1.82]
progress: [/192.168.1.33]0:1/1 100% [/192.168.1.82]0:1/1 100% total: 100% 0.011KiB/s (avg:
0.011KiB/s)
progress: [/192.168.1.33]0:1/1 100% [/192.168.1.82]0:1/1 100% total: 100% 0.000KiB/s (avg:
0.011KiB/s)
progress: [/192.168.1.33]0:1/1 100% [/192.168.1.82]0:1/1 100% total: 100% 0.000KiB/s (avg:
0.011KiB/s)
progress: [/192.168.1.33]0:1/1 100% [/192.168.1.82]0:1/1 100% total: 100% 0.000KiB/s (avg:
0.010KiB/s)

Summary statistics:
   Connections per host   : 1
   Total files transferred : 2
   Total bytes transferred : 0.150KiB
   Total duration        : 14398 ms
   Average transfer rate   : 0.010KiB/s
   Peak transfer rate    : 0.011KiB/s

cassandra@host4: $
```

As you can see from the above output, for *sstableloader*, we have provided the IP address of host4, which belongs to "*restoreclust*" cluster with two nodes. The data from the SSTable is streamed to all the hosts in the cluster. In this case, we have host4 and host5 as part of the "*restoreclust*" cluster.

```
cassandra@host4:~$ $CASSANDRA_HOME/bin/cqlsh -u cassandra -pcassandra 192.168.1.33
Connected to restoreclust at 192.168.1.33:9042.
[cqlsh 5.0.1 | Cassandra 3.10 | CQL spec 3.4.4 | Native protocol v4]
Use HELP for help.
cassandra@cqlsh:client> SELECT * FROM client.kode ;

 id | comment
----+----------
  7 |   code 7
  6 |   code 6
  9 |   code 9
 14 |  code 14

(4 rows)
cassandra@cqlsh:client>
```

After streaming from host1 SSTables, we do see that four rows were restored. When you run *sstableloader*, you see the below information messages in the system.log.

```
INFO  [STREAM-INIT-/192.168.1.33:46558] 2018-11-05 23:13:57,326 StreamResultFuture.java:116
- [Stream #5d9f49a0-e17a-11e8-b478-a501a3afd844 ID#0] Creating new streaming plan for Bulk
Load

INFO  [STREAM-INIT-/192.168.1.33:46558] 2018-11-05 23:13:57,643 StreamResultFuture.java:123
- [Stream #5d9f49a0-e17a-11e8-b478-a501a3afd844, ID#0] Received streaming plan for Bulk Load

INFO  [STREAM-INIT-/192.168.1.33:46557] 2018-11-05 23:13:57,647 StreamResultFuture.java:123
- [Stream #5d9f49a0-e17a-11e8-b478-a501a3afd844, ID#0] Received streaming plan for Bulk Load

INFO  [STREAM-IN-/192.168.1.33:46558] 2018-11-05 23:13:57,808 StreamResultFuture.java:173
- [Stream #5d9f49a0-e17a-11e8-b478-a501a3afd844 ID#0] Prepare completed. Receiving 1
files(0.075KiB), sending 0 files(0.000KiB)

INFO  [StreamReceiveTask:1] 2018-11-05 23:13:58,630 StreamResultFuture.java:187 - [Stream
#5d9f49a0-e17a-11e8-b478-a501a3afd844] Session with /192.168.1.33 is complete
```

INFO [StreamReceiveTask:1] 2018-11-05 23:13:58,679 StreamResultFuture.java:219 - [Stream #5d9f49a0-e17a-11e8-b478-a501a3afd844] All sessions completed

After running *sstableloader* to stream the data from host2 and host3, you will complete the entire table restore, as shown below.

```
cassandra@host4:$ sstableloader -d 192.168.1.33 /tmp/host2/client/kode
[...]
cassandra@host4:$ sstableloader -d 192.168.1.33 /tmp/host3/client/kode
[...]
cassandra@host4:~$ cqlsh -u cassandra -pcassandra 192.168.1.33
Connected to restoreclust at 192.168.1.33:9042.
[cqlsh 5.0.1 | Cassandra 3.10 | CQL spec 3.4.4 | Native protocol v4]
Use HELP for help.
cassandra@cqlsh> SELECT * FROM client.kode ;

 id | comment
----+----------
  5 |   code 5
 10 |  code 10
 13 |  code 13
 11 |  code 11
  1 |   code 1
  8 |   code 8
  2 |   code 2
  4 |   code 4
 15 |  code 15
  7 |   code 7
  6 |   code 6
  9 |   code 9
 14 |  code 14
 12 |  code 12
  3 |   code 3
```

(15 rows)
cassandra@cqlsh>

COPY Command

COPY command can be used to backup and restore data. Use tCOPY command when you would like to backup or restore a simple table with a small amount of data.

The following is the syntax to backup and restore from CSV files.

COPY <table> [column1, column2,...] TO <file> | STDOUT WITH <options> AND <options>

COPY <table> [column1, column2,...] FROM <file> | STDIN WITH <options> AND <options>

COPY command can be useful for backup and restore especially when you want to back up the data from a table before truncating. Later, you can restore the data to the same table or a different table. In a large cluster, if you have to take a snapshot of the table and later if you want to restore from that snapshot, the amount of work needed is more. COPY TO and COPY FROM will be faster, and you can do this from a single host.

CHAPTER 12

Cassandra Utilities

This chapter describes some of the command tools provided with Cassandra installation.

Cassandra-stress

Cassandra stress tool is a java based utility which you can use for load testing and benchmarking your Cassandra cluster. Under no circumstances, this is going to replace your actual application load testing and baselining. But you have a choice of writing your code or using *cassandra-stress*.

The *cassandra-stress* is easy to use. It's located in *$CASSANDRA_HOME/tools/bin/cassandra-stress*. When you run without user-defined mode, it creates keyspace *keyspace1* and table *standard1*, with the below definition

```
CREATE TABLE keyspace1.standard1 (
    key blob PRIMARY KEY,
    "C0" blob,
    "C1" blob,
    "C2" blob,
    "C3" blob,
    "C4" blob
```

```
) WITH COMPACT STORAGE
    AND bloom_filter_fp_chance = 0.01
    AND caching = {'keys': 'ALL', 'rows_per_partition': 'NONE'}
    AND comment = ''
    AND compaction = {'class': 'org.apache.cassandra.db.compaction.
SizeTieredCompactionStrategy', 'max_threshold': '32', 'min_threshold': '4'}
    AND compression = {'enabled': 'false'}
    AND crc_check_chance = 1.0
    AND dclocal_read_repair_chance = 0.1
    AND default_time_to_live = 0
    AND gc_grace_seconds = 864000
    AND max_index_interval = 2048
    AND memtable_flush_period_in_ms = 0
    AND min_index_interval = 128
    AND read_repair_chance = 0.0
    AND speculative_retry = '99PERCENTILE';
```

Cassandra-stress can be used to stress-test read-only load, write-only load, and mixed load.

Few example of *cassandra-stress*

Example 1. Write 100,000 writes on a given node.

```
$CASSANDRA_HOME/tools/bin/cassandra-stress write n=100000 -node 192.168.1.87
```

Example 2. Write 10,000 writes using 5 threads

```
$CASSANDRA_HOME/tools/bin/cassandra-stress write n=10000 -rate threads=5 -node
192.168.1.87
```

Example 3: Run mixed load of 25% writes and 75% reads with a consistency level of ONE. Below command also logs the results into a log file and generate graphs.

```
$CASSANDRA_HOME/tools/bin/cassandra-stress mixed ratio\(write=1,read=3\)
     n=10000
     cl=ONE
     -rate threads=3
     -node 192.168.1.77
     -log file=cs.log
     -graph file=cas-stress.graph
```

At the end of the stress test results are displayed by the command as below. All the results are written in the format of graphs, if you specify -graph option. In Figure 12.1 and 12.2, two graphs are displayed are generated for the above stress test.

```
Results:
Op rate                    :   252 op/s   [READ: 194 op/s, WRITE: 58 op/s]
Partition rate             :   252 pk/s   [READ: 194 pk/s, WRITE: 58 pk/s]
Row rate                   : 252 row/s [READ: 194 row/s, WRITE: 58 row/s]
Latency mean               :   11.6 ms [READ: 12.1 ms, WRITE: 10.0 ms]
Latency median             :   9.7 ms [READ: 10.1 ms, WRITE: 8.2 ms]
Latency 95th percentile :   25.4 ms [READ: 26.3 ms, WRITE: 21.6 ms]
Latency 99th percentile :   40.7 ms [READ: 42.7 ms, WRITE: 31.2 ms]
Latency 99.9th percentile: 81.4 ms [READ: 81.4 ms, WRITE: 71.8 ms]
Latency max                :   353.1 ms [READ: 352.6 ms, WRITE: 353.1 ms]
Total partitions           :   10,000 [READ: 7,690, WRITE: 2,310]
Total errors               :   0 [READ: 0, WRITE: 0]
Total GC count             :   0
Total GC memory            :   0.000 KiB
Total GC time              :   0.0 seconds
Avg GC time                :   NaN ms
StdDev GC time             :   0.0 ms
Total operation time       :   00:00:39
```

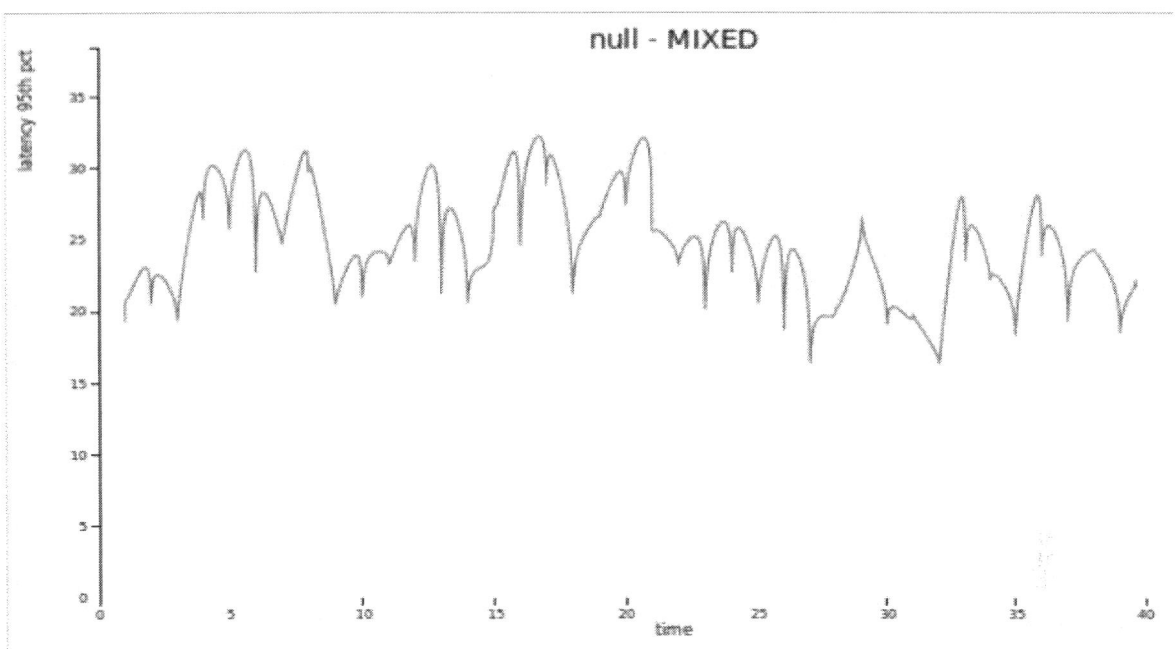

Figure 12.1: Latency 95th percentile graph 25.4 ms [READ: 26.3 ms, WRITE: 21.6 ms]

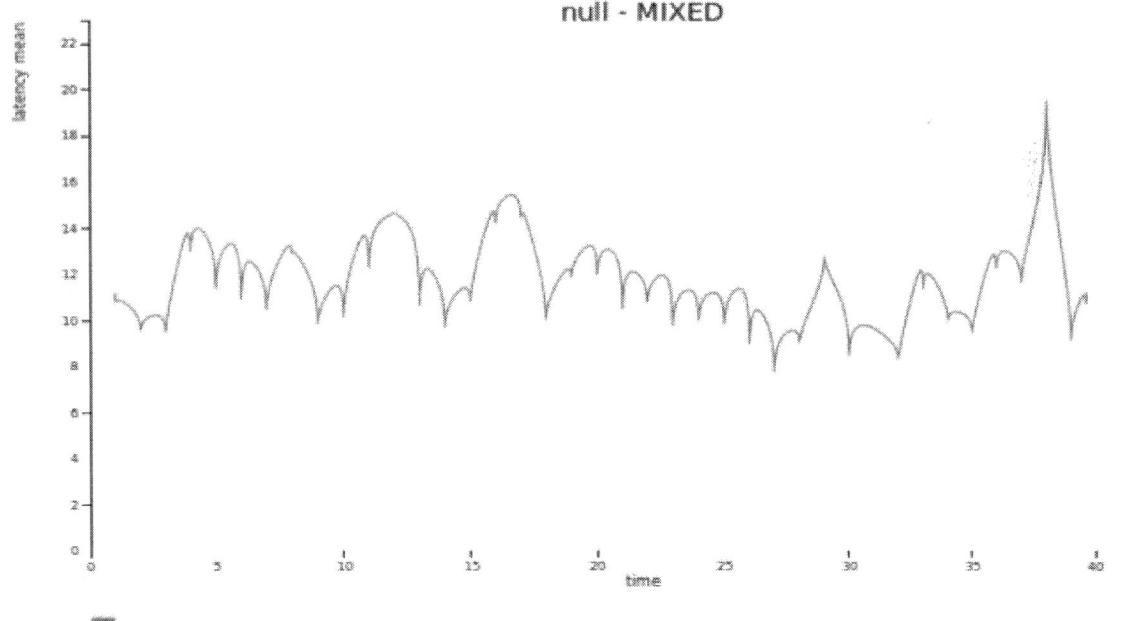

Figure 12.2: Latency mean graph 11.6 ms [READ: 12.1 ms, WRITE: 10.0 ms]

The Cassandra stress tool supports user mode test by using YAML based profiles. In the YAML you can define your schema, compaction strategies, keyspace setting.

sstabledump

Using *sstabledump*, you can look inside the SSTable on how the data is stored. You can dump the contents of an SSTable in JSON format or internal storage format. There are various options to dump the data, including for a single partition key.

Syntax : sstabledump [options] *<sstable file path>*

Let's look at a few examples, for a table customer, which has 3 rows and 2 tombstones as displayed by cqlsh below.

```
cassandra@cqlsh:demo> select * from customer;

 custno | address | name                      | status
--------+---------+---------------------------+--------
      5 |    Mike | 200 B rd, Etown,NJ,62648  |      A
      1 |    Jeff | 123 x rd, Atown,NJ,12345  |      A
      2 |  Warren | 345 y rd, Btown,NJ,12346  |      A
      4 |    Mark | 789 A rd, Dtown,NJ,12648  |      D
      3 | William | 567 z rd, Ctown,NJ,12348  |      I

(5 rows)

cassandra@cqlsh:demo> delete from customer where custno=5;
cassandra@cqlsh:demo> delete from customer where custno=4;
```

For all below examples, the SSTable path is /usr/local/cassandra/data/data/demo/customer-e9df3cb0bc7f11e8b1e22fe4ce31ab74, which has been removed for readability. Also additional empty line has been added in the outputs for readability.

sstabledump with -d option displays the internal representation of the data. In below output, you can see partition key, custno = 4 and 5 as tombstones.

```
cassandra@test_host: $ $CASSANDRA_HOME/tools/bin/sstabledump -d mc-3-big-Data.db

 [5]@0 deletedAt=1539915636937908, localDeletion=1539915636

[1]@19 Row[info=[ts=1537489875508463] ]: | [address=Jeff ts=1537489875508463], [name=123
x rd, Atown,NJ,12345 ts=1537489875508463], [status=A ts=1537489875508463]

[2]@77 Row[info=[ts=1537489875508463] ]: | [address=Warren ts=1537489875508463],
[name=345 y rd, Btown,NJ,12346 ts=1537489875508463], [status=A ts=1537489875508463]

[4]@137 deletedAt=1539915641315477, localDeletion=1539915641

[3]@156 Row[info=[ts=1537489875508463] ]: | [address=William ts=1537489875508463],
[name=567 z rd, Ctown,NJ,12348 ts=1537489875508463], [status=I ts=1537489875508463]
```

sstabledump without any option displays all the rows in JSON format. In below JSON output, you can see partition key, custno = 4 and 5 marked for deletion as tombstones. The delete time is used during compaction to remove these tombstones if they passed the *gc_grace_seconds*.

```
cassandra@test_host: $ $CASSANDRA_HOME/tools/bin/sstabledump mc-3-big-Data.db
[
  {
    "partition" : {
      "key" : [ "5" ],
      "position" : 0,
      "deletion_info" : { "marked_deleted" : "2018-10-19T02:20:36.937908Z", "local_delete_time" :
"2018-10-19T02:20:36Z" }
    }
  },
  {
    "partition" : {
```

```
  "key" : [ "1" ],
  "position" : 18
},
"rows" : [
  {
   "type" : "row",
   "position" : 37,
   "liveness_info" : { "tstamp" : "2018-09-21T00:31:15.508463Z" },
   "cells" : [
    { "name" : "address", "value" : "Jeff" },
    { "name" : "name", "value" : "123 x rd, Atown,NJ,12345" },
    { "name" : "status", "value" : "A" }
   ]
  }
 ]
},
{
  "partition" : {
   "key" : [ "2" ],
   "position" : 77
 },
 "rows" : [
  {
   "type" : "row",
   "position" : 95,
   "liveness_info" : { "tstamp" : "2018-09-21T00:31:15.508463Z" },
   "cells" : [
    { "name" : "address", "value" : "Warren" },
    { "name" : "name", "value" : "345 y rd, Btown,NJ,12346" },
    { "name" : "status", "value" : "A" }
   ]
  }
 ]
},
```

```
{
  "partition" : {
    "key" : [ "4" ],
    "position" : 137,
    "deletion_info" : { "marked_deleted" : "2018-10-19T02:20:41.315477Z", "local_delete_time" :
"2018-10-19T02:20:41Z" }
  }
},
{
  "partition" : {
    "key" : [ "3" ],
    "position" : 155
  },
  "rows" : [
    {
      "type" : "row",
      "position" : 174,
      "liveness_info" : { "tstamp" : "2018-09-21T00:31:15.508463Z" },
      "cells" : [
        { "name" : "address", "value" : "William" },
        { "name" : "name", "value" : "567 z rd, Ctown,NJ,12348" },
        { "name" : "status", "value" : "I" }
      ]
    }
  ]
}
```

If you want to just dump the partition keys, you can use -e option.

```
cassandra@test_host: $ $CASSANDRA_HOME/tools/bin/sstabledump -e mc-3-big-Data.db
[ [ "5" ], [ "1" ], [ "2" ], [ "4" ], [ "3" ] ]
```

Below *sstabledump* command dumps data for single key. "-k 1" below dumps the data for custno=1. Option -t displays the time in raw format.

```
cassandra@test_host: $ $CASSANDRA_HOME/tools/bin/sstabledump -t mc-3-big-Data.db -k 1
[
  {
    "partition" : {
      "key" : [ "1" ],
      "position" : 19
    },
    "rows" : [
      {
        "type" : "row",
        "position" : 37,
        "liveness_info" : { "tstamp" : "1537489875508463" },
        "cells" : [
          { "name" : "address", "value" : "Jeff" },
          { "name" : "name", "value" : "123 x rd, Atown,NJ,12345" },
          { "name" : "status", "value" : "A" }
        ]
      }
    ]
  }
]
```

sstableexpiredblockers

Utility *sstableexpiredblockers* will find out SSTables which are blocking an SSTable which contain only expired tombstones. During the compaction process, Cassandra can drop entire SSTables if they only have tombstones.

Syntax : sstableexpiredblockers [--dry-run] **keyspace table**

In our below example, we have *demo.tbl_tombstone*. In this, we inserted 25 rows and ran a *nodetool flush* to generate the first SSTable. Then we deleted these 25 rows and flushed again to create the second SSTable with all tombstones. Below output shows *sstabledump* of both the SSTable.

```
cassandra@host1:/usr/local/cassandra/data/data/demo/tbl_tombstone-
4ed5ee50eaea11e8a943d330b5c3dec0$ sstabledump -d mc-1-big-Data.db

[23]@0 Row[info=[ts=1542515417723890] ]: | [name=code 23 ts=1542515417723890]
[5]@33 Row[info=[ts=1542515417723890] ]: | [name=code 5 ts=1542515417723890]
[10]@65 Row[info=[ts=1542515417723890] ]: | [name=code 10 ts=1542515417723890]
[16]@98 Row[info=[ts=1542515417723890] ]: | [name=code 16 ts=1542515417723890]
[13]@131 Row[info=[ts=1542515417723890] ]: | [name=code 13 ts=1542515417723890]
[11]@164 Row[info=[ts=1542515417723890] ]: | [name=code 11 ts=1542515417723890]
[1]@197 Row[info=[ts=1542515417723890] ]: | [name=code 1 ts=1542515417723890]
[19]@229 Row[info=[ts=1542515417723890] ]: | [name=code 19 ts=1542515417723890]
[8]@262 Row[info=[ts=1542515417723890] ]: | [name=code 8 ts=1542515417723890]
[2]@294 Row[info=[ts=1542515417723890] ]: | [name=code 2 ts=1542515417723890]
[4]@326 Row[info=[ts=1542515417723890] ]: | [name=code 4 ts=1542515417723890]
[18]@358 Row[info=[ts=1542515417723890] ]: | [name=code 18 ts=1542515417723890]
[15]@391 Row[info=[ts=1542515417723890] ]: | [name=code 15 ts=1542515417723890]
[22]@424 Row[info=[ts=1542515417723890] ]: | [name=code 22 ts=1542515417723890]
[20]@457 Row[info=[ts=1542515417725645] ]: | [name=code 20 ts=1542515417725645]
[7]@491 Row[info=[ts=1542515417725645] ]: | [name=code 7 ts=1542515417725645]
[6]@524 Row[info=[ts=1542515417725645] ]: | [name=code 6 ts=1542515417725645]
[9]@557 Row[info=[ts=1542515417725645] ]: | [name=code 9 ts=1542515417725645]
[14]@590 Row[info=[ts=1542515417725645] ]: | [name=code 14 ts=1542515417725645]
[21]@624 Row[info=[ts=1542515417725645] ]: | [name=code 21 ts=1542515417725645]
[17]@658 Row[info=[ts=1542515417725645] ]: | [name=code 17 ts=1542515417725645]
[24]@692 Row[info=[ts=1542515417725645] ]: | [name=code 24 ts=1542515417725645]
[25]@726 Row[info=[ts=1542515417723890] ]: | [name=code 25 ts=1542515417723890]
[12]@759 Row[info=[ts=1542515417723890] ]: | [name=code 12 ts=1542515417723890]
[3]@792 Row[info=[ts=1542515417723890] ]: | [name=code 3 ts=1542515417723890]


cassandra@host1:/usr/local/cassandra/data/data/demo/tbl_tombstone-
4ed5ee50eaea11e8a943d330b5c3dec0$ $CASSANDRA_HOME/tools/bin/sstabledump -d
mc-2-big-Data.db

[23]@0 deletedAt=1542515530519281, localDeletion=1542515530
```

```
[5]@19 deletedAt=1542515530440822, localDeletion=1542515530
[10]@38 deletedAt=1542515530460825, localDeletion=1542515530
[16]@57 deletedAt=1542515530489218, localDeletion=1542515530
[13]@76 deletedAt=1542515530477853, localDeletion=1542515530
[11]@95 deletedAt=1542515530465563, localDeletion=1542515530
[1]@114 deletedAt=1542515530420256, localDeletion=1542515530
[19]@133 deletedAt=1542515530501680, localDeletion=1542515530
[8]@152 deletedAt=1542515530452131, localDeletion=1542515530
[2]@171 deletedAt=1542515530424543, localDeletion=1542515530
[4]@190 deletedAt=1542515530437572, localDeletion=1542515530
[18]@209 deletedAt=1542515530497694, localDeletion=1542515530
[15]@228 deletedAt=1542515530485196, localDeletion=1542515530
[22]@247 deletedAt=1542515530514677, localDeletion=1542515530
[20]@266 deletedAt=1542515530505698, localDeletion=1542515530
[7]@285 deletedAt=1542515530447528, localDeletion=1542515530
[6]@304 deletedAt=1542515530444063, localDeletion=1542515530
[9]@323 deletedAt=1542515530455916, localDeletion=1542515530
[14]@342 deletedAt=1542515530481210, localDeletion=1542515530
 [21]@380 deletedAt=1542515530508817, localDeletion=1542515530
[17]@399 deletedAt=1542515530493888, localDeletion=1542515530
[24]@418 deletedAt=1542515530522418, localDeletion=1542515530
[25]@437 deletedAt=1542515530526340, localDeletion=1542515530
[12]@456 deletedAt=1542515530471669, localDeletion=1542515530
[3]@475 deletedAt=1542515530429749, localDeletion=1542515530
```

SSTable mc-2-big-Data.db is full of expired tombstones, but mc-1-big-Data.db have older than the newest tombstones. When you run *sstableexpiredblockers*, it will show the blocking SSTable.

```
cassandra@host1: $ $CASSANDRA_HOME/tools/bin/sstableexpiredblockers demo tbl_tombstone

[BigTableReader(path='/usr/local/apache-cassandra-3.10/data/data/demo/tbl_tombstone-
4ed5ee50eaea11e8a943d330b5c3dec0/mc-1-big-Data.db') (minTS = 1542515417723890, maxTS
= 1542515417725645, maxLDT = 2147483647)], blocks 1 expired sstables from getting dropped:
```

[BigTableReader(path='/usr/local/apache-cassandra-3.10/data/data/demo/tbl_tombstone-4ed5ee50eaea11e8a943d330b5c3dec0/**mc-2-big-Data.db**') (minTS = 1542515530420256, maxTS = 1542515530530669, maxLDT = 1542515530)],

If you run manually major compaction, then the SSTable will be dropped during compaction.

sstablelevelreset

The sstablelevelreset can be run on a table with compaction strategy set as Leveled CompactionStrategy. This reset the level of the SSTable to 0 if it's currently more than 0. Use this when you want to change the minimum size of the SSTable. This will restart the compaction with new 'level 0' size.

Syntax : sstablelevelreset –really-reset keyspace table

Based on your use case you might want to reset the level of SSTables to 0 to force the compaction. For example, you have a use case where once in a few months, you want to go ahead and delete a lot of data manually. If this table is using LeveledCompactionStrategy, the tombstone data may occupy a lot of space at higher levels and may not compact immediately. This may lead to a lot of disk usage on the node. To force compaction of these SSTables, you can reset the level to 0 to force the compaction to evict the tombstones.

You can monitor number of SSTables at each level by running

nodetool tablestats keyspace.table

The *nodetool tablestats* output look for the line like "SSTables in each level: [35, 5, 1, 0, 0, 0, 0, 0, 0]."

In the above example, there are 35 SSTables at Level 0, 5 SSTables at Level 1 and 1 SSTable at Level 2 and so on.

sstableofflinerelevel

This can be run on a table with compaction strategy set as LevelledCompactionStrategy. When you experience a very heavy write workload like import of data or bootstrapping the node, it is possible that you could see many SSTables in level L0 and also excessively large. In this case, sometimes compactions also may never catch up. This may result in read latency & performance degradation. This tool can be used to optimally relevels the SSTables.

Synta: sstableofflinerelevel [--dry-run] *keyspace table*

Use the --dry run flag can to run in test mode and examine the tools results.

```
cassandra@host1:$ $CASSANDRA_HOME/tools/bin/sstableofflinerelevel --dry-run first_ks
customer1
For sstables in /usr/local/apache-cassandra-3.10/data/data/first_ks/
customer1-153d1210fb4111e8ac0d3550c4f85976:
Current leveling:
L0=2
Potential leveling:
L0=1
L1=1
```

sstablemetadata

Utility *sstablemetadata* prints the metadata about the given SSTable. It displays information such as – partitioner, tombstones and drop timestamp, SSTable level for LCS, cell size and bytes per row. It retrieves this information from Summary.db & Statistics.db. This report can be used to find out droppable tombstones in the SSTable as well as wide rows. Normally wide rows affect performance and put GC pressure during compactions.

Syntax : sstablemetadata [options] *<sstable file path>*

Estimated tombstone drop times displays number of tombstones are droppable at given epoch time.

cassandra@host1:/usr/local/cassandra/data/data/demo/tbl_tombstone-4ed5ee50eae-a11e8a943d330b5c3dec0$ $ sstablemetadata mc-2-big-Data.db

SSTable: /usr/local/apache-cassandra-3.10/data/data/demo/
tbl_tombstone-4ed5ee50eaea11e8a943d330b5c3dec0/mc-2-big
Partitioner: org.apache.cassandra.dht.Murmur3Partitioner
Bloom Filter FP chance: 0.010000
Minimum timestamp: 1542515530420256
Maximum timestamp: 1542515530530669
SSTable min local deletion time: 1542515530
SSTable max local deletion time: 1542515530
Compressor: org.apache.cassandra.io.compress.LZ4Compressor
Compression ratio: 0.5263157894736842
TTL min: 0
TTL max: 0
First token: -9157060164899361011 (key=23)
Last token: 9010454139840013625 (key=3)
minClustringValues: []
maxClustringValues: []
Estimated droppable tombstones: 1.0
SSTable Level: 0
Repaired at: 0
Replay positions covered: {CommitLogPosition(segmentId=1542327414988, position=1848615)=CommitLogPosition(segmentId=1542327414988, position=1849975)}
totalColumnsSet: 0
totalRows: 0
Estimated tombstone drop times:
1542515530:   25

Count	Row Size	Cell Count
1	0	26
2	0	0
3	0	0
[...]		

```
1179032288322         0
1414838745986         0
Estimated cardinality: 25
EncodingStats minTTL: 0
EncodingStats minLocalDeletionTime: 1542515530
EncodingStats minTimestamp: 1542515530420256
KeyType: org.apache.cassandra.db.marshal.Int32Type
ClusteringTypes: []
StaticColumns: {}
RegularColumns: {}
```

sstablerepairedset

This command is used to set the repairedAt status on a given set of SSTables. This meta data is used in incremental repairs.

```
Syntax: sstablerepairedset [--is-repaired | --is-unrepaired] [-f <sstable-list> | <sstables>]
```

Once you enable incremental repair and for any reason you want to turn it off, you can set unrepaired flag.

Before running the command, stop Cassandra on the node. If you want to set repaired status for all SSTables for an entire keyspace, you can run *find* command to generate a list of SSTable's and pass this file to *sstablerepairedset* command.

```
find $CASSANDRA_HOME/data/data/first_ks/* -iname "*Data.db" > first_ks_allTables_SSTables.txt
```

Let's look at an actual example. We will update the status of only one SSTable. The complete path of SSTable is stored in sstablelist.txt. You can run *sstablemetadata* to check the current repairedAt value of the SSTable.

```
$CASSANDRA_HOME/tools/bin/sstablemetadata /usr/local/cassandra/data/data/first_ks/custom-
er1-153d1210fb4111e8ac0d3550c4f85976/mc-1-big-Data.db | grep "Repaired at"
Repaired at: 0
```

As you see in the above ouput, repairedAt is 0. Once we set this value by running *sstablerepairedset*, it will update with the current timestamp, which you can see in the below output.

```
$CASSANDRA_HOME/tools/bin/sstablerepairedset --really-set --is-repaired -f sstablelist.txt

$CASSANDRA_HOME/tools/bin/sstablemetadata /usr/local/cassandra/data/data/first_ks/custom-
er1-153d1210fb4111e8ac0d3550c4f85976/mc-1-big-Data.db | grep "Repaired at"
Repaired at: 1544311850000
$
```

sstablesplit

Big SSTables can be split into smaller size using this command.

```
Syntax :  sstablesplit [-no-snapshot | -s <Max size in MB> SSTable_name
```

For sstablesplit, specify the size in MB. As a number, you do not need to give the unit. If you do not give the size, default is taken as 50MB. If the size of the SSTable is smaller than the size specified, *sstablesplit* will skip that SSTable from splitting.

Why do we split SSTable? When you force major compaction by running *nodetool compact*, on tables with SizeTieredCompactionStrategy, all the SSTables get compacted together as one large single SSTable. This large SSTable will likely never get compacted as it has to wait for similar size tables. This may affect the read performance on that node. In this situation, you can split the large SSTable into smaller ones.

Let's see an example to split a SSTable, which is 29 MB.

```
cassandra@host1:/usr/local/cassandra/data/data/demo/tablesplit-
c2392c30ec6c11e8953c855e44da35b5$ ls -l
total 31016
drwxrwxr-x  2 cassandra cassandra       4096 Nov 19 21:34   backups
-rw-rw-r--  2 cassandra cassandra      50475 Nov 20 16:12   mc-76-big-CompressionInfo.db
-rw-rw-r--  2 cassandra cassandra   29277108 Nov 20 16:12   mc-76-big-Data.db
```

```
-rw-rw-r--   2 cassandra cassandra         10 Nov 20 16:12  mc-76-big-Digest.crc32
-rw-rw-r--   2 cassandra cassandra     236192 Nov 20 16:12  mc-76-big-Filter.db
-rw-rw-r--   2 cassandra cassandra    2135303 Nov 20 16:12  mc-76-big-Index.db
-rw-rw-r--   2 cassandra cassandra      10190 Nov 20 16:12  mc-76-big-Statistics.db
-rw-rw-r--   2 cassandra cassandra      23576 Nov 20 16:12  mc-76-big-Summary.db
-rw-rw-r--   2 cassandra cassandra         92 Nov 20 16:12  mc-76-big-TOC.txt
drwxrwxr-x 4 cassandra cassandra       4096 Nov 20 17:25  snapshots
drwxrwxr-x 4 cassandra cassandra 4096 Nov 20 17:25 snapshots
```

Now run *sstablesplit* command. For the command, we have given size as parameter requesting to split the SSTables into 10 MB each. If you provide the option as *–no-snapshots*, *sstablesplit* will not take the snapshot backup before it splits the SSTable. In our case, since we did not mention this option, it has taken a snapshot backup.

```
cassandra@host1: $ sstablesplit --debug --size 10 /usr/local/cassandra/data/data/demo/
tablesplit-c2392c30ec6c11e8953c855e44da35b5/*

Skipping non sstable file /usr/local/cassandra/data/data/demo/
tablesplit-c2392c30ec6c11e8953c855e44da35b5/backups
Skipping non sstable file /usr/local/cassandra/data/data/demo/
tablesplit-c2392c30ec6c11e8953c855e44da35b5/snapshots
Pre-split sstables snapshotted into snapshot pre-split-1542775797669
cassandra@host1:/usr/local/cassandra/data/data/demo/tablesplit-c2392c30ec-
6c11e8953c855e44da35b5$ ls -l snapshots/
total 12
drwxrwxr-x 2 cassandra cassandra 4096 Nov 20 16:15 bigtable
drwxrwxr-x 2 cassandra cassandra 4096 Nov 20 17:26 nov20
drwxrwxr-x 2 cassandra cassandra 4096 Nov 20 23:49 pre-split-1542775797669
```

The command has split the SSTable into 3 SSTables as listed below.

```
cassandra@host1:/usr/local/cassandra/data/data/demo/tablesplit-c2392c30ec-
6c11e8953c855e44da35b5$ ls -lrt
total 31124
drwxrwxr-x   2 cassandra cassandra       4096  Nov 19 21:34  backups
```

```
drwxrwxr-x   5 cassandra cassandra      4096  Nov 20 23:49  snapshots
-rw-rw-r--   1 cassandra cassandra    740710  Nov 20 23:50  mc-77-big-Index.db
-rw-rw-r--   1 cassandra cassandra    740413  Nov 20 23:51  mc-78-big-Index.db
-rw-rw-r--   1 cassandra cassandra    586347  Nov 20 23:52  mc-79-big-Index.db
-rw-rw-r--   1 cassandra cassandra    118104  Nov 20 23:52  mc-77-big-Filter.db
-rw-rw-r--   1 cassandra cassandra      8472  Nov 20 23:52  mc-77-big-Summary.db
-rw-rw-r--   1 cassandra cassandra  10487440  Nov 20 23:52  mc-77-big-Data.db
-rw-rw-r--   1 cassandra cassandra        10  Nov 20 23:52  mc-77-big-Digest.crc32
-rw-rw-r--   1 cassandra cassandra     18115  Nov 20 23:52  mc-77-big-CompressionInfo.db
-rw-rw-r--   1 cassandra cassandra     10190  Nov 20 23:52  mc-77-big-Statistics.db
-rw-rw-r--   1 cassandra cassandra        92  Nov 20 23:52  mc-77-big-TOC.txt
-rw-rw-r--   1 cassandra cassandra    118104  Nov 20 23:52  mc-78-big-Filter.db
-rw-rw-r--   1 cassandra cassandra      8472  Nov 20 23:52  mc-78-big-Summary.db
-rw-rw-r--   1 cassandra cassandra  10486929  Nov 20 23:52  mc-78-big-Data.db
-rw-rw-r--   1 cassandra cassandra        10  Nov 20 23:52  mc-78-big-Digest.crc32
-rw-rw-r--   1 cassandra cassandra     18107  Nov 20 23:52  mc-78-big-CompressionInfo.db
-rw-rw-r--   1 cassandra cassandra     10190  Nov 20 23:52  mc-78-big-Statistics.db
-rw-rw-r--   1 cassandra cassandra        92  Nov 20 23:52  mc-78-big-TOC.txt
-rw-rw-r--   1 cassandra cassandra      6728  Nov 20 23:52  mc-79-big-Summary.db
-rw-rw-r--   1 cassandra cassandra    118104  Nov 20 23:52  mc-79-big-Filter.db
-rw-rw-r--   1 cassandra cassandra        10  Nov 20 23:52  mc-79-big-Digest.crc32
-rw-rw-r--   1 cassandra cassandra   8302195  Nov 20 23:52  mc-79-big-Data.db
-rw-rw-r--   1 cassandra cassandra     14355  Nov 20 23:52  mc-79-big-CompressionInfo.db
-rw-rw-r--   1 cassandra cassandra     10190  Nov 20 23:52  mc-79-big-Statistics.db
-rw-rw-r--   1 cassandra cassandra        92  Nov 20 23:22  mc-79-big-TOC.txt
cassandra@host1:/usr/local/cassandra/data/data/demo/
tablesplit-c2392c30ec6c11e8953c855e44da35b5$
```

sstableloader

The *sstableloader* also called as Cassandra bulk-loader, provides the ability to restore snapshots as part of recovery & load of existing SSTables from the same cluster or another cluster into the current cluster with different replication strategy and number of nodes.

> Syntax : sstableloader [options] <dir_path>

Note that the SSTable source folder paths must end with /[keyspace_name]/[table_name]. For example, if you want to load existing SSTables into keyspace.table called finance.customer table, you must store these in the path which ends with /finance/customer.

In this case, copy all the SSTables into say /usr/local/cassandra/bulkload/finance/customer directory.

You can provide *cassandra.yaml* file with -f command line option to set up streaming throughput, client and server encryption options. Only *server_encryption_options*, *stream_throughput_outbound_megabits_per_sec* is read from yaml. Refer to online documentation for all valid options.

Refer *Chapter 11 Backup & Restore* for an actual example.

sstablescrub

The *sstablescrub* can be used to fix corrupted SSTables. Cassandra internally and regularly checks SSTables while compacting and reading SSTables. If it detects any corruption, it logs the errors in the log files, with messages containing text like *CorruptSSTableException*, *CorruptBlockException*. When you notice corruption on the node, take the node offline and run *sstablescrub* for the table which reported as corrupt.

> Syntax : sstablescrub <options> <keyspace> <table_name>

The scrub when run, will take a pre-scrub snapshot first and rewrites all the corrupted SSTable for the given table. The corrupted SSTable will not be removed, and you need to remove them manually. Once you fix corruption, you can start the node and run repairs to fix the integrity of the data. If you have not set replication factor > 1 and corruption happens, you lose data as there is no way to repair it. In this case, your only option is to restore from latest backups, which may not have the most recent data.

```
$CASSANDRA_HOME/bin/sstablescrub --manifest-check --debug --verbose first_ks customer
Pre-scrub sstables snapshotted into snapshot pre-scrub-1544324016574
$
```

sstableupgrade

Upgrade the SSTable to the current version of Cassandra. This is typically run after you upgrade your Cassandra version. This rewrites the old version of SSTable to new version of Cassandra.

Syntax : sstableupgrade [options] <keyspace> <table> [snapshot]

The snapshot option will only upgrade the specified snapshot. Upgrading snapshots are required before attempting to restore a snapshot. This will replace the files in the given snapshot as well as break any hard links to live SSTables.

To upgrade snapshots, you can run *nodetool listsnapshots* to list all the snapshots. Once you have all the details, you can run

sstableupgrade keyspace table snapshot_name

sstableutil

This command will list SSTable files for the provided keyspace.table.

Syntax : sstableutil [options] keyspace table

Below output is modified to remove /usr/local/apache-cassandra-3.10 path from all listed files to fit into the screen.

```
cassandra@cc1:~$ $CASSANDRA_HOME/bin/sstableutil first_ks customer
Listing files...
/data/data/first_ks/customer-20465e30fa8f11e8ac0d3550c4f85976/mc-4-big-CompressionInfo.db
/data/data/first_ks/customer-20465e30fa8f11e8ac0d3550c4f85976/mc-4-big-Data.db
/data/data/first_ks/customer-20465e30fa8f11e8ac0d3550c4f85976/mc-4-big-Digest.crc32
/data/data/first_ks/customer-20465e30fa8f11e8ac0d3550c4f85976/mc-4-big-Filter.db
/data/data/first_ks/customer-20465e30fa8f11e8ac0d3550c4f85976/mc-4-big-Index.db
```

```
/data/data/first_ks/customer-20465e30fa8f11e8ac0d3550c4f85976/mc-4-big-Statistics.db
/data/data/first_ks/customer-20465e30fa8f11e8ac0d3550c4f85976/mc-4-big-Summary.db
/data/data/first_ks/customer-20465e30fa8f11e8ac0d3550c4f85976/mc-4-big-TOC.txt
```

You can use sstableutil in your maintenance script to make it dynamic. For example, to set "Repaired at" status for all the SSTables for all the tables in the Keyspace on all the nodes in the cluster, you could write a script. The below script is for demonstration only, and it does not do any error checking. Write such scripts cautiously.

```
# below cqlsh lists all the tables in keyspace first_ks to a text file tables.txt
$CASSANDRA_HOME/bin/cqlsh -e "select keyspace_name,table_name from system_schema.
tables where keyspace_name='first_ks'" | grep "first_ks"|awk -F"|" '{print $2}' > tables.txt

for host in `cat cluster_host.txt`   ← cluster_host.txt file contains all the ip for the cluster or
datacenter
do
    echo "Running on $host"
    echo ""
    for tbl in `cat tables.txt` ← this is from above text file
    do
        echo "Setting Repaired At for table first_ks.$tbl"
        sstableutil first_ks $tbl | grep "Data.db" > /tmp/sstablelist.txt
        sstablerepairedset --really-set --is-repaired -f sstablelist.txt
    done
done
```

sstableverify

The *sstableverify* utility verifies the SSTable and looks for data corruption or errors. Depending on the size of the SSTable, this might run longer and consumes a lot of memory. You may even need to increase memory before you run this on large SSTable.

```
Syntax : sstableverify [--debug | --extended | --help | --verbose] keyspace | table
```

Example

```
$CASSANDRA_HOME/bin/sstableverify --verbose --extended --debug first_ks customer

Verifying BigTableReader(path='/usr/local/apache-cassandra-3.10/data/data/first_ks/customer-
20465e30fa8f11e8ac0d3550c4f85976/mc-4-big-Data.db') (0.339KiB)
Checking computed hash of BigTableReader(path='/usr/local/apache-cassandra-3.10/data/data/
first_ks/customer-20465e30fa8f11e8ac0d3550c4f85976/mc-4-big-Data.db')
Extended Verify requested, proceeding to inspect values
Reading row at 0
row 000001f4 is 0.063KiB
Row 1 at 0 valid, moving to next row at 70
Reading row at 70
row 000000c8 is 0.064KiB
Row 2 at 70 valid, moving to next row at 142
Reading row at 142
row 00000064 is 0.063KiB
Row 3 at 142 valid, moving to next row at 212
Reading row at 212
row 00000190 is 0.060KiB
Row 4 at 212 valid, moving to next row at 279
Reading row at 279
row 0000012c is 0.061KiB
Row 5 at 279 valid, moving to next row at 347
Verify of BigTableReader(path='/usr/local/apache-cassandra-3.10/data/data/first_ks/customer-
20465e30fa8f11e8ac0d3550c4f85976/mc-4-big-Data.db') succeeded. All 5 rows read successfully
$
```

cqlsh

The cqlsh is a python script that starts the interact CQL shell for executing CQL (Cassandra Query Language) commands.

```
Syntax : cqlsh [options] [ host|IP_address [ port ] ]
```

315

Type $CASSANDRA_HOME/bin/cqlsh -**help** for detailed syntax and options for the cqlsh shell.

```
cassandra@cc1:~$ $CASSANDRA_HOME/bin/cqlsh
Connected to Test Cluster at 127.0.0.1:9042.
[cqlsh 5.0.1 | Cassandra 3.10 | CQL spec 3.4.4 | Native protocol v4]
Use HELP for help.
cqlsh>
```

Specifying a hostname or IP address after the *cqlsh* command connects the session to a specified Cassandra node. By default, CQL shell launches a session with the local host on 127.0.0.1. When no port is specified, the connection uses the default port: 9042. This is configured in *cassandra.yaml* as

native_transport_port: 9042

On startup, cqlsh shows cluster name, IP address and port it's connected to and version information. For the entire set of options, do check the online documentation. All DDL and DML commands which are covered in this chapter can be run through the cqlsh shell. There are some additional commands which are helpful and are listed below.

CQLSH output

You can redirect CQLSH output to a file for further processing. Below are couple of examples.

```
$ echo "SELECT * FROM first_ks.customer;"| cqlsh > output.txt
cassandra@cc1:~/cql$ cat output.txt

 custno | loginname | name   | phone                    | state
--------+-----------+--------+--------------------------+-------
    200 |  warren_2 | Warren | {'mobile': '321-6789'} |    NY
    100 |  bill_001 |   Bill | {'mobile': '123-4567'} |    NJ
    300 |    jeff00 |   Jeff | {'mobile': '123-9876'} |    NJ

(3 rows)
```

```
$ cqlsh -e "SELECT * FROM first_ks.customer;" > output.txt
$
$ cat output.txt

 custno | loginname | name   | phone                     | state
--------+-----------+--------+---------------------------+-------
    200 |  warren_2 | Warren | {'mobile': '321-6789'} |    NY
    100 |  bill_001 |   Bill | {'mobile': '123-4567'} |    NJ
    300 |    jeff00 |   Jeff | {'mobile': '123-9876'} |    NJ

(3 rows)
```

CAPTURE

The CAPTURE is a useful command to capture the output of cqlsh. This is equivalent to redirecting the cqlsh output at the command level. If you are interactively working on cql shell and if you want to capture different output to different files, it's easy to do without coming out of the shell.

```
cqlsh> CAPTURE 'customer_output.txt'
Now capturing query output to 'customer_output.txt'.
cqlsh> SELECT * FROM first_ks.customer;
cqlsh> CAPTURE OFF
cqlsh>
cqlsh> CAPTURE 'by_state.txt';
Now capturing query output to 'by_state.txt'.
cqlsh> SELECT * FROM first_ks.cust_by_state;
cqlsh> CAPTURE OFF
cqlsh> exit
$ cat customer_output.txt
```

```
 custno | loginname | name   | phone                    | state
--------+-----------+--------+--------------------------+-------
    200 |   warren_2 | Warren | {'mobile': '321-6789'} |    NY
    100 |   bill_001 |   Bill | {'mobile': '123-4567'} |    NJ
    300 |     jeff00 |   Jeff | {'mobile': '123-9876'} |    NJ

(3 rows)
$ cat by_state.txt

 state | custno | loginname | name   | phone
-------+--------+-----------+--------+--------------------------
    NJ |    100 |  bill_001 |   Bill | {'mobile': '123-4567'}
    NJ |    300 |    jeff00 |   Jeff | {'mobile': '123-9876'}
    NY |    200 |  warren_2 | Warren | {'mobile': '321-6789'}

(3 rows)
$
```

EXPAND

EXPAND on/off enable or disable vertical printing of the rows. If you enable, it is a useful and convenient way to read long rows of data. Also, this is useful if you want to convert the output to a key-value pair in your scripting.

```
cqlsh:first_ks> SELECT * FROM customer ;

 custno | loginname | name   | phone                    | state
--------+-----------+--------+--------------------------+-------
    200 |   warren_2 | Warren | {'mobile': '321-6789'} |    NY
    100 |   bill_001 |   Bill | {'mobile': '123-4567'} |    NJ
    300 |     jeff00 |   Jeff | {'mobile': '123-9876'} |    NJ

(3 rows)
```

```
cqlsh:first_ks> EXPAND ON;
Now Expanded output is enabled
cqlsh:first_ks> SELECT * FROM customer ;

@ Row 1
-----------+-----------------------
 custno    | 200
 loginname | warren_2
 name      | Warren
 phone     | {'mobile': '321-6789'}
 state     | NY

@ Row 2
-----------+-----------------------
 custno    | 100
 loginname | bill_001
 name      | Bill
 phone     | {'mobile': '123-4567'}
 state     | NJ

@ Row 3
-----------+-----------------------
 custno    | 300
 loginname | jeff00
 name      | Jeff
 phone     | {'mobile': '123-9876'}
 state     | NJ

(3 rows)
cqlsh:first_ks>
```

PAGING

PAGING ON displays 100 lines and prompt with more. Run PAGING OFF to turn off this prompting. If you are capturing the output to a file or redirecting *cqlsh* output, use this option. The current status can be found by PAGING without any option.

```
cqlsh> paging
Query paging is currently enabled. Use PAGING OFF to disable
Page size: 100
cqlsh>
```

Below command runs PAGING OFF and redirects the output. The FROM cust_by_state is not a table, but it's a materialized view. In the current version, COPY TO does not allow you to export data from the view. You can use *cqlsh* to export the results from the view.

```
$ cqlsh -e "PAGING OFF; SELECT * FROM first_ks.cust_by_state;" > output.txt

$ cat output.txt
Disabled Query paging.

 state | custno | loginname | name    | phone
-------+--------+-----------+---------+----------------------
    NJ |    100 |  bill_001 |    Bill | {'mobile': '123-4567'}
    NJ |    300 |    jeff00 |    Jeff | {'mobile': '123-9876'}
    NY |    200 |  warren_2 |  Warren | {'mobile': '321-6789'}

(3 rows)
```

SOURCE

The SOURCE command read the content of the file and executes it. This is equivalent of giving -f <filename> for *cqlsh* command.

```
cassandra@cc1:~/cql$ cat cust.cql
SELECT * FROM first_ks.customer WHERE custno IN (100,200);


cassandra@cc1:~/cql$ $CASSANDRA_HOME/bin/cqlsh localhost


Connected to Test Cluster at localhost:9042.
[cqlsh 5.0.1 | Cassandra 3.10 | CQL spec 3.4.4 | Native protocol v4]
Use HELP for help.
cqlsh> source 'cust.cql';


 custno | loginname | name    | phone                  | state
--------+-----------+---------+------------------------+-------
    100 |  bill_001 |    Bill | {'mobile': '123-4567'} |   NJ
    200 | warren_2  |  Warren | {'mobile': '321-6789'} |   NY


(2 rows)
cqlsh>
```

There are few other *cqlsh* commands which are listed in the below output, which are self-explanatory.

```
cassandra@cc1: $ $CASSANDRA_HOME/bin/cqlsh localhost
Connected to Test Cluster at localhost:9042.
[cqlsh 5.0.1 | Cassandra 3.10 | CQL spec 3.4.4 | Native protocol v4]
Use HELP for help.
cqlsh>
cqlsh> show version;
[cqlsh 5.0.1 | Cassandra 3.10 | CQL spec 3.4.4 | Native protocol v4]
cqlsh> show host;
Connected to Test Cluster at 127.0.0.1:9042.
cqlsh> describe cluster;


Cluster: Test Cluster
Partitioner: Murmur3Partitioner
```

```
cqlsh> consistency;
Current consistency level is ONE.
cqlsh> consistency LOCAL_QUORUM;
Consistency level set to LOCAL_QUORUM.
cqlsh> consistency;
Current consistency level is LOCAL_QUORUM.
```

TRACING

TRACING ON/OFF enables or disables tracing of the queries. Queries run with TRACING ON creates a tracing session and results are stored in two tables - *events* & *sessions* in the *system_traces* keyspace.

```
cqlsh> select count(*) from first_ks.cust_by_state;

 count
-------
    3

(1 rows)

Warnings :
Aggregation query used without partition key

Tracing session: 04a0b580-fbdf-11e8-90b9-8313280638c7

[...removed tracing details...]

qlsh:system_traces> EXPAND ON;
Now Expanded output is enabled
cqlsh:system_traces> SELECT * FROM sessions
                WHERE session_id=04a0b580-fbdf-11e8-90b9-8313280638c7;
```

```
@ Row 1
--------------+-------------------------------------------------------
----------------------------------------------------------------------
--------------
 session_id   | 04a0b580-fbdf-11e8-90b9-8313280638c7
 client       | 127.0.0.1
 command      | QUERY
 coordinator  | 127.0.0.1
 duration     | 64553
 parameters   | {'consistency_level': 'ONE', 'page_size': '100',
'query': 'select count(*) from first_ks.cust_by_state;',
'serial_consistency_level': 'SERIAL'}

 request      | Execute CQL3 query
 started_at   | 2018-12-09 18:19:50.872000+0000

(1 rows)
cqlsh:system_traces> EXPAND OFF;
Disabled Expanded output.
cqlsh:system_traces> SELECT activity FROM events
                 WHERE session_id=04a0b580-fbdf-11e8-90b9-8313280638c7;


 activity
----------------------------------------------------------------------
                       Parsing select count(*) from first_ks.cust_by_state;
                                                        Preparing statement
                                                   Computing ranges to query
    Submitting range requests on 1 ranges with a concurrency of 1 (614.4 rows per range expected)
              Executing seq scan across 2 sstables for (min(-9223372036854775808),
                                              min(-9223372036854775808))
                                          Submitted 1 concurrent range requests
                                             Read 3 live and 0 tombstone cells

(7 rows)
```

cqlsh session

The *cqlsh* session reads *cqlshrc* file from *~/.cassandra* when it launches. You can pre-configure many options in *~/.cassandra/cqlshrc* file. The listed options with comments are self-explanatory.

```
cassandra@cc1:~/.cassandra$ cat cqlshrc

[ui]
;; Whether or not to display query results with colors
color = off

;; Used for displaying timestamps (and reading them with COPY)
datetimeformat = %Y-%m-%d %H:%M:%S%z

[connection]

;; The host to connect to
;hostname = 127.0.0.1
hostname = localhost

;; The port to connect to (9042 is the native protocol default)
port = 9042

;; A timeout in seconds for opening new connections
; timeout = 10

;; A timeout in seconds for executing queries. If your query is taking more than 10 seconds and
;;timing out, you can change the behavior by setting request_timeout. Its updated as 600 seconds
request_timeout = 600

[copy]
;; For COPY TO, controls whether the first line in the CSV output file will
;; contain the column names.  For COPY FROM, specifies whether the first
;; line in the CSV file contains column names.
header = false
```

```
;;number of processes is set to 2
numprocesses=2

[authentication]
;; set up credentials to automatically log in when CQL shell starts and/or choose a keyspace.
username=dba
password=dba123
keyspace=first_ks
cassandra@cc1:~/.cassandra
```

In the same directory, *~/.cassandra*, you can see two more files, which records all the commands typed in *cqlsh* shell and history of *nodetool*. This is quite useful if you want to go back and check prior commands. Make sure to protect this directory and files to *cassandra* user as they contain passwords.

```
cassandra@cc1:~/.cassandra$ ls -l
total 40
-rw------- 1 cassandra cassandra 24742 Dec  9 15:31 cqlsh_history
-rw-rw-r-- 1 cassandra cassandra   776 Dec  9 15:32 cqlshrc
-rw-rw-r-- 1 cassandra cassandra  3170 Dec  9 00:24 nodetool.history
```

nodetool

The nodetool utility is the gateway to your Cassandra cluster. It is broadly and frequently used for managing your cluster. The nodetool has over 100 commands, and we will not list all the commands here. Depending on the Cassandra version you are using, some commands may not exist in older versions. You can type nodetool help for a complete list of commands supported in your version.

All the *nodetool* commands can be grouped in performing certain tasks. For example, commands such as assassinate, removenode, cleanup, join, rebuild, refresh, decommission & viewbuildstatus are used for node management. Next set of commands cleanup, clearsnapshot, disablebackup, drain, enablebackup, flush, import, listsnapshots & snapshot are used for backup related tasks.

There are a group of commands to 'get' current settings and 'set' commands to change the settings.

For example, *getcompactionthroughput* can display the current cap on compaction throughput. If you want to dynamically change the compaction throughput, use *setcompactionthroughuput*.

```
cassandra@host1:~$ nodetool getcompactionthroughput
Current compaction throughput: 16 MB/s
cassandra@host1:~$ nodetool setcompactionthroughput 64
cassandra@host1:~$ nodetool getcompactionthroughput
Current compaction throughput: 64 MB/s
```

Below are some commonly used nodetool options:

status

nodetool status is mostly used to check the status of each node in the cluster.

```
$ nodetool status

Datacenter: NewYork_DC
=======================
Status=Up/Down
|/ State=Normal/Leaving/Joining/Moving
--   Address       Load      Tokens  Owns      Host ID                               Rack
                                     (effective)
UN  192.168.1.72  149.52 KiB  2      8.4%      d667b029-d5c3-4c14-90aa-a5b547880863  rack1
UN  192.168.1.77  144.17 KiB  2      25.2%     e02d6b99-1776-41d6-97ba-7ad0994496c2  rack1
UN  192.168.1.81  169.07 KiB  2      66.4%     d7a52bdf-5711-4d29-a3c2-abd6c6aefafc  rack1
```

In the output, the first letter represents Status U (up) or D (down) and the second letter represents state N (normal), L (leaving), J (joining), M (moving).

If you are running a large cluster with over 100 nodes in the cluster, sometimes it is difficult to list nodes which are not UN (up and normal). Similarly, you may want to display downed nodes (DN). Below are a few simple scripts which can help in monitoring.

nodetool status | grep -v "^UN"   Display nodes which are not UN.

nodetool status | grep -c "^DN"   Get the count of number of nodes down.

nodetool status | grep -c "^UN"   Get the count of number of nodes up.

ring

```
$ nodetool ring

Datacenter: NewYork_DC
==========
Address        Rack    Status  State   Load        Owns      Token
                                                              2868830891279948088
192.168.1.81  rack1   Up      Normal  163.66 KiB  66.40%    -8149832100167230518
192.168.1.77  rack1   Up      Normal  139.08 KiB  25.20%    -5395472283733381655
192.168.1.72  rack1   Up      Normal  140.24 KiB  8.39%     -4670984523451443789
192.168.1.77  rack1   Up      Normal  139.08 KiB  25.20%    -2776392500669656502
192.168.1.72  rack1   Up      Normal  140.24 KiB  8.39%     -1952338433292696309
192.168.1.81  rack1   Up      Normal  163.66 KiB  66.40%    2868830891279948088
```

The *nodetool ring* display token assignment, load and owns percentage. If you are using a single token cluster, this output becomes very important when you downsize the cluster or add new nodes. Load represents the amount of data in Cassandra data directory excluding all the snapshot subdirectories. Data that is not cleaned up, but still exists in SSTables is included in the load. Owns is the percentage of the data owned by the node. Owns includes replicated data.

describecluster

This command is used to validate the schema disagreement. If you are making DDL changes and if the schema version mismatch, it will show in the output. Also if any nodes are unreachable, it will show in the output. It also shows cluster information at the top of the output.

There are many commands which you need to use carefully. The commands such as *cleanup*, *clearsnapshot*, *compact*, *decommission*, *rebuild*, *stop*, *truncatehints* & few others can cause an outage if you issue on a wrong node by mistake. So it is always good practice to run hostname & *nodetool describecluster* to make sure you are on the right cluster and the right node.

```
cassandra@host1:~$ hostname
host1
cassandra@host1:~$ hostname -I
192.168.1.77
cassandra@host1:~$ nodetool describecluster
Cluster Information:
    Name: CADG_c
    Snitch: org.apache.cassandra.locator.DynamicEndpointSnitch
    Partitioner: org.apache.cassandra.dht.Murmur3Partitioner
    Schema versions:
        0a33b449-9aa2-31c0-8292-d4b985d1f640: [192.168.1.72, 192.168.1.77, 192.168.1.81]
```

Throughout this book there are many examples of *nodetool*, which you can refer.

CHAPTER 13

Best Practices

Following are the few best practices. This chapter is not going to cover all, but it will give an idea for you to come up with your list of best practices.

Delete Data

As we read about 'tombstones' in Data Modeling chapter, careful considerations must be made while designing the tables. In one of the shop, the use case was such that, the application was inserting millions of rows in a staging keyspace. Once rows inserted, they were running some intermediate calculations, and at the end of the day, a batch job used to insert these rows into another keyspace as a final validated data. All this was looking good until they went into production. The issue was, they were deleting all the rows from the table in the staging keyspace once the data was inserted into the final keyspace. As you are expecting, yes they had tombstone problems. All their scripts running SELECT to do calculations on staging keyspace were started running very slow due to a spike in read latency. This caused the production outage, and they have to change the script from deleting rows to TRUNCATE table. This solved their immediate problems, but frequent truncate table started creating the snapshots, which began filling the disk space. To overcome that, they created a cron job to remove the snapshot for that staging keyspace table.

In the above case, the entire code and design of the process were driven by RDBMS background. As a Best practice, check your process along with the data model to make sure it does not create bottleneck once it goes to production. To improve this process, the following changes were done.

The staging keyspace RF was set at 3 on all dc. This was changed and limited to only one local dc. The reason behind is, staging data can be reinserted any time if required, and it was not needed on all the dc. This saved the disk space requirements on other datacenters.

The way deletes works in a distributed database like Cassandra is different than RDBMS. As a best practice, review your data modeling to make sure deletes can be limited by design. Talk to developers to review the code, like the one explained above. Making awareness is very important especially developers are coming from an RDBMS background.

When you run select, Cassandra fetches these tombstones and keep them in memory, to make sure that other replicas know about the deleted data. If your workload generates lot of tombstones, this can cause heap pressure and performance problems.

Compaction Strategy

Compaction is the process which merges multiple SSTables into one larger SSTable. Compaction strategy you are going to use matters a lot based on if the table is read heavy or write heavy and type of the disk you are using. Use Leveled Compaction Strategy (LCS) if you are using SSD and for read heavy use case. Use Size Tiered Compaction Strategy (STCS) for write heavy or if you are using spinning disks. Use Time Window Compaction Strategy (TWCS) for time series data.

Server Time (ntpd)

Cassandra is a distributed database running on multiple nodes. The way it replicates the data and achieves eventual consistency is based on the write time of the data. Everything that is written has a timestamp. What makes it highly distributable makes it also vulnerable if clocks on the nodes in the cluster are out of synchronization. The timestamp Cassandra writes is given by the node and coordinator node. So it is vital to make sure all your servers (nodes) in the cluster have the correct time and in synchronization.

Always install *ntpd*. The *ntpd* program is an operating system daemon which sets and maintains the system time of day in synchronism with Internet standard time servers. You can periodically monitor if any server is drifting and take appropriate action. When you configure NTP daemon, make sure that all your nodes are synchronized with one dedicated instance for NTP which can be in synchronized with an external server.

Pay attention to this critical configuration. Keep your server clocks in sync. Cassandra uses a concept called "Last Write Wins". Whenever a write happens, the timestamp is assigned by the coordinator node, and it is written with each column value. If your nodes clocks become out-of-sync, this could cause a major issue with your data. Let's look at an example.

Assume we have two nodes – nodeA and nodeB. nodeA is in synchronization with the real-time, whereas nodeB is 10 seconds behind the real time. This means at real-time 8:30:00.000, nodeB time will be 8:29:50.000.

Now let's say

nodeA: INSERTS a partition at 8:30:00.000. After exactly 5 seconds, a request to delete the same row comes through nodeB.

nodeB: DELETE the same partition at 8:30.05.000 but writes the timestamp as 8:29.55.000.

In a real scenario, the partition was INSERTED, and due to some action, the row was DELETEd right away. But due to the clock is out of sync, this row never gets deleted, and this leads to a data mismatch scenario.

auto_snapshot

By default, *auto_snapshot* is set to 'true', and Cassandra will create a snapshot of a table that you truncate or drop. This is a safety feature to recover accidental truncate or drop table and must be set to 'true' in production as a best practice. This can be set to 'false' on non-production clusters, as mostly, these environments will be running truncate and drop many times. Note that, snapshots created by *auto_snapshot* will not be removed automatically.

SSD Disks

Performance in Cassandra is directly related to the underlying disks. The disk is heavily used during writes, reads, compactions & during repairs.

When it comes to choosing and configuring disks, review the following guidelines.

Shared storage is not recommended. If all your Cassandra nodes in the cluster are pointing to same shared storage, then this could be a single point of failure. Also as Cassandra uses disk very aggressively, shared storage may not be able to keep up with the IOPS and throughput at the same time. The exception is when you are using virtualization.

If you are using spinning disks, configure at least two drives per node, one for the data directory and the second one for a commit log. If you mix commit log and data directories on the same disk, you might see additional disk latency.

If you are using SSD, it's ok to have commit log and data directories on the same mount point.

Snitch

Snitch is configured in cassandra.yaml with the property name endpoint_snitch. Snitch is used for determining the relative host proximity. A snitch determines which datacenters and racks, the nodes belong to. The replication strategy places the replicas based on the information provided by the snitch and Cassandra does it best not to have more than one replica on the same rack.

As a best practice, do not configure your production cluster with *SimpleSnitch*. This is true even when you may have single datacenter. *GossipingPropertyFileSnitch* is recommended over *PropertyFileSnitch*.

In *PropertyFileSnitch*: Datacenter and rack locations are determined by a static file *cassandra-topology.properties*, which contains topology information.

In *GossipingPropertyFileSnitch*, the rack and datacenter are configured in *cassandra-rackdc.properties* file and the node identify its own location. This information propagated to other nodes via gossip. When you add or decommission nodes or datacenter, maintaining this configuration is very easy. Since each node joining the cluster identify its own datacenter & rack information in the *cassandra-rackdc.properties* file, you don't need to update this information on all other hosts in the cluster.

For example, say you have a prod_cluster with 2 datacenters as below.

DC-EAST
host-e1, host-e2, host-e3, host-e4, host-e5 & host-e6

DC-WEST
host-w1, host-w2, host-w3, host-w4, host-w5 & host-w6.

If you are using GossipingPropertyFileSnitch, each node will have just following entry in its *cassandra-rackdc.properties*, which self-identify its datacenter and rack information.

For example, on host-e1,

dc=DC-EAST
rack=RAC1

If you are adding another datacenter, you don't need to update the *cassandra-rackdc.properties* file on the existing nodes in DC-EAST or DC-WEST. Whereas, if you are using PropertyFileSnitch, the datacenter and rack configuration are maintained in *cassandra-topology.properties* static file in the following format. This file needs to be on all the nodes in the cluster.

#DC-EAST
<host-e1_ip>=DC_EAST:RACK1
<host-e2_ip>=DC_EAST:RACK2
<host-e3_ip>=DC_EAST:RACK3
<host-e4_ip>=DC_EAST:RACK1
<host-e5_ip>=DC_EAST:RACK2
<host-e6_ip>=DC_EAST:RACK3

#DC-WEST

```
<host-w1_ip>=DC_WEST:RACK1
<host-w2_ip>=DC_WEST:RACK2
<host-w3_ip>=DC_WEST:RACK3
<host-w4_ip>=DC_WEST:RACK1
<host-w5_ip>=DC_WEST:RACK2
<host-w6_ip>=DC_WEST:RACK3
```

If you are decommissioning any nodes or adding a new datacenter, you need to modify this file on all the nodes in the cluster and restart the cluster.

Replication factor for system_auth.

If we turn on authentication in a cluster, the first thing we need to do is increase the replication factor of the *system_auth* keyspace from the default of 1 to the number of nodes in the datacenter. If we keep the default RF=1, we will not be able to login to the cluster if that node goes down. The *system_auth* uses QUORUM level consistency when checking authentication for default user 'cassandra'. For all other users, it will be checking with LOCAL_ONE.

By default, "system_auth" keyspace is configured with SimpleStrategy. It is recommended and best practice to change this to NetworkTopologyStrategy and set RF to the number of nodes in the datacenter. For example, if you are running a multi-dc with NY & NJ each with 9 nodes, then ALTER the keyspace as follows

```
ALTER KEYSPACE system_auth WITH
replication = {'class': 'NetworkTopologyStrategy', 'NY': 9, 'NJ': 9};
```

Cache tuning
Key Cache Tuning

As you read Cassandra's read path, row cache and Key Cache play an important role in Cassandra reads. Proper allocation of memory to these caches may improve read latency.

When the Key Cache is configured correctly, and the hit rate is close to 100%, it avoids that many physical I/Os. The '*nodetool info*' will give you information about key cache hit rate.

```
$ $CASSANDRA_HOME/bin/nodetool info
ID                       : f5b07323-214f-4a78-8640-c3ed1b61c15d
Gossip active            : true
Thrift active            : true
Native Transport active: true
Load                     : 110.61 GB
Generation No            : 1551928383
Uptime (seconds)         : 9837600
Heap Memory (MB)         : 6324.21 / 16384.00
Off Heap Memory (MB)     : 1037.87
Data Center              : datacenter1
Rack                     : RAC1
Exceptions               : 0
Key Cache                : size 104857592 (bytes), capacity 104857600
(bytes), 35149691430 hits, 50820492787 requests, 0.729 recent hit rate,
14400 save period in seconds
Row Cache                : size 0 (bytes), capacity 0 (bytes), 0 hits, 0
requests, NaN recent hit rate, 0 save period in seconds
[...]
$
```

If your hit rate for Key Cache is consistently falling below 80-85%, review and allocate more memory. This is configured in *cassandra.yaml* as *key_cache_size_in_mb*. This also can be set dynamically without starting the node by running *nodetool setcachecapacity*.

Row Cache

The row cache holds the entire content of a row in memory, and by default, it is set to 0. Row cache can give significant read performance, but it is memory-intensive. By default, row cache is disabled. It is ideal for small tables or tables which are frequently accessed. Also, you need to avoid configuring row cache for tables which are updated regularly. The reason, when a row is updated, it will remove the row from the cache.

Bloom filters

Bloom filters help reads to determine if the SSTable has a given partition key. It is used only for index scan queries and not for range scans. Bloom filter setting range from 0.0 to 1.0. The default value for *bloom_filter_fp_chance* is 0.1 for tables using *LeveledCompactionStrategy* and 0.01 for all other compaction strategy. Setting the value closer to 0 requires more memory. If you are not using SSD disks or you are using disks with low IOPS, allocating more memory to bloom filter may reduce your disk I/o thus improving read latency.

If *nodetool tablestats* output reports a higher number of "Bloom filter false positives", consider altering the table to change *bloom_filter_fp_chance* to a lower value.

```
ALTER TABLE keyspace.your_table WITH bloom_filter_fp_chance=0.01
```

A higher number of "Bloom filter false positives" means Number of false positives, which occur when the bloom filter said the row existed, but it did not exist.

Operational

These are some simple operational best practices which can help avoid any human errors, which can cause outages.

Always verify cluster performance before and after changes to make sure change looks good. It cannot be just a smoke test. A smoke test is good for functional testing. You want to measure the performance impact happening due to the change. Don't evaluate the change on how you feel about it, but always go by the metrics. Having a baseline metrics is very important when you want to measure any kind of impact due to the change.

Always make changes in the lower environment before moving the change to the production cluster. If you do not have a non-production environment, you should seriously consider building it now. The cost of having one additional set of environment always better than cost you have to pay. If there is an outage which could cost the business in terms of money and reputation. Along with your production environment, ideally, you should have a development/QA and Staging environment. It is important to have a staging environment at the same version level as production. Deployment in a staging environment will help catch any glitches/issues before deploying changes to production.

When you are making changes, ideally implement changes one at a time. The reason is, if you see cluster performance degrade after changes applied, you may not know and confirm which change is working and which change is causing the degrade of the performance.

Preparedness is always best when it comes to change management. Have runbooks for every change. The Runbooks should be written at a level, where you almost cut and paste the commands. This avoids many human errors.

Before making any changes always run *nodetool describecluster* to make sure you are on the right node and right cluster before making any changes. As all we know, we have many putty or shell open and doing many things in parallel. The last thing you want to do is, decommission a production cluster node instead of a development cluster node just because you ran the command in a hurry. This mistake can be very costly.

Avoid generic user id

In some shops its common practice to have a generic application user id's across environment. For example,

app_read_only
app_write_only
app_admin

Best practice is to have environment specific naming convention such as

app_prod_read_only
app_prod_write_only
app_prod_admin

app_qa_read_only
app_qa_write_only
app_qa_admin

Don't have the same password for a given id across the environment. This avoids many human errors. In one of my client, they were using generic id across all environment such as 'app_write_only account'. For an application load testing, they used to point to Cassandra staging cluster and run few tests. One day, unfortunately, they were pointing the load test to Cassandra production cluster and wrote a lot of test data. It took a few days to clean up the unwanted data written to the production cluster. Implementing some best practices can safeguard your environment.

Datacenter wise implementation

Whenever you apply any changes, do it datacenter wise. If you have multiple datacenter setup, work on only one datacenter first. This way you can isolate other datacenters. I believe this is one of the main reason your cluster must be configured as multiple datacenters. Along with this, your application should have the ability to stop and start the read and write traffic for each datacenter independently.

Monitoring

Monitoring Cassandra cluster is most important tasks as an administrator or DBA. No one needs to tell the importance of monitoring. Monitoring is done for two types of issues. First, one is prevention monitoring and alerting so that you can avoid an outage. For example, disk getting full or on one of the node memory utilization is high. Second, the outage is already has happened and alerted for it. For example, one or more nodes are down.

For cluster monitoring and alerts you can use various tools. Those tools will be giving you a high-level view on what happening in your cluster and nodes. Few important things to monitor -

- Disk space
- CPU on the host
- Node down or unreachable
- Cassandra log monitoring
- Server clock synchronization
- Full GC

Along with the above monitoring related to Cassandra, you need detail application metrics and dashboards. This is required to understand granular level details. These metrics and dashboards will be helpful along with Cassandra metrics to know how well your application is performing.

You want to make sure to setup log aggregation. It's essential that you aggregate all logs from all the nodes to a central location and they can be searchable. For this, you can use Splunk, logtash/kibana or Graylog. Along with Cassandra system.log and /var/log/messages, you can write some keyspace level read and write statistics to a file and aggregate it, so that you can give a facility to chart various data items.

For example, you can collect read throughput, write throughput, read latency, write latency at the node level and write to a log aggregator. This information can be searched, and the graph can be plotted for a given keyspace or data center. These monitoring and information will be convenient in troubleshooting.

The *nodetool* command can be used as one of the main monitoring and troubleshooting tool. The following section will discuss some useful monitoring and troubleshooting commands.

nodetool status

Provides status of the cluster and information such as node status, load, host id, rack. You can use this command (nodetool status | grep -c "^DN") in your monitoring script to generate appropriate alerts or actions.

nodetool info

Provides information about uptime, load, datacenter, rack, heap memory info, key cache, row cache.

nodetool describecluster

Provides cluster name, snitch, partitioner and schema version of a cluster.

Opscenter

If you are using DataStax DSE, the first monitoring tool you are going to use is OpsCenter. OpsCenter is monitoring and visual management tool. It simplifies the administration of the cluster and performs some of the below tasks.

- Viewing historical performance through Dashboards
- Configuring nodes
- Adding and expanding clusters
- Monitoring clusters
- Management services such as Repair Service, Backup Service, Capacity Service & Best practices service.

For detailed product information, refer https://www.datastax.com/products/datastax-opscenter

Below are the couple of screen shot of the OpsCenter 6.5.1

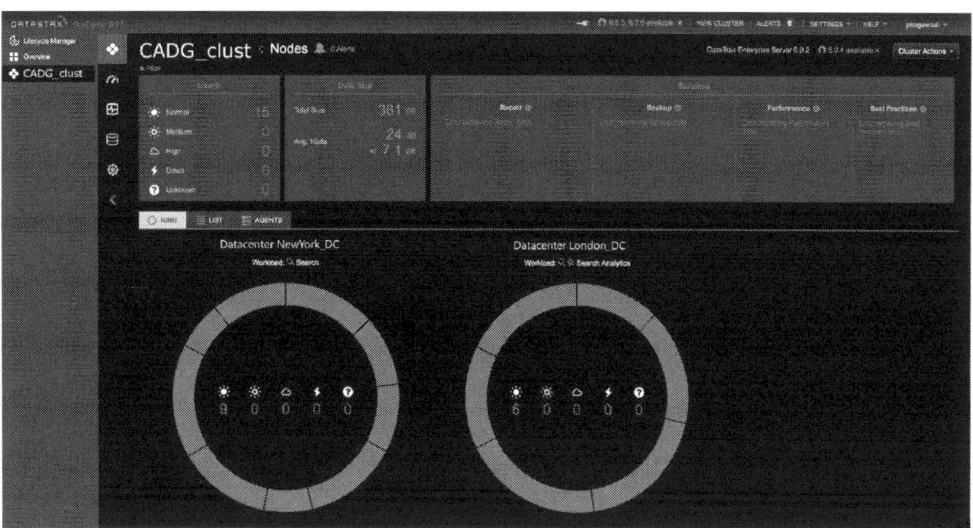

Figure 13.1 : Datastax OpsCenter – ring view.

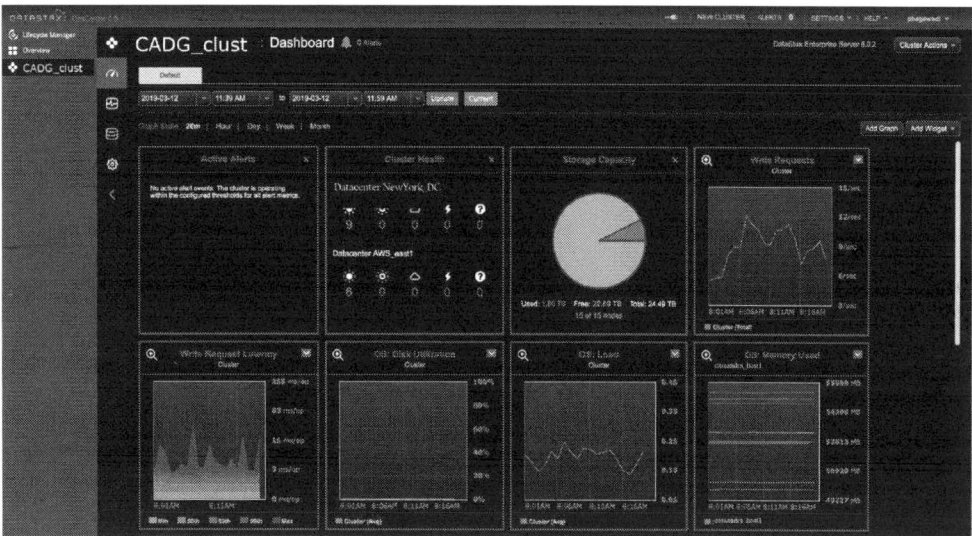

Figure 13.2 : Datastax OpsCenter - Dashboard

* * *

CHAPTER 14
Trouble Shooting

Troubleshooting Cassandra cluster first starts with the best practices. What do I mean? You are troubleshooting an issue means; maybe you did not follow the best practices. It could be an environment related issue. It could be a change issue. It could be an application issue or just the volume of the data. It could be a human error.

Best practices start with designing the cluster with proper configurations. If you are building a new environment, obviously you cannot come up with the best configurations and practices in the beginning. But as you see issues and troubleshoot them and fix it, you go back and update your cluster deployment code, best practices document and run books.

In this chapter, we will go through a few generic troubleshooting scenarios. Some of the points covered here may or may not apply to your use case or environment. As you troubleshoot the issues, it is recommended that you document them with as many details as possible, which includes actual commands used to fix it and the output of the commands & screenshots. This habit of documenting will be beneficial for you and your team members to address similar issues.

Node Down

There could be several reason nodes could go down. The node could be going through the load and momentarily it was unreachable and flapping. In this case no need to start or restart Cassandra on the node.

Run nodetool status to check which node is down. If you have a lot of nodes in the cluster, it will be difficult to locate the downed node. In this case, you can run nodetool status | grep DN.

```
$ nodetool status

Datacenter: NewYork_DC
=======================
Status=Up/Down
|/ State=Normal/Leaving/Joining/Moving
--   Address       Load         Tokens  Owns        Host ID                                Rack
                                        (effective)
UN  192.168.1.72  149.52 KiB   2         8.4%       d667b029-d5c3-4c14-90aa-a5b547880863   rack1
UN  192.168.1.77  144.17 KiB   2        25.2%       e02d6b99-1776-41d6-97ba-7ad0994496c2   rack1
DN  192.168.1.81  169.07 KiB   2        66.4%       d7a52bdf-5711-4d29-a3c2-abd6c6aefafc   rack1

$ nodetool status | grep DN
DN  192.168.1.81  169.07 KiB   2        66.4%       d7a52bdf-5711-4d29-a3c2-abd6c6aefafc   rack1
```

If you are using Datastax OpsCenter and you concluded node is down through the OpsCenter, run above command to make sure node is actually down. Sometimes OpsCenter agent may have some issues, and it may appear as the node is down in the OpsCenter.

Reason for node down could be due to a hardware issue, like disk issue, physical box or VM is down. Many times physical machine or virtual machine on which Cassandra is running reboot itself. If you have configured auto-start Cassandra on OS restarts, by the time you check, you may notice that node is already up. In this case, you can check host uptime to confirm if the host/VM got rebooted. If the host is not reachable, this could be a network issue or host may be down.

The node could be down due to the memory issue. If your nodes are frequently going down due to a memory issue, you would see OutOfMemoryErrors in your system.log. This indicates that your heap size is under configured for your data size and processing.

Out of memory issue is due to java heap exception. This may happen when the node tried to compact a large row and ran out of memory. Check how much memory you have allocated to

Cassandra. If you have additional memory on the node, increase it and restart Cassandra on the node.

Your issue may be the number of concurrent compactors. The *concurrent_compactors* defaults to the smaller of (number of disks, number of cores), with a minimum of 2 and a maximum of 8. The number of concurrent compaction processes allowed to run simultaneously on a node, which does not include validation compactions for repairs. Currently configured memory may not be sufficient for these simultaneous compactions. In this case, you can reduce this to a lower number. Below output shows an example of lowering concurrent compactions from 4 to 2.

```
$ nodetool |grep compactors
   getconcurrentcompactors    Get the number of concurrent compactors in the system.
   setconcurrentcompactors    Set number of concurrent compactors in the system.
$ nodetool getconcurrentcompactors
Current concurrent compactors in the system is:
4
$ nodetool setconcurrentcompactors 2
$ nodetool getconcurrentcompactors
Current concurrent compactors in the system is:
2
$
```

Disk Full

Disk full is a very common issue. In Cassandra, the majority of the time disk fills up due to data directory is full. Some of the common reason disks fill up, and the solution is listed below.

Snapshot backups take a significant amount of space. When the snapshot is run, it creates a hard link to each SSTable. These files cannot be deleted unless you remove these snapshots (means remove hard links). Removing snapshots can be done by removing these files, or you can run *nodetool clearsnapshot* command.

Adding new nodes to the cluster brings down the node density as new nodes take ownership of the equal share of tokens and the data. This data is streamed from the existing nodes to the new nodes joining the cluster. But note that the data which is steamed and now not owned by the node is not deleted. You need to run *nodetool cleanup* to remove this data. The *nodetool cleanup* cleans up keyspace and partition keys (tokens) no longer belonging to a node. Similarly, when you reduce replication factor (RF), say 5 to 3, the nodes owning the 4th and 5th copy of the data is not cleaned up automatically. You need to run cleanup to remove this data.

You may be running out of disk capacity. This is a pure capacity issue, and you need to add new nodes to the cluster. If you cannot add more disk space to the node or cannot add nodes to the cluster, review your current RF for all keyspace and plan to reduce the RF and run a cleanup. It is strongly recommended that, examine how reducing RF affects the consistency in all your applications. This is a very serious change need proper verification, and it is DBA's job to bring this discussion.

You can run *du* command in *data_file_directory* to verify which keyspace has taken more space and from there you can check the particular table which might be causing the disk to be filled up.

```
$ cd $CASSANDRA_HOME/data/data
/usr/local/cassandra/data/data$ du -sch *
48K        customer
48K        data_modeling
264K       demo
26M        keyspace1
52K        stresscql
448K       system
180K       system_auth
64K        system_distributed
344K       system_schema
20K        system_traces
27M        total
/usr/local/cassandra/data/data$
```

Read Latency High

Cassandra writes are designed to be fast at the expense of reads. When Cassandra node receives a read request for a given table, the row must be combined from all the SSTables on that node and unflushed data from the memtables. Memory structures like row cache, key cache and bloom filters can be optimized for the reads. If you see high read latency for a particular table, this could be due to the following reasons.

SSTable count is high

When you have a lot of SSTables for a given table, the read performance will degrade as it has to read all the SSTables. If you are updating the data frequently, depending on the volume of updates and if those updates are for the same partitions, your data will be spread among many SSTables.

If your use case and design are updating the data in the same partition frequently at different interval of times, you should consider using LevelledCompactionStrategy with that table. This will keep the same partition data together in the same SSTable within the same level which significantly improves the read performance. Within each level, SSTables are guaranteed to be non-overlapping. Do consider to test this in lower environments as a best practice.

You can run *nodetool tablehistograms* which provides statistics about a table including partition size, SSTable count & read/write latency. The latencies displayed by *tablehistograms* are the time it takes for replica node to retrieve the data and return to the coordinator. In the below output, reading the data from the disk and returning to coordinator finishes in 786.43 microseconds 99 percentile of the time. 99 percentile of partitions has 310 bytes. The SSTables column is how many SSTables are touched on a read, so 99 percentile of read requests are looking at 2 SSTables.

```
$CASSANDRA_HOME/bin/nodetool tablehistograms customer_ks customer_tran
customer_ks/customer_tran
```

Percentile	SSTables	Write Latency (micros)	Read Latency (micros)	Partition Size (bytes)	Cell Count
50%	0.00	229.38	131.07	258	4

75%	0.00	262.14	196.61	258	4
95%	1.00	458.75	524.29	258	4
98%	2.00	524.29	655.36	258	4
99%	**2.00**	**524.29**	**786.43**	**310**	**4**
Min	0.00	98.30	32.77	25	0
Max	2.00	786.43	12582.91	372	4

A high number of SSTable count per node along with SSTable merge can lead to an increase in read latency. You can use CQL tracing to see if this is the case. Below output is just an example of TRACING ON. As you can see in the below output, this particular query has to read 4 SSTables to retrieve the results.

```
cassandra@cqlsh> TRACING ON;
Now Tracing is enabled
cassandra@cqlsh> SELECT custno,name,status FROM demo.customer WHERE custno=100;


 custno | name   | status
--------+--------+--------
    100 | Joe W  |    x


(1 rows)


Tracing session: 1b62bfe0-0669-11e9-a706-67507c40ce96
[...] output removed and SELECT on system_traces.events displayed for
cassandra@cqlsh:system_traces> SELECT activity, thread
                      FROM events
                      WHERE session_id = 1b62bfe0-0669-11e9-a706-67507c40ce96;


 activity                                                          | thread
-------------------------------------------------------------------+--------------------------
 Parsing SELECT custno,name,status FROM demo.customer WHERE custno=100; |
Native-Transport-Requests-1
                      Preparing statement                          | Native-Transport-
Requests-1
                      Executing single-partition query on customer |         ReadStage-2
```

Acquiring sstable references |	ReadStage-2
Merging memtable contents |	ReadStage-2
Merging data from sstable 7 |	ReadStage-2
Partition index with 0 entries found for sstable 7 |	ReadStage-2
Merging data from sstable 6 |	ReadStage-2
Partition index with 0 entries found for sstable 6 |	ReadStage-2
Merging data from sstable 5 |	ReadStage-2
Partition index with 0 entries found for sstable 5 |	ReadStage-2
Merging data from sstable 4 |	ReadStage-2
Partition index with 0 entries found for sstable 4 |	ReadStage-2
Read 1 live and 0 tombstone cells |	ReadStage-2

(14 rows)
cassandra@cqlsh:system_traces>

Analyze read latency using *tablehistograms* & *proxyhistograms*. Once you identify the node in question, you can further analyze few tables on that node. If you are using OpsCenter, you can identify the node which is experiencing high load. If you know which table is causing the issue, then you can directly focus on troubleshooting that table. If you do not know which table is generating read latency and causing the node to use high CPU, you can run *nodetool tablestats* <keyspace> to identify the tables which have high local read latency. Below is an example output. As you can see, on this node, the table *customer_tran* has 14 SSTables and "Local read latency" is 20 ms, which is very high. You might want to run *sstablemetadata* on each SSTable to see the droppable tombstones.

```
$CASSANDRA_HOME/bin/nodetool tablestats customer_ks
Total number of tables: 63
----------------
Keyspace : customer_ks
    Read Count: 105245109
    Read Latency: 0.7359123610580326 ms
    Write Count: 14507976
    Write Latency: 0.34491732285744064 ms
    Pending Flushes: 0
```

```
Table: customer_tran
SSTable count: 14
Space used (live): 25141200728
Space used (total): 25141200728
Space used by snapshots (total): 46697449238
Off heap memory used (total): 298231224
SSTable Compression Ratio: 0.4453076175593084
Number of keys (estimate): 170009666
Memtable cell count: 31312
Memtable data size: 6477192
Memtable off heap memory used: 0
Memtable switch count: 1344
Local read count: 82711607
Local read latency: 20.136 ms
Local write count: 10119600
Local write latency: 0.291 ms
Pending flushes: 0
Percent repaired: 0.0
Bloom filter false positives: 6156647
Bloom filter false ratio: 1.00000
Bloom filter space used: 292248048
Bloom filter off heap memory used: 292247936
Index summary off heap memory used: 0
Compression metadata off heap memory used: 5983288
Compacted partition minimum bytes: 25
Compacted partition maximum bytes: 372
Compacted partition mean bytes: 230
Average live cells per slice (last five minutes): 1.0
Maximum live cells per slice (last five minutes): 1
Average tombstones per slice (last five minutes): 5.0
Maximum tombstones per slice (last five minutes): 1
Dropped Mutations: 0
```

The *nodetool proxyhistograms* shows the full request latency recorded by the coordinator.

Secondary Index with high cardinality.

If you are seeing the performance impact on a specific table and seeing read latency, check whether you have a secondary index on that table? At a high level, indexes look like normal tables with an indexed column as the partition key. But they are not. Cassandra secondary indexes are not distributed like tables. Check if you have an index on a high cardinality column. High cardinality columns such as SSN, email which is more distinct, becomes expensive when you query. You may have to go back to your data modeling and see if you can maintain this as a table instead of index.

Refer Secondary Index in *Chapter 5, Cassandra Data Modeling.*

Large Rows

Depending on the use case, wide rows may be one of the reasons for your read latency and query timeouts. As you read in *"Chapter 5. Cassandra Data modeling"*, if the *cust_by_state* table has 30 million rows and out of which 20 million rows inserted with the *state* as "NJ", 1/3 or the table will be residing on one node as one large single partition. Retrieving this row from that single node also put pressure on network and garbage collection.

Look for "large row" compaction messages *in system.log* and run *nodetool tablehistograms* to identify the large row partition. If your use case allows you to change the data modeling, you can add an additional column to the partition key to break up the large row. This may need many changes to your application code.

If you are seeing GC pause on the node where large rows reside, increasing heap little bit may help.

Slow disk or disk issues

Average wait on most SSDs are below 5-10 ms and on spinning disks are below 200ms. You can run "iostat -x -t 5", which shows the averages for 5 seconds intervals. If you start seeing a higher number for %iowait means, there could be disk or storage issues, and the node is starting to get I/O bound.

Sporadic read latency

If some of your standard queries are sporadically running slow and running extra few milliseconds, check your driver to make sure you are using DC aware policy. If your Cassandra cluster has multiple DC in different regions, the latency between the regions could be an additional of 75-200 milliseconds. If your client driver is not configured with a DC aware policy, your driver could randomly communicate and pick a coordinator node in a local region node or a node from another region. Say your read latency for a query is 5 ms, and whenever driver picks a coordinator from another region, the additional latency will be added to that query. This could be a reason why sporadically you see the latency of 5 ms and 100+ ms for the same query.

Select returning wrong result

Note that Cassandra is a distributed database with eventual consistency. Consistency is sacrificed for partition tolerance and high availability. If you suspect that SELECT is not returning the correct data, it could be an issue with CONSISTENCY. The reason for this is Cassandra's eventual consistency. Two identical queries can give you different results depending on which coordinator node is queried. The chances are that your application code is running SELECT with consistency LOCAL_ONE. What is your driver's default consistency level? Make necessary adjustments to the code. Based on your use case, ideally, it's best practice to write at QUORUM and read QUORUM. This will always give correct results. If you are using multi-dc, you can write at LOCAL_QUORUM and read at LOCAL_QUORUM.

If your consistency is correct and still getting incorrect results, check your server times and make sure all the nodes clock is synchronized correctly. Refer "Server Time (ntpd)" in *Chapter 13, Best Practices*.

Truncated Table

Scenario: Someone by mistake truncated a table.

Most of the times the accidental truncate table happens due to human error. Human error can be avoided by following operational best practices. Many times, individuals with the 'MODIFY' privilege has truncated a table in production cluster without realizing that he or she has logged into the production cluster. For such situations, make sure to follow the best practice of setting *auto_snapshot* = 'true'. When *auto_snapshot* is set to 'true', Cassandra will take a snapshot before truncating the table. This will be very useful to recover the truncated data.

Below are the steps to recover the entire table.

Before Truncate

Below output shows demo.test table has 3 rows and has only one SSTable.

```
$ pwd
/usr/local/cassandra/data/data/demo/test-cd5a6da04e3c11e8a1db33414edc3696
$ ls -l
total 48
drwxrwxr-x 2 cassandra cassandra  4096 May  2 2018  backups
-rw-rw-r--  1 cassandra cassandra    31 Oct 13 09:49  manifest.json
-rw-rw-r--  1 cassandra cassandra    51 Dec 23 20:23  mc-17-big-CompressionInfo.db
-rw-rw-r--  1 cassandra cassandra   158 Dec 23 20:23  mc-17-big-Data.db
-rw-rw-r--  1 cassandra cassandra    10 Dec 23 20:23  mc-17-big-Digest.crc32
-rw-rw-r--  1 cassandra cassandra    24 Dec 23 20:23  mc-17-big-Filter.db
-rw-rw-r--  1 cassandra cassandra    41 Dec 23 20:23  mc-17-big-Index.db
-rw-rw-r--  1 cassandra cassandra  4753 Dec 23 20:23  mc-17-big-Statistics.db
-rw-rw-r--  1 cassandra cassandra    56 Dec 23 20:23  mc-17-big-Summary.db
-rw-rw-r--  1 cassandra cassandra    92 Dec 23 20:23  mc-17-big-TOC.txt
-rw-rw-r--  1 cassandra cassandra   818 Oct 13 09:49  schema.cql
```

```
$
$ $CASSANDRA_HOME/bin/cqlsh -u cassandra -p cassandra 192.168.1.87
Connected to testclust at 192.168.1.87:9042.
[cqlsh 5.0.1 | Cassandra 3.10 | CQL spec 3.4.4 | Native protocol v4]
Use HELP for help.
cassandra@cqlsh> SELECT * FROM demo.test;

 id | city     | status
----+----------+--------
  1 | New York |      2
  2 |    Paris |      X
  3 |    Tokyo |      X

(3 rows)
cassandra@cqlsh>
```

Truncate table.

Now simulate a truncate table. Table demo.test truncated and 0 rows found. Since *auto_snapshot* is 'true', truncate table has created snapshots and took the backup of original SSTable mc-17-big* into snapshots/ truncated-1545616164974-test/

When we recover the truncated data, these SSTables will be copied back to data directory.

```
cassandra@cqlsh> TRUNCATE demo.test;
cassandra@cqlsh> SELECT * FROM demo.test;

 id | city | status
----+------+--------

(0 rows)
cassandra@cqlsh>
```

```
$ pwd
/usr/local/cassandra/data/data/demo/test-cd5a6da04e3c11e8a1db33414edc3696
$ ls -l
total 16
drwxrwxr-x 2 cassandra cassandra  4096 May  2  2018 backups
-rw-rw-r--  1 cassandra cassandra    31 Oct 13 09:49 manifest.json
-rw-rw-r--  1 cassandra cassandra   818 Oct 13 09:49 schema.cql
drwxrwxr-x 3 cassandra cassandra  4096 Dec 23 20:49 snapshots
$ ls -l snapshots/
total 4
drwxrwxr-x 2 cassandra cassandra 4096 Dec 23 20:49 truncated-1545616164974-test
$ ls -l snapshots/truncated-1545616164974-test/
total 44
-rw-rw-r-- 1 cassandra cassandra   32 Dec 23 20:49 manifest.json
-rw-rw-r-- 1 cassandra cassandra   51 Dec 23 20:23 mc-17-big-CompressionInfo.db
-rw-rw-r-- 1 cassandra cassandra  158 Dec 23 20:23 mc-17-big-Data.db
-rw-rw-r-- 1 cassandra cassandra   10 Dec 23 20:23 mc-17-big-Digest.crc32
-rw-rw-r-- 1 cassandra cassandra   24 Dec 23 20:23 mc-17-big-Filter.db
-rw-rw-r-- 1 cassandra cassandra   41 Dec 23 20:23 mc-17-big-Index.db
-rw-rw-r-- 1 cassandra cassandra 4753 Dec 23 20:23 mc-17-big-Statistics.db
-rw-rw-r-- 1 cassandra cassandra   56 Dec 23 20:23 mc-17-big-Summary.db
-rw-rw-r-- 1 cassandra cassandra   92 Dec 23 20:23 mc-17-big-TOC.txt
-rw-rw-r-- 1 cassandra cassandra  818 Dec 23 20:49 schema.cql
$
```

INSERT DATA

In an ideal scenario, when a table gets truncated due to a human error, the write processes from applications will be still writing the data to that table. As part of this recovery, we need to make sure that, when we recover the truncated data, we also preserve the new data that has been inserted as well.

To simulate this, we will insert some rows in the table after truncation. Run *nodetool flush* command to create new SSTable. As you can see, it has created new SSTable with mc-18-big-*. This is the data we need to preserve when we recover truncated data which had 3 rows.

```
cassandra@cqlsh> INSERT INTO demo.test (id,city,status) VALUES ( 4,'London','Y' );
cassandra@cqlsh> INSERT INTO demo.test (id,city,status) VALUES ( 5,'Bangalore','Y' );
cassandra@cqlsh> SELECT * FROM demo.test;

 id | city      | status
----+-----------+--------
  5 | Bangalore |      Y
  4 |    London |      Y

(2 rows)

$ pwd
/usr/local/cassandra/data/data/demo/test-cd5a6da04e3c11e8a1db33414edc3696

$ $CASSANDRA_HOME/bin/nodetool flush
$ ls -l
total 52
drwxrwxr-x 2 cassandra cassandra 4096 May  2 2018 backups
-rw-rw-r-- 1 cassandra cassandra   31 Oct 13 09:49 manifest.json
-rw-rw-r-- 1 cassandra cassandra   43 Dec 23 21:02 mc-18-big-CompressionInfo.db
-rw-rw-r-- 1 cassandra cassandra   70 Dec 23 21:02 mc-18-big-Data.db
-rw-rw-r-- 1 cassandra cassandra   10 Dec 23 21:02 mc-18-big-Digest.crc32
-rw-rw-r-- 1 cassandra cassandra   16 Dec 23 21:02 mc-18-big-Filter.db
-rw-rw-r-- 1 cassandra cassandra   16 Dec 23 21:02 mc-18-big-Index.db
-rw-rw-r-- 1 cassandra cassandra 4658 Dec 23 21:02 mc-18-big-Statistics.db
-rw-rw-r-- 1 cassandra cassandra   56 Dec 23 21:02 mc-18-big-Summary.db
-rw-rw-r-- 1 cassandra cassandra   92 Dec 23 21:02 mc-18-big-TOC.txt
-rw-rw-r-- 1 cassandra cassandra  818 Oct 13 09:49 schema.cql
drwxrwxr-x 3 cassandra cassandra 4096 Dec 23 20:49 snapshots
```

Recover Truncated Data

Recover the data is done by copying the SSTable from truncated snapshot directory to the actual data directory for the demo.test table. The SSTables with mc-17-big* tables contain data before the table was truncated.

```
$ pwd
/usr/local/cassandra/data/data/demo/test-cd5a6da04e3c11e8a1db33414edc3696
$ ls -l
total 52
drwxrwxr-x 2 cassandra cassandra 4096 May  2  2018 backups
-rw-rw-r--  1 cassandra cassandra   31 Oct 13 09:49 manifest.json
-rw-rw-r--  1 cassandra cassandra   43 Dec 23 21:02 mc-18-big-CompressionInfo.db
-rw-rw-r--  1 cassandra cassandra   70 Dec 23 21:02 mc-18-big-Data.db
-rw-rw-r--  1 cassandra cassandra   10 Dec 23 21:02 mc-18-big-Digest.crc32
-rw-rw-r--  1 cassandra cassandra   16 Dec 23 21:02 mc-18-big-Filter.db
-rw-rw-r--  1 cassandra cassandra   16 Dec 23 21:02 mc-18-big-Index.db
-rw-rw-r--  1 cassandra cassandra 4658 Dec 23 21:02 mc-18-big-Statistics.db
-rw-rw-r--  1 cassandra cassandra   56 Dec 23 21:02 mc-18-big-Summary.db
-rw-rw-r--  1 cassandra cassandra   92 Dec 23 21:02 mc-18-big-TOC.txt
-rw-rw-r--  1 cassandra cassandra  818 Oct 13 09:49 schema.cql
drwxrwxr-x 3 cassandra cassandra 4096 Dec 23 20:49 snapshots

$ cp snapshots/truncated-1545616164974-test/* .
$ ls -l
total 88
drwxrwxr-x 2 cassandra cassandra 4096 May  2  2018 backups
-rw-rw-r--  1 cassandra cassandra   32 Dec 23 21:08 manifest.json
-rw-rw-r--  1 cassandra cassandra   51 Dec 23 21:08 mc-17-big-CompressionInfo.db
-rw-rw-r--  1 cassandra cassandra  158 Dec 23 21:08 mc-17-big-Data.db
-rw-rw-r--  1 cassandra cassandra   10 Dec 23 21:08 mc-17-big-Digest.crc32
-rw-rw-r--  1 cassandra cassandra   24 Dec 23 21:08 mc-17-big-Filter.db
-rw-rw-r--  1 cassandra cassandra   41 Dec 23 21:08 mc-17-big-Index.db
-rw-rw-r--  1 cassandra cassandra 4753 Dec 23 21:08 mc-17-big-Statistics.db
-rw-rw-r--  1 cassandra cassandra   56 Dec 23 21:08 mc-17-big-Summary.db
```

```
-rw-rw-r--   1 cassandra cassandra     92 Dec 23 21:08 mc-17-big-TOC.txt
-rw-rw-r--   1 cassandra cassandra     43 Dec 23 21:02 mc-18-big-CompressionInfo.db
-rw-rw-r--   1 cassandra cassandra     70 Dec 23 21:02 mc-18-big-Data.db
-rw-rw-r--   1 cassandra cassandra     10 Dec 23 21:02 mc-18-big-Digest.crc32
-rw-rw-r--   1 cassandra cassandra     16 Dec 23 21:02 mc-18-big-Filter.db
-rw-rw-r--   1 cassandra cassandra     16 Dec 23 21:02 mc-18-big-Index.db
-rw-rw-r--   1 cassandra cassandra   4658 Dec 23 21:02 mc-18-big-Statistics.db
-rw-rw-r--   1 cassandra cassandra     56 Dec 23 21:02 mc-18-big-Summary.db
-rw-rw-r--   1 cassandra cassandra     92 Dec 23 21:02 mc-18-big-TOC.txt
-rw-rw-r--   1 cassandra cassandra    818 Dec 23 21:08 schema.cql
drwxrwxr-x 3 cassandra cassandra   4096 Dec 23 20:49 snapshots
$
```

Once data is copied, run **nodetool refresh** command. Truncated data along with new data both are recovered through these steps.

```
cassandra@cqlsh> SELECT * FROM demo.test;

 id | city      | status
----+-----------+--------
  5 | Bangalore |      Y
  4 |    London |      Y

(2 rows)
cassandra@cqlsh> exit

$CASSANDRA_HOME/bin/nodetool refresh demo test

$ $CASSANDRA_HOME/bin/cqlsh -u cassandra -p cassandra 192.168.1.87
Connected to testclust at 192.168.1.87:9042.
[cqlsh 5.0.1 | Cassandra 3.10 | CQL spec 3.4.4 | Native protocol v4]
Use HELP for help.
cassandra@cqlsh> SELECT * FROM demo.test;
```

```
 id | city      | status
----+-----------+--------
  5 | Bangalore |      Y
  1 |  New York |      2
  2 |     Paris |      X
  4 |    London |      Y
  3 |     Tokyo |      X

(5 rows)
cassandra@cqlsh>
```

Note that, as a demonstration, in this example, it is done only on a single node cluster. If you have multiple node and multiple DC, you need to do this on each node. When you are copying the SSTables from snapshot directory to data directory, make sure that there are no duplicate SSTable names. If there are, you may overwrite the SSTable and lose some data. In this case, rename those SSTable with a different numeric number.

Tombstone warnings / failure threshold

If you are getting tombstone warnings or failures in your Cassandra system.log, check the tombstone warning and failure thresholds in *cassandra.yaml* file. By default, the threshold is set as listed below.

tombstone_warn_threshold: 1000
tombstone_failure_threshold: 100000

This can be increased to a higher number to resolve the issue. In one of the use case, we increased this to 1,000,000 from 100,000 for failure threshold. We made this change after making sure we are confident about this number and memory. Following are excerpts from the *cassandra.yaml*.

When executing a scan, within or across a partition, we need to keep the
tombstones seen in memory so we can return them to the coordinator, which
will use them to make sure other replicas also know about the deleted rows.

358

With workloads that generate a lot of tombstones, this can cause performance
problems and even exaust the server heap.
(http://www.datastax.com/dev/blog/cassandra-anti-patterns-queues-and-queue-like-datasets)
Adjust the thresholds here if you understand the dangers and want to
scan more tombstones anyway. These thresholds may also be adjusted at runtime
using the StorageService mbean.

As you read in earlier chapters, tombstones in Cassandra are deleted markers. They take up the storage space and are cleaned up only during compactions after *gc_grace_seconds* of delay, which is typically 10 days. Querying tables with a large number of tombstones cause performance issues and put pressure on the heap.

To troubleshoot this scenario, you need to evict these tombstones from the table and also address any data modeling issues if any. Because if you have underlying data modeling issue, after a while, you will be again in the same situation.

These tombstones will be disappearing after *gc_grace_seconds* property set on the table, which is typically 10 days. This means manual compaction will not remove tombstones until *gc_grace_seconds* has elapsed from the time of deletion. Cassandra does not guarantee that tombstones will be removed right after *gc_grace_seconds*. The reason is the SSTable containing tombstone may not be compacted, and even if it's compacted it may not clear these tombstones as SSTable data may be shadowed in another SSTable (Refer *sstableexpiredblockers* in *Chapter 12. Cassandra Utilities*). You have few options listed below, but do test them before you perform these on the production cluster.

-Run major compactions by running *nodetool compact*. You can run *sstablesplit* after major compaction to split the single large table if required. (Refer *sstablesplit* in *Chapter 12. Cassandra Utilities*).

-If your table sizes are not too big, you can alter the table to change the compaction strategy and alter it back.

If the issue is with data modeling, you need to fix it. Are you frequently deleting the data? Are you inserting 'null', which is generating these tombstones? If you are using a third party application, is it using materialized views, which is creating tombstones to maintain secondary index tables? You can enable probabilistic tracing on one or few nodes to see what the deletes are.

nodetool settraceprobability --[value is a probability between 0 and 1]

A probability of 1.0 will trace everything. A value of 0.1 will trace about 10% of the statements. The trace information is stored in a *system_traces* keyspace that holds two tables – *sessions* and *events*. Setting it to 1.0 will overwhelm the cluster, and it is not recommended.

Until you fix your data modeling, you can alter the table and set *tombstone_compaction_interval, tombstone_threashold* & *tombstone_compaction_interval* for aggressive compaction (Refer Tombstone compaction in *Chapter 10. Cassandra Architecture II*). Lower the *gc_grace_seconds* for the table from default 10 days to few hours so that those can be cleared during compaction earlier.

CHAPTER 15

Upgrade Cassandra

Upgrading Cassandra and keeping it up to date is required for many reasons. Upgrading Cassandra just for the sake of it is never a reasonable justification. The benefit of upgrading should outweigh the risks, time and money.

Cassandra is classified as AP system, meaning that availability and partition tolerance are considered more important than the consistency. This is true when you upgrade Cassandra. You can upgrade Cassandra with zero downtime. For this, you need to make sure that you have proper replication factor setup and quorum consistency.

In this chapter, we will upgrade an actual one node Cassandra cluster from 3.10 to 3.11.3. The upgrade method followed here is manual. In large installations, you can't upgrade each node manually, but you will be using the homegrown script or automation software such as Ansible.

Why upgrade Cassandra?

It's easier for future upgrade. The greater the gap between your current Cassandra version and the target version, it becomes more complex, and even multiple upgrades are necessary.

The main reason in many cases will be for vendor support and bug fixes. If you want to keep the applications running and avoid any additional support fees, you need to be up to date with the version being supported. If your current version is the end of life and bugs fix patches are not being released anymore, your application will be in trouble. In these situations, you will be pressed for an immediate upgrade, and you will not have enough time for proper testing of the new version.

Preparation

Once upgrade version is decided and verified that you can upgrade from current version to the new version, prepare a checklist of all the items needs to be checked, like java version, os version, driver compatibility, compatibility of all other software tools and monitoring you are using with the new version of Cassandra. Check if any feature is deprecated or any command deprecated which could affect one of your functionality.

The best practice is never to implement anything in production without testing in the lower environment. Before even upgrading your development environment, create a test cluster with the current Cassandra version and first try your upgrade here. If your shop is using AWS, it's easy to spin off a few nodes and try the upgrade. Your upgrade in the test environment will be to identify basic issues you may face so that it can be fixed before the actual upgrade in any environment.

Once the upgrade is tested in a test environment, upgrade in development cluster followed by staging cluster. Your staging cluster should be as close as possible to the production cluster in terms of data centers, monitoring, functional testing applications and any other component which is used in the production cluster.

If you have a multi-datacenter cluster, upgrade every node in one datacenter, before upgrading another datacenter. Upgrades must be done one node at a time. This way, if you have set up proper RF such as 3 and you are using LOCAL_QUORUM or QUORUM, your rolling upgrade will not impact the application. The best way is taking the read and write traffic away from the datacenter which you are upgrading.

Make sure that each node has ample free disk space. The last thing you need is a disk full issue during the upgrade.

The experience from lower environment upgrade will help you to prepare a proper upgrade document. Cross verify this upgrade document with your production cluster.

Schedule upgrade during low usage hours when the cluster is NOT under heavy load.

Upgrade Steps
Backup

Ensure to take configuration backups like your cassandra.yaml, JVM options, and all other necessary files. If you have your code on git or any other such system, it's much better.

Take complete schema backup.

Take snapshot back up on all the nodes in the cluster.

Below output shows, complete schema backup has taken and nodetool snapshot has taken. Make sure to take snapshot back up on all the nodes.

```
cassandra@casupgrade:~$ echo "describe full schema;" | cqlsh -u cassandra -p cassandra
192.168.1.22 > full_schema.cql
cassandra@casupgrade:~$ ls -l full_schema.cql
-rw-rw-r-- 1 cassandra cassandra 38037 Dec 15 22:16 full_schema.cql


cassandra@casupgrade:~$ $CASSANDRA_HOME/bin/nodetool snapshot -t before_upgrade
Requested creating snapshot(s) for [all keyspaces] with snapshot name [before_upgrade] and options {skipFlush=false}
Snapshot directory: before_upgrade
cassandra@casupgrade:~$
```

Upgrade restrictions

There are general restrictions need to be followed during entire upgrade.

- Cluster operations like repairs needs to be stopped during upgrade. Repairs cannot be performed on a mixed version cluster.
- Do not decommission any nodes or bootstrap new nodes.
- Do not run any DDL commands or make any security related changes
- Do not truncate any tables.
- If you are using SOLR, do not update schema (schema.xml) or reindex.

Upgrade

If you have multi datacenters, upgrade one datacenter at a time. You can redirect your read and write application away from this datacenter during the time of the upgrade. This is one of the reasons that you should build your production cluster as a multi-datacenter. If you have only one datacenter, you can still perform the upgrade as a rolling upgrade. So at any given point of time, only one node will be unreachable, and your QUORUM reads will not fail.

Following steps needs to be performed on each node in the datacenter and it is preferred to do one node at a time.

Download software

Go to http://cassandra.apache.org/download/ and select latest version of apache Cassandra. In this case it will be 3.11.3. Select one of the http site and *wget* the software.

```
cassandra@casupgrade:~$ wget http://apache.cs.utah.edu/cassandra/3.11.3/apache-cassandra-
3.11.3-bin.tar.gz
--2018-12-15 22:50:46--  http://apache.cs.utah.edu/cassandra/3.11.3/apache-cassandra-3.11.3-
bin.tar.gz
Resolving apache.cs.utah.edu (apache.cs.utah.edu)... 155.98.64.87
Connecting to apache.cs.utah.edu (apache.cs.utah.edu)|155.98.64.87|:80... connected.
HTTP request sent, awaiting response... 200 OK
Length: 37317433 (36M) [application/x-gzip]
Saving to: `apache-cassandra-3.11.3-bin.tar.gz.1'

100%[=====================================================================
===========================================================================>]
37,317,433   898K/s   in 59s
2018-12-15 22:51:45 (622 KB/s) - `apache-cassandra-3.11.3-bin.tar.gz.1' saved
[37317433/37317433]

cassandra@casupgrade:~$ ls -l apache-cassandra-3.1*
-rw-rw-r-- 1 cassandra cassandra 37608621 Feb  3 2017 apache-cassandra-3.10-bin.tar.gz
```

```
-rw-rw-r-- 1 cassandra cassandra 37317433 Aug  1 13:19 apache-cassandra-3.11.3-bin.tar.gz
cassandra@casupgrade:~$
```

Once the new version is downloaded, tar the file and change the ownership to *cassandra*.

```
sudo tar -xvf apache-cassandra-3.11.3-bin.tar.gz -C /usr/local/
sudo chown -R cassandra:cassandra /usr/local/apache-cassandra-3.11.3/
```

Stop Cassandra

Before stopping Cassandra make sure to run *nodetool drain*. The *nodetool drain* will flush all the data to SSTables and stop listening to the connections from clients and other nodes.

```
nodetool drain
```

Configuration file update

Your new binary installation will have configuration files with all the defaults. The build we did in this book did not follow a best practice standard in terms of where do you store your configuration files and data files. Both configuration and data files are configured under $CASSANDRA_HOME, which is not best practice. Our original path for 'conf' directory is

```
cassandra@casupgrade:~$ cd $CASSANDRA_HOME /conf
cassandra@casupgrade:/usr/local/cassandra/conf$ pwd -P
/usr/local/apache-cassandra-3.10/conf
```

In this case, since we are upgrading from 3.10 to 3.11.3, the new *cassandra.yaml* file for 3.11.3 version is installed in */usr/local/apache-cassandra-3.11.3/conf*. These files need to be overwritten by the original file from */usr/local/apache-cassandra-3.10/conf*.

For a larger cluster with tens or hundreds of nodes, ideally, you will be using homegrown automation or software like git and ansible code to deploy the proper tar file, *cassandra.yaml* file and *cassandra-rackdc.properties* or other files.

Copy configuration files from old version to new version.

```
cassandra@casupgrade: $ cd /usr/local/apache-cassandra-3.11.3/conf
$ cp $CASSANDRA_HOME/conf/cassandra-rackdc.properties .
$ cp $CASSANDRA_HOME/conf/cassandra.yaml .
```

Change Symbolic link

Change symbolic link for /usr/local/cassandra from apache-cassandra-3.10 to new version apache-cassandra-3.11.3. For this remove the existing soft link and create new soft link.

```
cassandra@cascassandra@casupgrade:/usr/local$ pwd
/usr/local
cassandra@casupgrade:/usr/local$ ls -l | grep cassandra
drwxr-xr-x 12 cassandra cassandra 4096 Jul 16 22:59 apache-cassandra-3.10
drwxr-xr-x 12 cassandra cassandra 4096 Oct 22 23:22 apache-cassandra-3.11.3
lrwxrwxrwx  1 cassandra cassandra   33 Dec 15 21:42 cassandra -> /usr/local/apache-cassandra-3.10/

cassandra@casupgrade:/usr/local$ sudo rm cassandra
cassandra@casupgrade:/usr/local$ ls -l | grep cassandra
drwxr-xr-x 12 cassandra cassandra 4096 Jul 16 22:59 apache-cassandra-3.10
drwxr-xr-x 12 cassandra cassandra 4096 Oct 22 23:22 apache-cassandra-3.11.3

cassandra@casupgrade:/usr/local$ sudo ln -s /usr/local/apache-cassandra-3.11.3/ /usr/local/
cassandra

cassandra@casupgrade:/usr/local$ ls -l | grep cassandra
drwxr-xr-x 12 cassandra cassandra 4096 Jul 16 22:59 apache-cassandra-3.10
drwxr-xr-x 12 cassandra cassandra 4096 Oct 22 23:22 apache-cassandra-3.11.3
lrwxrwxrwx  1 root    root     35 Dec 15 23:03 cassandra -> /usr/local/apache-cassandra-3.11.3/
```

Once new soft link is created, change the ownership of the folders to 'cassandra' id.

```
cassandra@casupgrade:/usr/local$ sudo chown -R cassandra:cassandra /usr/local/
apache-cassandra-3.11.3/

cassandra@casupgrade:/usr/local$ sudo chown -R cassandra:cassandra /usr/local/cassandra

cassandra@casupgrade:/usr/local$ ls -l | grep cassandra
drwxr-xr-x 12 cassandra cassandra 4096 Jul 16 22:59 apache-cassandra-3.10
drwxr-xr-x 12 cassandra cassandra 4096 Oct 22 23:22 apache-cassandra-3.11.3
lrwxrwxrwx 1 cassandra cassandra 35 Dec 15 23:03 cassandra -> /usr/local/
apache-cassandra-3.11.3/
cassandra@casupgrade:/usr/local$
```

Both Cassandra 3.10 binary and 3.11.3 binary are installed in *usr/local*. $CASSANDRA_HOME, which is *usr/local/cassandra* is a symbolic link to 3.10 binary. As you see in the above screen, we are removing the link to 3.10 binary and reestablishing to 3.11.3 binary and changing the ownership to Cassandra. This way, whenever you upgrade, you don't need to change $CASSANDRA_HOME.

In the below output, performing a quick check to make sure the symbolic link is pointing to the new version (3.11.3), seed, cluster name, all IP addresses are correct.

```
cassandra@casupgrade:/usr/local$ cd $CASSANDRA_HOME/conf
cassandra@casupgrade:/usr/local/cassandra/conf$ pwd -P
/usr/local/apache-cassandra-3.11.3/conf

cassandra@casupgrade:/usr/local/cassandra/conf$ grep seeds cassandra.yaml
     # seeds is actually a comma-delimited list of addresses.
     - seeds: "192.168.1.22"

cassandra@casupgrade:/usr/local/cassandra/conf$ grep cluster_name cassandra.yaml
cluster_name: 'casupgrade'

cassandra@casupgrade:/usr/local/cassandra/conf$ grep "_address" cassandra.yaml | grep
"192.168"
listen_address: 192.168.1.22
```

```
broadcast_address: 192.168.1.22
rpc_address: 192.168.1.22


cassandra@casupgrade:/usr/local/cassandra/conf$
```

In our installation, we did not follow the best practice, and we went with default values for storing data in $CASSANDRA_HOME/data/data. Ideally, this should be independent of the Casandra binary folder. In this case, we need to copy the entire data directory from /usr/local/apache-cassandra-3.10/data to /usr/local/apache-cassandra-3.11.3/data.

So let's copy the data before we restart Cassandra 3.11.3.

```
cassandra@casupgrade:~$ cd $CASSANDRA_HOME
cassandra@casupgrade:/usr/local/cassandra$ pwd -P
/usr/local/apache-cassandra-3.11.3 ← new version.
cassandra@casupgrade:/usr/local/cassandra$ # copy entire data directory from old version
cassandra@casupgrade:/usr/local/cassandra$ cp -R /usr/local/apache-cassandra-3.10/data .
cassandra@casupgrade:/usr/local/cassandra$ cd data
cassandra@casupgrade:/usr/local/cassandra/data$ ls -l
total 16
drwxrwxr-x 2 cassandra cassandra 4096 Dec 18 00:12 commitlog
drwxrwxr-x 8 cassandra cassandra 4096 Dec 18 00:12 data
drwxrwxr-x 2 cassandra cassandra 4096 Dec 18 00:12 hints
drwxrwxr-x 2 cassandra cassandra 4096 Dec 18 00:12 saved_caches
cassandra@casupgrade:/usr/local/cassandra/data$ cd data
cassandra@casupgrade:/usr/local/cassandra/data/data$ ls -l
total 24
drwxrwxr-x 4 cassandra cassandra 4096 Dec 18 00:12 demo
drwxrwxr-x 26 cassandra cassandra 4096 Dec 18 00:12 system
drwxrwxr-x 6 cassandra cassandra 4096 Dec 18 00:12 system_auth
drwxrwxr-x 5 cassandra cassandra 4096 Dec 18 00:12 system_distributed
drwxrwxr-x 12 cassandra cassandra 4096 Dec 18 00:12 system_schema
drwxrwxr-x 4 cassandra cassandra 4096 Dec 18 00:12 system_traces
cassandra@casupgrade:/usr/local/cassandra/data/data$
```

Note that, the above steps are not required if you change below default directory from $CASSANDRA_HOME/data to a location which is outside the binary installation.

```
cassandra@casupgrade:/usr/local/cassandra/conf$ pwd
/usr/local/cassandra/conf
cassandra@casupgrade:/usr/local/cassandra/conf$
cassandra@casupgrade:/usr/local/cassandra/conf$ grep "default directory" cassandra.yaml
# If not set, the default directory is $CASSANDRA_HOME/data/hints.
# If not set, the default directory is $CASSANDRA_HOME/data/data.
# If not set, the default directory is $CASSANDRA_HOME/data/commitlog.
# separate spindle than the data directories. If not set, the default directory is
# If not set, the default directory is $CASSANDRA_HOME/data/saved_caches.
```

Start Cassandra

Now CASSANDRA_HOME is pointing to new version 3.11.3, and we have copied and verified all the configuration files, and we have copied the entire data directory.

Note that, in your environment, you will not be copying data or overwriting cassandra.yaml, jvm.options, rack-dc or topology files. Those files should not be overwritten when you install new binaries. The upgrade example in this book is for learning and demonstration purpose only.

For any reason, your staging or production cluster is configured this way; it is time for you to reconfigure during the upgrade

Now start Cassandra with new version. You will see few messages like below

INFO [main] 2018-12-18 00:20:54,120 SystemKeyspace.java:1362 - Detected version upgrade from 3.10 to 3.11.3, snapshotting system keyspace

INFO [main] 2018-12-18 00:20:56,257 StorageService.java:600 - Populating token metadata from system tables

sstableupgrade

Syntax: sstableupgrade [options] <keyspace> <cf> [snapshot]

This tool rewrites all the SSTables for given keyspace.table to match the current version of Cassandra. If there is no significant difference in the versions, it skips the upgrade of SSTables. In this case, upgrade of Cassandra from 3.10 to 3.11.3 does not need upgrading SSTable as you can see from the below output.

```
cassandra@casupgrade:/usr/local/cassandra/bin$ ./sstableupgrade demo customer
Found 0 sstables that need upgrading.
cassandra@casupgrade:/usr/local/cassandra/bin$
```

For any reason, you upgraded to a new major version, and if you want to load the old major version SSTable through sstableloader, you need to run sstableupgrade on those snapshots first.

In this example of upgrading a single node cluster, it does not give a complete idea of upgrading SSTables in a large cluster. Upgrading SSTable is going to take a lot of time depends on your data size and type of hardware and disks. To speed up the *sstableupgrade*, you can set the compaction throughput to a higher value or set it to 0 to disable throttling. If your SSTables are large, it's the best thing is to run the upgrade in background mode with *nohup*.

```
$nodetool setcompactionthroughput 0
```

There is no progress bar to monitor the status of the *sstableupgrade*, but you can monitor the data directory for the given *keyspace.table* for a specific file extension.

NOTE: If you have written any custom scripts around naming convention of the SSTabes, make sure to update those scripts. Upgrade from 3.10 to 3.11.3 does not change the SSTable format version name such as
mc-1-big-Data.db
The "mc" indicates the SSTable format version. The word "big" was added to Cassandra SSTable files starting in Cassandra 2.2. But do make a note of this and pay attention to your home-grown scripts.

If you do not see any issue or errors during the upgrade, you can continue upgrading the next node in the datacenter, and you can run the SSTable upgrade during low usage hours on the node.

Verification

Once Cassandra starts with new version, you can run *nodetool gossipinfo* to make sure the node has been upgraded.

Also login by *cqlsh* to check the version of Cassandra.

During and after upgrade check Cassandra error logs to make sure there are no errors.

```
cassandra@casupgrade:~$ $CASSANDRA_HOME/bin/nodetool gossipinfo
/192.168.1.22
  generation:1545110461
  heartbeat:3978
  STATUS:27:NORMAL,-2216002491950792111
  LOAD:3932:161352.0
  SCHEMA:23:5d4f0ac8-dcf8-3be0-bc04-70ba8e73badd
  DC:8:dc
  RACK:10:rack1
  RELEASE_VERSION:4:3.11.3
  INTERNAL_IP:6:192.168.1.22
  RPC_ADDRESS:3:192.168.1.22
  NET_VERSION:1:11
  HOST_ID:2:a5619105-66c0-4857-97b6-86fda072b760
  RPC_READY:40:true
  TOKENS:26:<hidden>

cassandra@casupgrade:~$
```

Run *nodetool describecluster* to make sure all nodes are up in the cluster.

```
cassandra@casupgrade:~$ $CASSANDRA_HOME/bin/nodetool describecluster
Cluster Information:
    Name: casupgrade
    Snitch: org.apache.cassandra.locator.GossipingPropertyFileSnitch
    DynamicEndPointSnitch: enabled
    Partitioner: org.apache.cassandra.dht.Murmur3Partitioner
    Schema versions:
        5d4f0ac8-dcf8-3be0-bc04-70ba8e73badd: [192.168.1.22]

cassandra@casupgrade:~$
```

372

Index

Printed in Great Britain
by Amazon